The United Nations and the Regions

United Nations University Series on Regionalism

Volume 3

Series Editors:

PHILIPPE DE LOMBAERDE AND LUK VAN LANGENHOVE

The United Nations University Series on Regionalism, launched by UNU-CRIS and Springer, offers a platform for innovative work on (supra-national) regionalism from a global and inter-disciplinary perspective. It includes the policy-oriented *World Reports on Regional Integration*, published in collaboration with other UN agencies, but it is also open for theoretical, methodological and empirical contributions from academics and policy-makers worldwide.

Book proposals will be reviewed by an International Editorial Board.

The series editors are particularly interested in book proposals dealing with:

- comparative regionalism;
- comparative work on regional organizations;
- inter-regionalism;
- the role of regions in a multi-level governance context;
- the interactions between the UN and the regions;
- the regional dimensions of the reform processes of multilateral institutions;
- the dynamics of cross-border micro-regions and their interactions with supra-national regions;
- methodological issues in regionalism studies.

Accepted book proposals can receive editorial support from UNU-CRIS for the preparation of manuscripts.

Please send book proposals to: pdelombaerde@cris.unu.edu and lvanlangenhove@cris.unu.edu.

For further volumes:
http://www.springer.com/series/7716

Philippe De Lombaerde • Francis Baert
Tânia Felício
Editors

The United Nations and the Regions

Third World Report on Regional Integration

Springer

Editors
Philippe De Lombaerde
United Nations University Institute on
Comparative Regional Integration Studies
(UNU-CRIS) Potterierei, 72
8000 Brugge
Belgium

Francis Baert
United Nations University Institute on
Comparative Regional Integration Studies
(UNU-CRIS) Potterierei, 72
8000 Brugge
Belgium

Tânia Felício
United Nations Integrated Mission in Timor
Leste (UNMIT)
Dili
Timor Leste

ISBN 978-94-007-2750-2 e-ISBN 978-94-007-2751-9
DOI 10.1007/978-94-007-2751-9
Springer Dordrecht Heidelberg London New York

Library of Congress Control Number: 2011944647

Printed on acid-free paper

Springer is part of Springer Science+Business Media (www.springer.com)

Acknowledgments

The editors are grateful to Oscar Guinea Ibáñez and Liesbeth Martens for their outstanding job in revising and formatting the manuscript, to Daniele Marchesi for his help in an earlier stage of the project, and to Lurong Chen for preparing the Statistical Annex.

We are also thankful to Esther Otten and staff at Springer.

Bruges — Francis Baert
Dili — Tânia Felício
Bruges — Philippe De Lombaerde

Contents

List of Contributors

Ademola Abass United Nations University Institute on Comparative Regional Integration Studies (UNU-CRIS), Bruges, Belgium

Francis Baert United Nations University Institute on Comparative Regional Integration Studies (UNU-CRIS), Bruges, Belgium

Centre for European Studies, University of Ghent, Ghent, Belgium

Holly Benner The World Bank, Washington, DC, USA

Franziska Brantner European Parliament, Brussel, Belgium

Hans Günter Brauch Free University of Berlin, Berlin, Germany

Jean-Marc Coicaud Rutgers University, Newark, USA (formerly with UNU Office, New York)

Bob Deacon University of Sheffield, United Nations University Institute on Comparative Regional Integration Studies (UNU-CRIS), Bruges, Belgium

Philippe De Lombaerde United Nations University Institute on Comparative Regional Integration Studies (UNU-CRIS), Bruges, Belgium

Edith Drieskens International Relations, Leuven University, Leuven, Belgium

Annette Fath-Lihic Senior Programme Manager, International IDEA, Stockholm, Sweden

Tânia Felício UN Integrated Mission in Timor Leste (UNMIT), Dilli, Timor Leste (formerly with UNU-CRIS, Bruges, Belgium)

Richard Gowan Centre on International Cooperation, New York University, New York, USA

Kennedy Graham Member of Parliament, Wellington, New Zealand

Geert Haghebaert Delegation of European Commission, Maputo, Mozambique

Robert Kissack Institut Barcelona d'Estudis Internacionals (IBEI), Barcelona, Spain

Hans Köchler University of Innsbruck, Innsbruck, Austria

Eric Maertens UNU-CRIS, Bruges, Belgium (formerly with the ILO, Geneva)

Edgard Moncayo Jiménez Centro de Investigaciones y Estudios, Facultad de Ciencias Administrativas, Económicas y Contables, Universidad Central, Bogotá, Colombia

United Nations University Institute on Comparative Regional Integration Studies (UNU-CRIS), Bruges, Belgium

Amre Moussa Secretary-General League of Arab States (2001–2011), Cairo, Egypt

Marie Muller University of Pretoria, Pretoria, South Africa

Carlos Pascual Formerly with the Brookings Institution, Washington, DC, USA

Vesselin Popovski United Nations University-ISP, Tokyo, Japan

Maxi Schoeman University of Pretoria, Pretoria, South Africa

Joseph E. Schwartzberg University of Minnesota, Minnesota, USA

See Seng Tan Rajaratnam School of International Studies, Nanyang Technological University, Singapore, Singapore

Rodrigo Tavares United Nations University Institute on Comparative Regional Integration Studies (UNU-CRIS), Bruges, Belgium

Luk Van Langenhove United Nations University Institute on Comparative Regional Integration Studies (UNU-CRIS), Bruges, Belgium

Jin Zhang Formerly with UNU-ONY , New York , USA

Abbreviations

ACS	Association of Caribbean States
AFTA	ASEAN Free Trade Area
ALBA	Bolivarian Alternative for Latin America
AMIS	African Union Mission in Sudan
AMISOM	African Union Mission in Somalia
APEC	Asia-Pacific Economic Cooperation
APSA	African Peace and Security Architecture
ARF	Asian Resource Foundation
ARIA	Assessing Regional Integration in Africa
ASEAN	Association of Southeast Asian Nations
ASF	African Standby Force
AU	African Union
AUPST	African Union Peace Support Team
CAFTA	Central America Free Trade Agreement
CARICOM	Caribbean Community
CBMs	Confidence Building Measures
CDEMA	CARICOM's Disaster Emergency Management Agency
CDERA	Caribbean Disaster Emergency Response Agency
CDM	Comprehensive Disaster Management
CDRU	Regional Coordination Centre for the CARICOM Disaster Relief Unit
CERF	Central Emergency Response Fund
CEWARN	Conflict Early Warning and Response Mechanism
CHS	Commission on Human Security
CIDA	Canadian International Development Agency
CIS	Commonwealth of Independent States
COE	Council of Europe
CPC	Caribbean Program Coordination
CPLP	Community of Portuguese Speaking Countries
CRID	Regional Disaster Information Centre
CSCE	Conference for Security and Cooperation in Europe

DFID	UK Department for International Development
DPA	Department of Political Affairs
DPKO	Department of Peacekeeping Operations
DRC	Democratic Republic of Congo
DRR	Disaster Risk Reduction
EC	European Community
ECA	Economic Commission for Africa
ECAFE	Economic Commission for Asia and the Far East
ECC	Eastern Caribbean Countries
ECCAS	Economic Community of Central African States
ECDG/DM	Eastern Caribbean Donor Group for Disaster Management
ECE	Economic Commission for Europe
ECLAC	Economic Commission for Latin America and the Caribbean
ECOMOG	ECOWAS Monitoring Group
ECOSOC	Economic and Social Council
ECOWAS	Economic Community of West African States
ECSWA	Economic and Social Commission for Western Asia
EDF	European Development Fund
EFTA	European Free Trade Association
EPAs	Economic Partnership Agreements
ESCAP	Economic and Social Commission for Asia and the Pacific
EU	European Union
EULEX	European Union Rule of Law Mission
FAO	Food and Agriculture Organization
FHS	Friends of Human Security
G77	Group of 77
G8	Group of 8
GA	General Assembly
GLF	Global Leaders Forum
GNP	Gross National Product
HLMs	High-Level Meetings
HLP	High-Level Panel
HRC	Human Rights Council
HSN	Human Security Network
IACNDR	Inter-American Network for Disaster Mitigation
IADB	Inter-American Development Bank
IASC	UN Inter-Agency Standing Committee
ICOW	Issue Correlates of War
IEBL	Inter-Entity Boundary Line
IFOR	Implementation Force
IGAD	Intergovernmental Authority on Development
ILO	International Labour Organization
IMF	International Monetary Fund
IPCC	Intergovernmental Panel on Climate Change
ISDR	UN International Strategy for Disaster Reduction

LAS	League of Arab States
MDG	UN Millennium Development Goals
MEHSEC	Mediterranean Environmental and Human Security Initiative
MERCOSUR	Mercado Común del Sur (Southern Common Market)
MGI	Managing Global Insecurity Project
NAFTA	North American Free Trade Area
NAM	Non-Aligned Movement
NATO	North Atlantic Treaty Organization
NGO	Non-Governmental Organization
NPFL	National Patriotic Front of Liberia
OAS	Organization of American States
OCHA	Office for the Coordination of Humanitarian Affairs
ODA	Official Development Assistance
OECD	Organization for Economic Cooperation and Development
OECS	Organization of Eastern Caribbean States
OFDA	Office of Foreign Disaster Assistance
OIC	Organization of the Islamic Conference
OMC	Open Method of Coordination
ONUMOZ	United Nations Operation in Mozambique
OSCE	Organization for Security and Cooperation in Europe
PAHO	Pan American Health Organization
PCRD	Post Conflict Reconstruction and Development
PED	Program on Emergency Preparedness and Disaster Relief
PIF	Pacific Islands Forum
PRODIAF	Promotion of Social Dialogue in Francophone Africa
PRSPs	Poverty Reduction Strategy Papers
PSOD	Peace Support Operation Department
R2P	Responsibility to Protect
RECs	Regional Economic Communities
RO	Regional Organizations
SAARC	South Asian Association for Regional Cooperation
SADC	Southern African Development Community
SC	Security Council
SDB	Sustainable Development Board
SEANWFZ	Southeast Asian Nuclear Weapons Free Zone
SPMU	Strategic Planning/Management Cell
SUMA	Supply Management System
SWC	UN System-Wide Coherence
TCRP	Triennial Comprehensive Policy Review
UMA	L'Union du Maghreb arabe (Arab Maghreb Union)
UN	United Nations
UNAMID	AU/UN Hybrid Operation in Darfur
UNASUR	Unión de Naciones Suramericanas (Union of South American Nations)
UNCH	United Nations Charter

UNCTAD	United Nations Conference on Trade and Development
UNDAC	United Nations Disaster Assessment and Coordination
UNDP	United Nations Development Program
UNDPA	United Nations Department of Political Affairs
UNEF	United Nations Emergency Force
UNEP	United Nations Environment Program
UNESCO	United Nations Educational, Scientific and Cultural Organization
UNESOB	UN Economic and Social Office in Beirut
UNGA	United Nations General Assembly
UNHRC	United Nations Human Rights Council
UNICEF	United Nations Children's Fund
UNITA	União Nacional para a Independência Total de Angola
UNMIK	United Nations Interim Administration Mission in Kosovo
UNMIT	United Nations Integrated Mission in Timor-Leste
UNOMIL	United Nations Observer Mission in Liberia
UNPROFOR	United Nations Protection Mission in Yugoslavia
UNSC	United Nations Security Council
UNTAC	United Nations Transitional Authority in Cambodia
UNTAET	United Nations Transitional Administration in East Timor
UNU-CRIS	United Nations University Institute on Comparative Regional Integration Studies
VC	Voting Cohesion
WB	The World Bank
WCSDG	World Commission on the Social Dimension of Globalization
WEOG	Western Europe and Others Group
WHO	World Health Organization
WMO	World Meteorological Organization
WSOD	World Summit Outcome Document
WTO	World Trade Organization
ZOPFAN	Zone of Peace, Freedom and Neutrality

List of Figures

List of Tables

Chapter 1
Introduction

Francis Baert, Tânia Felício, and Philippe De Lombaerde

> *Today, existing regional organisations, like the EU, the African Union for instance, undoubtedly have a key role to play in global governance, as platforms to forge consensus on global issues at continental or regional level. The United Nations acknowledges this role and has close relations with these organisations.*
>
> Joseph Deiss, President of the United Nations General Assembly, 8 June 2011 (EurActiv 2011)

In an increasingly global but concomitantly regionalised world, global governance and the work of the global body – the United Nations (UN) – are no longer made up solely of interstate cooperation. New forms of governance emerge with consequences in the global arena, and clearly regional governance is one.[1] Regional governance has been in ascendancy in the past few decades (or definitely so since

F. Baert (✉)
United Nations University Institute on Comparative Regional Integration Studies (UNU-CRIS), Bruges, Belgium

Centre for European Studies, University of Ghent, Ghent, Belgium
e-mail: fbaert@cris.unu.edu

T. Felício
United Nations Integrated Mission in Timor Leste (UNMIT), Dili, Timor Leste

P. De Lombaerde
United Nations University Institute on Comparative Regional Integration Studies (UNU-CRIS), Bruges, Belgium

P. De Lombaerde et al. (eds.), *The United Nations and the Regions: Third World Report on Regional Integration*, United Nations University Series on Regionalism 3, DOI 10.1007/978-94-007-2751-9_1, © Springer Science+Business Media B.V. 2012

the end of the Cold War) in various fields, namely economy, trade, finance, health, development, environment – and very clearly so – in peace and security. The influence of this new form of governance (whether it is based on cooperative arrangements or deeper integration) on the development, the present management and the foreseeable reforms of the global body deserves a closer look.

In effect, recent developments illustrate very well the growing interaction between the UN and the regions. In May 2011, the UN General Assembly (UNGA) adopted Resolution 65/276 on the participation of the European Union (EU) in the work of the UN. Although the EU internal structure will still need to adapt to this new situation, the resolution gives for the first time to a regional body the right to intervene in the intergovernmental equality of the UNGA. It is not unthinkable that other regions will want to follow this example.[2] Concerned with the gross and systematic violation of human rights, the UN Security Council (UNSC) authorised in Resolution 1973 coercive actions in Libya in March 2011. The UNSC makes explicit reference to the crucial roles played by the League of Arab States (LAS), the African Union (AU) and the Organization of the Islamic Conference (OIC). In the same month, reference is made to the deployment of election observers by the Economic Community of West African States (ECOWAS), the EU, the West African Economic and Monetary Union (UEMOA) and the International Organization of la Francophonie (OIF) in the runoff of the second round of the presidential elections in Côte d'Ivoire (UNSC 2011).[3]

This book is not primarily about the normative questions related to whether the regional level is 'optimal' (i.e. superior compared to other levels) for governance and policy-making in particular policy areas, as, for example, discussed in the literature on regional public goods,[4] optimum currency areas[5] or fiscal federalism.[6] Rather, the book takes a pragmatic approach and starts from the observation that in the postwar history (and especially the most recent decades), supranational regions have de facto become more important and that governance and policy-making has become spread over different layers of governance (from local to global). The rise of the regions can often be linked to the challenges posed by globalisation and is, in turn, challenging the conceptual and institutional foundations of the Westphalian system (Cooper et al. 2008). The UN, as a club of states, is also essentially based on this logic. Although the UN has recognised the emerging regional reality since its origin, and links between the UN and the institutionalised regions have multiplied, it is clear that the linkages between the UN and the regions are still on the global political agenda, and that it will be an important issue to consider when talking and deciding upon reforms of the UN system in the future. It is in this context that this book aims to contribute to the discussions on the roles that regions might play in the UN system of the (near) future. It should be emphasised right from the start that, consistent with the mandate of UNU, this is an academic exercise which does not reflect in any way official positions of the UN, any UN agency, UNU or UN member states. The authors of the individual contributions to this academic exercise are personally responsible for the contents of their respective chapters. At the same time, the ambition of the book goes beyond juxtaposing opinions of a number of academics and other experts. The book aims at contributing analytical insights to the debates, or in other words, to 'problematise' the relationship between the UN and the regions. In our opinion, this is done at different levels. Spread over different chapters, the book – first of all – constitutes a stocktaking exercise of how linkages between the UN and the regions have developed, both historically and across policy domains. It will be demonstrated that these linkages are multiple, that they take different forms and shapes, and that they continuously evolve. The roles of the regions in the UN will be shown to be diverse, unstructured, independently built and multifaceted. Different concepts of regions are also used in different fields of the UN's work, and the cooperation with and representation of the regions at the global body have varied considerably. As suggested in the book, it is thereby useful to distinguish between issues of regional representation and operational issues. The former are broadly interpreted by us and include not only direct formal regional representation (as suggested in some reform proposals) but also indirect representation (through member states) and 'lighter' forms of representation such as (regional) voting coordination at the UNGA or UNSC, dialogue processes involving regional organisations and so on. The operational issues refer to the interaction and cooperation of the UN agencies on the ground with regional organisations, on the one hand, and the regional coordination of UN operations and creation of regional structures (such as the UN Regional Economic Commissions), on the other hand.

1.1 Definitional Issues: The Academic Perspective

If one is to study the role of regions in the UN, one should first address the definitional issue(s). What do we mean by regions? In the academic literature, one notices that scholars have been struggling with the conceptual framework for decades. The literature on regionalism is by and large disarticulated and crossing numerous academic (sub-)disciplines (De Lombaerde et al. 2010; Mansfield and Solingen 2010; Nye 1971; Russett 1967; Söderbaum 2009; Tavares 2004). The concept of region is therefore often used differently in different disciplines. For example, in the fields of geography or development, regions are usually seen as sub-national entities. Economists focus their attention on regional trade agreements, regional development banks, customs unions or regional currency areas. In international relations and international law, regions are usually treated as supranational subsystems of the international system – as emerging regional formations with their own dynamics. A new phenomenon is the emergence of 'clusters' of megacities, with a population above ten million, who by their proximity emerge into novel regional spaces and formats. *The Guardian* recently spoke in this regard of the emergence of 'mega-regions'. One of the most impressive examples is the Hong Kong-Shenhzen-Guangzhou region in China, home to about 120 million people. The United Nations Human Settlement Programme (UNHABITAT) monitors this process closely (UNHABITAT 2008). And although a vast majority of the world population will be living in cities, one should be aware of the huge economic, environmental and societal challenges this encompasses (Koonings and Kruijt 2009).

Deutsch defines regions as 'groups of countries markedly interdependent over a wide range of different dimensions'[7]; Nye views a region as 'a limited number of states linked together by a geographical relationship and by a degree of mutual interdependence' (Nye 1968: 68). Even when one is zooming in on the formalised or institutionalised supranational regions (i.e. regional organisations), one is faced with a much more heterogeneous set of cases/objects than is usually the case in comparative politics (Genna and De Lombaerde 2010). This is related to the proliferation of often overlapping regional arrangements, the experimentation with different organisational models and the lack of standardising mechanisms (such as international law or diplomatic practice). In other words, regions (and regional integration processes) are 'moving targets' (Hettne 2005: 544). When comparing the first wave of regional integration (centred around the 1960s) with the second wave (since the 1990s), one sees a rapid increase of the number of new initiatives, as illustrated by the figures of WTO notifications of regional trade agreements, but also qualitative differences (deeper integration, multidimensional arrangements) (Breslin et al. 2002; Hettne and Söderbaum 2004).

However, the so-called new regionalism does not only refer to the changing characteristics of the regional phenomenon, it also refers to new (and more sophisticated) ways of looking at regions and understanding regionalisation patterns (De Lombaerde 2003). Comparative and interdisciplinary approaches have become more important. Gradually, the process characteristics of the regional phenomenon became more emphasised, and the regionalisation process began more and more to be seen as a complex and multidimensional process of societal transformation involving a variety of actors, not just states. Both formal (de jure) and informal (de facto) regions were considered (Breslin et al. 2002). Illustrative of the new approaches, Jessop (2003: 183) argued that 'rather than [to] seek an elusive objective [...] criterion for defining a region, one should treat regions as emergent, socially constituted phenomena'. Hettne and Söderbaum (2000: 461) share this view with their introduction of the notion of 'regionness', the process whereby a geographical area is transformed from a passive object to an active subject capable of articulating the transnational interests of the emerging region. Tavares (2004) defines 'region' as 'a cognitive construction that spills over borders, based on territoriality, with a certain degree of singularity, socially moulded by a body of different actors, and motivated by different (and sometimes contradictory) principles'. Other authors look at the different levels of analysis when attempting to define region (a level between state and global levels of governance). Another useful categorisation is advanced by Van Langenhove (2003, 2011), involving unity, identity and boundary delimitation. He introduces two related concepts of 'regionhood' (what distinguishes one region from another) and 'regionality' (the historical, geographical, economic, cultural and social conditions that comprise such distinctions).

Many more definitions have been proposed and as we have argued elsewhere (De Lombaerde et al. 2010), conceptual pluralism is inevitable. It is rather the research question at stake and the discursive context which will guide us to a relevant definition.

In this book, which is concerned with the relations between the UN and the regions, the latter will understandably mostly be assimilated with the institutionalised regions (regional organisations). However, the new insights from academia help us to better understand the connections between these organisations and their (historical, institutional, social, political…) context and to better evaluate the role they might play globally.

1.1.1 Definitional Issues in the UN

The regions were – in some way or another – part of the UN from its inception and are present in their different forms in the Charter and in the development of the UN structures and agencies (Graham and Felício 2006). The visible regional aspects of the global body are the regional economic commissions – linked to the UN Economic and Social Council (ECOSOC), the regional electoral groupings linked to the UNSC and the UNGA, and the cooperation with regional arrangements or agencies as foreseen in Chapter VIII of its Charter.

But even if the regions have been present since the inception of the global body, they were never properly defined or understood. When it was time for the UN Charter drafters to define the concept of region, regional agency and regional arrangement, the parties were unable to do so – for lack of empirical examples, or most likely to allow for more flexibility and pragmatism in the creation of new regional forms. Maybe also because of this '*UNdefinition*', the following years witnessed the development of UN regional structures plus regional organisations, arrangements, treaties and agencies, in a totally independent fashion, growing in different directions, with different memberships, mandates and areas of operation which have lead to today's complex and confusing cooperation structures.

Therefore, the UN Charter does not define the 'region', its framers having decided, after much fruitless effort, against any self-restricting ordinance of that kind. The UN Charter speaks only of cooperation with 'regional agencies or arrangements', without further dwelling on their distinction, being unable to define what is a region, regional agency or regional arrangement, and therefore leaving it open for future developments. There is no other mention of regional representation in the Charter, leaving whatever internal regional structure to develop in an ad hoc manner.

The closest adherence to the most basic concept of region in the political world is maintained by the UN economic regional commissions of which there are five (Berthelot 2004). Yet, even the economic commissions lose clarity from the outset as the imperatives of global and regional politics confound apparent geographical simplicities. Of the five commissions, only one, the Economic Commission for Africa (ECA), is a 'pure' regional body whose 53 members are exclusively regional (African) and comprehensively form a region (Africa).[8] The other four are political hybrids. Asia is split into two commissions – Asia-Pacific, the Economic and Social Commission for Asia and the Pacific (ESCAP) and West Asia, the Economic and Social Commission for Western Asia (ESCWA). In ESCAP, four exogenous metropolitan countries are 'non-regional members' (Britain, France, the Netherlands and the United States).[9] ESCWA includes two African countries, Egypt and Sudan, which are also a member of ECA.[10] Within the Economic Commission for Latin America and the Caribbean (ECLA), eight exogenous countries are non-regional members (Britain, France, the Netherlands, the United States, Canada, Italy, Portugal and Spain).[11] The European body, the Economic Commission for Europe (ECE), is perhaps the biggest hybrid of all. It includes the membership of Israel, the five Central Asian countries (also members of ESCAP), Moldova and three Caucasian countries.[12] For their parts, Russia and Turkey are seen to be 'within the geographical scope' of two regions (Europe and Asia) and thus 'regional members' of two regional commissions.

Furthermore, their mandates are not identical. For example, whilst the Economic Commission for Europe aims at economic 'co-operation and integration' of member countries and their 'policy convergence',[13] the others omit reference to integration, confining themselves to 'facilitating co-operation in economic and social development' (Asia-Pacific),[14] 'facilitating concerted action' for dealing with economic problems arising from World War II (Latin America-Caribbean)[15] and 'raising the level of economic activity and levels of living' (Africa).[16]

Thus, in what might have been supposed to be the clearest example of region – UN economic commissions – no light is shed on the inherent meaning of the concept of 'region' for the practical purposes of international diplomacy or regional/global cooperation and governance.

Adding to the confusion on a regional concept or structure for the UN system is the set of regional electoral groups (also referred to as 'groupings') of Member States at the UN (Thakur 1999). These groups are 'unofficial', having been developed in 1963 in order to achieve a more 'equitable representation' in the Security Council and other UN organs.[17] As a result of this, UN Member States are divided into five 'regional groups' for electoral purposes, namely: African Group, Asian Group, Eastern European Group (EEG), Western European and Other States Group (WEOG), and Latin American and Caribbean Group (GRULAC). These groupings reflect yet another 'hybrid' of geography and political concerns. Europe is split between East and West (reflecting the Cold War whose termination has not yet, over two decades later, been reflected in any new electoral formulation). North America is in WEOG, as are two 'antipodean' countries (Australia and New Zealand), and also Turkey. Turkey, however, also 'fully participates' in the Asian group, but for electoral purposes, it is only considered a member of WEOG. Cyprus, which has just joined the EU, is 'in Asia'.[18] There are a few states that did not belong to any group, recently joined or are only loosely affiliated to one of the groups. South Africa had previously been excluded from the group system, but after the end of apartheid was welcomed into the African group. Estonia became a member of the UN in 1991 but only joined the EEG in May 2004. Kiribati (geographically in Oceania) is not a member of any regional group, despite other Oceania nations belonging to the Asian group. Although a member of the UN since 1999, Kiribati has never delegated a permanent representative to the UN. The United States, for its part, advises that 'it is not a member of any regional group', but it attends WEOG (Western Europe and Others) meetings 'as an observer' and is considered to be a member of that group for electoral purposes, leaving to the imagination what other purpose 'membership' would serve. Israel was rejected from the Asian group by the Arab member states and sought affiliation with the WEOG. In May 2000, Israel became a temporary member of this group, as Israel still prefers to join the Asian group. It still has to be seen what will happen with potential new UN members like Kosovo,[19] Southern Sudan[20] and Palestine.[21]

Clearly, the electoral grouping at the UN does nothing to add clarity to the institutional regional issues. On the other hand, the grouping does have significance for security behaviour, insofar as the voting patterns on peace and security issues bears a correlation with electoral breakdowns.

Within the UN System, most bodies apply the electoral group division to demarcate their regional policies. But even here one can observe certain differences. The website of the United Nations Children's Fund (UNICEF) divides countries up in the following regions: Central and Eastern Europe and the Commonwealth of Independent States (CIS) countries, East Asia and the Pacific, Eastern and Southern Africa, Industrialised countries, Latin America and the Caribbean, Middle East and North Africa, South Asia and finally West and Central Africa. This division of the world in particular groups is reflected in the publications of UNICEF, for instance the latest the *State of the World's Children Report 2011*. The World Bank Group adopts yet again a different regional categorisation, comprised of six regions, namely sub-Saharan Africa, North Africa and Middle East, Europe and Central Asia, South Asia, East Asia and Pacific and Latin America and Caribbean. Clearly, regionalism should be taken to respond to the organisational perceptions – whether economic, electoral or security. The World Meteorological Organization (WMO) came up with the most sophisticated demarcations of their regional groups. Members are divided in six groups, called regional associations, each indicated with a Roman number and geographically defined with latitudes and longitudes in Annex II to the WMO Convention.[22] WMO also recognises non-UN member states as WMO member. It is certainly not the only institution within the UN System to do that (one can think of the Holy See or the particular case of the European Communities). But in this specific case, there are six 'additional' members that are commonly referred to as 'territories': British Caribbean Territories, French Polynesia, Hong Kong, Macao, New Caledonia and the Netherlands Antilles and Aruba. Additional divisions in the UN System can be observed when one looks at the implementation of policies on the ground. The United Nations Development Programme (UNDP) has five administrative bureaus, covering Africa, the Arab States, Asia and the Pacific, Europe and the CIS and, finally, Latin America and the Caribbean.[23]

1.2 Bringing the Regions (Further) In: The Case of Peace and Security

The question that might arise is – if the regions are still such an undefined heterogeneous concept, why then the focus on regional action and cooperation with the regions? But indeed, academia and policy-makers alike have been increasingly interested in the regional phenomena and the regional governance approach. The fact is that the international system has been changing in such a way – with the fragmentation of the state and the emergence of new regional actors with an increasing role in development, economic and security governance – that a new concept of regional/global cooperation has become clear and clearly necessary. A number of arguments can be put forward to help understand and strengthen it.

If one looks at the field of peace and security, for example a natural field to study the regionalisation of the UN (considering its primary objective of saving humanity from the scourge of war), one will realise that security itself has become multilevel: less nationally bounded, easily having global ramifications and very often regional in nature. Not only do conflicts spill over and become regional, their consequences gain regional proportions. The same is easily understood for the fields of economy, trade, finance, development, social impacts of immigration and so on.

Governance needs to accommodate the changes in the international system, which has become multilevel, and focusing on the regional level for response. At the same time, regions themselves are changing and becoming more organised in every field – involving political, cultural, and economic and security issues in the broadest contemporary sense – and transforming international organisations. Some organisations have developed from purely economic organs to peacekeepers or even peace enforcers, showing comparative advantages in faster response to conflict and addressing its roots, whilst others have grown from a collective security mandate into much broader, development-related fields.

According to Peou (2001: 89), 'facing so many challenges in security', the UN has a better chance of achieving its goals by helping to build effective regional organisations and security communities. This new form of security governance must be one that enhances the role of the regions, profits their comparative advantages by giving them further responsibilities, but also that keeps the legitimacy of the global body, especially in security, and helps promote cooperation not only between the regional and the global level but also in between the regions to help create a cooperative environment where regions are not competing block-to-block but becoming building blocks of a reformed new multilateral governance system.

Theoretically, regional organisations are pertinent instruments of regional peace and prosperity in two ways. First of all, regional integration processes are an engine for peace – as put forward by the neo-functionalists. Diplomacy, economic and cultural exchange, possibly also soft power rather than military means, are the currency of interactions. Furthermore, the integration process overcomes simple proximity and cooperation in which it slowly intermingles sovereignties, which further blur borders and make peace and security not only expected but crucial for every member of the integration process. The advantage of creating a zone of peace and prosperity or a 'security community'[24] becomes obvious to all its members who already acknowledged the need to lose parts of their sovereignty for achieving common interests and overcoming common threats, as is the case of the EU. Secondly, the geographical changes in conflict make the regional approach logical. The regionalisation of conflict has become a reason for region-building. Regional bodies have an interest to prevent, contain or solve conflicts in their region because of the disastrous humanitarian and development effects – not the least – because of the spillover effects into the region (Hettne 2008: 410).

The ascendancy in regionalism shows that the way to overcome the present crisis in the traditional form of governance portrayed by the UN – intergovernmental multilateralism – is to accept it (regionalism) and build on it. An effective universal organisation for the promotion of peace and development presupposes the existence of a high degree of integration in the world community. And regional organisations can be seen as building blocks for an effective world community. Regional organisations are not to be judged a priori as anti-United Nations or as undermining global organisations, but as stepping stones to this global community of organisations.[25]

The recent discussions on the crisis of multilateralism bring in regional solutions in order to overcome it. Furthermore, the policy-makers within the UN stress the need for an enhanced role of regional groupings. In order to catch up with reality, the theory on international cooperation has to incorporate the regional concepts into multilateralism. As Akindele so well put already in 1976, 'In an international system which already has a universal organization to perform world-wide functions, the ideal is to have regional organisations which actually are regional in their membership, areas of cooperation, and significance, and which confine their activities to well-defined areas corresponding to their circles of membership. The principles of regionalism and universality might then be simultaneously applied to the organization of world peace with a minimum of conflict of competence and jurisdiction' (Akindele 1976: 9).

1.3 Structure and Contents of This Book

This third volume in the series of UNU world reports on regional integration will look at the present place of the regions at the UN, both endogenously (in UN structures) and exogenously (through cooperation with specific organisations with a regional nature), and analyse present and future avenues for the enhancement of the role of the regions at the UN and in the cooperation with the world organisation.

The book is divided in three parts. Part I deals with regional actorness and representation. The first two chapters set the scene. Pascual and Benner (Chap. 2) look at the issue of sovereignty, its validity as a principle in a globalised world, how regional understandings of sovereignty – in different world regions – have evolved over time, and the ways in which regional organisations can contribute to a new understanding sovereignty. Moncayo Jiménez (Chap. 3) looks in detail at the role played by the ECLAC in promoting and supporting regional integration to illustrate the historical contribution of the UN to the formation of regions in different parts of the world and reflect on its role in the future. Kissack (Chap. 4) looks at representational issues and questions the usefulness of assessing regional actorness through the analysis of voting behaviour in the UNGA, thereby focusing on the case of human rights issues. He also enquires whether regional-bloc mentality is becoming stronger or weaker. Drieskens (Chap 5) further problematises the complexities of regional representation at the UNSC and its difficult measurement. She zooms thereby in on the actorness of the EU. Schwartzberg (Chap. 6) addresses UNSC reform, proposes guidelines for devising proposals for reforming representation at the UNSC and develops a proposal based on weighted regional representation. Köchler (Chap. 7) also looks at UN reform and the place of the regions in it.

The second and third parts are devoted to the operational level and the role that is given to the regions by the UN and searched for by the regions and regional organisations themselves in dealing with specific issues. Part II of the book is devoted to the cooperation between the UN and regional organisations in the area of peace and security.

Van Langenhove, Felício and Abass (Chap. 8) look at the high-level meetings (HLMs) with the UN Secretary-General and the joint meetings with the UNSC, and cooperation between the UN and regional organisations in peace and security. The former Secretary-General of LAS, Amre Moussa, reflects on the functional relationship between the UN and the LAS and points to the possibilities to deepen it further (Chap. 9). Abass (Chap. 10) looks at the historical development of cooperation between the UN and regional organisations in peace and security and assesses its legal basis. Tavares (Chap. 11) and Coicaud and Zhang (Chap. 12) provide critical approaches to the cooperation with regional organisation, looking at the shortcomings and limitations of regional organisations in this field (capacities, resources, mandates, impartiality, etc.) and asking for caution. Popovski and Fath-Lihic (Chap. 13) look further into the prospects for 'hybrid missions', and analyse the cases of UNAMID and EULEX. The following two contributions deal with specific organisations and their cooperation with the world body in peace and security: Tan's chapter on the Association of Southeast Asian Nations (ASEAN) and Muller and Schoeman's chapter on AU.

Part III is devoted to cooperation between the UN and the regions in the broader areas of human security, sustainable development and human rights, departing in Chap. 16 (Brauch) from the re-conceptualisation of security and the need to expand the debate on regional/global cooperation – from the peace and security focus of 1945 present in the UN Charter to the so-called human security and soft security issues of the twenty-first century, such as environment and human rights. Brauch builds on this point through an analysis of cooperation on the Mediterranean region. Graham and Maertens give further insight on how the global body needs to bring regional thinking into its structures in a more streamlined and coordinated manner, discussing the recent report on system-wide coherence. Once again, the authors ask the reader for an examination of how the UN needs to reform according to a more regionalised world. Deacon (Chap. 19) looks at social policies and how they are developed at the regional level, whilst Haghebaert (Chap. 20) takes a look at yet another field – health sector and disaster management – also looking at a specific region – the Caribbean. Gowan and Brantner (Chap. 21) focus on the Human Rights Council (HRC) and address the question whether the promotion of universal human rights by the UN is compatible with maintaining an equitable balance of power between regions.

Finally, some general conclusions are presented by the editors of this volume.

Notes

1. Unless stated otherwise, 'regional' refers in this book to the supranational regional level.
2. The European Communities have been an observer within the UNGA since 1974. After the ratification of the Lisbon Treaty in December 2009, that recognises the EU's juridical personality, the newly set-up diplomatic service of the EU, the European External Action Service (EEAS) has been working to enhance the EU's representation in the UN System. For more information on the role of the EU, see the chapters by Kissack and Drieskens in this volume. Good introductions into the relationship between the European Communities and the UN System are Kissack (2010), Laatikainen and Smith (2006) and Wouters et al. (2006).
3. See, for example, Bolderson (2011).
4. See, for example, Arce and Sandler (2002); Estevadeordal et al. (2005); and De Lombaerde and Van Langenhove (2011).
5. See, for example, Mundell (1961), Blejer et al. (1997) and Vinhas de Souza and Weidinger Sosdean (2011).
6. See, for example, Oates (1999).
7. Cited in Nye (1968).
8. For the full membership, see http://www.uneca.org/. And although the contemporary ECA is 'purely' regional, there were historical attempts to propose a rather hybrid form. ECA experienced a difficult birth. It took 13 years to convince colonial powers to accept it. Compromise proposals like the one from India to establish an economic commission for *North Africa and Ethiopia* were hindered (Adedeji 2009: 375 – emphasis added).
9. For the full membership, see http://www.unescap.org/about/member.asp.
10. For the full membership, see http://www.escwa.un.org/.
11. See http://www.eclac.cl/cgi-bin/getprod.asp?xml=/noticias/paginas/7/21497/P21497.xml&xsl=/tpl-i/p18f-st.xsl&base=/tpl-i/top-bottom_acerca.xsl.
12. See http://www.unece.org/oes/nutshell/member_States_representatives.htm.
13. ECOSOC res. 36 (IV) 1947.
14. ECOSOC res. 37 (IV) 1947.
15. ECOSOC res. 106 (VI) 1948.
16. ECOSOC res. 671A (XXV) 1958.
17. UNGA res. 1991 (XVIII), 17 December 1963.
18. This has been explained by Cyprus officials on the grounds that coexistence with Turkey in the WEO group was politically unacceptable.
19. Kosovo declared independence from Serbia on 17 February 2008. Many states recognised its independence, but not all. The international community is quite divided on this matter. For instance Brazil, China, Cyprus, Greece, India, Indonesia, Russia or Spain does not recognise the independence. A request for an advisory opinion was referred to the International Court of Justice (ICJ) on request of the UNGA. The ICJ delivered its advisory opinion on 22 July 2010 where it declared that the declaration of independence of 17 February 2008 did not violate general international law. See Ryngaert (2010) for a legal examination of some of the controversies regarding this matter.
20. A referendum on independence for Southern Sudan was held in January 2011 with 99% of the electorate option for secession. The president of Sudan accepted the results, and Southern Sudan became is independent on 9 July 2011.
21. The Palestinian Authority (PA) applied for UN membership during the UNGA session in September 2011. The likelihood that this would be accepted is rather small, but the PA could still be granted observer status as non-member state, which would entail recognition of the sovereignty of the Palestinian state (Abrams 2011).
22. For instance, regional association IV North America, Central America and the Caribbean is demarcated in the following manner:
    Southern limit

From the point 10°N, 35°W along latitude 10°N to the point 10°N, 62°W, thence westwards along the territorial waters of the coast and islands of Venezuela and Colombia to the coastal boundary of Panama and Colombia, thence along that boundary to the Pacific Coast, thence to the point 5°N, 80°W, thence westwards along latitude 5°N to the point 5°N, 120°W

Eastern limit

From the point 10°N, 35°W northwards along longitude 35°W to the point 59°N, 35°W, thence westwards along latitude 59°N to the point 59°N, 55°W, thence along the central line of Davis Strait, Baffin Bay, Smith Sound, Kane Basin, to the Arctic Ocean

Western limit

From the point 5°N, 120°W to the point 30°N, 140°W, thence westwards along latitude 30°N to the point 30°N and the 180th meridian, thence northwards along the International Date Line

23. http://www.beta.undp.org/undp/en/home.html.
24. For a definition of the concept of security community, see Deutsch et al. (1957) and Adler and Barnett (1998).
25. See Akindele (1976: 14–15) for this discussion.

References

Abrams, E. (2011) *Can the United Nations make Palestine a state? Council on Foreign Relations*, 23 June, http://blogs.cfr.org/abrams/2011/06/23/can-the-united-nations-make-palestine-a-state/

Adedeji, A. (2009). The UN Economic Commission for Africa. In A. Adebajo (Ed.), *From global apartheid to global village. Africa and the United Nations* (pp. 373–398). Scottsville: University of KwaZulu-Natal Press.

Adler, E., & Barnett, M. (1998). *Security communities*. Cambridge: Cambridge University Press.

Akindele, R. A. (1976). *The organization and promotion of world peace: A study of universal-regional relationships*. Toronto: University of Toronto Press.

Arce, D. G., & Sandler, T. (2002). *Regional public goods: Typologies, provision, financing, and development assistance*. Stockholm: Almkvist and Wiksell International/EGDI.

Berthelot, Y. (2004). *Unity and diversity in development ideas. Perspectives from the UN regional commissions*. Bloomington/Indianapolis: Indiana University Press.

Blejer, M., et al. (1997). *Optimum currency areas. New analytical and policy developments*. Washington, DC: IMF.

Bolderson, C. (2011, May 15). *Why UN acted over Libya and Ivory Coast – but not Syria*, BBC News. www.bbc.co.uk.

Breslin, S., Higgott, R., & Rosamond, B. (2002). Regions in comparative perspective. In S. Breslin, C. W. Hughes, N. Philips, & B. Rosamond (Eds.), *New regionalisms in the global political economy* (pp. 1–19). London: Routledge.

Cooper, A. F., Hughes, C., & De Lombaerde, P. (Eds.). (2008). *Regionalisation and global governance. The taming of globalisation*. Abingdon: Routledge.

De Lombaerde, P. (2003). Book review of new regionalism in the global political economy. *Journal of Common Market Studies, 41*(5), 968–969.

De Lombaerde, P., & Van Langenhove, L. (2011). Monitoring and evaluating the provision of (donor-funded) regional public goods. *Regions & Cohesion, 1*(1), 101–123.

De Lombaerde, P., Söderbaum, F., Van Langenhove, L., & Baert, F. (2010). The problem of comparison in comparative regionalism. *Review of International Studies, 36*(3), 731–753.

Deutsch, K. W., et al. (1957). *Political community and the North Atlantic area*. Princeton: Princeton University Press.

Estevadeordal, E., Frantz, B., & Nguyen, T. R. (Eds.). (2005). *Regional public goods – From theory to practice*. Washington, DC: Inter-American Development Bank/Asian Development Bank IDB.

EurActiv. (2011, June 8). *GA chief: Negotiations to reform UN Security Council must start now*. EurActiv, http://www.euractiv.com/en/global-europe/ga-chief-negotiations-reform-un-security-council-start-interview-505422.

Genna, G., & De Lombaerde, P. (2010). The small *N* methodological challenges of analyzing regional integration. *Journal of European Integration, 32*(6), 583–595.

Graham, K., & Felício, T. (2006). *Regional security and global governance: A study of interactions between regional agencies and the UN Security Council*. Brussels: VUB Brussels University Press.

Hettne, B. (2005). Beyond the new regionalism. *New Political Economy, 10*(4), 543–571.

Hettne, B. (2008). Security regionalism in theory and practice. In H. G. Brauch et al. (Eds.), *Globalization and environmental challenges*. Berlin/Heidelberg: Springer.

Hettne, B., & Söderbaum, F. (2000). Theorising the rise of regionness. *New Political Economy, 5*(3), 457–474.

Hettne, B., & Söderbaum, F. (2004). *Regional cooperation. A tool for addressing regional and global challenges* (9). Göteborg: International Task Force on Global Public Goods.

Jessop, R. (2003). The political economy of scale and the construction of cross-border regions. In F. Söderbaum & T. M. Shaw (Eds.), *Theories of new regionalism* (A Palgrave reader). Basingstoke: Palgrave.

Kissack, R. (2010). *Pursuing effective multilateralism: The European Union, international organizations and the politics of decision making*. Basingstoke: Palgrave.

Koonings, K., & Kruijt, D. (Eds.). (2009). *Megacities. The politics of urban exclusion and violence in the global south*. London: Zed Books.

Laatikainen, K., & Smith, K. E. (Eds.). (2006). *Intersecting multilateralisms: The European Union and the United Nations*. Houndmills/Basingstoke/Hampshire: Palgrave Macmillan.

Mansfield, E. D., & Solingen, E. (2010). Regionalism. *Annual Review of Political Science, 13*, 145–153.

Mundell, R. A. (1961). A theory of optimum currency areas. *American Economic Review, 51*(4), 509–517.

Nye, J. (1968). *International regionalism: Selected readings*. New York: Little, Brown.

Nye, J. (1971). *Peace in parts: Integration and conflict in regional organization*. Boston: Little, Brown and Company.

Oates, W. (1999). An essay on fiscal federalism. *Journal of Economic Literature, 37*(3), 1120–1149.

Peou, S. (2001). Security community building for a better global governance.

Russett, B. (1967). *International regions and international system: Study in political ecology*. Chicago: Rand McNally.

Ryngaert, C. (2010). The ICJ's advisory opinion on Kosovo's declaration of independence: A missed opportunity? *Netherlands International Law Review, LVII*, 481–494.

Söderbaum, F. (2009). Comparative regional integration and regionalism. In T. Landman & N. Robinson (Eds.), *The Sage handbook of comparative politics* (pp. 477–496). Los Angeles: Sage.

Tavares, R. (2004). The state of the art of regionalism: The past, present and future of a discipline. *UNU-CRIS Working Papers* (10).

Thakur, R. (ed.). (1999, March 26). *What is equitable geographic representation in the twenty-first century*. Report of a seminar held by the International Peace Academy and the United Nations University, New York, USA.

UNHABITAT. (2008). *Harmonious cities. State of the world's cities 2008/2009*. London: Earthscan.

UNSC. (2011, March 30). *Twenty-seventh progress report of the Secretary-General on the United Nations Operation in Côte d'Ivoire* (S/2011/211). United Nations Security Council.

Van Langenhove, L. (2003). Theorising regionhood. *UNU-CRIS Working Papers* (1).

Van Langenhove, L. (2011). *Building regions*. London: Ashgate.

Vinhas de Souza, L., & Weidinger Sosdean, C. (2011). Optimum currency area criteria. In P. De Lombaerde, R. Flôres, L. Iapadre, & M. Schulz (Eds.), *The regional integration manual. Quantitative and qualitative methods* (pp. 179–197). London: Routledge.

Wouters, J., Hoffmeister, F., & Ruys, T. (Eds.). (2006). *The United Nations and the European Union: An ever stronger partnership*. The Hague: TMC Asser Press.

Part I
Regional Actorness and Representation

Chapter 2
Sovereignty's Evolution: The Role of Regions – Regional Convergence in a Transnational World*

Carlos Pascual and Holly Benner

2.1 Introduction

During the last great negotiation to build international order in the post–World War II era, the creators of the United Nations heralded the principle of state sovereignty as the foundation of a stable international security system. Over 60 years later, profound changes have taken place in the world. From nuclear proliferation, terrorism and infectious disease to conflict and climate change, twenty-first century threats defy borders. Sovereignty is not obsolete as a concept. But sovereignty premised on borders serving as inviolable boundaries simply does not function in a world where money, ideas, capital, labour and even pollution know no bounds. Our ability to govern the planet requires the international community to reinvent its understanding of sovereignty. This chapter addresses how regional organisations can build on diverse experiences to provide the building blocks that put a new understanding of sovereignty to work.

Traditional, or Westphalian sovereignty, developed as a norm in an era where unequal powers and never-ending intervention had threatened global stability. Founders of the United Nations viewed disrespect of national borders as a liability. Sovereignty needed to be reinforced and borders made sacrosanct for a predictable, peaceful and prosperous world. Article 2(1) of the UN Charter states that the organisation is based on the principle of the sovereign equality of all its members. Article 2(7) reinforces the corresponding principle of non-intervention.[1]

* This chapter was written prior to Carlos Pascual's entry into the US Government.

C. Pascual
Formerly with the Brookings Institution, Washington, DC, USA

H. Benner (✉)
The World Bank, Washington, DC, USA
e-mail: hbenner@worldbank.org

P. De Lombaerde et al. (eds.), *The United Nations and the Regions: Third World Report on Regional Integration*, United Nations University Series on Regionalism 3,
DOI 10.1007/978-94-007-2751-9_2, © Springer Science+Business Media B.V. 2012

Globalisation has presented unprecedented challenges and opportunities. The ability to tap into global markets for capital, technology and labour has allowed the private sector to amass wealth unfathomable 50 years ago, and it has helped lift hundreds of millions out of poverty in emerging economies such as China, India and Brazil. Yet the very transnational nature of globalisation has also challenged the precepts that shaped international order and multilateral institutions since World War II. Where the private sector prospered, official institutions have floundered. If states seek to reap the benefits of this 'global age', a fundamental adjustment of global norms and conceptions of sovereignty will be necessary as the foundation for the revitalisation of the multilateral security system.

For guidance, we should look to evolving conceptions of sovereignty incubated at the regional level: from European success in 'pooling sovereignty' to the vibrant debate sparked by African leaders on 'sovereignty as responsibility'. Flush with many of the world's new great powers, evolving Asian conceptions of sovereignty and non-interference will figure centrally in future global norms. Weak 'regional architecture' is also instructive. While many of today's most acute transnational threats – from nuclear proliferation to terrorism and conflict – converge in the Middle East, principles for regional engagement and cooperative arrangements lag woefully behind, arguably making the broader Middle East the most dangerous region in the world today.

Hence, the premise we present in this chapter: for new global norms on sovereignty to take root, they must emanate from diverse regions, and they are best supported through effective regional structures. Regions are bound by shared threats, serve as first responders, are often most adroit at employing diplomatic persuasion and pressure, with vested interests in regional stability. States within a region are often bound in common environmental systems and face common disease burdens and terrorist group activity. Responsible regional organisations can facilitate cooperation, regularise relations, deliver tough messages and build confidence. Regional interventions constrained further outbreaks of violence during Ukraine's Orange Revolution in 2004, and after Kenya's contested elections in 2008. An ad hoc grouping of regional actors has orchestrated the best chance for the denuclearisation of the Korean Peninsula. Conversely, weak regional responses have exacerbated the crises now faced in Zimbabwe and Myanmar.

2.2 Pooling Sovereignty in Europe

The European experience has demonstrated at both a regional and global level the benefits of regional integration and 'pooled sovereignty'. The EU now has an even larger economy and even greater trade flows with the outside world than the United States. The euro competes with the dollar as a global currency. Supranational institutions, such as the European Court of Justice, the European Commission and the European Central Bank, can override national authorities in defined areas. The reason is simple: the gains in economic prosperity and stability. Even so, the initial

Irish rejection of the Lisbon Treaty in June 2008 also underscores that shared sovereignty is controversial – even in a state that may have gained most from its EU membership.

The mandate and role of the Conference for Security and Cooperation in Europe (later the Organisation for Security and Cooperation in Europe (OSCE)) has also been instructive. Most fundamentally, by establishing respect for national borders, OSCE helped build trust between Western and Soviet blocs during the Cold War, and in many respects, this mutual recognition of borders helped avoid violence after the collapse of the Warsaw Pact and the Soviet Union. In the post–Cold War phase, its specific agenda of intrusive and sanctions-backed military confidence building measures (CBMs) to prevent interstate conflicts, preventive diplomacy and election monitoring and assistance in post-conflict settings initiated early understandings that regional assistance for economic, social and political development *within* states was directly tied to regional stability. And despite these successes, the OSCE is today at risk of unravelling, especially due to Russia's efforts to hinder the OSCE's ability to uphold human rights standards established in the organisation's foundational charter.

From Europe, three lessons are clear. First, stability and development within states was aided by the creation of a regional neighbourhood. The prospect for membership in the North Atlantic Treaty Organisation (NATO) and the EU can be considered the world's most successful experiment in democracy promotion. Second, borders and sovereignty are not irrelevant. When states do not understand the benefits of shared sovereignty (Ireland's rejection of the Lisbon Treaty in 2008), or use shared sovereignty as an excuse for weak national policies (France and Netherlands' rejection of the European Constitution in 2005), or resent external scrutiny of the domestic actions (Russia's opposition to OSCE election monitoring in 2008), they will resist vesting power in regional organisations, even when they have benefited. Do not expect progress on new understandings of sovereignty to be linear. Third, and perhaps most importantly for other regions moving forward, integration in Europe worked because the larger powers in the region recognised the potential benefit of tying themselves to a regional architecture (Fukuyama 2005; Krasner 2001).

2.3 Redefining Sovereignty in Africa

Strikingly, the African experience in the post–Cold War era has sparked the most vibrant debate in shaping sovereignty norms. The debate over the contours of sovereignty in Africa has led to the most significant modification of our understanding at sovereignty at the global level, a new definition that can be perceived as an even greater challenge to traditional sovereignty than the European Union experiment (Gandois 2008).

The original charter of the Organisation of African Unity (OAU) exalted sovereignty and non-interference in an effort to make fragile African borders permanent and unquestionable in the post-independence era (Deng et al. 1996). But the reality of state fragility across the continent, permeable borders to flows of insurgents, refugees and arms and internal conflicts that threatened regional neighbourhoods, demanded mechanisms of 'shared sovereignty'. Interventions to address humanitarian need and mediate conflict throughout the 1990s – such as the Economic Community of West African States (ECOWAS) Monitoring Group (ECOMOG) in Liberia – began a march to a redefinition of Westphalian sovereignty for Africa.

In May 1991, President Museveni of Uganda, Chairman of the AU, and Olusegun Obasanjo, Chairman of the African Leadership Forum, gathered African Heads of State for a Conference on Security, Stability and Development Cooperation in Africa to shape the Charter of the African Union (AU) and its Peace and Security Council. The conference was inspired by the Helsinki process in Europe in the 1970s. Salim Salim, Secretary-General of the OAU, said the OAU should take the lead in transcending the traditional view of sovereignty by 'building on the African values of kinship solidarity and the notion that every African is his brother's keeper. We should talk about the need for accountability of governments and of their national and international responsibilities. In the process we shall be redefining sovereignty' (Deng et al. 1996). Salim promoted the OAU mechanism for conflict prevention and resolution as a way for states to intervene swiftly, building norms for preventive action to save lives, while promoting democracy, human rights protection and good governance.

Building on these concepts, Francis Deng, African Statesman and Representative of the United Nations (UN) Secretary-General on Internally Displaced Persons, enunciated the concept of 'responsible sovereignty' in 1993 as a form of state responsibility to one's own displaced population. Deng argued that if a state did not want the international community to intervene, it should provide for the security and well-being of the populations within its borders. If a state refused these protections, the international community had a right, and even a responsibility, to become involved (Cohen 2008). The African Union (AU) is currently developing a legally binding instrument based on the Guiding Principles on Internal Displacement, the first international standards for internally displaced persons (IDPs) whose foundation is sovereignty as responsibility (Cohen 2008: xiii).

Building on these African foundations, an international panel led by Gareth Evans and Mahmoud Sahnoun called on states in 2002 to uphold the 'responsibility to protect' (R2P) as a new international norm. The 2004 report of the UN Secretary-General's High-Level Panel on Threats, Challenges and Change subsequently endorsed the responsibility to protect at a global level (United Nations 2004). In 2005, the African Group at the UN, led by South Africa, won General Assembly endorsement of the principle as an international norm by 191 member states. The World Summit Outcome document asserts that 'states are expected first and foremost to protect their own populations but if they are unwilling or unable to do so – and citizens are subjected to genocide, ethnic cleansing or war crimes – responsibility shifts to the international community which is expected to take collective action' (United Nations 2004). The African Group has begun to articulate its own unique perspective on the protection of civilians, emphasising early warning, the moral imperative to stop genocide and a continuum of responses from prevention to reaction and post-conflict rebuilding. Security Council Resolution 1706 first applied the R2P concept to a specific situation – Darfur (Cohen 2008: xv).

However, in the African context, the 'responsibility to protect' has not always been matched by the 'capacity to protect'. African regional organisations have been under-resourced for the scale of need. African peacekeepers deployed to Darfur had to depend on other countries providing external lift. Many troops needed uniforms and equipment. The AU had little experience in command and control or intelligence. At a political level, while the principles of mutual scrutiny and responsible sovereignty are enshrined, South Africa's unwillingness to exert pressure on Zimbabwe when President Mugabe demonstrated his intent to steal national elections in June 2008, underscored the ability of large actors to unravel an emerging regional consensus.

2.4 Talk Shops in Asia

The Association of Southeast Asian Nations (ASEAN), founded in 1967, has traditionally embraced non-interference, 'common security', the promotion of economic growth and respect for national sovereignty as treasured operating principles. While Asia has held national sovereignty sacrosanct, the Asian financial crisis was a wake-up call that underscored the transnational nature of today's threats and their potential impact on economic development (Acharya 2007). In the wake of the financial crisis, a frenzy of additional regional institution building occurred that now includes the Asia-Pacific Economic Cooperation (APEC), the ASEAN Free Trade Area (AFTA), the Asian Resource Foundation (ARF), ASEAN plus three (China, Japan and South Korea) and the East Asia Summit among others.

In contrast to the European Union (EU), a great degree of distrust exists among the major players in Asia, driven in part by the changing power balances among Japan, China, India, Russia and the United States. This history combined with regional aversion to confrontations that could derail economic interests has resulted in a deep respect for traditional sovereignty and a reluctance to impose formal pressure on state behaviour. Instead, Asia has relied on informal cooperation and the creation of multiple regional arrangements to promote dialogue.

Until the recent passage of the ASEAN charter, there was no legal basis for integration into the ASEAN framework. Rather, states relied on 'soft institutionalism' to socialise states to regional norms. Asian institutions have relied on informal relationships and a shared quest for growth to underpin multilateral cooperation. Many Asian leaders deemed the 'ASEAN way' as more effective because of its avoidance of legalism and emphasis on consultations and consensus building (Acharya and Johnston 2007).

The 'ASEAN way's' limitations arise when it becomes necessary to secure collective action in a crisis. While security cooperation mechanisms such as ARF exist, ASEAN lacks policy instruments, such as the Organisation of American States' Inter-American Democratic Charter, to discourage democratic backsliding or coups. This became evident during Thailand's 2006 military coup: ASEAN nations remained silent (Acharya 2007). ASEAN has also not contributed to regional peacekeeping or peace building efforts such as in Afghanistan and East Timor, in contrast to the AU or EU in their regions.

Still Asian sovereignty norms are evolving. Indonesia allowed ASEAN members to observe the peace process in Aceh. In 2007, ASEAN summit discussions on an ASEAN Charter included the idea that decisions could be made by majority voting and that sanctions could be taken against members breaking the rules. This presented a substantial break from ASEAN's norms of consensus and non-interference (Rolfe 2007). Surin Pitsuwan, the new Secretary-General of ASEAN, has in the past expressed interest in ASEAN taking a greater role in political issues such as Myanmar and other transnational issues such as financial crises, drug trafficking and regional environmental threats (Acharya 2007).

Further impetus may come from a combination of economic, social and cultural marginalisation alongside suboptimal governance structures in places such as Mindanao, southern Thailand and Malaysia. Asian regional institutions may have to confront these traditionally 'domestic' problems and set aside 'non-interference' to deal with domestic issues that threaten regional stability (Ibid.). From another direction, with a disproportionate number of new global powers coming from Asia, global structures (the UN Security Council, World Bank, IMF and G8) will have to make space for Asian representation. Asian organisations and states will play a stronger role in governing regional and global institutions. Inevitably they will face some of the same tensions as Europe as individual states weigh the benefits of stability and predictability against transparency and external scrutiny.

2.5 Chasing Sovereignty in the Middle East

Egypt, Iraq, Lebanon, Saudi Arabia, Syria, Jordan and Yemen formed the Arab League in 1945 as a first step towards Arab unity at about the same time as the initiation of the European community. Yet 60 years later, while Europe has achieved unprecedented regional integration, economic prosperity and regional stability, the Arab League, despite having grown to include 22 countries, has barely gotten out of the blocks.

When the Arab states gained independence in mid-1940s, a defining issue in inter-Arab politics became how to reconcile the existence of separate sovereign states with a commitment to pan-Arabism that viewed borders as artificial and demanded unification. Sentiments of pan-Arabism also at times meant Arab leaders felt licensed to involve themselves in each other's domestic affairs, complicating the search for shared norms of non-interference upon which a stable regional order could be based.

With the decline of pan-Arabism, states in the regions embraced sovereignty and independence, yet borders and statehood remain in dispute (Barnett 1995). Most acute are unresolved issues between Israel and the Palestinians and Lebanon and Syria. Lebanon and Syria are in constant tension. Saddam's invasion of Kuwait in 1991 is still a reminder of tensions among Sunni states. The American invasion of Iraq has been hugely destabilising, as Arab states have no interest in Shi'a dominance in Iraq or greater Iranian influence in the region. Such festering conflicts and disputes across borders have impeded the emergence of a regional structure or norms that can overcome current political dynamics.

Arguably, the Arab League's Charter exacerbates the challenge of building effective regional structures. Article VII, for example, states that unanimous decisions are binding on all member states, but majority decisions are binding only on those states that have accepted them. In other words, members can do as they like. The charter also says each member is free to implement the League's decisions according to its respective laws leaving much open to interpretation. Finally, in a region fraught with authoritarian regimes, corrupt governance and human rights abuses, the charter requires members to 'respect the systems of government established in the other member states and regard them as the exclusive concerns of those states'. Even in Asia, there is growing recognition that national political, economic and social development affects regional stability.

2.6 The Future of Sovereignty: Lessons from the Regions

As the protection of traditional sovereignty was the lynchpin of the 1945 vision of world order, a new conception of sovereignty must underpin efforts to revitalise the United Nations in the face of twenty-first century challenges. In this new 'global age', the nation state remains the undeniable core unit of the international system, but sovereignty must be re-assessed and re-defined.

The Managing Global Insecurity Project (MGI), drawing on diverse regional experiences, has argued that a new era of international cooperation should be built on the principle of *responsible sovereignty: the idea that to manage transnational threats, states must be willing to take responsibility for the external effects of their domestic actions – that sovereignty entails obligations and duties towards other sovereign states as well as to one's own citizens.*[2] To protect national interests and the environment within their borders, even to protect national sovereignty states must negotiate rules and norms to guide actions that reverberate beyond national boundaries.

Africa and the EU have demonstrated that states can benefit from such a reconceptualisation of sovereignty that takes into account their interests across borders. Shared sovereignty has brought wealth and stability to Europe. In Africa, greater national responsibility, and now a willingness to exercise responsibility regionally, has allowed 17 non oil-producing countries (representing about 35% of Africa's population) to grow at about 5% on average for the past 10 years.[3]

That said, borders and national interests matter. The CSCE and post–Cold War experience demonstrated that agreement on national borders was crucial to underpin other forms of cooperation. That lesson still begs to be learned in the Middle East.

Within regions, cooperation among large powers, and their willingness to exert pressure, is crucial. Since October 2006, a common agenda among China, Japan, South Korea and the United States, and a willingness to combine pressure and benefits, have turned the North Korean nuclear nightmare into a potential diplomatic success story. In Africa, just one major power out of sync with the region has undermined regional efforts to achieve legitimate elections in Zimbabwe.

It is possible to achieve new norms and practices when states realise that it is in their self-interest. Activities that were rare and politically infeasible violations of sovereignty during the Cold War are now the UN's most important contribution to international peace and security – diplomacy to prevent civil conflicts, mediation to resolve civil wars, peacekeeping to end civil wars and transitional authority to help ensure that peace is sustainable after civil wars (Jones et al. 2009).

Looking forward, the new 'great power' stewards of the international system will increasingly reside in Asia: the Asian regional experience will play centrally in the perspectives and principles these actors bring to the global stage and efforts to revitalise and reform international institutions for the twenty-first century. Similarly, the Middle East will be a vortex of the challenges that will define the global security environment over the next decades – from nuclear proliferation to economic development to terrorism. A critical gap in regional dialogue and debate on what sovereignty means in this volatile region must be filled, with ramifications for both regional and global stability.

Notes

1. The Charter of the United Nations was signed on 26 June 1945 and came into force on 24 October 1945.
2. MGI is a joint initiative by the Brookings Institution, the Center on International Cooperation at New York University and the Center for International Security and Cooperation at Stanford University which aims to provide recommendations and generate political momentum for the next American President, the United Nations and key international partners to launch a strategic effort to revitalise the multilateral security system in 2009. The recommendations follow over a year of research, analysis and consultations with policymakers and experts from the United States, Asia, Africa, Europe, the Middle East and Latin America and reflect the input of MGI's advisory group, composed of American and international leaders. See Jones et al. (2009).
3. http://allafrica.com/stories/200806200815.html

References

Acharya, A. (2007, August 15). ASEAN at 40: Mid-life rejuvenation? *Foreign Affairs*.

Acharya, A., & Johnston, A. I. (Eds.). (2007). *Crafting cooperation: Regional international institutions in comparative perspective*. Cambridge: Cambridge University Press.

Barnett, M. (1995). Sovereignty, nationalism, and regional order in the Arab state system. *International Organizations, 49*(3), 479–510.

Cohen, R. (2008). Humanitarian imperatives are transforming sovereignty. *Northwestern Journal of International Affairs, 10*(1), 2–12.

Deng, F. M., Kimaro, S., Lyons, T., Rothchild, D., & Zartman, I. W. (1996). *Sovereignty as responsibility*. Washington, DC: Brookings Institution Press.

Fukuyama, F. (2005). Re-envisioning Asia. *Foreign Affairs, 84*(1), 75–87.

Gandois, H. (2008, March 16–30). *Sovereignty as responsibility: Theory and practice in Africa.* Prepared for delivery at the Annual Meeting of the International Studies Association, University of Oxford, Oxford.

Jones, B., Pascual, C., & Stedman, S. (2009). *Power and responsibility: International order in an era of transnational threat.* Washington, DC: Brookings Institution Press.

Krasner, S. (2001). Think again: Sovereignty. *Foreign Policy, 80*(1), 178–190.

Rolfe, J. (2007). A complex of structures: Functional diversity, regional consolidation, and community development in the Asia-Pacific. *Asian Affairs: An American Review, 33*(4), 217–234.

United Nations. (2004). *A more secure world: Our shared responsibility. Report of the Secretary-General's High-Level Panel on Threats, Challenges and Change.* New York: United Nations.

Chapter 3
The Contribution of the Regional UN Economic Commissions to Regional Integration Processes: The Case of ECLAC

Edgard Moncayo Jiménez

3.1 Introduction

This chapter deals with the role the regional UN Economic Commissions have played in support of regional integration processes in the past and explores their possible role in the future. Indeed, all regional UN Commissions (i.e. ECLAC, ECA, ESCWA, ESCAP and UNECE) have a track record of support to regional cooperation and integration in different policy areas, although there is some variation in terms of intensity, modalities as well as direction of this support. The regional commission which has probably been most prominent in this area is ECLAC. The role that this commission has played and is playing in this area is analysed in depth in this chapter, as it is a good starting point for a more general reflection on the potential role of the regional commissions in the future.

The intention of creating a common sociopolitical, economic and cultural space has always been a constant in Latin American history. In counterpoint to local – (sometimes) nationalist – tendencies, a clear inclination towards regional integration can be observed since the beginning of the republican era.[1]

During the first half of the nineteenth century, some of the most distinguished leaders of the emancipating processes in Hispanic America promoted several initiatives in order to achieve the political and economic union of the newly formed sovereign states. These proposals were mainly motivated by the common defence against the potential threat of an incursion by the Holy Alliance (Austria, Russia and Prussia), which since 1815 tried to restrain democracy in Europe and in the

E. Moncayo Jiménez (✉)
Centro de Investigaciones y Estudios, Facultad de Ciencias Administrativas, Económicas y Contables, Universidad Central, Bogotá, Colombia

United Nations University Institute on Comparative Regional Integration Studies (UNU-CRIS), Bruges, Belgium
e-mail: edgardmoncayo@yahoo.com

P. De Lombaerde et al. (eds.), *The United Nations and the Regions: Third World Report on Regional Integration*, United Nations University Series on Regionalism 3, DOI 10.1007/978-94-007-2751-9_3,

New World. Furthermore, these initiatives were also aimed at the consolidation of the rising democracy and the economic positioning in the emerging international division of labour.[2]

The most outstanding project in the Latin American integration protohistory was the Amphictyonic Congress of Panama in 1826, promoted by the Liberator Simón Bolívar. A Treaty of Union League and Perpetual Confederation was signed at the Congress, with the aim of creating a confederation intended to unite themselves 'against every attempt of foreign dominance'. The event held in Panama attracted delegates from current Colombia, Ecuador, Panama, Venezuela and Peru (Andean countries); Costa Rica, Guatemala, Honduras, Nicaragua, El Salvador (Central American); and Mexico. The absence of the southern nations, the covert opposition from the United States (US),[3] the common fears from the Bolivarian countries themselves and the participants' lack of political will to ratify the treaty turned the Congress of Panama into one of Bolivar's thwarted dreams.

The Congress of Panama can be described by the contemporary integration discourse as an initiative focused on a continental union scheme to achieve the convergence of the different integration processes between nations during the third decade of the nineteenth century. Such integration processes included Great Colombia (formed by Nueva Granada (current Colombia), Venezuela and Ecuador), the United Provinces of Central America (Federal Republic of Central America) (formed by Guatemala, El Salvador, Honduras, Nicaragua and Costa Rica) and the United Provinces of Rio de la Plata (formed by current Argentina, Bolivia, Paraguay and Uruguay).

This period of integrationist euphoria was followed by a new and long cycle, marked not only by sharp nationalisms but sadly also by numerous conflicts between several nations in the region. The fragmenting forces penetrated at a national level, causing internal frictions and divisions who have not yet been solved. Consequently, the territorial issue in its internal and external dimensions has been at the centre of Latin American history over the years.

With the exception of sporadic regrouping attempts in the second half of the nineteenth century,[4] only after the Second World War would Latin America restore the lost path of integration.

3.2 First Wave of Latin American Regionalism

In an international context characterised on the political scene by the Cold War and on the economic scene by the beginning of a period distinguished by positive economic growth and world trade that would last for 30 years, the early regionalism in Latin America found its concrete expression in the Latin American Free Trade Association – LAFTA (1960), the Central American Common Market (1960), the Caribbean Free Trade Association – CARIFTA (1968)[5] and the Cartagena Agreement (1969).

This first generation of integrationist schemes in the region, contemporary to the European integration process, had a common denominator: the liberalisation of trade. In the case of the Cartagena Agreement (Andean Group), the Central American Common Market (1960) and the CARICOM (1973), the goal was the establishment of a common market, through the previous creation of a customs union. These treaties, especially the Central American and Andean ones, pursued long-term development goals based on large-scale industrialisation and productive complementarity amongst associate states. The achievement of these objectives required an active role of the state.

Argentina, Brazil, Chile and Uruguay already enjoyed a considerable amount of exchanges and trade, boosted by free trade and payment agreements between themselves. Thus, they played a determinant role in the shaping of LAFTA whose membership also included Bolivia, Colombia, Ecuador, Mexico, Paraguay, Peru and Venezuela (Wionczek 1964a).

Unlike the European experience, where the political impulse was essential ('we're [EEC] not in business, we're in politics'[6]), Latin American post-war regionalism originated from purely economic considerations.[7] Therefore, the obstacles to the process of import substitution, the generalised difficulties in the balance of payments, the narrowness of internal markets (worsened with the unequal distribution of income) and the need to enhance employment creation in order to absorb the demographic explosion were amongst the factors that led Latin America to look for alternatives for reaching economic growth and social development based on regional cooperation. Furthermore, the Treaty of Rome, signed in 1957, was expected to restrict the Latin American exports to Europe.

In this regard, the role of the Economic Commission for Latin America – ECLAC – was fundamental. ECLAC was established in 1948, after a decision of the United Nations in 1947. During the 1950s, ECLAC framed a systematic and coherent approach to Latin American development.

Based on the 'Economic Survey of Latin America, 1948' and Raul Prebish's seminal contribution 'Economic Development of Latin America and its Principal Problems', published in 1949 (as a prologue of the 'Economic Survey...'[8]) and being supported by a group of remarkable intellectuals under the leadership of Prebish himself, ECLAC developed the well-known 'Latin American structuralism' theory, building a truly integrated concept of development. Thus, ECLAC's theoretical framework dealt with growth, capital accumulation, structural change, technological progress, income distribution and international integration of the peripheral economies (Rodríguez 2000).

The main ideas of ECLAC at the time were closely linked to the proposals developed by structuralist authors such as Kuznets, Hirschman, Myrdal and Kaldor, and therefore, industrialisation was thought to represent the most appropriate means to achieve higher levels of development. These common approaches and the influence of those authors in development policies across many peripheral countries (in Latin America, Egypt, India, etc.) represented what Ranis (2004) called the 'Post-War consensus'.[9]

ECLAC's understanding of industrialisation found several justifications. First, the need for an endogenous source of growth in order to overcome the external restrictions caused by the deterioration on the terms of trade. Second, the importance of generating their own technological changes due to the asymmetric concentration of innovation and benefits in the industrialised countries. Third, the need to increase employment in order to absorb the excess of labour supply with low productivity in the agricultural sector.

Finally, the strengthening of the industrialised sector, full employment and the increase of productivity and wages would contribute to improve the income distribution and to overcome long-term structural poverty (Fitzgerald 1998).

In the four above-mentioned aspects, the participation of the state through trade policies, productive incentives, coordination and planning of public investment were essential.

It should be observed that, unlike stated by the literature criticising ECLAC, the Commission has never proposed an autarchic model. On the one hand, already in the early 1960s ECLAC proposed an export strategy for manufactures through intra–Latin American trade and through the suppression of tariff barriers in core countries (Bielschowsky 1998: 23).[10] The means to achieve these goals were, respectively, Latin American integration schemes and the creation of the United Nations Conference on Trade and Development (UNCTAD) in 1964, under the leadership of Prebish himself.

In the framework of this conference, the core countries established a system of unilateral tariff preferences in favour of developing countries in 1971 (Generalised System of Preferences).

This context reveals the reasons propelling ECLAC to focus on Latin American integration. The purpose was the liberalisation of commercial exchanges between countries in the region to overcome the limitations of national markets through the use of economies of scale and the expansion of the horizons of import substitution to the regional level (Wionczek 1964 b: XVII). The initial contribution of ECLAC to regional integration was the 'Economic Survey of Latin America, 1949', as well as some studies on Latin American trade within the region and worldwide, drafted by specialised working groups. Moreover, ECLAC encouraged the Central American integration process initiated in 1951, which achieved its first contractual formulation with the 'General Treaty on Central American Economic Integration', signed in Managua in 1960.

ECLAC's work in that period was compiled in the report 'The Latin American Common Market and the multilateral payment systems', presented by the Executive Secretary in 1959.[11] According to the document '[…] the common market aims at the creation of a new model for Latin American trade more suitable to meet the need for industrialisation and reduce external vulnerability' (CEPAL 1959: 330).[12]

It is remarkable that the document rejects any plan or pretension of self-sufficiency in a clear, categorical and resolute way. On the contrary, the idea of integration as a platform to improve the international inclusion of Latin America is stressed throughout the report:

> The need for industrialisation in these countries is undeniable. It is also indisputable that by intending to fulfil this objective within small countries, there will be a deprivation – in a much higher level than with bigger countries – of specialisation opportunities and lower costs which can only be attained inside a common market. This market should be organised in such a way that it stimulates industrial expansion of the region's less developed countries [...] the common market will contribute to reduce the cost of production and boost industrial manufacture exports [...] Latin American Common Market policy, as it has been conceived, is far from being against international trade, but on the contrary supporting it
>
> (CEPAL 1959: 330–337)[13]

Besides, ECLAC's integrationist proposals were not hostile to foreign direct investment: '[...] foreign capital will have a vital role in the next years. Therefore, it will help to create the necessary conditions for Latin America endogenous growth' (CEPAL 1959: 345).[14] Nevertheless, the report states that a restructuring of trade policies in the core countries is required in order to achieve the double goal of boosting trade with the rest of the world and trade within the region:

> [...] a readjustment of trade policy [of industrialised centres] will be necessary [...] without it, the Latin American common market cannot by itself promote trade with the big centres. If Latin America's trade flow towards the latter centres continues to be composed solely by traditional products, still bounded by current barriers, the quantity of imports coming from those big centres will be the same with or without the common market, and only its composition would have changed. However, if the readjustment of trade policy would improve the conditions for primary exports and open new opportunities for industrial exports, the Latin American common market could apply all its potential to increase trade
>
> (CEPAL 1959: 37)[15]

Regarding operational aspects, ECLAC proposed an integration model with the following characteristics:

- A common market opens to all other Latin American countries, with a common external tariff and universal product coverage, to be achieved in stages.
- Harmonisation of industrial policies and agreements of industrial complementation, in order to encourage the advanced phase of import substitution.
- Special treatment to relatively less-developed countries and to the traditional agriculture sector.
- Safeguard clauses for sensitive products and compensation mechanisms to assure an equitable distribution of benefits.
- A multilateral payments agreement.
- State-led integration with an active role for the private sector.

The above-mentioned Treaty of Montevideo (1960) reflected the majority of elements of ECLAC's proposal, though in a 'light' version due to the fact that the southern countries (Argentina, Uruguay, Brazil and Chile) had proposed a scheme with a narrower scope, in which only trade liberalisation was pursued. According to Wionczek (1964a: 71):

> Therefore, the final formula accepted by the seven promoting countries[16] showed all the characteristics of a transaction. Some consider that its biggest virtue is to avoid a political and economic rupture in Latin America, for which the conditions for a serious long-term regional economical cooperation should be created.[17]

Also in 1960, the 'General Treaty on Central American Economic Integration' was signed in Managua (Nicaragua) by Guatemala, El Salvador, Honduras and Nicaragua,[18] culminating a process that started in the preceding decade with the active support from ECLAC. The Treaty of Managua was more ambitious than the Treaty of Montevideo since the former aimed at the creation of a common market, a customs union, an accelerated programme of trade liberalisation, an industrial development plan and cooperation in areas such as infrastructure and investment financing. In order to pursue the latter, the Central American Bank for Economic Integration (1960) was created. A multilateral payment system was also established in 1961. And in 1964, the 'Agreement for the Establishment of the Central American Monetary Union' was formalised although it was never fully implemented.

The reactions from the international community to the first generation of Latin American integration processes were diverse. Whereas the USA – unlike in the case of European integration – had held an ambiguous and fearful position towards Latin America's integration efforts and towards ECLAC itself, it decided to endorse LAFTA and the Treaty of Managua during the Conference of Punta del Este (Uruguay) in 1961. In this meeting of the Inter-American System,[19] summoned by the initiative of President Kennedy to multilateralise the Alliance for Progress, the US delegation proposed the inclusion in the final text of the 'Charter of Punta del Este' of the following declaration according to which one of the purposes of the Alliance for Progress was:

> To strengthen existing agreements on economic integration, with a view to the ultimate fulfilment of aspirations for Latin American common market that will expand and diversify trade among the Latin American countries and thus contribute to the economic growth of the region.

An entire section of the charter is devoted to the means by which the Alliance for Progress would contribute to the economic integration of Latin America (Levinson and De Onis 1970: 170).[19]

The GATT and the International Monetary Fund (IMF) adopted totally opposed positions. The first, following the precedent established by the Treaty of Rome, declared LAFTA compatible with its rules on free trade. The latter, by contrast, rejected the establishment of payment and compensation mechanisms in the framework of LAFTA arguing that it could lead to bilateralism and delay the region's course to convertibility and liberalisation of trade and payments already underway (Dell 1966: cap. IX).

According to Fernando H. Cardozo (1977), the 1960s were the 'Golden Age' of ECLAC. There was a full convergence between its ideas on industrialisation-driven development and the need to enlarge markets through integration, on the one hand, and the actually adopted policies by the Latin American countries. Maria da Conceição Tavares (1998), a prominent Brazilian economist from the ECLAC school of thought, rightfully synthesises ECLAC's position on integration:

> In sum, regional economical integration was conceived, as shown in ECLAC's original documents, as a strategic vector intended to break out of the prevailing lack of dynamism and productivity in the Latin American economy. It would project itself in three interdepen-

> dent dimensions: the acceleration of growth, the expansion and diversification of exports, and the progress of industrialisation
>
> (Tavares 1998: 202)[20]

In the first years of LAFTA, the liberalisation of commercial exchanges was very slow, and it was mainly concentrated on raw materials and foodstuff coming from Argentina and Brazil and, on a smaller scale, from Uruguay and Paraguay (Cline 1983: 317). This led Colombia's President Lleras Restrepo and Chile's President Frei to propose to the other Andean countries a more ambitious sub-regional agreement. In 1969, Bolivia, Colombia, Chile, Ecuador and Peru concluded the Cartagena Agreement (Andean Group), also joined by Venezuela in 1973 (whereas Chile left in 1976).[21]

The aim of the Andean Group was not the creation of a self-sufficient space detached from LAFTA. On the contrary, it aimed at the strengthening of commercial bonds and productive complementation between the members of the Association. Nevertheless, its integration model was more advanced than the LAFTA one.

The Andean Group aspired to become a common market with harmonised economic policies towards third countries by means of a common external tariff and a common regime for foreign direct investment (FDI) and technology. Furthermore, the Andean Group saw as one of its major objectives balanced sub-regional growth, formalised in a regime of preferential treatment for the less developed countries (i.e. Bolivia and Ecuador) in all the programmes of the agreement. Amongst its main mechanisms, a policy of integrated industrial development was foreseen to jointly carry out programmes in new industrial sectors.[22]

In 1973, Prebish declared enthusiastically that the scheme of the Cartagena Agreement overcame many of LAFTA's limitations:

> I believe that the existence and the development of the Andean Group will help to clarify more than one doubt or sceptical opinion regarding the Latin American attitude. It is positive that the Cartagena Agreement has made use of the LAFTA experience, trying to overcome and correct the previously mentioned flaws
>
> (Prebisch 1973: 35)[23]

One of the strengths of the Andean Group underlined by Prebish was the existence of an Executive Secretariat which, similarly to ECLAC, had the legal and technical capability to act in accordance with the collective objectives and independently from the member states' interests (Prebisch 1973: 34–35). Devlin and Estevadeordal (2001: 2) argue that the Andean model of integration is a good synthesis of the first wave of Latin American regionalism.

Since its beginning, Latin America integration faced huge obstacles, such as those related to the accentuated differences in levels of income and productive development between the countries involved in the process. Unlike the European Economic Community which departed from relatively homogeneous national structures combined with strong economic interdependence (building on century-old ties), Latin America showed a high degree of 'structural heterogeneity', in Aníbal Pinto's words. This author explains that the economies in the region were characterised by the coexistence of several 'modern poles' – composed by export activities (primary commodities) and industrial activities, with good productivity performance – and 'primitive' production systems which had not experienced structural changes since colonial times (Pinto 1970).

Consequently, almost half of Latin American population was far away from the dynamics of the modern capitalist market integration was aiming for.

A second element that hindered the evolution of Latin American integration was the lack of commitment from the governmental elites of the region regarding the adoption of harmonised macroeconomic policies. In practice, each country continued elaborating exchange rate, fiscal and monetary policies addressing their domestic needs, disregarding the declared objectives of intensifying cooperation within the region. In third place, there were the difficulties associated with the adopted integration models: exclusive trade orientation and weak institutional basis in LAFTA, unrealistic objectives in terms of joint industrialisation and very complex institutional structures in the cases of the Andean Group and the Central American Common Market.

Last but not least, the import substitution strategy (ISI) was incoherently pushed forward. Some of the most serious limitations of this strategy in Latin America were the existence of tariff patterns that provided exaggerated protection to consumer goods that discouraged the internal production of machinery and other equipments, lack of interest in export development, excessive intrusion by multinational companies and absence of endogenous technical progress. In these circumstances, the 'modern' industrial sector was unable to deploy Kaldor's virtuous cycles, which had characterised industrialisation in advanced countries, at the regional level, as had been proposed by ECLAC.

In spite of this, during the 1960s and the 1970s, Latin American integration achieved some significant successes. The intra-regional trade share (measured by exports) in LAFTA's member states went from 6.7% in 1961 to 14.0% in 1980 (Aladi 1983),[24] growing even more in the Central American Common Market.[25] The Andean Group developed a solid institutional base including an investment bank (*Corporación Andina de Fomento*).

However, the profound disturbances in the world economy which took place in the 1970s and 1980s led to the failure of the first wave of Latin American regionalism. Thus, this period is often identified by ECLAC as 'the lost decade' for the development of the region.

Amongst other factors, the 1973 and 1979 oil shocks, the fiscal crisis of the mid-1970s and the abandonment by the USA of the Bretton Woods rules on fixed parities, meant for developed countries the end of an expansive cycle known in economic history as the 'golden age'.

Simultaneously with falling economic activity and productivity, oil prices were increased by OPEC in 1973. The corresponding need for international banks to recycle exceeding funds from oil producing countries led to a massive expansion of the international movements of capital. This astonishing increase of capital transactions, together with the technological revolution in central countries, established the beginning of the current phase of globalisation.

Such processes were accompanied by an ideological shift in favour of the free market under the leadership of President Reagan and Prime Minister Thatcher. This shift was further reinforced by the implosion of the Soviet Union and the generalised collapse of the socialist regimes.

In conclusion, this period did not mean – as previously noted – an 'age of change' but rather a 'change of age', and in this transition, Latin America got the worst of it. Developed countries faced the emerging challenges with a new range of fossil energy-saving technological innovations and made the transition towards an information- and knowledge-based economy. On their side, the Southeast Asian region succeeded in consolidating its industrial export model benefiting from a wide access to the North American market.

Latin America, on the contrary, became trapped in the landslide of Eurodollars and petrodollars that flooded the region with unconditional loans and negative interest rates in the 1970s. Later, in the 1980s, a complete change occurred and massive volumes of financial resources were withdrawn, sinking the region for a whole decade. Besides, high-debt service payments, with remarkably high interest rates, were accompanied by a generalised worsening of the terms of trade, a reduction of the demand for primary commodities in the North and, consequently, a restricted access to fresh capital resources.

In this period of the world economic history (1980–1990), developed countries registered an annual 2.0% per capita growth and decisively entered a new stage of globalisation and technological changes. Asia achieved the highest growth in the post-war period (4.9%),[26] successfully entering in productive activities with high technological content. Paradoxically, Latin America experienced on average a tightening of –0.1% of per capita GDP and suffered a severe regression in all political and structural dimensions of its development process.

This situation was exacerbated by the structural adjustment programmes adopted by Latin American governments in order to face the crisis. These programmes provided a severe reduction of public spending – especially in the social sector – and on imports, causing a deep recession and also a generalised deterioration of the social indicators. As a result, between 1980 and 1990, the regional GDP per capita fell by 9%, and the real minimum wage dropped 31%, whilst poverty and extreme poverty increased by 5% and 3%, respectively.[27] In addition to those recessive adjustment policies, the IMF and The World Bank introduced 'conditionality' clauses in the financing operations.

The devastation produced by the Latin American debt crisis during the 1980s seriously damaged the main pillars of the development model that Latin America had been following until then: industrialisation based on import substitution, state intervention and economic integration.

The dismantling of industrialisation policies, which started in the 1970s in the Southern Cone (Argentina, Uruguay and Chile) (Ramos 1986), became a general trend in Latin America during the years of the debt crisis. The countries of the region were convinced that the industrialisation process was worn out and has caused serious distortions in the structure of relative prices in their economies. Unilateral trade liberalisation was initiated by Bolivia, Mexico and Costa Rica and spread to the rest of the countries of the region in the beginning of the 1990s (French-Davis 2005: 50).

It is undeniable that import substitution industrialisation showed indeed serious limitations and was affected by significant incoherencies, as ECLAC had timely warned. However, in the same period, Latin America also witnessed significant progress on all its development fronts, described by the World Bank – in its first World Development Report (1978) – as 'a substantial improvement of the historical record' (Brutton 1998:916). Additionally, as Chang (2003) clearly states, almost all currently developed economies used intensively several forms of protectionism in order to achieve their economic take-off. This is what happened also in the recent case of South East Asian industrialisation (Aoki et al. 1998).

In addition to the trade liberalisation, a reduction of the functions of the state was implemented, as prescribed by the neoliberal paradigm that began to prevail during that period in Latin America. The concept of a 'developmental state', with an active role through planning, the protection of the internal market, fiscal policy and direct investment in strategic sectors, was gradually replaced by a 'smaller state' via privatisation, fiscal orthodoxy and market deregulation.[28] In regard to the new economic growth strategy, this was captured by the often repeated *dictum* 'the best industrial policy is *no* industrial policy' (Ocampo 2008: 47).

In such a context, it was to be expected that the integration model aimed at boosting the import substitution strategy at the regional level also entered into a crisis. It was a real 'identity crisis' since the integration process lost its way due to the lack of higher industrialisation objectives and active state leadership.

3.3 The Second Latin American Regionalism

The above-mentioned transformations in the world economy and changes in development policies in Latin America, associated with a worldwide revaluation of regionalism, led to Latin America's 'second regionalism' in the 1990s.

Although up until then globalisation was expected to stimulate multilateralism, during that period, there was a movement towards regional integration agreements at an international level, as noted by Diana Tussie: 'It could be argued that, paradoxically, globalisation has not accelerated but has actually slowed down the development of the multilateral trading system over the last decade' (Tussie 1998: 81).Therefore, by that time, more than 90% of the members at the WTO were participating in regional integration agreements. This paradox could be explained, as suggested by Charles Oman (1996), by the fact that national states wanted to take part in economic internationalisation without endangering their autonomy to manage their commercial flows.

The limitations of GATT multilateralism[29] at that time, the consolidation of the European Union (EU) with the Treaty of Maastricht of 1992, the adoption of the euro and the accession of ten new member states also played a role in the renewed importance of regionalism and the 'second regionalism' wave (Bhagwati 1991). Regarding the accessions of the new EU member states, it has been observed that the enlargement or extension of the existing regional agreements gives an incentive for non-members either to apply for membership, so that they are not left aside, or engage in new agreements (i.e. a 'domino effect' occurs, according to Baldwin, 1993).

In the case of Latin America, this second regionalism wave was due, amongst other factors, to the new position adopted by the USA. As previously mentioned, this country had been a champion of free trade and multilateralism since the end of the Second World War and, therefore, sceptic and many times opposed towards Latin American integration. However, the USA considerably changed its trade policy and began showing a growing interest towards regional integration initiatives. First, the Caribbean Initiative was launched in 1983. Subsequently, bilateral free trade agreements with Israel and Canada were concluded in 1985 and 1989, respectively. Moreover, the USA joined APEC in 1989. Finally, in 1992, the North American Free Trade Agreement (NAFTA) was put in place with Mexico and Canada (Panagariya 1998). The culminating point of this new American attitude towards regionalism took place in 1990, when the administration of President Bush Sr introduced the Americas Initiative, proposing a continental scale free trade area.[30]

Other relevant causes behind this renewed inclination towards regionalism were the consolidation of certain structural reforms that were already underway, the necessity of attracting FDI and the interest in undertaking functional cooperation initiatives in fields such as infrastructure and energy.

The transformation of LAFTA into the Latin American Integration Association (LAIA) in 1980 can be regarded as the first Latin American movement towards the new regionalism. This treaty initially proposed as long-term objective the creation of a Latin American Common Market, although in practical terms it became an overly open and flexible scheme where almost everything was possible: multilateral and bilateral agreements between member countries or between the latter and other Latin American countries, and the inclusion of issues not just related to trade but also to agriculture, tourism, science, technology or economic complementarities, amongst others. None of them included deadlines or specific chronograms (Vieira 2008: 103–107).

In the following years, several other agreements were signed: the Group of Three (G-3) between Colombia, Mexico and Venezuela (1989), the Common Market of the Southern Cone (MERCOSUR) between Argentina, Brazil, Uruguay and Paraguay (1991),[31] the transformation of the Andean Group into the Andean Community (1997) and the transformation of CARICOM (2002). In addition, NAFTA was signed between Canada, Mexico and the USA in 1994, representing the first integration scheme between the latter and a Latin American country. From that moment onwards, these North–south interregional agreements became one of the most characteristic elements of the new stage of Latin American regionalism.

This collection of integration schemes showed some common characteristics, which enables us to label them as 'second regionalism'. These common factors included wider product coverage and 'depth' of the agreements, liberalisation of FDI, enhanced participation of private sector and, above all, search for compatibility between a reasonable protection of the integrated market and the efficient insertion in the international markets.[32] In conclusion, the new agreements were *pro-market, pro-trade, pro-competition and pro-FDI.*

Table 3.1 First versus second regionalism

First regionalism	Second or open regionalism
Functional auxiliary instrument of ISI in order to expand protected markets	Functional for the strategy of insertion in the world's economy – third way towards the global liberalisation of markets
Agreements between countries with similar development levels (North-North or South-South)	Agreements between developed and less developed countries (North-South)
Hostility of the USA	Active support from the USA
Superficial integration (industrial goods, tariffs)	Deep integration (all products, services, investment and competition regimes)
Restrictions to FDI	Attraction of FDI
Economic scope	Economic, social and political scope
Governmental initiative	Active participation from private companies
Resource allocation through planning and political negotiation	Market-based allocation of resources
Differentiated treatment of least developed countries	Equal norms, although with different adjustment periods

Source: Author's elaboration, based on Lawrence (1997)

A synoptic comparison between first and second (open) regionalism is represented in Table 3.1.

In the context of above-mentioned changes in the international environment and in the orientations of development and integration policies in Latin America, ECLAC, following its historical-structuralist method, adjusted its position according to the sequence of historical events. Thus, ECLAC first proposed expansive adjustment policies and debt renegotiation and afterwards, a new strategy oriented towards long-term growth (CEPAL 1990b).

The core of this new strategic vision – inspired by the work of Fernando Fajnzylber (1983, 1988, 1990) – was a renewed proposal for industrialisation based on the creation of an endogenous core of technical progress,[33] needed in order to achieve 'genuine' competitiveness in the international market. The 'productive transformation with social equity', which articulated ECLAC's contributions, also granted an essential role to an equitable income distribution considering the latter determines consumption patterns and hence savings and investment rates which influence the relationship between capital and production (Bielschowsky 1998).

According to the document 'Productive transformation with social equity' (CEPAL 1990):

> [t]he productive transformation with social equity can be achieved in the context of better international competitiveness. Such competitiveness should rely more on a deliberate and systematic incorporation of technical progress in the productive process (with the corresponding productivity increases) than on shrinking of real wages. Thus, greater recognition of the learning dimension and of the diffusion of the available knowledge at the international level is needed, a prerogative hardly ever used by the region in the past [...]
>
> Industrialisation constitutes the core of the productive transformation, mainly because it supports technical progress, and also because, due to the new circumstances, policies have to beyond the former narrow sectoral approach. Instead, industrialisation should aim to

> connect itself with the primary and services sectors in order to integrate the productive system and contribute to the progressive harmonisation of productivity levels. The overcoming of sectoral entrapment is one of the keys of the productive transformation and the new stage of industrialisation
>
> (CEPAL 1990: 14)

As mentioned before, ECLAC's theoretical approach in the three previous decades was known as 'structuralism'; therefore, the new proposals from the 1980s and 1990s were accordingly named 'neo-structuralism':

> After the analytical recoil experienced under the dominance of the monetarist approach, there should be, in our opinion, a revitalisation of the structuralist tradition by incorporating therein a systematic concern about the design of economic policies. Macroeconomic equilibria, coordination between the short-term and the long-term, coordination between private and public sectors, building-up of more equitable production and management structures, and the adoption of strategies and policies aiming for an enhanced national autonomy are very important aspects. This is what could be described as 'neo-structuralism'. Its most defining characteristic consists of offering selective policies instead of the theoretically neutral neo-liberal policies
>
> (French-Davis 1988: 39)[34]

Whereas the first Latin American regionalism emerged in the theoretical framework of ECLAC's structuralism, the second generation of regional and sub-regional integration agreements found its conceptual support in the notion of 'open regionalism', derived from 'neo-structuralism' and developed by ECLAC in the first half of the 1990s. According to ECLAC in 1994:

> 'Open regionalism' is defined as the process that follows the conciliation of both phenomena [...] interdependence as the result of special preferential agreements and interdependence driven by trade liberalisation in general. Open regionalism intends to reconcile explicit integration policies with other – complementary – policies pursuing international competitiveness. What makes open regionalism differ from the opening-up of the economy and non-discriminatory export promotion is a preferential ingredient, reflected in integration agreements and reinforced by geographic and cultural proximity between the countries in the region.
>
> A complementary objective of open regionalism is to become a building-block of favouring a more open and transparent international economy, instead of being an obstacle that hinders it and limiting the options of Latin America and Caribbean countries
>
> (CEPAL 1994: 12–13)[35]

Consequently, the wider opening to international markets, as one of the innovative elements in the approach of 'productive transformation with social equity', was reflected in ECLAC's 'open regionalism' framework. Additionally, regarding Baghwati's question (1991) on whether multilateralism and regionalism are complementary or supplementary, ECLAC opted for the first. Thus, according to ECLAC's new views, integration is a 'building block' rather than a 'stumbling block' for a free and competitive international market.

According to Pizarro (1999: 34), this change in ECLAC's point of view meant that Latin American integration continues to represent a valid instrument not longer for industrialisation based on import substitution but for growth based on international trade. Furthermore, the role of the state – another of ECLAC's major principles of integration – was consequently weakened.

Palacio observed on a critical tone:

> The concept of open regionalism at the end of the 20th century represents a change in the paradigm of regional integration. Regional integration no longer aims to support national industrial development but, on the contrary, to create trade at the multilateral level. In this new paradigm, not only trade in goods but also trade in service is relevant, as well as other issues that had not been covered by the old regionalism agenda. This new regional integration paradigm is no longer State-centred. Instead, it attempts to discipline State intervention through a new governance model ruled by markets and international capital
>
> (Palacio 2006: 4)[36]

The idea of open regionalism also found enthusiastic reception in international organisations such as the World Bank and the Inter-American Development Bank (IADB). According to the World Bank:

> In sum, there are both political economy and purely economic arguments that support the political decision to move forward with unilateral trade liberalisation and regionalism. In any event, there is little doubt that they were part and parcel of the same political decision to integrate LAC economies into the global economy, and we could even argue that one process would not have happened without the other in many LAC countries. There is, thus, a case to judge jointly the outcome of both processes and not to attempt an artificial separation in the analysis
>
> (World Bank 1998: 6)

The IADB (2002) sustained that:

> The regional initiatives that emerged in the 1990s have been characterised as the 'new regionalism.' This is because the role of regional integration has changed dramatically with respect to the early post-war episode. The new regionalism is an integral part of an overall structural policy shift in Latin America towards more open, market-based economies, operating in a democratic system.
>
> (IADB 2002: 4)[37]

A strong dissenting opinion in the academic world was Baghwati's, who, concerned by the negative effects of free trade agreements on trade liberalisation at a multilateral level, sustained that:

> An FTA, because of the *inherent* discrimination that it implies in freeing trade, is different from free trade. Indeed, its flip side is protectionist-protectionist against non-members, against whom the relative protection is increased because barriers fall in favour of members, while the ones against non-members remain in place
>
> (Baghwati 1995: 13)

Based on this premise, Baghwati recommended the following:

> The policy option for the United States is entirely clear. We should revert to exclusive focus on multilateralism and MFN-based trade liberalisation, asking the South American nations to join in the multilateral opening of markets through a variety of initiatives, while pursuing 'regionalism' and its separate objectives through non-PTA means. In short, we should renounce the FTAA gracefully, easing into an Americas Initiative that focuses, like APEC,

> on issues like security, democracy, human rights, drug trafficking, customs procedures and a whole host of issues of hemispheric interest, while becoming a regional platform for launching multilateral trade liberalisation initiatives
>
> (Baghwati 1995: 18)

The movement towards integration in Latin America experienced a period of intensification during the 1990s. Open regionalism was clearly in the convergence of two tendencies: the US stance on regionalism – induced by changes in its relative position in worldwide geopolitics – and Latin America's stance towards the market economy and international trade.

Amid such converging interests, the Bush Sr administration proposed the creation of a free trade zone 'spreading from the port of Anchorage [Alaska] to Tierra del Fuego' (Enterprise for the Americas Initiative). With the aim to achieve this goal, the USA announced that they were willing to enter free trade agreements with Latin American and Caribbean countries, giving priority to Mexico (ECLAC 1990).

The USA formed in 1992 the North American Free Trade Association – NAFTA – with Canada and Mexico and summoned, in December 1994, the Summit of the Americas in Miami. The signing of NAFTA unfolded a new series of regional integration agreements in the American hemisphere. Whilst in the period from 1960 (year of LAFTA's creation) until 1992, five agreements of this nature had been signed; between 1992 and 2008, more than 60 agreements were concluded.[38] Moreover, the former five agreements were 'opened up' to adopt the model of the second regionalism.

The most active countries in the context of open regionalism were Mexico and Chile. After joining NAFTA in 1992, Mexico initiated similar schemes with Costa Rica, Colombia and Venezuela (in the framework of the Group of the Three) and with El Salvador, Guatemala and Honduras (which formed the Northern Triangle). Furthermore, Mexico extended its network of trade agreements to all the industrialised countries with whom it shared economical relations (except Japan),[39] through different agreements with the European Union and with the European Free Trade Association (EFTA).

In the same way, Chile, already an associated member of MERCOSUR, signed regional trade agreements with Mexico, Venezuela, Bolivia, Ecuador, Panama, Colombia, Peru, Costa Rica, the Central America Common Market, Canada and the USA. In addition, Chile has also been especially interested in the relations with Asian countries, its main trade partners, and has consequently signed several agreements with Japan, North Korea, China and India.

In the early 1990s, the dense network of agreements between American nations – which gave birth to the 'spaghetti bowl' metaphor – seemed to fit in the greater hemispheric scheme previously suggested by the USA through the Free Trade Area of the Americas (FTAA). The negotiations on the FTAA started in 1994 and were expected to be concluded in 2005.

However, after the promising beginning, the process leading to the creation of the FTAA – the most ambitious external policy initiative in the Americas since the 1950s – came to a standstill due to several factors such as the failure of the Doha Round in Cancun (2003).[40] The USA conferred to the WTO framework the negotiations on subsidies, antidumping and agricultural aid, and therefore, the failure of the Doha Round made the negotiation of such issues in the framework of the FTAA unmanageable. This deadlock, in turn, gave way to new bilateral agreements between Latin American countries – Chile, Central America, Colombia, Panama and Peru – and the USA, threatening the previous agreements between themselves.

In fact, the signing of bilateral agreements by Peru (2005) and Colombia (2006)[41] caused the withdrawal of Venezuela from the Andean Community, leaving this regional bloc plunged in the most serious crisis in its history.

Thus, the results of the new regionalism could not match the initial expectations. In an article written by Devlin and Estevadeordal (2001), the authors optimistically stated that:

> The New Regionalism contrasts fundamentally with the old. Its instrumental role is geared to supporting structural reforms to make economies more open, market based, competitive and democratic [...] the scope of liberalizing disciplines in the New Regionalism tends toward a comprehensive, more rapid, universal and sustained system in terms of effective application. The New Regionalism also is designed to attract foreign investment, not to restrict or control it. Moreover the new Regionalism has more functional and cost effective institutional arrangements. Finally, the new initiatives better support important non-economic objectives such as peace, democracy and effective participation in international forums
>
> (Estevadeordal 2001: 21)

Nowadays, a wide consensus exists regarding the fact that the neoliberal structural reforms inspired by the Washington Consensus did not succeed in driving Latin America towards accelerated growth and sustainable social development. Besides, the democratic systems of the region still suffer from an enormous deficit in terms of social equity and institutional development (O'Donnel 2008). Furthermore, there was a disturbing appearance of authoritarianism, nationalism and power perpetuation tendencies of different nature.

Obviously, the expected evolution towards 'a comprehensive, more rapid, universal and sustained system in terms of effective application' did not occur. The 'spaghetti bowl' grew exponentially and turned the current regionalism in this hemisphere into a great amalgam of uncoordinated FTAs signed by the USA and several Latin American countries, the debilitated first regionalism schemes and a *compact* matrix of bilateral agreements amongst almost every country.

This complex framework is completed by nearly 30 agreements with countries outside the region and several integration programmes focused on infrastructure and energy (Vaillant 2007).[42] In spite of all these developments, intra-regional exports – in relation to the total – decreased during the current decade from an average of 17% for the period 1990–1999 to 16.8% in 2006 (Sàez 2005: 18), and the participation of Latin America in world's GDP and trade is still very limited.

During the period of open regionalism, Latin America could not be said to play an effective role in the international forums. On the contrary, some authors as Sáez (2005) unveil the institutional weaknesses affecting the process of trade policymaking in Latin America, as well as the low influence of the region in multilateral negotiations at the WTO.

In this confusing scenario, the real possibilities of achieving a convergence of the different integration processes in the regions, bringing to life an effective South American Community (2007),[43] are extremely remote. This is even more obvious with the involvement of 'alternative' or 'post-liberal' integration initiatives such as the Bolivarian Alternative for the Americas – ALBA – signed in Havana (2004).[44]

3.4 'Post-NeoLiberal' Regionalism: Beyond Open Regionalism

In the 1980s and 1990s, as mentioned, the decline of state-led industrialisation and the consequent loss of purpose and identity of the first Latin American regionalism led to the generalised adoption of open regionalism, already boosted in other latitudes. Nowadays, in a *corsi e ricorsi* movement, so common throughout history, the poor results yielded by the neoliberal reforms and the debilitation of open regionalism are shifting development and integration policies again away from the neoliberal postulates and especially from the emphasis on the role of trade and FDI for growth.

Concerning the evaluation of the policies inspired by the Washington Consensus, it seems relevant to quote an enthusiastic and influential neoliberal from the 1990s, who now reconsiders: '[…] assuming that the list of priorities for reform is the same for every country seems more and more unfounded… there is increasing evidence that the empirical connection between wide reform packages and growth is fragile' (Hausman and Velasco 2007: 72–73).

Haussmann[45] does not limit himself to criticising the structural reforms:

> The obstacles to productive transformation can be an important cause in understanding the lack of economic growth in many countries. Therefore, it will not be of a great help to keep favouring horizontal policies with few dimensions. Inevitably, *policies will have again to actively promote economical activity*, a change that could cause legitimate worries over the possible repetition of the mistakes made in the past
>
> (Hausman 2008: 114)

A large group of academic development experts share Haussmann's concern about productive transformation. These include José Antonio Ocampo, Dani Rodrik, Ha-Joon Chang, Alice Amsden and Anthony Thirlwall, who continue – in a way – the 'neo-structuralist' tradition.

The reflection of this recent version of structuralism on Latin American integration are several 'post-neoliberal' initiatives aimed at transcending the model of open regionalism. Within this 'third Latin American regionalism', two trends can be identified: one inspired by a 'neo-structuralist' agenda aimed at promoting productive transformation in the region and a second trend focused on the conformation of blocks of countries with ideological affinities (Motta and Rios 2007).

The concrete expression of the above-mentioned first trend is the creation of the South American Community of Nations in 2004, recently (2008) transformed in the

Union of South American Nations – UNASUR. This scheme holds a 'positive' vision of integration and focuses on the creation of a new regional production platform, thus abandoning the emphasis given to mere trade liberalisation. Furthermore, UNASUR, led by Brazil, proposes to act preferably in political, social, environmental and security areas. On the other hand, the movement searching to promote an 'alternative' integration based upon an ideological convergence of Latin American socialist regimes is being lead by President Chávez of Venezuela, who promotes a '21st century socialism' and the creation of ample South-South Alliances in order to face the US hegemony (Sanahuja 2009).

Beyond the obvious differences in these approaches, the two initiatives share common elements such as the 'return of the state', the concern about the social dimension (poverty, inequality and asymmetries in levels of development), military security, energy cooperation and the recovery of a 'policy space' in order to implement autonomous domestic policies.

Thus, Latin America is in-between the end of the open regionalism model and the two new proposals, strongly differentiated in terms of leadership, scope and political and ideological orientation. Therefore, a substantial contribution from ECLAC would be desirable, given its role in the past as theoretical and cognitive reference guiding the regional integration policies. In spite of its continuous intellectual production throughout the last decade, focused for example, on a better comprehension of the effects of neoliberal reforms, as well as providing information in order to deal with the financial crisis and social and productive transformation policies,[46] ECLAC has not expressed yet a global vision on development synchronised with the circumstances of the current times. Nor has ECLAC suggested any proposal on any integration model in order to overcome this stage of open regionalism, although it does have monitored the development of every integration process underway.

3.5 Conclusion

Latin American integration has entered a new existential crisis with the discredit and weakening of the policies promoted by the Washington Consensus. Thus, open regionalism risks becoming irrelevant. After an integration stage mainly focused on trade liberalisation for nearly two decades, the region moves again towards integration models focusing on development objectives based on productive transformation and genuine competitiveness.

The current proposals – basically UNASUR and ALBA – fail to present an alternative integration model since they appear to compete between them and to suffer from profound internal contradictions. Furthermore, they lack correspondence between the ambitious objectives – aiming at every dimension of development and external policy – and intergovernmental decision-making, consensus and presidential diplomacy. In sum, weak institutions, lacking binding legal force and supranational capacity, are further obstacles to move into more advanced stages of integration.

Notwithstanding these shortcomings, such initiatives still raise political and academic debate on integration and its relation with socioeconomic development, paving the way to more progressive and innovative visions. That is to say, the 'reason for integration', that had become impoverished by processes based exclusively on trade liberalisation, where tariff preference margins are anyway close to zero.

In this context, the contribution of ECLAC can be extremely important in matters such as a new generation of productive transformation policies; social rights, citizenship and social cohesion; energetic integration; and the new configuration of the world economy. All these issues are included in the new agenda on integration, on which ECLAC has already accumulated a huge amount of analytical and theoretical capacity.

Notes

1. The following paragraphs are based on Vieira (2004).
2. The Central American José Cecilio del Valle (1970–1834) proposed, for example, the creation of a Pan-American federation concluding with a general trade agreement.
3. In 1823, the USA, who since its independence had adopted a neutral position in the independency wars in the south of the continent, proclaimed the 'Monroe Doctrine', starting a new era, not yet finished, characterised by the US intervention in the rest of the continent. The USA sent its delegates to the Congress of Panama. However, due to certain circumstances, they did not participate actively in its deliberations.
4. In 1980, the International Union of American Republics (called Pan-American Union since 1810) was created in Washington. This is the beginning of the continental political and economic cooperation called 'Pan-Americanism'.
5. In 1973, CARIFTA was turned into the Caribbean Community – CARICOM.
6. Speech from Prof. Hallstein, at the time President of the Commission of the EEC, in the Joint Meeting of Harvard University and Massachusetts Institute of Technology, on 22 May 1961. Quoted by Dell (1966: 45).
7. Also different from the above-mentioned integrationist projects from the first half of the nineteenth century.
8. This work was recognised by Hirschman as the 'Latin-American Manifest' (Gurrieri 1982: 14).
9. In a different analytical framework, Marxist economists, such as Paul Baran (1957), proposed industrialisation as the path for future economic development.
10. Indeed, Latin American manufacture exports increased sharply (more than 10%) between 1960 and 1973 (Halperin et al. 2002: 362).
11. This report was drafted by Raul Prebish, at the time Executive Secretary of ECLAC.
12. Our translation.
13. Our translation.
14. Our translation.
15. Our translation.
16. The Treaty of Montevideo was originally signed by Argentina, Brazil, Chile, Mexico, Paraguay, Peru and Uruguay. Later on, Colombia, Ecuador and Venezuela also joined.
17. Our translation.
18. Costa Rica joined in 1962.
19. In a new meeting at Punta del Este in 1967, summoned by President Johnson, the Chiefs of State of the Pan-American Union agreed to form a Latin American Market, with financial sup-

port from the USA, over a 15-year period beginning in 1970 (Levinson and De Onis 1970: 174).

20. Our translation.
21. Colombia, Ecuador and Venezuela constituted the Great Colombia in the beginning of the nineteenth century.
22. Puyana (1984) presents a complete analysis of the first phases and achievements of the Andean Group.
23. Our translation.
24. The biggest part of these exchanges was operating within the Multilateral Compensation and Reciprocal Credit Agreement, signed in 1969 by the central banks of all contractual parties of LAFTA and the Dominican Republic. On the concept and measurement of intra-regional trade shares, see, for example, Iapadre (2006).
25. In the CACM, the intra-regional trade share (measured by exports) went from 8% in 1962 to 25.4% in 1980 (Halperin et al. 2002: 375).
26. ECLAC (2003: 29)
27. Halperin et al. (2002: 395)
28. Salazar (1991) presents a good extensive overview of the paradigm shift on the role of the State in Latin America during this period.
29. Until the mid-1980s, when the new regionalism starts taking form, the Uruguay Round which resulted in the transformation of the GATT in to the WTO had not yet been concluded.
30. Garay (1997) presents a good analysis on the context, causes and (potential) consequences of the Free Trade Area of the Americas (FTAA).
31. Chile and Bolivia became associate members as of 1996 and 1997, respectively. Since Argentina, Brazil, Uruguay and Paraguay had been the main promoters of LAFTA, MERCOSUR represents an alignment of these countries with the new Latin American integration context. MERCOSUR had its origins in a bilateral agreement signed in 1986 between Argentina and Brazil in the framework of LAIA.
32. For a complete analysis of the second regionalism wave in Latin America, see De Lombaerde and Garay (2008).
33. Some similarity should be noted between this approach and 'endogenous growth theories', which, at that time, were being developed by North-American academia. See Romer (1990) and Lucas (1988).
34. Our translation.
35. Towards the end of the 1970s, the concept of 'open regionalism' was originally presented by Masayoshi Ohika, at the time Japan's prime minister, who proposed to engage in an 'open regional cooperation in accordance with the new era of globalisation' in order to overcome the political and economic differences between the Asia-Pacific countries. This initiative was materialised in a consultation mechanism leading to the Asia Pacific Economic Cooperation – APEC – which includes 'open regionalism' as one of its basic principles (Okita 1992).
36. Our translation.
37. Our translation.
38. Including the Partial Scope Agreements (PSA) negotiated at the Latin American Integration Association – LAIA – and the extra-regional agreements subscribed by the Latin American countries (Durán et al. 2007: 10).
39. Nevertheless, Mexico is a member of APEC.
40. As well as the Doha Round in Cancun, the FTAA faced a strong popular opposition (Lander 2004).
41. The FTA between Colombia and the USA has not been approved the US Congress yet.
42. Vaillant qualifies these agreements, especially the North–south ones (with the EU and with the USA), as inefficient and futile.
43. In 2004, in order to improve the convergence of the different regional processes, the Third Presidential Summit at Cuzco (Peru) agreed on creating a South American Community.
44. Venezuela and Cuba established ALBA in 2004. Later, Nicaragua and Bolivia joined. In this framework, the People's Trade Treaty – TCP – was signed in Havana in 2006.

45. In his role of Chief Economist at the Inter-American Development Bank in the 1990s, Ricardo Haussmann was a firm advocate of the neo-liberal reforms.
46. On this subject, the document 'Structural Change and Productivity Growth, 20 Years Later. Old Problems, New Opportunities', directed by Fernando Fajnzylber, is an attempt to update ECLAC's work on productive transformation of the 1980s.

References

ALADI. (1983). Evolución y estructura del intercambio comercial de los países que integran la ALADI. *Doc/ALADI/Sec/Estudios* (5).

Aoki, M. et al. (Eds) (1998). *The role of government in East Asian Economic Development*. Oxford: Clarendon Press.

Baldwin, R. (1993). A Domino Theory of Regionalism. *NBER Working Paper* (4465).

Baran, P. (1957). *The political economy of growth*. Nueva York: Monthly Review Press.

Bhagwati, J. (1991). *The world trading system at risk*. Princeton: Princeton University Press.

Bhagwati, J. (1995). US Trade Policy: the infatuation with Free Trade Areas. In Bhagwati, J., & A.O. Krueger (Eds.), *The dangerous drift to Preferential Trade Agreements* (pp; 1–18). washington DC: American enterprise institute for Public Policy Research.

BID. (2002). *Más allá de las fronteras. El nuevo regionalismo en América Latina*. Washington, DC: Banco Interamericano de Desarrollo. http://www.iadb.org/res/pub_desc.cfm?pub_id=B-2002

Bielschowsky, R. (1998). Cincuenta años del pensamiento de la Cepal. In CEPAL, *Cincuenta años de pensamiento de la Cepal. Textos seleccionados*. Tomo I. Santiago de Chile: FCE and CEPAL.

Brutton, H. J. (1998). A reconsideration of import substitution. *Journal of Economic Literature, 36*, 903–936.

Cardozo, F. H. (1977). La originalidad de la Cepal: La Cepal y la idea del desarrollo. *Revista de la Cepal,* 9. Santiago de Chile: CEPAL.

CEPAL. (1959). *El mercado común latinoamericano y el régimen de pagos multilaterales en el mercado común latinoamericano*. Santiago de Chile: Naciones Unidas.

CEPAL. (1990). *Transformación productiva con equidad*. Santiago de Chile: Naciones Unidas.

CEPAL. (1994). *El regionalismo abierto en América Latina y el Caribe. La integración económica al servicio de la transformación productiva con equidad*. Santiago de Chile: Naciones Unidas.

Chang, H.-J. (2003). *Rethinking development economics*. London: Anthem Press.

Cline, W. R. (1983). El interés de América Latina en la integración económica. In E. R. Conessa (Ed.), *Términos de intercambio y tarifa óptima en América Latina* (pp. 23–33). Buenos Aires: BID and Intal.

Da Motta, P., & Rios, S. P. (2007). *O regionalismo pós-liberal, na América do Sol: origens, iniciativas e dilemas* (*Serie Comercio Internacional*, Vol. 2). Santiago de Chile: CEPAL.

De Lombaerde, P., & Garay, L. J. (2008). El nuevo regionalismo en América Latina. In P. De Lombaerde, S. Kochi, & J. Briceño (Eds.), *Del regionalismo latinoamericano a la integración interregional* (pp. 3–35). Madrid: Fundación Carolina and Siglo XXI.

Dell, S. (1966). *Experiencias de la integración económica en América Latina*. Mexico DF: Centro de Estudios Latinoamericanos.

Devlin, R., & Estevadeordal, A. (2001). What's new in the new regionalism in the Americas? *Intal ITD–STA Working Paper* (6).

Devlin, R., & Estevadeordal, A. (2001). What's new in the new regionalism in the Americas? *Intal ITD–STA Working Paper* (6).

Durán Lima, J. E., de Miguel, J., & Schuschny, A. R. (2007). Trade agreements by Colombia, ecuador and peru with the United States: Effects on Trade, Production and Welfare. *CEPAL Review*, (91), 67–93.

ECLAC. (2003). *A decade of light and shadow. Latin America and the Caribbean in the 1990s*. Santiago de Chile: United Nations.

Fajnzylber, F. (1983). *La industrialización trunca de América Latina*. Mexico DF: Editorial Nueva Imagen.

Fajnzylber, F. (1988). Competitividad internacional: evolución y lecciones. *Revista de la Cepal*, 36.

Fajnzylber, F. (1990). Industrialización en América Latina: De la 'caja negra' al 'casillero vacio'. *Cuadernos de la Cepal*, 60.

FitzGerald, V. (1998). La Cepal y la teoría de la industrialización (*Revista de la Cepal*, extraordinary issue), Santiago de Chile: CEPAL.

French-Davis, R. (1988). Esbozo de un planteamiento neoestructuralista. *Revista de la Cepal*, 34.

French-Davis, R. (2005). *Macroeconomía, comercio y finanzas* (2nd ed.). Bogota: CEPAL/Mayol.

Garay, L. J. (1997). Regionalismo e integración en las América. In R. Bouzas (Ed.), *Regionalismo e integración económica. Instituciones y procesos comparados*. Buenos Aires: Grupo Editor Latinoamericano.

Gurrieri, A. (1982). *La obra de Prebish en la Cepal*. México DF: FCE.

Halperin, T., et al. (2002). *Historia Económica de América Latina. Desde la independencia a nuestros días*. Barcelona: Crítica.

Hausman, R. (2008). El futuro de la estrategia de crecimiento de América Latina. In O. Altimir, E. Iglesias, & J. L. Machinea (Eds.), *Hacia la revisión de los paradigmas del desarrollo en América Latina*. Santiago de Chile: CEPAL and Segib.

Hausman, R., & Velasco, A. (2007). Crecimiento lento en América Latina ¿resultados comunes, causas comunes? In J. L. Machinea & N. Serra (Eds.), *Visiones del desarrollo en América Latina* (pp. 15–76). Santiago de Chile: CEPAL and Fundación Cidob.

Iapadre, L. (2006). Regional integration agreements and the geography of world trade. Statistical indicators and empirical evidence. In P. De Lombaerde (Ed.), *Assessment and measurement of regional integration* (pp. 65–85). London: Routledge.

Lander, E. (2004). Modelos alternativos de integración? Proyectos neoliberales y resistencias populares. *OSAL*, (15), 45–56.

Lawrence, R. Z. (1997). Preferential trading agreements: The traditional and the new. In A. Ghalal & B. Hoekman (Eds.), *Regional partners in global markets. Limits and possibilities of the Euro-Med agreements* (pp. 13–34). London/Cairo: CEPR.

Levinson, J., & De Onis, J. (1970). *The alliance that lost its way*. San Antonio: Quadrangle Press.

Lucas, R., Jr. (1988). On the mechanics of economic development. *Journal of Monetary Economics, 22*, 3–42.

O'Donnel, G. (2008). Los desafíos actuales de la democracia y el desarrollo. In O. Altimir, E. Iglesias, & J. L. Machinea (Eds.), *Hacia la revisión de los paradigmas del desarrollo en América Latina*. Santiago de Chile: CEPAL and Segib.

Ocampo, J. A. (2008). Etapas del Pensamiento sobre el desarrollo de América Latina. In O. Altimir, E. Iglesias, & J. L. Machinea (Eds.), *Hacia la revisión de los paradigmas del desarrollo en América Latina*. Santiago de Chile: CEPAL and Segib.

Okita, S. (1992). *Regionalism and the Asia-Pacific development outlook*. Paper presented at International Seminar on the Pacific: An Integral Part of the World, the Ocean of the XXI Century, Santiago de Chile.

Oman, C. (1996). *Los desafíos políticos de la globalización y la regionalización*. Lima: Fundación Friedrich Ebert.

Palacio, P. (2006). La industrialización nacional y el papel del Estado, en el viejo regionalismo y en el nuevo regionalismo abierto americano: un cambio de paradigma. *Observatorio de la Economía Latinoamericana* (57). http://www.eumed.net/cursecon/Lecocat/la/

Panagariya, A. (1998). The regionalism debate: An overview. *World Economy, 22*(4), 455–476.

Pinto, A. (1970). Naturaleza e implicaciones de la 'heterogeneidad estructural' de la América Latina. *El Trimestre Económico, 37*(1).

Pizarro, R. (1999). *Comparative analysis of regionalism in Latin America and Asia-Pacific* (*Serie Comercio Internacional*, Vol. 6). Santiago de Chile: CEPAL.
Prebisch, R. (1973). La integración económica en América Latina. In E. Wyndlam-White et al. (Eds.), *La integración latinoamericana en una etapa de decisiones*. Buenos Aires: BID and Intal.
Puyana, A. (1984). *Economic integration among unequal partners. The case of the Andean Group*. New York: Pergamon Press.
Ramos, J. (1986). *Neoconservative economics in the southern cone of Latin America, 1974–1983*. Baltimore: The John Hopkins University Press.
Ranis, G. (2004). The evolution of development thinking: Theory and Policy, *Economic Growth Center Discussion Paper*, Yale University, (886).
Rodríguez, O. (2000). *El estructuralismo latinoamericano*. Mexico DF: Siglo XXI and CEPAL.
Romer, P. (1990). Endogenous technological change. *Journal of Political Economy, 98*(2), 71–102.
Sáez, S. (2005). *Trade policy making in Latin America: A compared analysis* (Serie Comercio Internacional, Vol. 55). Santiago de Chile: CEPAL.
Salazar, J. M. (1991). El papel del Estado y del mercado en el desarrollo económico. In O. Sunkel (Ed.), *El desarrollo desde dentro. Un enfoque neoestructuralista para la América Latina*. Mexico DF: El trimestre Económico and FCE.
Sanahuja, J. A. (2009). Del 'regionalismo abierto' al 'regionalismo post-neoliberal'. Crisis y cambio en la integración regional en América Latina. *Anuario de la Integración Regional de América Latina y el Gran Caribe, 7*, 11–54, Buenos Aires: Coordinadora Regional de Investigaciones Económicas y Sociales.
Tavares, M. C. (1998). La Cepal y la integración económica de América Latina. *Revista de la Cepal*, número extraordinario, 213–228. Santiago de Chile: CEPAL.
Tussie, D. (1998). In the whirlwind of globalization and multilateralism: The case of emerging regionalism in Latin America. In W. D. Coleman & R. D. Geoffrey (Eds.), *Regionalism & global economic integration: Europe, Asia and the Americas*. New York: Routledge.
Vaillant, M. (2007). *Convergencias y divergencias en la integración sudamericana* (Serie Comercio Internacional, Vol. 83). Santiago de Chile: CEPAL.
Vieira, E. (2004). *La integración de América Latina: del Congreso Anfictiónico de Panamá en 1926 a una comunidad latinoamericana o sudamericana de Naciones en el año 2010*. Bogota: Editorial Pontificia Universidad Javeriana.
Vieira, E. (2008). *La formación de espacios regionales en la integración de América Latina*. Bogota: Universidad Javeriana and Convenio Andrés Bello.
Wionczek, M. (1964a). Historia del tratado de Montevideo. In M. Wionczek (Ed.), *Integración de América Latina. Experiencias y Perspectivas* (pp. 53–93). Mexico DF: FCE.
Wionczek, M. (1964b). *Integración de América Latina. Experiencias y Perspectivas*. Mexico DF: FCE.
World Bank. (1978). *Word development report*. Washington, DC: The World Bank.
World Bank. (1998). *Trade towards open regionalism*. Annual conference on Development in Latin American and the Caribbean 1997, Washington, DC.

Chapter 4
Breaking the Deadlock of Regional Bloc Politics: Cross-Regional Coalitions and Human Rights in the UNGA

Robert Kissack

4.1 Introduction

Let us begin with a simple question: what 'regions' are we talking about? The membership of the UN Organisation is divided into five regional constituencies from which representative states are nominated to serve on the various bodies where membership is restricted – such as the Security Council, ECOSOC and the Human Rights Council.[1] Alternatively, a region can be a self-selected and exclusive group of states with economic, political or ideational ties. Regional organisations such as the European Union (EU), MERCOSUR or Association of South East Asian Nations (ASEAN) clearly fit this definition as having limited membership set predominantly, but not exclusively, by geographic criteria.[2] Much has been written about the relationship between these sorts of regional organisation and universal organisations such as the UN, its specialised agencies or the World Trade Organisation. There are three dominant theoretical perspectives on their relationship. The first, federalism, advocates the principal of subsidiary in which regional organisations serve specific political purposes that neither universal organisations, nor nation states, can adequately do. The second, functionalism, regards regional organisations as stepping stones towards universal membership of universal organisations and is concerned with the 'administration of things, not the governance of men' (Mitrany 1943). A third way of understanding the relationship between regional and universal organisations is to see regional organisations supersede their member states as the primary actors at the world level, which is neofunctional in intellectual ancestry.

If we broaden our horizons to consider other groups of states that have considerable influence in international politics, the overlapping of 'region' in the UN sense of constituency, and 'regional' as a limited international organisation of sovereign

R. Kissack (✉)
Institut Barcelona d'Estudis Internacionals (IBEI), Barcelona, Spain
e-mail: rkissack@ibei.org

P. De Lombaerde et al. (eds.), *The United Nations and the Regions: Third World Report on Regional Integration*, United Nations University Series on Regionalism 3,
DOI 10.1007/978-94-007-2751-9_4, © Springer Science+Business Media B.V. 2012

states, runs into trouble because of considerable slippage over the term ‘regional’. The Group of Eight (G8) serves as a relatively informal environment in which the eight coordinate their policies prior to their participation in international organisations. Membership is determined by economic and political clout on the world stage, not by geography, yet is a ‘region’ in the sense of constituting the (self-selected) most important countries on the planet.[3]

Their influence over the international financial institutions is evidenced by the fact that major policy decisions concerning the IMF and World Bank are agreed at the G8 and then adopted ‘by consensus’ in Washington (Dreher and Vreeland forthcoming). The future of the post–Kyoto environmental regime was mapped out in at the G8 summit in Germany (2007),[4] and G8 pre-negotiations will be an essential ingredient in any grand bargain agreed in Copenhagen at the end of 2009. Whether the G8 can successfully present a *fait accompli* to the international community is debatable, but it remains their preferred strategy of engagement with the other 184 members of the UN in areas of high salience.[5] There are two other important examples to consider. The Organisation of the Islamic Conference (OIC) has members from all five UN regions.[6] It promotes the political and economic well-being of states with Muslim majority or minority populations. The European Union has clearly stated geographical limits (insofar as the European Court of Justice ruled that all members must be on the European continent), yet inside the UN, it spans three regional constituencies (WEOG, Eastern Europe and Asia). The G8, OIC and EU are all important, limited membership organisations and challenge us to think about how a ‘region’ should be defined as a self-selecting (i.e. non-universal) group of states.

Given the limited space available, the scope of this contribution is limited to presenting three interrelated arguments. The first is to question the usefulness of measuring regional actorness through the analysis of voting behaviour, a preoccupation of EU studies for many years. Instead, I will argue that we should be focusing on the political capacity of the region to promote its interests beyond its constituency and in the broader context of UN politics. Failing to do so and remaining concerned with regional actorness is tantamount to reinventing the wheel with regard to the study of ‘blocs’, the partisan characteristic of the UN system during the Cold War. Second, by drawing on empirical research and interviews with regard to the promotion of human rights in the UN Third Committee and General Assembly, I will argue that practitioners in New York are seeking to undermine the regional-bloc mentality, rather than continuing to use it. The success of the 2007 UNGA Resolution calling for a moratorium on the death penalty was in a large part due to its cross-regional co-authorship, the purpose of which was to *break* the logic of regions acting as cohesive blocs. Third and by way of a conclusion, I will contextualise my argument in the broader debate about multilateralism.

4.2 Actorness, Blocs and Politics

What can we learn from studying the voting behaviour of states from different regions in the UNGA or United Nations Security Council (UNSC)? How confident can we be that seeing evidence of cohesive voting is evidence of volitional coordination pertaining to promoting the region as an actor in the UN system? The defence of this approach is based on the assumption that states within regional groups coordinate their positions prior to important roll-call votes and strategically vote *en masse*, either to maximise their aggregate weight or to send a message to other states, their domestic constituents and anyone else interested, that region X has a cohesive voice on issue Y. The European Union has for many years regarded as a virtue the numerous (1,000+) annual coordination meetings held in New York between its member states and their 95% frequency of voting cohesion (European Union 2004) although fails to mention that this figure includes votes adopted by consensus, where *all* UN members are in agreement (Laatikainen 2004). There are at least two major problems with this analytical approach, one concerning the methodology and the other concerning the utility. Taking the methodological concerns first, voting records alone do not shine a light on the coordination process behind the scenes. If the members of a regional group vote cohesively as a result of coincidence, past practice or instructions from national capitals, it is difficult to reasonably argue anything more than the group has homogeneous interests. Conversely, when voting records show non-cohesiveness, one cannot automatically rule out the possibility that extensive coordination *did* take place but ultimately yielded nothing.[7] A regional group exhibits 'actorness' when it undertakes a political process designed to produce an output furthering the interests of the collective. Actorness implies agency, the capacity to use free will to consciously decide upon courses of action to take. It is for this reason that the analysis of voting records alone is not enough to demonstrate convincingly the existence of actorness within a region. It must be supplemented by some form of evidence of coordination that can demonstrate the volitional intention associated with agency (Kissack 2007).

'Important as the understanding of individual and group voting behaviour undoubtedly is, such analysis does not provide us with comprehensive knowledge of General Assembly politics' (Keohane 1967: 221). This quote from Robert Keohane captures the essence of the second major problem of studying voting records and is related to its utility. Keohane instead advocates looking at the political process, which he defines as 'the exercise of political influence in the service of national politics' (Keohane 1967: 221). Laatikainen and Degrand-Guillaud argue along a similar line, where 'being effective at the UN is less an exercise in *policy-making* than in *politics*' [emphasis in original] (Laatikainen and Degrand-Guillaud 2009: 11). They continue, saying that the 'ongoing effort to make the EU a stronger actor is less critical in this context than fostering like-mindedness on a range of issues of vital global importance. Persuasion, not leverage, is the essence of UN diplomacy' (Guillaud 2009: 12). This line of argument can be expanded to all regions that aspire to being actors in the UN system, not simply the EU. When roll-call voting takes place (and on many important issues consensus is preferred), it is often at the *end* of the political process and serves either to formalise a decision, force recalcitrant states to publicly display their position, apply pressure to those still holding out for concessions or to accept differences and move on. The study of voting as a form of decision-making must be contextualised in the organisational structure, as well as part of a larger political process that links across many areas beyond the specific issue at hand (Kissack forthcoming).

Keohane's comments, despite being written over 40 years ago, remain pertinent today because the analysis of regional voting patterns is similar to the analysis of voting 'blocs'. Much of the history of the UN up until 1990 can be written in terms of bloc-politics. In the first 15 years, the majority of states supported the USA, and a minority Soviet-dominated bloc opposed American hegemony. After 1960, decolonisation swelled UN membership with newly independent states in Africa, Asia and the Caribbean, as well as admitting more Eastern European states. The formation of the G77 on economic issues, and the Non-Aligned Movement (NAM) on political questions such as decolonisation and disarmament, attracted many South American states into its gravitational pull and away from the USA. Three worlds, Western, Soviet and the G77/NAM 'third world' thus formed the blocs that dominated politics in the UN for three decades. As the Soviet Union realised that there was demand for an alternative economic model to capitalism among the G77, it found allies in the South ready to use their majority to apply pressure on the West. '"Bloc" bids fair to join "veto" at the top of the list of opprobrious terms in the international vocabulary of the West' (Claude 1984: 135). Nevertheless, both East and West were coalitions 'formed through the threats and promises of one Member' (Keohane 1967: 223), providing bribes and punishments for support and defection respectively. The G77 operates somewhat differently with India, Pakistan, Egypt, Cuba and Yugoslavia, all providing leadership, although other members served as conduits for coordination based on the capabilities and experience of a particular mission. The limited staffing and financial resources of G77 member missions greatly increase their reliance on 'like-minded' states as trusted advocates of how to vote. East, West and G77 were all defined by their distinct ideological orientations and all exhibited actorness.

4.3 Human Rights Promotion and the 'Breaking' of Regional Blocs

In the 62nd session of the General Assembly in December 2007, a resolution was passed by 104 votes in favour to 51 against calling for a moratorium on the use of the death penalty.[8] One year earlier, the government of Finland read a statement during the plenary of the 61st session of the UNGA calling for the abolition of the death penalty, co-signed by 85 states. Prior to that, in 1999, efforts to draft a resolution against the use of the death penalty had come to an unceremonious end in the Third Committee (social, humanitarian and cultural) when opponents of the text secured the insertion of a 'wrecking amendment' that reasserted the right of non-intervention in domestic politics offered in Article 2(7) of the UN Charter (Bantekas and Hodgkinson 2000). In the intervening period, a number of resolutions against the death penalty were successfully passed in the UN Commission on Human Rights, where an institutional bias in membership towards states from the WEOG, Eastern Europe and Latin American regions ensured they enjoyed slender majorities. The creation of the Human Rights Council (HRC) in 2005 resulted in an overall reduction in membership (from 53 to 47) and a proportional increase in states from Asia and Africa, making the OIC highly influential HRC (Smith 2008). The EU has suffered from a decline in influence in the UNGA over the last decade, measured as a percentage of votes on HR issues in which it is on the losing side (Gowan and Brantner 2008). The picture painted is of the EU becoming marginalised and an 'axis of sovereignty' becoming ever more influential. The only point of positive to be found, it would seem, is in the progress made on passing the resolution on the death penalty. So how did it succeed here while failing elsewhere?

I have elaborated in greater detail elsewhere the mechanism through which the resolution was passed, focusing on the role of the Presidency, the Italian government, NGO advocacy and expert knowledge and the co-authoring structure (Kissack 2008). It is the last of these four that I shall expand upon here. The original text of the resolution was drafted by a group of ten states, two from each of the five UN regions.[9] Apart from the Lusophone connection that the Portuguese brought to the group, their composition was specifically intended to demonstrate the universality of the resolution and pre-empt counterarguments from retentionist opponents that this was a western HR ideal being exported globally. Interviews with diplomats involved make it clear that the co-authors from Africa and Asia received much criticism from their regional constituents for their involvement and fought hard to argue the case against staunch internal opposition. The cross-regional initiative was designed to *break* the stranglehold of leading states in the African and Asian groups monopolising the regional position.[10] The same approach is being used again, this time in the 2008 statement read out by Argentina in the General Assembly calling for full respect of human rights regardless of sexual orientation or gender identity.[11] The alignment of the US government with this statement in March 2009 brings the total number of signatures to 67, still a considerable way short of the 97 needed to win a majority in the UNGA, but once again strategically promoted across the five UN regions in an attempt to show the universal support for the action. Whether a resolution is sought in the short or medium term is as yet undecided, however, the way forward of the sponsoring states is through the reiteration of its cross-regional support that contradicts the logic of cohesive regional actors.

4.4 Conclusions and Reflections on Multilateralism

How do regional groups fit into the architecture of the multilateral system? As has been made clear above, voting patterns alone do not reveal regional actorness; instead, one must identify the political process through which a region undertakes volitional coordinated action. The nature of the political coordination process is crucial in assessing the degree of 'fit' between the region as an actor and the multilateral system. Regions that resemble the blocs of old, centred round a core state that expected its satellites to follow its position contravene the qualitative dimension of multilateralism identified by John Ruggie of non-discrimination between members (Ruggie 1992: 569). Relations between states in such blocs more closely resemble hub-and-spoke, asymmetrical bilateralism. This description best fits the USSR, and to a less extent the USA, than it does the Global South. In an idealised way, the EU is fundamentally different to this system, where its coordinated position is the product of dialogue between members, founded on '"generalised" principles of conduct' (Ruggie 1992: 571). But in reality, EU cohesion does break down on issues of fundamental national importance, and this, perversely, allows each state to participate in the UN as sovereign equals.

The recent strategy of the EU member states and others that support progressive human rights promotion in the UNGA has been to build a large coalition across the five UN regions. This is intended to prevent opponents from 'capturing' regions and securing mass votes in support of their position. The 'breaking' of a regional bloc vote is intended to allow diversity of opinion to be heard, thus reiterating the values of multilateralism as equal participation over the asymmetrical bilateralism often exhibited in blocs. When regions bridge the gap between sovereign state and universal international organisation according to multilateral principles, they should be valued. When they serve as frameworks through which powerful states wield voting power, they should be challenged. In all cases, we must look at the political process rather than satisfy ourselves with voting records alone.

Notes

1. The five regional groups are African states, Asian states, Eastern European states, Western European and other states and Latin American and Caribbean states.
2. The EU's Copenhagen Criteria stipulate minimal democratic standards for members.
3. Transformation to the G20 does not alter this assessment and in fact demonstrates its wider appreciation among those states admitted.
4. http://www.g-8.de/Webs/G8/EN/Homepage/home.html (accessed 31 May 2009).
5. The presentation of a package deal was often the basis of GATT trade agreements. The process was carried over into the WTO, where prior to the 2003 Cancun meeting, the EU and the US had resolved their differences over agricultural subsidies, one of the major sticking points. However, a change in the balance of power within the WTO meant that it was not enough. See Falke (2005).
6. The majority of the 57 member states are in the Asia and Africa regions; however, Turkey (WEOG), Albania (Eastern Europe) and Suriname (Latin America) are also members. http://www.oic-oci.org/member_states.asp (accessed 31 May 2009).
7. One must also consider the dynamics of particular voting systems and their relationship to the structure of a given organisation. In the International Labour Organisation (ILO), the EU member states frequently coordinate during the drafting of labour standards, only to vote non-cohesively in the subsequent plenary session. A credible explanation for this behaviour is that drafting locks in the content of the instrument and is where the EU wishes to be most influential. The subsequent plenary vote, by contrast, is little more than a formality, and EU member states (like all ILO members) are able to freeride on the assumption of the vote passing in order to satisfy domestic constituents (Kissack 2009).
8. The resolution calling for a moratorium on the death penalty (A/62/439/Add.2) was adopted by a recorded of vote of 104 in favour to 54 against, with 29 abstentions. 18 December 2007. UN press document GA10678.

9. Portugal and New Zealand from WEOG, Croatia and Albania from Eastern Europe, Mexico and Brazil from Latin America, East Timor and the Philippines from Asia and Angola and Gabon from Africa.
10. Vocal opponents included Syria, Pakistan, Iran, Singapore, (Asia) Egypt and Libya (Africa), all of which belong to the Organisation of the Islamic Conference (OIC).
11. The EU French Presidency set up a website: http://www.droitslgbt2008.fr/acueil/index.php (accessed 23 May 2009). Afterwards, Syria read out what has become referred to as a 'counter-statement', signed by 57 states (predominantly from the IOC). They accept universal human rights but not accept that states are obliged to protect the rights of lesbian, gay, bisexual and transgender (LGBT) peoples because such 'behaviours' are not genetic and should not be linked to existing HR instruments, http://www.un.org/news/Press/docs/2008/ga10801.doc.htm (accessed 23 May 2009).

References

Bantekas, I., & Hodgkinson, P. (2000). Capital punishment at the United Nations: Recent developments. *Criminal Law Forum, 11*(1), 23–34.

Claude, I. (1984). *Swords into plowshares: The progress and problems of international organization* (4th ed.). New York: Random House.

Dreher, A., & Vreeland, J. R. (forthcoming). *The political economy of the United Nations Security Council*. Cambridge: Cambridge University Press.

European Union. (2004). *The enlarging European Union at the United Nations: Making multilateralism matter*. Luxembourg: Office of Official Publications of the European Communities.

Falke, A. (2005). EU-USA trade relations in the Doha development round: Market access verses a post-modern trade policy agenda. *European Foreign Affairs Review, 10*, 339–357.

Gowan, R., & Brantner, F. (2008). *A global force for human rights? An audit of European power at the UN*. Brussels: European Council of Foreign Relations.

Keohane, R. (1967). The study of political influence in the general assembly. *International Organization, 21*(2), 221–237.

Kissack, R. (2007). *European Union member state coordination in the United Nations system: towards a methodology for analysis*. LSE EFPU Working Paper (1).

Kissack, R. (2008). *Outreach, Overstretch or Underhand? Strategies for cross-regional consensus in support of a UN General Assembly Resolution on a Moratorium on the use of the death penalty*. LSE EFPU Working Paper (2).

Kissack, R. (2009). When European Union member state voting cohesion does not matter: Lessons learnt about majoritarian decision-making from the ILO. *Studia Diplomatica, 7*(1), 55–74.

Kissack, R. (forthcoming). *The European Union and the multilateral system: Myth and reality of 'effective multilateralism*. Basingstoke: Palgrave.

Laatikainen, K. V. (2004). Assessing the EU as an actor in the UN: Authority, cohesion, recognition and autonomy. *CFSP FORUM, 2*(1), 4–9.

Laatikainen, K. V., & Degrand-Guillaud, A. (2009, March). *Two logics, One treaty: The Lisbon Treaty and EU Foreign Policy in Brussels and at the United Nations*. Paper presented at 50th International Studies Association Convention, New York.

Mitrany, D. (1943). *A working peace system*. London: Royal Institute for International Affairs.

Ruggie, J. G. (1992). Multilateralism: The anatomy of an institution. *International Organization, 46*(3), 561–598.

Smith, K. E. (2008, March). *Speaking with one voice but having little impact: The EU at the UN's Human Rights Council*. Paper presented at 49th International Studies Association Convention, San Francisco.

Chapter 5
Measuring Regional Actorness at the UN Security Council: The EU as a Paragon of Complexity

Edith Drieskens

5.1 Introduction

Scholars studying *regional actorness* at the United Nations (UN) often rely on voting records to prove their point, in particular in relation to the performance of the European Union (EU) and its member states at the UN General Assembly (UNGA).[1] Voting information has been used frequently for evaluating the implementation of the EU's Common Foreign and Security Policy (CFSP), with cohesion being seen as a proxy for success. That is hardly surprising: not only are those records publicly accessible, they are consistent over time and thus well suited for statistical analysis (Kissack 2007: 7).

However, a note of caution is in order. Kissack already indicated that such measuring ignores the type of vote being cast. Moreover, in issue areas where the level of consensus between the UN members is high, so is the likelihood of consensus between the EU member states. Like Smith, Kissack warns that there is usually little consideration of what voting is about and of how difficult it was to get a unified position (Smith 2005: 60). Also, Jørgensen notes that the most interesting things about UN voting are to be found in the explanations for voting rather than in the votes themselves (Jørgensen 2004: 20).

Adding to that criticism and zooming in on the UN Security Council (UNSC), we demonstrate that voting cohesion does not have the same explanatory power for all UN bodies: it may be a powerful tool for measuring regional actorness at the UNGA, but not for the UNSC. We develop our argument by undertaking a review of the complexities faced by scholars studying the manifestation of regional

E. Drieskens (✉)
International Relations, Leuven University, Leuven, Belgium
e-mail: Edith.Drieskens@soc.kuleuven.be

P. De Lombaerde et al. (eds.), *The United Nations and the Regions: Third World Report on Regional Integration*, United Nations University Series on Regionalism 3,
DOI 10.1007/978-94-007-2751-9_5,

actorness within that framework, focusing on the EU and its member states. We conclude by suggesting an agenda for research on regional actorness at the UNSC, raising the question if the EU is as sui generis as it claims.

5.2 Defining Regional Actorness

Shaping the cooperation between the UNSC and regional *arrangements* and *agencies*, Chapter VIII of the UN Charter (UNCH) has been the starting point for most scholars studying the regional dimension of UNSC policy- and decision making. For many of them, it has also been the end point.

That is quite remarkable, especially from an EU point of view. Indeed, while the EU has been a loyal participant in the meetings that have been organised by the UN Secretary-General and UNSC under the umbrella of Chapter VIII, it has never been a strong supporter of that rather ritualistic interpretation.[2] As a matter of fact, the occasional meetings at UN Headquarters have not given it a voice in the UNSC's decision-making process, at least not one that is similar to its serving member states.

Those member states, and states more generally, will remain the core players at the UNSC in the years to come. Unlike some other contributors to the volume, we argue that the prospects for a regional form of representation are non-existing (Drieskens 2009). Granted, regional representation has been defined as an issue to be included in the reform discussions, and a more equitable geographical representation has been mentioned by those countries favouring an expansion of the membership.[3] However, the intergovernmental nature of the UN system, the diversity between the various groupings and the disagreements within those groupings, do not make the introduction of regional seats a realistic option. In fact, *not* changing the allocation basis of seats seems to be one of the few things that most UN members can agree upon. The same goes for the EU member states: whereas some have been advocating a single representation of the EU at the UNSC, most of them seem to support Germany's bid for a permanent seat.

Also, the Lisbon Treaty, which entered into force on 1 December 2009 and aims to increase the EU's international profile and performance, does not point in the direction of a single EU seat. A careful reading of the new provisions reveals that the actual decision-making process remains in the hands of the EU member states, even if the representation of some of their decisions may be delegated to the new *High Representative of the Union for Foreign Affairs and Security Policy*. In that regard, the new Article 34 of the EU Treaty (*ex* Article 19) determines that when the EU has defined a position on a subject that is on the UNSC's agenda, the new representative will be invited to present it.

The introduction of that representative has been informed by existing practice, like the *EU Delegation to the UN* replacing the rotating EU Presidency as the EU's spokesperson in open debates at the UNSC. Indeed, Javier Solana, the EU's former *High Representative for the CFSP*, addressed the UNSC at the invitation of the serving EU member states – be it only a limited number of times. Whereas the new provision turns the invitation into an obligation, the new external representative is only tasked with representing foreign policy decisions that are agreed upon by the EU member states.

In fact, the Lisbon Treaty leaves no doubt concerning the impact of the new provisions. Following *Declaration 14 concerning the common foreign and security policy*, which is attached to the Lisbon Treaty, the provisions will not affect the existing legal basis, responsibilities and powers of the EU member states in relation to their participation in international organisations, including their membership of the UNSC. Put differently, also after Lisbon, the EU's actorness at the UNSC remains dependent upon the serving EU member states and their representation behaviour (Drieskens 2008, 2009).

5.3 Measuring Regional Actorness

Such indirect focus on the extent to which the members of the UNSC take their regional memberships into account does not make things easier for scholars exploring the regional dimension of the UNSC's decision-making practice. Looking into the EU and its member states, three complicating factors can be identified.

5.3.1 Membership

First of all, unlike in the UNGA, only a limited number of the EU member states serve at a certain moment in time at the UNSC.

France and the UK are represented on a permanent basis; the others may obtain a seat for a period of 2 years if the members of the UNGA elect them, usually following nomination by the regional groups. The EU-15 (i.e. Austria, Belgium, Denmark, Finland, France, Germany, Greece, Ireland, Italy, Luxembourg, the Netherlands, Portugal, Sweden, Spain and the UK) and Malta are part of Western European and Others Group (WEOG). With the exception of Cyprus, which belongs to the Asian Group, the other countries that joined the EU on 1 May 2004 are part of the Eastern European Group (EEG; i.e. Czech Republic, Estonia, Hungary, Latvia, Lithuania, Poland, Slovakia and Slovenia). The same goes for the EU's youngest members: Romania and Bulgaria.

Reflecting the Cold War division between East and West, the groups can be seen as relics of the past. However, neither the EU institutions nor the EU member states have been raising their composition. That should be no surprise. After all, the successive enlargements of the EU have had a positive effect on the number of EU member states serving on the UNSC (see Table 5.1). Moreover, given the EU's enlargement plans, there is still potential for growth (see Table 5.2).

Yet Brussels-driven election dynamics are absent in New York, both in terms of presenting and electing candidates. Giving an overview of the countries with the

Table 5.1 Indirect EU representation at the UNSC 1957–2009

	PM		%PM	EM		%EM	%UNSCM
1957 (UNSC11, EU6)	FR		20			5.6	12.1
1958	FR						
1959	FR			IT			
1960	FR			IT			
1961	FR						
1962	FR						
1963	FR						
1964	FR						
1965	FR			NL			
1966 (UNSC15)	FR			NL		7.1	8.0
1967	FR						
1968	FR						
1969	FR						
1970	FR						
1971	FR			BE	IT		
1972	FR			BE	IT		
1973 (EU9)	FR	UK	40			5	16.7
1974	FR	UK					
1975	FR	UK		IT			
1976	FR	UK		IT			
1977	FR	UK		DE			
1978	FR	UK		DE			
1979	FR	UK					
1980	FR	UK					
1981 (EU10)	FR	UK		IE		10	20
1982	FR	UK		IE			
1983	FR	UK		NL			
1984	FR	UK		NL			
1985	FR	UK		DK			
1986 (EU12)	FR	UK		DK		10	20
1987	FR	UK		DE	IT		
1988	FR	UK		DE	IT		
1989	FR	UK					
1990	FR	UK					
1991	FR	UK		BE			
1992	FR	UK		BE			
1993	FR	UK		ES			
1994	FR	UK		ES			
1995 (EU15)	FR	UK		DE	IT	15.6	23.7
1996	FR	UK		DE	IT		

(continued)

Table 5.1 (continued)

	PM		%PM	EM			%EM	%UNSCM
1997	FR	UK		PT	SW			
1998	FR	UK		PT	SW			
1999	FR	UK		NL				
2000	FR	UK		NL				
2001	FR	UK		IE				
2002	FR	UK		IE				
2003	FR	UK		DE	ES			
2004 (EU25)	FR	UK		DE	ES		23.3	28.9
2005	FR	UK		DK	GR			
2006	FR	UK		DK	GR	SK		
2007 (EU27)	FR	UK		BE	IT	SK	20	26.7
2008	FR	UK		BE	IT			
2009	FR	UK		AT				

Note: This table illustrates that since the accession of Romania and Bulgaria, the EU member states occupy – on average – 26.7% of the seats in the UNSC (%UNSCM), making up 40% of the permanent members (%PM) and 20% of the elected members (%EM). In other words, the EU member states occupy on average two permanent and two non-permanent seats at the UNSC. While the first percentage has remained unchanged since the accession of the UK in 1973, the latter has been increasing following the accession of new members, at least until Romania and Bulgaria joined the EU in 2007. In the early years of European integration (1957–1965), the members of the then European Economic Community only counted for 12.1% of the UNSC membership – for 20% of the permanent members and 5.6% of the elected members, respectively. In the first column, the successive stages of EU and UNSC enlargement are printed in bold. In 1965, the membership of the UNSC was extended with four elected members, even though the amendment only entered into force in 1966

Table 5.2 Candidates for a non-permanent seat at the UNSC 2011–2019

	WEOG (2 seats every 2 years)	EEG (1 seat every 2 years)	Asian group (1 seat every year)	
2011	CA, *DE, PT*		IN, KZ	
2012		AM, AZ, *HU, SI*		FJ, KG, PK
2013	AU, *FI, LU*		BT, KH, KR	
2014		GE, *LT*		SA
2015	*ES*, NZ		MY	
2016		UA		BD
2017	*IT, NL, SE*		TH	
2018		*BG, PL*		YE
2019	*BE*, IL		MV	

Note: This table provides an overview of the candidates for a non-permanent seat at the UNSC for the coming years. EU member states that have announced their candidacy for a non-permanent seat at the UNSC are printed in italics. Candidates aspiring EU membership (candidate countries and potential candidate countries) are indicated with an asterisk. Situation as of 1 July 2010

ambition of serving at the UNSC in the coming years, Table 5.2 shows that their EU membership does not impede EU member states from running against each other, both within WEOG and the EEG. Not only the dispersion over various regional groups but also diverging views on UNSC reform may explain so.[4]

Table 5.2 also shows that the composition of the group of EU member states serving at the UNSC is changing almost every year, with the WEOG members being elected in the *even* years and the EEG seat being assigned in the *uneven* ones. As a result, when relying on voting cohesion for evaluating EU actorness at the UNSC, one can only measure the degree to which a variable group of EU member states – with France and the UK being the only 'permanent members' – vote in a similar way at a certain point in time. That observation also brings us to the second complexity for scholars analysing the regional dynamics in the UNSC: its consensus-oriented decision-making practice.

5.3.2 Decision-Making

Working with voting cohesion, one can only measure the degree to which a number of EU member states that belong to two – and if Cyprus is elected three – different regional groups vote similarly on draft resolutions that are formally introduced. Because the UNSC largely operates by consensus and divisive issues are rarely pushed to a vote, one can only gain insight into the tip of the proverbial decision-making iceberg.[5] Again, the numbers speak for themselves.

Table 5.3 shows that of the 664 resolutions that were introduced between 1 January 1997 and 31 December 2006, the EU member states showed a different voting – i.e. abstention – pattern in only 12 cases, resulting in an average voting cohesion of 98.2% (%VC).[6] Also, the decisive issues seem to run parallel with those in the UNGA, with the Middle East Peace Process being the most important one (Biscop and Drieskens 2006). More specifically, France decided not to follow its EU colleagues in 1997 and 1999 when a draft resolution on Iraq was introduced. In 1997, it abstained (S/RES/1134); 2 years later, it decided not to take part in the vote (S/RES/1280). In addition, in the period researched, seven draft resolutions dealing with the Israeli-Palestinian conflict resulted in different abstention patterns between the EU member states serving.[7] All seven initiatives were blocked by the US delegation.

The other three drafts that caused disunity between the EU member states were introduced in 2003 and related to (1) the conflict in Liberia (S/RES/1497), (2) the Lockerbie case (S/RES/1506) and (3) the International Criminal Court's procedures (S/RES/487). The Iraq crisis that paralysed the UNSC that year for many weeks and divided the EU member states in an 'old' and 'new' Europe remains thus invisible. That can be explained by the fact that the USA decided not to call for a vote and illustrates again the disadvantages to the use of voting records.

Table 5.3 EU voting cohesion at the UNSC 1997–2006

	# EUMS	¬P EUMS	# RES	% VC	Issue	Y	N	A	NP
97	4	PT, SE	57	98.2	Iraq [S/RES/1134]	10	0	5 (FR)	0
98	4	PT, SE	73	100.0					
99	3	NL	67	98.5	Iraq [S/RES/1280]	11	0	3	1 (FR)
00	3	NL	52	100.0					
01	3	IE	54	98.1	MEPP (Mar)	12	1	2 (UK)	0
02	3	IE	70	100.0					
03	4	ES, DE	69	92.8	MEPP (Sep)	11	1	3 (DE, UK)	0
					MEPP (Oct)	10	1	4 (DE, UK)	0
					ICC [S/RES/1487]	12	0	3 (DE, FR)	0
					Libya [S/RES/1497]	13	0	2 (FR)	0
					Liberia [S/RES/1506]	12	0	3 (DE, FR)	0
04	4	ES, DE	62	96.8	MEPP (Mar)	11	1	3 (DE, UK)	0
					MEPP (Oct)	11	1	3 (DE, UK)	0
05	4	DK, GR	71	100.0					
06	5	DK, GR, SK	89	97.8	MEPP (Jul)	10	1	4 (DK, SK, UK)	0
					MEPP (Nov)	10	1	4 (DK, SK, UK)	0
			664	**98.2**	**12**				

Note: This table presents for the years between 1997 and 2006 the number of EU member states serving on the UNSC (#EUMS) and identifies the EU member states sitting on a non-permanent basis (¬P EUMS). It shows the number of draft resolutions tabled (#RES) and the percentage of voting cohesion between the EU member states serving (%VC). It also identifies the policy issues (issue) for which these countries showed a different voting (i.e. abstention) pattern. If the draft resolution in question was adopted, the document number is indicated; if not, only the month in which the text was vetoed is. As known, UNSC members can vote yes (Y), no (N), abstain (A) or not participate in the vote (NP). If one of the five permanent members casts a negative vote, a draft resolution is vetoed. Data based on the annual voting practices in the United Nations reports of the US State Department's Bureau of International Organisation Affairs [online available at: www.state.gov/p/io/res/rpt/index.htm]

5.3.3 Representation

The foregoing has focused on how the limited membership of the UNSC, and its consensual working practice complicates things for scholars analysing the EU's actorness within that body, especially in comparison to their colleagues focusing upon the UNGA. Turning to the third obstacle, the EU reality at the UNSC is also different from the UNGA because the serving EU member states are not involved in EU coordination. At most, they are involved in EU representation, with their representation behaviour being subject to EU rules.

The above-mentioned Article 34 of the EU Treaty shapes the representation behaviour of the EU member states in international organisations and at international conferences. The provision starts with a general coordination requirement, before focusing on settings in which not all EU member states are represented and the UNSC in particular. Those member states that are sitting at the UNSC will 'concert' and keep the others 'fully informed'. Moreover, they have to 'ensure the defence' of the positions and interests of the EU, be it 'without prejudice to their responsibilities under the UN Charter'.[8]

The practice that follows from those provisions is one of sharing information. The provisions have been implemented in New York through (1) weekly information briefings in which the EU member states with a seat at the UNSC inform their colleagues and (2) monthly lunches between the member states serving each time at both ambassadorial and expert level. While the first format is about *information*, the latter may lead to *coordination*. However, this coordination is always *informal*, ad hoc and *procedural in nature*. Substantive EU coordination remains the privilege of the national capitals, with Brussels being a necessary intermediate stop for the formulation of EU positions.

That knowledge underlines the necessity of relying on process tracing and systematic case-study research in order to make valid claims about the EU's actorness within that body and about regional actorness more generally. Conclusions will thus always be conditional: they will only be valid for a specific decision-making context in which only some of the EU member states were present.

5.4 Evaluating Regional Actorness

The limitations of measuring voting cohesions may also explain – at least to a certain extent – why the body of research on EU representation and coordination at the UNSC is rather limited, especially in comparison to the UNGA. While the collections by Laatikainen and Smith (2006) and Wouters et al. (2006) are valuable attempts to narrow the gap in literature on EU-UN relations, the field remains somewhat thin.

Even if the academic interest into the EU's foreign policy at the UNSC has been growing, the empirical analysis of the decision-making practice remains cursory. Research has been limited to a factual description of the membership or a historical reconstruction of the relevant legal provisions (Drieskens 2009; Drieskens et al. 2007). Much of the existing research has been focusing on the special position of France and the UK as permanent members. By contrast, the positions of the EU member states serving on an elected basis and the role of the EU institutions are not discussed in great detail. Moreover, as the UNGA has often been used as a point of reference, most conclusions are of a rather general nature, stressing what EU actorness at the UNSC is *not.*

The implementation of the Lisbon Treaty has been given a new impulse to the literature on EU-UN relations, like the European Security Strategy (2003) and its plea for 'effective multilateralism'. Scholars are exploring the question how the new provisions on external representation will be implemented in the multilateral context of the UN. Whereas the implementation of those provisions may inspire questions about the EU's representation at the UNSC, their main impact is on the UNGA, not only because the role of the rotating EU Presidency was more developed within that context but also because the EU claims there additional rights and privileges (Drieskens and Wouters 2009).

When the Lisbon Treaty entered into force, the European Community (EC), which enjoyed observer status within the UNGA, ceased to exist and was replaced by the EU. The EU has not been satisfied with merely taking over the status of the former EC, but wants – we write early July 2010 – its post-Lisbon foreign policy status being matched with an enhanced status at the UN. The EU's wish list is rather long, yet most wanted (because most symbolically) is the right to participate in the UNGA's general debate, allowing the EU to speak in an early stage. Because such upgrade implies the adoption of a resolution by the UNGA, the EU will have to convince the other members of the UN of its sui generis character, of its uniqueness.

Whereas the EU has been increasingly presented as an example for other regional groupings (Jørgensen and Rosamond 2002; Acharya and Johnston 2007), little systematic research has been done on how unique the EU reality really is, including within the context of the UN. Few researchers have looked into the question if the EU's foreign policy ambitions are also reflected in policy practice, whether that practice is more developed than that of other regional actors.

However, as Smith has argued, comparing EU foreign policy cooperation with similar efforts in other regions could result in explanations for cooperation within the EU (Smith 2007: 4). Indeed, while the EU is often seen as the most successful experiment in regional integration, at the UN there are groupings that are more united than the EU member states. Referring to the African Group and the Organisation of the Islamic Conference, she added the question 'What is going on there and how does it compare to what is going on within the EU?' to her list of questions that should guide the study of EU foreign policy in the years to come (Smith 2007: 10).

The EU has often been seen as a unique case, as an *n of 1*, even if early theorists like Deutsch, Haas or Nye were convinced that the study of the European case could generate hypotheses for the study of regional integration more generally (Rosamond 2000: 16). While those theorists were well aware of the contextual differences among the various processes of regional integration, they thought of the European integration process as being part of a larger universe of possible cases (Caporaso et al. 1997: 1–5).[9]

Looking into the question if the EU represents an *n of 1*, Caporaso explains the treatment of the EU as a special case by referring to 'disciplinary pressures', the 'increasing academic division of labour' as well as the 'increasing complexity' of the European integration project itself. Whereas some have perceived a lack of comparable cases (De Lombaerde et al. 2010), in his view, differences are 'something to be explained', providing 'variation'. Likewise, Marks notes that the EU's uniqueness does not exclude trying to understand it from a comparative perspective because what matters is 'the existence of underlying dimensions on which one may place the EU alongside other cases'. On a similar vein, Pollack argues that if we shift the focus away from integration to other variables, the EU merely represents 'one of a number of cases'.

Continuing on the same line, as for the manifestation of regional actorness at the UNSC, scholars could look into the question whether the election of the non-EU members has a regional dimension and analyse the extent to which those countries take into account their regional memberships within the UNSC. Such comparative approach will not only increase our knowledge about the EU's actorness at the UNSC but also about the regional realities at the UN in New York more generally.

5.5 Conclusion

Focusing on the EU and its member states, this chapter first looked into the obstacles to the use of voting cohesion for measuring regional actorness in the context of the UNSC: the limited membership of the UNSC, its consensus-oriented decision making and the EU practice being one of representation. We then argued that the understanding of the regional reality in New York will not only benefit from such indirect focus on regional actorness, looking into the serving countries, but also from taking a comparative stance, comparing the EU's foreign policy practice to that of other regional players. Indeed, the EU's self-identification as a sui generis actor should not stop researchers from testing the validity of those claims, quite contrary.

Notes

1. Following Sjöstedt's definition of 'actor capacity', we define the notion of actorness as 'the capacity to behave actively and deliberately in relation to others in the international system' (Sjöstedt 1977: 16). Regional actorness refers then to the actor capacity of a region, referring to 'a limited number of states linked together by a geographical relationship and by a degree of mutual interdependence' (Nye 1971: vii).
2. On the evolution of the Chapter VIII Process, *see* Tavares (2009).

3. Article 23 UNCH stipulates that the members of the UNGA have to take into account the contribution of those countries to the maintenance of international peace and security and to the other purposes of the UN, as well as 'an equitable geographical distribution'.
4. While the table also includes the future candidates for the Asian Group, it is rather unlikely that Cyprus will be able to secure the Asian seat because of the voting arrangements that are in place and, more importantly, the membership of Turkey.
5. Security Council Report has suggested that the number of presidential statements may be used as an indicator for evaluating the UNSC's more informal activities (Security Council Report 2010).
6. Technically speaking, 663 resolutions and one (not adopted) decision were introduced, i.e. to allow the Former Republic of Yugoslavia to participate in the discussions on the situation in the Balkans in June 2000.
7. These draft resolutions were voted upon on 14 December 2001, 16 September 2003, 14 October 2003, 24 March 2004, 5 October 2004, 13 July 2006 and 11 November 2006, respectively.
8. On the origins of the disclaimer clause, *see* Drieskens (2010); on the modifications introduced by the Lisbon Treaty, *see* Drieskens (2008).
9. Caporaso, Marks, Moravcsik and Pollack expressed their views on the *n of 1* problem in a 1997 essay in ECSA Review. On the lack of comparative research in the study of regionalism more generally, *see* De Lombaerde et al. (2010).

References

Acharya, A., & Johnston, A. I. (Eds.). (2007). *Crafting cooperation: Regional international institutions in comparative perspective*. Cambridge: Cambridge University Press.

Biscop, S., & Drieskens, E. (2006). Effective multilateralism and collective security: Empowering the UN. In K. Laatikainen & K. E. Smith (Eds.), *Intersecting multilateralisms: The European Union and the United Nations* (pp. 115–132). Houndmills: Palgrave Macmillan.

Caporaso, J. A., et al. (1997). Does the European Union represent an *n* of 1? *ECSA Review, X*(3), 1–5.

De Lombaerde, P., Söderbaum, F., Van Langenhove, L., & Baert, F. (2010). The problem of comparison in comparative regionalism. *Review of International Studies, 36*(3), 731–753.

Drieskens, E. (2008). EU actorness at the UN Security Council: A principal-agent comparison of the legal situation before and after Lisbon. *European Journal of Law Reform, 10*(4), 575–594.

Drieskens, E. (2009). Walking on eggshells: Non-permanent members searching for a EU perspective at the UN Security Council. In J. Wouters et al. (Eds.), *Belgium in the UN Security Council: Reflections on the 2007–2008 membership* (pp. 185–195). Antwerp: Intersentia.

Drieskens, E. (2010). Beyond Chapter VIII: Limits and opportunities of regional representation at the UN Security Council. *International Organisations Law Review, 7*(1), 149–169.

Drieskens, E., & Wouters, J. (2009). Epilogue: Looking backward, going forward. In J. Wouters et al. (Eds.), *Belgium in the UN Security Council: Reflections on the 2007–2008 membership* (pp. 187–190). Antwerp: Intersentia.

Drieskens, E., et al. (2007). In search of a European dimension in the UN Security Council. *The International Spectator, XLII*(3), 421–430.

Jørgensen, K. E. (2004). Theorizing the European Union's foreign policy. In B. Tonra & T. Christiansen (Eds.), *Rethinking European foreign policy* (pp. 10–25). Manchester: Manchester University Press.

Jørgensen, K. E., & Rosamond, B. (2002). Europe: Regional laboratory for a global polity? In M. Ougaard & R. Higgott (Eds.), *Towards a global polity* (pp. 189–206). London: Frank Cass Publishers.

Kissack, R. (2007). *European Union Member States coordination in the United Nations system: Towards a methodology for analysis* (European Foreign Policy Unit Working Paper 20071/1).

Laatikainen, K., & Smith, K. (Eds.). (2006). *Intersecting multilateralisms: The European Union and the United Nations*. Houndmills: Palgrave Macmillan.
Nye, J. (1971). *Peace in parts: Integration and conflict in regional organization*. Boston: Little, Brown and Company.
Rosamond, B. (2000). *Theories of European integration*. Houndmills: Palgrave Macmillan.
Security Council Report (2010). Reduced Security Council decision-making in 2009: A year of decline – Or are the statistics misleading? *Update Report* (14).
Sjöstedt, G. (1977). *The external role of the European Community*. Westmead: Saxon House.
Smith, C. (2005). *Politics and process at the United Nations. The global dance*. London: Lynne Rienner Publishers.
Smith, K. E. (2007, October 19). *The EU in the world: Future research agendas*. Anna Lindh award lecture. Brussels.
Tavares, R. (2009). *Regional security: The capacity of international organizations*. London: Routledge.
Wouters, J., et al. (Eds.). (2006). *The United Nations and the European Union: An ever stronger partnership*. The Hague: TMC Asser Press.

Chapter 6
Weighted Regional Representation as a Basis for Security Council Reform[1]

Joseph E. Schwartzberg

6.1 Introduction: Time for a New Paradigm

In recent years, we have witnessed – in the deliberations of the UN General Assembly, in diplomatic negotiations outside the UN and in various academic forums – a plethora of ineffectual attempts to devise a broadly acceptable accord for making the Security Council more representative of the world's nations and peoples.[2] Almost all such proposals call for an expanded membership with permanent and rotating seats allocated, as at present, to specific member nations. While there is widespread acknowledgment of the excessive power wielded by nations of the 'global North', there is considerable disagreement on the regional allocation of seats and on which nations deserve new permanent or, in some formulations, 'semi-permanent' seats.[3] Nor is there much accord on which seat holders shall be endowed with the veto and how the veto power might be responsibly employed.

Virtually every proposal put forward by individual nations or blocs of nations is a self-serving attempt at enhancing the power of the proposing parties, with little regard for the overall good of humanity. All such proposals would anoint a select few nations with membership in what is, in effect, a governing club and preserve a major gap in power between the anointed few and all remaining nations.

With respect to rotating seats, the proposals advanced have, almost without exception, failed to address four notable deficiencies: First, some 75 of the UN's 192 member nations have yet to serve a single term in the Security Council. Second, seat holders seldom seek to determine, much less articulate, the views of other nations of the regions they supposedly represent. Third, the weakness of many seat holders renders them susceptible to unwarranted influence by major powers, who frequently resort to bribery and coercion to influence their votes. Finally, because

J.E. Schwartzberg (✉)
University of Minnesota, Minnesota, USA
e-mail: schwa004@umn.edu

P. De Lombaerde et al. (eds.), *The United Nations and the Regions: Third World Report on Regional Integration*, United Nations University Series on Regionalism 3,
DOI 10.1007/978-94-007-2751-9_6, © Springer Science+Business Media B.V. 2012

of the archaic, increasingly dysfunctional Westphalian concept of the 'sovereign equality of nations', the votes of such Council members as Djibouti, Guyana and Malta (all with populations well below a million) have counted the same as those of such global giants as India and Japan.

The problems referred to above are all soluble. But their solution calls for acceptance of a new paradigm, one that sheds slavish adherence to the 'sovereign equality of nations' mantra and recognises instead the growing importance of major world regions in global affairs and establishes a more realistically congruent relationship between voting strength in the UN and power in the real world outside the arena of the UN itself.[4] In the absence of such a credible relationship, Security Council decisions will lack legitimacy and continue to be ignored whenever doing so suits the purpose of sufficiently powerful nations. This chapter puts forward a logical, regionally based paradigm for allocating power in the Security Council that is more appropriate to the needs of the twenty-first century than the arbitrary, increasingly anachronistic formulation imposed in 1945 by the five major victors in World War II.

6.2 Guidelines for the Allocation of Voting Power

Listed below are guidelines for devising an equitable system of weighted regional voting in the UN Security Council:

First, the number of regions should be sufficient to facilitate adequate expression of the world's diversity, yet not so great as to preclude expeditious decision making.

Second, each region should have a population, territorial extent, and/or economic importance such that the legitimacy of its representation in the Security Council will not be seriously questioned.

Third, regional boundaries should be drawn to maximise internal homogeneity in regard to multiple factors: culture, religion, language, economic interests and recent historical experience.

Fourth, the composition of each region should minimise co-membership therein of nations that are long-standing antagonists.

Fifth, ideally, no single nation within a multinational region should have greater decision-making power than all the other members combined.

Sixth, individual nations, especially those on the periphery of a proposed region, should have the right to request membership in another region, but with no guarantee that such a request will be honoured.

Seventh, regional contiguity is desirable, but not essential.

Eighth, regions shall be periodically alterable in light of ongoing political, demographic and economic changes.

Ninth, allocation of weighted votes in the new system must not create so great a departure from the present system as to be unacceptable to the nations or blocs that presently wield the greatest political influence.

6.3 Proposed Regions and Weighting Formula

I here propose a system with twelve 'regions', four consisting of single nations with a combined demographic and economic weight above a specified threshold, and eight multinational regions. Although the threshold for single-nation representation and the inclusiveness of multinational regions would initially be determined by a committee of the UN General Assembly, individual nations therein would be allowed to request transfer from one region to another subject to the approval of the region within which membership is sought. Figure 6.1 presents the set of regions that, in my judgment, would prove optimal. It reflects, to a remarkable degree, regional organisations that already exist (e.g. the EU, Arab League, ASEAN, AU, OAS, etc.). The name of one region, the 'Westminster League', comprised of Canada, Australia and New Zealand, is an invention of the author. As need arises, the General Assembly would be empowered to recommend alterations in regional boundaries without resort to amending the UN Charter.

Each region would have one seat in the Security Council, and the holder of that seat would cast a weighted vote.[5] The weights assigned (W) would be the average of three terms in the following equation:

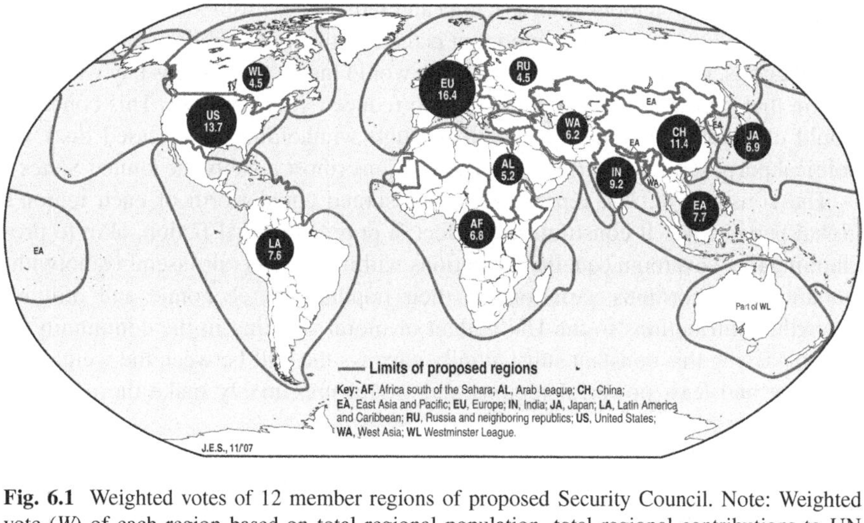

Fig. 6.1 Weighted votes of 12 member regions of proposed Security Council. Note: Weighted vote (W) of each region based on total regional population, total regional contributions to UN budget and regional constant according to the formula: $W = (P + C + 8.33)/3$

$$W = \frac{P + C + 8.33\%}{3} \tag{6.1}$$

wherein P represents the region's population as a percentage of the total population of all UN member states, C represents the region's total contributions to the UN budget as a percentage of the total budget (with contributions being uniformly assessed in proportion to GDP) and 8.33% is a constant signifying that the global perspective of each of the 12 regions is equally worthy of respect. Decisions of the Security Council on procedural matters would require a total weighted vote exceeding 50%, while actions on most substantive matters would require a two-thirds majority (66.7%), with the concurrent approval of regions whose combined populations totalled at least 50% of the world's total. On certain matters (e.g. imposition of sanctions, armed intervention), super-majorities exceeding 66.7% might be required. On no vote would vetoes be admissible.

The validity of the equation's population term is intuitively obvious. It embodies the democratic principle, now conspicuously lacking in the both the General Assembly, with its one state – one vote voting system, and in the Security Council, with its anachronistic and unfair privileged status for the P-5. The specific values assigned would, of course, be periodically adjusted, say every 10 years, in light of differential rates of population change around the world.

The GDP-based contributions term reflects the capacity of nations and regions to be effective.[6] This is consistent with Article 23 of the Charter, which stipulates that SC selection shall pay 'due regard in the first instance to the contribution of Members of the United Nations to the maintenance of peace and security and to the other purposes of the organisation'. From a pragmatic perspective, the world's wealthier countries would have little incentive to accept the proposed new system if there were no counterweight to the population term, which greatly privileges populous, but relatively poor, nations such as China and India (notwithstanding their currently burgeoning economies). Also important is the fact that the formula is based on *paid* contributions, not rates of assessment. This would insure that nations pay what they owe in that failure to do so would result in reduced voting weight. This condition would eliminate economic blackmail through withholding of assessed dues for political purposes, as practised by certain nations (most notably the United States).

The constant, 8.33%, represents the presumed equal worth of each region's global perspective. It constitutes, in effect, a pragmatic legal fiction, akin to proclaiming the 'sovereign equality' of nations within the General Assembly, notwithstanding the enormous variations in their populations, economic and military strength, contributions to the UN budget or moral standing in the community of nations. Using this constant substantially narrows the gulf between the weights of the most and least powerful regions and would presumably make the proposed system more widely acceptable.

An important consequence of applying the proposed voting formula is that it would establish a Security Council with a nearly equal balance between the five developed regions constituting the global North (i.e. Europe, the USA, Japan, Russia

Table 6.1 Regions to be represented in a reformed Security Council

Regions (see Fig. 6.1)	No. of UN members	Population 2006 (%)	Total GDP 2006 (%)	Area%	Weighted vote (%)
Africa	43	10.70	1.32	15.1	6.78
Arab League	21	4.91	2.24	10.6	5.16
China	1	20.42	5.47	7.2	11.41
East Asia +	29	10.62	4.06	5.3	7.67
Europe	41	8.31	32.64	3.8	16.43
India	1	17.35	1.83	2.4	9.17
Japan	1	1.98	10.29	0.3	6.87
Latin America +	33	8.71	5.63	5.3	7.56
Russia +	6	3.26	2.02	13.5	4.54
United States	1	4.64	28.26	7	13.74
West Asia	12	8.22	1.89	6.0	6.15
Westminster League	3	0.89	4.36	13.5	4.53
Total	192	100.00	100.00	100.0	100.00

Note: Some regional names are here abbreviated; more complete names appear on the map in Fig. 6.1. Data on number of members and area do not figure in the calculation of voting weights

and the Westminster League), with a combined weight of 46.11%, and the seven remaining regions of the global South (roughly the so-called G-77 + China), with a combined weight of 53.89%. Since binding votes on substantive matters would require a two-thirds majority, the practical effect of this near equivalence is that on issues involving a North–south division of opinion, it would be necessary for the two camps to engage in genuine dialogue to forge workable and widely acceptable compromises.

Another advantage of the proposed system is that it would enormously reduce the current problem of influencing votes through coercion and bribery in that great powers would find such tactics far more difficult to employ with multinational regions than with individual weak and scattered states.

Space considerations preclude discussion of the factors providing cohesion to the eight multinational regions indicated on Fig. 6.1 and Table 6.1, but it should be obvious that some, such as Europe and the Westminster League, are presently much more cohesive than others such as West Asia and East Asia and the Pacific. But in all regions, it seems probable that processes of globalisation and the need for intra-regional interaction will combine to diminish existing intra-and inter-regional disparities.

A region that might prove to be especially problematic is 'Russia and Neighbouring Republics'. The neighbours in question are five culturally European republics (Armenia, Belarus, Georgia, Moldova and Ukraine) of the former USSR. Because their combined political weight would be substantially less than that of Russia alone, they might regard themselves in a permanent minority position and seek to opt out of the region in favour of inclusion within the much larger, but more liberal and less monolithic European region. Were that to occur, the weight of the European region would be increased to 16.88, while that of Russia, reduced to a single-nation entity, would be reduced to 4.090.

Table 6.2 Likely areas of overlap between proposed regions

Region 1 (to which listed countries were initially assigned)	Region 2	Likely area of overlap
Arab League	Africa	Ten Arab League members in northern and eastern Africa
Arab League	West Asia	Iraq or parts thereof in the event of partition
East Asia and Pacific	Westminster League	Six small Pacific island states with strong ties to Australia and New Zealand; less likely: Papua New Guinea and Solomon Islands
Europe	Westminster League	United Kingdom and Ireland
Latin America and Caribbean	Westminster League	Eleven small former British dependencies in Caribbean region plus Guyana
Russia and Neighbouring Republics	Europe	Armenia, Belarus, Georgia, Moldova and Ukraine
West Asia	East Asia+	Bangladesh
West Asia	Europe	Turkey
West Asia	Russia and Neighbouring Republics	Kazakhstan; less likely: Azerbaijan, Kyrgyzstan, Tajikistan, Turkmenistan and Uzbekistan

6.4 Representation with Overlapping Regional Membership

To this point, we have presumed that each of the world's nations would have membership in only one region. But numerous nations have significant ties to more than one of the regions indicated on Fig. 6.1. Turkey, for example, aspires to be a member of the European Union, but might also wish to retain a voice in the affairs of the West Asian region, in which it would be especially influential. Similarly, the United Kingdom, among the more important members of the European Union, might also wish to play a role in the Westminster League. And the ten African members of the Arab League might wish to maintain their bond with the 43 other nations comprising the African region.

Table 6.2 indicates the areas of the world that, in the author's view, might wish to belong to two regions for purposes of representation in the SC if a workable system for doing so were in place.

In all likelihood, however, some of the 45 countries noted above would reject the opportunity for dual regional membership. It is also conceivable that circumstances might lead other countries to exercise the choice to do so.

Although allowing national affiliations with only one region would make for a simpler system than one in which nations could simultaneously belong to two regions, there is no reason in principle why the latter could not be established. The key to establishing a just and workable system would be to establish rules whereby a country choosing membership in two regions would have its weight in decision making divided between the two so that its overall contribution to SC decision making would be the same as if it were in only one region.

A final provision in respect to nations with overlapping regional memberships would be that they could be elected to the Security Council as representatives of either one of the two regions to which they belong, but not of both simultaneously.

6.5 Means of Selection and Functioning of Representatives and Alternates

The means of selecting and instructing seat holders in a Security Council with universal weighted regional representation would vary considerably from those presently employed. Necessary conditions would be that the representatives: (1) make a bona fide effort to represent fairly the wishes of their region rather than those of their respective countries, (2) be accountable to all countries in the region for their actions on the Council; and (3) be subject to recall if they failed egregiously to carry out the trust placed in them. Additionally, whatever the selection system might be, it would entail different rules for single-nation and multination regions. Finally, it would be desirable to maintain the General Assembly's role in the final selections for multimember regions.

A minimum departure from present practice would have each of the four single-nation regions select its own representative, just as the P-5 powers do now, while each multination region would nominate, by whatever method it wished, either a single preferred country or several countries from among which the General Assembly would select one.

A more innovative, competitive and democratic system would have each multinational region, by a method of its own choosing, nominate, in June of an election year, from two to five specific nations or two to five individuals (but not more than one individual per nation) to represent it. The General Assembly would then consider the merits of candidates on each regional list and elect in September a representative as well as an alternate. If no candidate received an absolute majority on the first ballot, the candidate with the lowest vote total would be eliminated, and the process would be repeated until one candidate emerged with an absolute majority. Terms would commence the following January.

The recommended procedure would promote meritocracy in that nations within a region would put forward as potential candidates only highly capable individuals or countries held in high international regard, knowing that poorly qualified nominees would garner little support from other member nations in the region and stand little chance of election by the General Assembly as a whole, Additionally, once chosen, Security Council delegates would strive to be responsive to the concerns of all countries in the region they represented and would be accountable for all their official actions and votes. Failure to satisfy the expectations of a substantial segment of their regional constituents would possibly result in their recall and would greatly reduce one's chances for re-election to the Security Council if consecutive terms were to be allowed.

Meritocracy is important in a system of regional representation because it increases the likelihood of election of worthy candidates from small, internationally responsible nations in preference to those from larger, more powerful, but possibly less virtuous, regional hegemons. As representatives of their respective regions, they would, of course, wield far more influence than if they were serving in the Security Council as it is presently constituted.

Additionally, a representative's power would depend not only on the weight of the vote that she/he might cast but also on the persuasiveness and moral and legal content of her/his arguments. Thus, a weak region with an eloquent spokesperson and a strong case might stand a good chance of winning sufficient support for a given position even in the face of strenuous opposition from certain regions with higher weighted votes. One would therefore anticipate that the proposed system would lead to greater emergence on the world scene of globally acclaimed statespersons and that such individuals would continue to play key roles in shaping world opinion long after concluding their respective terms on the Security Council.

As at present, representatives and their alternates would be guided by the foreign ministries of the nations they represent. In multinational regions, this would presuppose frequent consultation with and among the ministries of the countries comprising the region. Not long ago, this would have been impossible, but in an age of electronic communication, such difficulties can rather easily be overcome or greatly mitigated.[7] While much of the deliberation of issues before the Security Council would be handled via the Internet, it would be in the general interest of the region also to have periodic face-to-face summit meetings to formulate general regional policies.

In general, alternates would assume the role of delegates when the latter were, for whatever reason, unable to serve. Additionally, a region's delegation could request additional speakers to present particular positions when, for political reasons, it became impossible for the delegate or alternate to do so.

Each multinational region would find it necessary to formulate procedural rules to guide Security Council representatives and alternates. Each, presumably, would wish to devise its own formula for casting weighted national votes within the region itself. There would be no necessity for all to adopt the same system. Space considerations preclude discussion of the many possible solutions to this problem.

Once national voting weights have been determined, each multinational region would also have to establish rules on voting. For example, the rules might call for simple majorities on procedural matters, two-thirds majorities on most substantive matters and three-fourths majorities on Security Council resolutions calling for armed intervention in a given area.

Members of multinational regions would presumably wish to consult not only on issues likely to come before the Security Council but also on those within the purview of the General Assembly and other organs of the UN system. They could also use such meetings to discuss matters for which the UN bears little or no responsibility (e.g. trade regimes, environmental and energy issues, multinational river basin development, educational and cultural exchanges, migration rules, pandemic diseases, etc.). Thus, the system of regional representation would promote regional cooperation in general and foster greater regional integration.

Obviously, consultation and cooperation ought not to be limited to the regions established for purposes of Security Council representation. There is, for example, no reason why the nations of NAFTA (the North American Free Trade Area) or of SAARC (the South Asian Association for Regional Cooperation) should not continue to carry out all the functions that those organisations now address even though the member states lie in two or more Security Council regions. Nor should there be any bar to prevent members of any region from inviting participation from extra-regional states in deliberating a question of mutual concern.

6.6 Advantages of the Proposed System

We may now summarise the advantages of the proposed Security Council reforms in comparison to the present and other possible systems:

- The system provides universal participation in decision making.
- The system is nondiscriminatory. No nation would be singled out by name for permanent representation, as is now the case with the P-5; rather a nation would have to meet specified objective criteria to have a seat in its own right.
- Weighted votes would be objectively determined by a rational and simple mathematical formula.
- Regionally weighted votes provide a more realistic reflection of power than in any other system of representation.
- The system is flexible, providing for periodic adjustments of voting weights based on relative changes in population and economic power.
- When changing voting weights and the composition of regions, adjustments would not require Charter amendment.
- The system would establish a workable balance between the global North and the global South.
- Regions represented would have far more political, economic and cultural coherence than do the five broad regions from which Security Council members are presently elected.
- The system gives individual nations substantial latitude in choosing the region(s) to which they wish to belong.
- The system would encourage nations to pay their dues in full since failure to do so would reduce a region's weighted vote; this would put an end to fiscal blackmail.
- Even regions with the low weighted votes would be sufficiently strong to preclude the likelihood of bribery and coercion, both of which currently compromise the legitimacy of many Security Council votes.

- The system would heighten the prospect of small nations playing significant roles in world affairs.
- The system of nominating candidates and selecting seat holders by the General Assembly promotes meritocracy and a sense of global community.
- The selection system is also more democratic.
- The system would cast able diplomats into the role of global statespersons.
- Necessary regular regional consultation on matters coming before the Security Council would also promote regional consultation and cooperation in matters outside the purview of the United Nations.
- The system allows each region to establish its own rules for determining policies and instructing Security Council representatives.
- By enhancing the weight of key nations' Security Council votes, the proposed system offers a more acceptable alternative than other reform proposals for persuading presently veto-wielding nations to give up the veto.

6.7 Conclusion

A paradigm shift is needed, but paradigm shifts are not easily accomplished. Logic and fairness alone may not suffice to overcome the political inertia resulting from apathy, ignorance and the vested interest of major powers in the status quo. Yet, political systems and institutions can and do change. Over time, structural deficiencies often build up internal stresses that make change unavoidable. Alternatively, systems may respond to catastrophic events such as World Wars I and II, which respectively led to the creation of the League of Nations and the United Nations. Nobody can forecast with certainty what the next climactic event(s) will be: A monumental stroke of terrorism? World War III? An unprecedented natural catastrophe? Widespread famine? A global energy crisis? Whatever the precipitating circumstances may be, our planet would be well served to have a plan for global governance to deal with them. If our leaders, prodded by civil society, are sufficiently wise, they will anticipate the changes and improve government mechanisms accordingly. How the Security Council functions is but one part of a much larger governance mosaic, but it is a vital part. This essay provides a blueprint for a fairer and more workable system.

Notes

1. This chapter is essentially an abridgement, with minor modifications, of a much longer essay, 'Universal Regional Representation as a Basis for Security Council Reform', presented at the 20th Annual Meeting of the Academic Council on the United Nations System at the Ralph Bunche Institute for International Studies, CUNY Graduate Center, New York, in June 2007. The longer essay may be obtained by contacting the author at schwa004@umn.edu or downloaded from the Center for War/Peace Studies website, www.cwps.org. The 2007 essay was itself the culmination of a series of publications by the author and critical responses to those works, beginning with 'Towards a more representative and effective Security Council', *Political*

Geography, vol. 13, no. 6, 1994, 483–491. The most detailed of the intermediate works in question is the monograph, *Revitalizing the United Nations: Weighted Voting as a Vehicle for United Nations reform,* New York and the Hague: Institute for Global Policy, World Federalist Movement, 2004. This work may be downloaded from the WFM website, www.wfm.org or the websites of Civitatis International, www.civitatis.org; Citizens for Global Solutions, www.globalsolutions.org.

2. For an extensive, but incomplete, list, see Manuel Fröhlich, Klaus Hüfner and Alfredo Marker, Reform des Sicherheitsrats: Modelle, Kriterien und Kennziffer (Reform of the UN Security Council: Models, Criteria and Index Numbers), Berlin: Deutsche Gesellschaft für die Vereinten Nationen, Blaue Reihe Nr. 94, 2005. This compendium provides essential data on 25 proposals for the period 2003–2005 as well as 57 others for earlier years and indicates for each the agency responsible for the proposal, the principal recommendations and the published sources in which the proposal is described. Additional proposals are cited in the essay cited in note 1.
3. The most important documents in which these concepts are developed are: A more secure world: our shared responsibility, Report of the High-level Panel on Threats, Challenges and Change, United Nations General Assembly, A/59/565, 29 November, 2004; and Kofi Annan, In larger freedom: towards development, security and human rights for all; Report of the Secretary-General, United Nations General Assembly, A/59/2005, 21 March 2005. A critique of the SC reform recommendations of the former of these two documents (applicable also to the latter) is provided in Joseph E. Schwartzberg, 'Getting It Wrong on Security Council Reform', paper presented at the annual meeting of the Academic Council on the United Nations System, Ottawa, Canada, June 2005.
4. An excellent discussion of the importance of regions and regionalism in global governance is provided in Kennedy Graham and Tânia Felicio, Regional Security and Global Governance, Brussels: VUB Press, 2006. This work includes an annex suggesting the composition of a reformed 24-seat Security Council based on regional security arrangements. An alternative proposal, remarkably similar to the those recommended by the author in 1997, 2004 and in this essay (see note 1) is that of Kemal Dervis, in cooperation with Ceren Özer, A Better Globalization: Legitimacy, Governance, and Reform, Washington, DC: Center for Global Development, 2005, which advocates a 14-seat Security Council with regionally weighted voting.
5. The case for weighted voting with illustrations of where and how it has been used are fully discussed in Paul C. Szasz, Alternative Voting systems in International Organizations and the Binding Triad Proposal to Improve U.N. General Assembly Decision-Taking, Wayne, NJ: Center for U.N. Reform Education, Monograph # 17, 2001.
6. Readers may question the recommendation that contributions be strictly proportional to GNP, rather than following the slightly progressive system now in effect. Apart from the anomalous privileging of the United States, which – as a result of intense political pressure – became the only wealthy country to be assessed at a rate less than its proportional share of the gross world product (22% as opposed to roughly 28%), the system entails a needlessly complicated formula to provide meagre economic savings to poor countries that could be better served by wiser redistributive measures in the allocation of UN revenues.
7. Some indication of how regional deliberations might be undertaken is provided by the virtual parliament, established in 2003, which already links hundreds of legislators from many parts of the world. See http://www.e-parl.net.

Chapter 7
Regionalisation, Transnational Democracy and United Nations Reform: A Viewpoint

Hans Köchler

7.1 Introduction

Regional organisations can contribute to the reform and, in particular, democratisation of the United Nations Organisation in two distinct ways: (1) *through their very existence* – since regional cooperation across national borders, especially in its institutionalised form, strengthens the tendency towards global *multipolarity*, the only form of world order in which the UN can properly function as intergovernmental organisation that is built on the philosophy of collective action ('collective security') – and (2) through the development of procedures of *democratic decision-making* in a transnational space – as in the case of the European Union – that can serve as exemplary standards for intergovernmental cooperation and the rule of law at the global level. These procedural matters include, inter alia, regulations for the separation of powers, the distinct role of legislative (parliamentary) branches in transnational structures, weighted voting, etc.

7.2 Regionalisation and Global Multipolarity

During the first four decades of its existence, the UN had to act within the framework of an essentially *bipolar* balance of power. Because of the veto right of the Security Council's five permanent members, including the two major players of that era, the organisation was unable to act efficiently on important issues of its mandate, especially in the field of international security. The UN's 'forced inaction' in major conflict situations has been widely regretted as a sign of paralysis of the world organisation due to the East–west conflict.

H. Köchler (✉)
University of Innsbruck, Innsbruck, Austria
e-mail: hans.koechler@uibk.ac.at

P. De Lombaerde et al. (eds.), *The United Nations and the Regions: Third World Report on Regional Integration*, United Nations University Series on Regionalism 3,
DOI 10.1007/978-94-007-2751-9_7,

This structural problem could not be addressed in the existing statutory framework, with the special voting rights under Art. 27 of the Charter that allowed the two great powers to neutralise each other. There is hardly any disagreement that the veto principle in and of itself is not compatible with the sovereign equality of states, one of the basic norms of the UN Charter. More specifically, the provision according to which all decisions of the Security Council on other than procedural matters require the consent of the five permanent members cannot be reconciled with democratic decision-making; decisions reached under this provision constitute – to put it mildly – a rather inadequate form of 'weighted voting'.

The structural change of the international order that has taken shape within the last one and a half decades (i.e. since the end of the Cold War) has further aggravated the situation. In matters of war and peace, the United Nations Organisation has, if only temporarily, to operate in the absence of a balance of power, a state of affairs that has made the veto rule even more detrimental in terms of the efficacy as well as legitimacy of the international order. Within a unipolar system, there are very few, if any, incentives for the most influential member state not to resort to the veto power whenever that country deems it advantageous for its national interests – and there are almost no impediments to unilateral action (outside the framework of the UN) in situations where other permanent members might be prepared to object a certain enforcement action under Chapter VII.

Under these circumstances, it appears to be the predicament of the world organisation that it has to act *multilaterally* – according to the Charter's doctrine of collective security – in an actually *unilateral* (political) framework. It is not surprising that this contradictory mission has led not only to a loss of efficiency, but a serious erosion of legitimacy of the world organisation.

The only antidote to this constellation – in which the UN is prevented from carrying out its mandate in a consistent manner, i.e. is actually incapacitated – will be the gradual emergence of a *new balance of power*. The formation of regional groupings – and the strengthening of existing ones – may be an essential contribution to such a development. Ideally, regional structures in all corners of the globe could be the pillars of a multipolar world order for the twenty-first century, in which the United Nations Organisation is enabled to accomplish its mission in conformity with the Charter's idealistic mandate ('that armed force shall not be used, save in the common interest').

As part of a major reform of the organisation – that has to be aimed at making it more *representative* and *democratic* at the same time – regional organisations (such as the European Union) could eventually take the place of the traditional veto-wielding nation-states. It goes without saying that such a restructuring of the organisation, and in particular of the permanent membership in the Security Council, has to be undertaken on the basis of geographically balanced representation. This will imply the redefinition of the very notion of 'permanent membership' in the sense of a *collective membership of regions* – an organisational model that will ensure a global distribution of power that is substantially more fair than the present one, which is a legacy of the power constellation of 1945. (In the case of Europe, this would mean the replacement of two individual permanent members [nation-states] by an intergovernmental and partly supranational entity, namely the EU, that includes the two.) Regional organisations in other parts of the world – such as the African Union – may assume a similar role when they will have achieved sufficient internal cohesion. This development will have special importance on those continents which, so far, have been totally unrepresented in the category of permanent membership – namely Africa and Latin America.

It is obvious that a redrafting of the UN Charter along the principles of 'regional representation' is an elusive task under the present distribution of power and authority. As we know by now, even the less ambitious reform proposals of the Secretary-General's High Level Panel (2005) have no chance of realisation. (The Charter's Art. 108 is in fact an insurmountable procedural obstacle.) It is important, however, to highlight the impact that regional groupings could have in a future scenario in which a way out may have to be sought of the impasse resulting from the Charter's incorporating a balance of power of an earlier era. In case of a major reform of the Charter, which will have to include reform of the Security Council as a top priority, regional structures – whether intergovernmental or supranational or both – will present a viable organisational alternative to the singular nation-state membership in the Council.

Absent such a structural change, even the mere existence of regional groupings, at different levels of cohesion and organisational density, will have a positive impact on the UN's day-to-day functioning, helping to reduce, at least informally, the often regretted 'democratic deficit'. The more forms of regional cooperation and regional organisations exist, the better able will individual UN member states – belonging to those regional groupings – be to avoid being marginalised in matters affecting their national interests, not only in the field of security and peace, but also regarding economic and social development. The same holds true for measures of peace and security under Chapter VIII of the UN Charter. The more structures of efficient regional cooperation and decision-making are in place, the less likely will it be that the Security Council will have to act – or be tempted to intervene – under the provisions of Chapter VII (which are essentially measures of last resort). As recent history has documented, compulsory measures (including the use of force) under Art. 41ff may jeopardise an often delicate regional balance of power and lead to long-term destabilisation of 'geographical' regions that, would they have been able to act as 'political' regions (i.e. would there have been an effective regional organisation), might have escaped that fate. It is here where the principle of *subsidiarity*, often overlooked in international affairs, comes to play. Supranational regions could indeed breathe new life into the provisions of Chapter VIII and give concrete meaning to the principle of subsidiarity, particularly in matters of international security.

Furthermore, membership within a regional structure often provides an opportunity of a de facto, if not de jure, collective representation at the global level, something which smaller and medium states can ill afford to neglect under the conditions of an uneven distribution of power and wealth. At the same time, the debates and decision-making procedures in the fora of the United Nations Organisation will be more balanced in terms of the Charter's idealistic commitment towards 'sovereign equality' – since otherwise isolated member states can voice their concerns more effectively within a regional framework.

Generally speaking, only genuine *multipolarity* in terms of power relations can finally introduce elements of an urgently needed *separation of powers* into a system where, so far, the Security Council in many instances not only acts as supreme executive, but legislative organ as well. The only realistic method by which, under the present circumstances, such a multipolar order can be promoted is through the intensification of regional cooperation at all levels and the strengthening of regional organisations on all continents. Such a process will also give new relevance to the 'transnational paradigm' which is incorporated in the Preamble to the UN Charter and which should be taken as a guideline for the restructuring of international relations in the twenty-first century.

7.3 Regionalisation and Transnational Democracy

As regards decision-making procedures at the transnational level and the contribution regional organisations can make to the democratisation of international relations, the experience of the European Union may, to a certain extent, also be relevant for the UN or at least provide some ideas for the ongoing reform debate. It is safe to assume that, as far as organisational aspects are concerned, the methods practised by a regional organisation comprising 27 states with over 490 million citizens may, in principle, also be applied to a worldwide organisation.

The fundamental challenge faced by any intergovernmental organisation, whether regional or global, lies in finding a formula which is doing justice to the principle of *equal rights* of all citizens in an environment which is determined by the sovereign equality of states (as collective units of citizens). How can the democratic maxim of equality (in the sense of equal voting rights at the domestic level) be adapted to the *transnational* level?

The principle of 'one state – one vote' expresses the sovereignty of states; only rather indirectly can it be related to the sovereignty of the citizen (insofar as 'individual sovereignty' is mediated by the state as the citizen's international agent). As is obvious in the structure of the UN General Assembly, this creates a huge imbalance and raises questions of democratic legitimacy – since a vote on behalf of a community of over a billion citizens will have the same weight as that made on behalf a few thousand. In view of the Preamble's solemn exclamation – 'We the peoples of the United Nations' – there is no doubt that a body thus composed is faced with the question as to how to be truly representative of the *citizens of the world*. The imbalance in terms of popular representation is further exacerbated by the veto power of only five member states in the Security Council, the supreme executive organ of the organisation.

A solution to this dilemma may lie in the introduction of a kind of *weighted-voting* formula – especially in the form of *double majority* provisions – for decisions to be taken by the delegates as the representatives of states (whether in the General Assembly or in the Security Council), similar to the voting regulations practised in the European Union – the refinement of which has been debated extensively in the course of the reform process of the latter. To 'measure' the 'weight' of a (state) vote in relation to the population represented in that vote is an appropriate democratic procedure (since the very rationale of democracy is the preservation of the dignity of the human being as citizen with equal rights). Ideally, a weighted-voting formula of some sort, in combination with a double majority requirement, could open a way out of the present impasse in terms of Security Council reform. The veto rule of Art. 27 of the UN Charter has, in actual fact, been an undemocratic formula of 'weighted' voting according to which the individual votes of five member states are given precedence, not in terms of their population but of the power which they enjoyed in a particular historical constellation.

Should a voting model in analogy to the double majority regulations in the EU Council of Ministers (that would imply the effective abrogation of the unanimity requirement among the five permanent members) not be feasible for reasons that lie in the genesis of the organisation, the UN member states may consider to redefine the Charter's veto provision in the sense of a *unanimity requirement among the global regions*. In the case of the region covered by the European Union, this would entail that the two 'European' seats are merged into one permanent seat, to be occupied on the basis of rotation among all member states, large or small, of this regional group. Similar procedures could apply to other regions once they have reached a sufficient state of cohesion and visibility as international actors (e.g. the Association of Southeast Asian Nations or, eventually, the African Union).

A further measure that may be considered is the creation – in analogy to the European Parliament – of a 'parliamentary assembly' of the UN with the number of deputies, within certain margins, being proportional to the population size of the respective member *state* or, where adequate arrangements exist, the respective *region* (comprising smaller member states that would otherwise be left out of the equation). Such an arrangement would be more in conformity with democratic representation than the present state-centred structure. However, such an assembly will have to be more than a deliberative (consultative) organ if it is to fit into a system of a transnational *separation of powers*, something which is indispensable for the international rule of law and, thus, for the legitimacy and long-term prospects of the United Nations Organisation.

7.4 Conclusion

All these elements of a 'grand' reform of the world organisation have regard to the vision of a genuine *multipolar* world order – that is to emerge in the future – and are expression of an approach that goes beyond traditional forms of intergovernmental cooperation among nation-states, seen as isolated entities, towards transnational and supranational forms of organisation. The *supranational* element has first been introduced into the international system by regional groupings that saw in it an important means of effective representation of their member states' 'national' interests. This is even more so in the 'globalised' environment at the beginning of the twenty-first century. Although the supranational paradigm is being implemented, at varying degrees, by regional organisations, in particular the European Union, it is still lacking in the world organisation. International realpolitik – more specifically an imbalance in power relations – has prevented any reform measures in that regard.

It goes without saying that, under the present conditions, the blueprint of a 'regional' reorganisation of the UN – in the sense of (1) structure and composition of membership (including regional groupings) and (2) regionalisation of the decision-making, in particular in the Security Council – is only an idealistic vision. However, the absence of a global balance of power – one of the factors that have made major reform efforts elusive – is only a transient stage of world affairs. At the social, cultural (or civilisational) and economic levels, the global reality is undeniably *multipolar* even now.

Under the condition that no catastrophic military confrontation between the major global players occurs (the avoidance of which is the raison d'être of the UN), sufficiently coherent regional groupings (such as the European Union) could become the catalyst of change within the global system, providing new impetus to the democratic reform of the UN and, thus, ensuring the organisation's long-term viability. As new actors on the international scene – in addition to the traditional nation-states – they may (1) gradually introduce an element of political multipolarity into an otherwise unipolar order and (2) demonstrate that the paradigm of democracy can also be implemented, albeit with modifications, in the framework of large transnational, virtually universal, organisations such as the UN. Successful 'regionalisation' of the global system could not only provide a much-needed impetus to the emergence of a multipolar balance of power but also contribute to the solution of one of the most difficult problems of international order, namely how to reconcile the requirements of *state* sovereignty with the sovereign status of the *citizen*.

Part II
Regional Organisations and Peace and Security

Chapter 8
The UN and Regional Organisations for Peace: Tracking a Slippery Partnership

LukVan Langenhove, Tânia Felício, and Ademola Abass

8.1 Introduction

The United Nations (UN) is in principle exclusively based upon state membership. This means that only states and no other entities of governance can be members of the UN. However, developments in regional integration have led to the emergence of new forms of governance and new entities with concerted voices – which do cooperate with and are represented within the UN system. A number of regional organisations have even obtained observer status within the global organisation. A special case is the European Union, having attained voting rights in the WTO (World Trade Organisation) and FAO (Food and Agriculture Organisation) plus full participation in the UN Convention on Climate Change. This shows that regional governance is not seen as incompatible with UN global governance. So much that, as previously stated, the UN Charter even foresees a potential role for regional organisations in the area of peace and security, and this has led to much discussion on how the existing regional organisations can and should cooperate with the global body in this field and how this cooperation should be framed and structured, considering the lack of clarity provided in the Charter.

L. Van Langenhove (✉)
United Nations University Institute on Comparative Regional Integration Studies (UNU-CRIS), Bruges, Belgium
e-mail: lvanlangenhove@cris.unu.edu

T. Felício
United Nations Integrated Mission in Timor Leste (UNMIT), Dili, Timor Leste

A. Abass
United Nations University Institute on Comparative Regional Integration Studies (UNU-CRIS), Bruges, Belgium

P. De Lombaerde et al. (eds.), *The United Nations and the Regions: Third World Report on Regional Integration*, United Nations University Series on Regionalism 3, DOI 10.1007/978-94-007-2751-9_8,

This chapter discusses the recent dialogue and cooperation between the UN and regional organisations at the level of the UN Secretariat and the Security Council. It will be argued that between 1992 and 2006, an attempt was made to move the UN/ regional organisations relationship from a sporadic and spontaneous phase to a more organised and systematic collaboration based upon Chapter VIII of the UN Charter. Several countries including Greece, Romania, Belgium and South Africa have used their Security Council membership period to stimulate this process. Within the UN, Secretary-General Kofi Annan repeatedly called for a greater role for regional organisations in conflict prevention, management and resolution. His successor, Secretary-General Ban Ki-Moon, appears more inclined towards strengthening UN collaboration with the African Union than deepening the relationship between the UN and regional organisations in general.

As previously noted, the most formal form of regionalism or regional representation in the UN system is the one embodied by Chapter VIII of the UN Charter. Under this chapter, regional organisations are empowered to assist the UN in the field of peace and security in their respective regions. Several organisations such as the Organisation of the American States (OAS), the Arab League or the Organisation of African Unity (OAU) were oriented to such a conflict-control role, but their endeavours had limited importance during the Cold War since they were founded on the principles of sovereignty and noninterference in regions dominated by interstate conflicts. In the aftermath of the Cold War, however, the security agenda has become 'considerably less monolithic and global, and considerably more diverse, regional and local, in character than the old one' (Buzan 2000: 12). This is due not only to the demise of the East–west confrontation but was also inspired by the explosion of new security threats at local or regional level (sometimes called 'low intensity conflicts') and of threats beyond military conflicts but related to political, social, economical or environmental concerns. These developments have spurred renewed attention to the potential role played by regional organisations in this field.

A number of regional actors, seduced by the potentially positive effects of economic integration and suffering the negative effects of globalisation, started acknowledging the advantages of giving away little bits of their sovereignty for regional stability. At the same time, a renewed interest in the global level and in the possibility of a new approach in terms of international peacebuilding was generated. However, as the deterrence of the Cold War disappeared and a new form of conflict (intra-state) mushroomed around the world, the UN grew increasingly unable to maintain peace and security on its own. The weak financial conditions, poor peacekeeping record in the 1990s (Somalia, Bosnia, Haiti) and political pressure from Western powers for reform hindered the feasibility of the UN as a self-sufficient conflict management tool.

As pointed out by Haas (1969: 93), 'regional security arrangements grow in direct proportion to disappointment with the UN collective security system'. The clear limitations of the global body have compelled the UN to empower regional organisations to manage their own conflicts, and a framework for cooperation, which can be easily defined as a regional-global security mechanism, has been growing steadily since the 1990s. The shift in both the content and nature of security has brought with it a growing interest in regional organisations as actors for peace and security. But the efficiency of each of such regional actors 'seems to depend on its credibility, as well as its political, military and economic power' (Laakso 2002: 5). There have been both successes and failures, and there is a debate about whether regional initiatives are either 'stumbling blocks' or 'building blocks' for a global multilateral approach to peace and security. Nonetheless, as the potential of regional initiatives became recognised, the UN has gradually taken up an interest in regional organisations (Thakur and Van Langenhove 2008).

In addition to the objectives already identified, this chapter will also look at the basis, development and present state of the formal cooperation between the UN and regional organisations, analysing how they are formally represented and how they are relating to the global body in peace and security.

8.2 Chapter VIII: Cooperation with Regional Agencies and Arrangements

When the UN Charter was signed, the choice of the Allied powers was to set up a universal security structure with a small opening for regions (allowed under Chapter VIII of the Charter). Regional organisations were in fact almost nonexistent (only the Arab and the American states had created 'regional' systems at the time), so the contextual basis for such cooperation was very limited. And this might have been one of the reasons why there was so much discussion on Chapter VIII and so little definition on the terms used in its articles.

The basis and legal implications of Chapter VIII have been thoroughly and extensively analysed by a great number of scholars such as Simma (1995), Abass (2004), Goodrich (1949), Padelford (1954: 203–216), Bebr (1955: 166–184), Eide (1966), Akindele (1976) and Graham and Felício (2006), just to name a few. Drawn up over 60 years ago, the UN Charter is a document of its time, reflecting the tension between 'universalism' and 'regionalism' in such way that the drafters sought an institutional formula that both facilitated, but at the same time delimited, the role of regional organisations in peace and security, especially when military force is involved.

Definitions and strategic choices over a more or less regional UN were present in the discussions of the UN Charter framers since the early planning for a new world organisation during World War II. The issue of 'security regionalism' was a subject of considerable dispute among the framers of the initial outline within the US State Department, and then among the other victors of the World War II: the UK (favouring regionalism and even envisaging a series of regional councils under the roof of the UN) (Grewe 1995: 7–9; Schlesinger 2003: 49–66), the USA and the USSR (at Dumbarton Oaks, the USA reached a compromise agreement with the UK, later endorsed by the USSR, acknowledging the possibility of regional agencies), Latin American countries (which wanted their own regional security system) and France (persuaded by the USA to drop its 'regional concerns' in exchange for a permanent seat) (Schlesinger 2003; Simma 1995). The Latin America bloc in particular mounted pressure against the provision in the draft charter that would accord the Security Council power to veto any action by a regional body, apprehensive about the prospect of a foreign power attacking them with the benefit of a Security Council veto on any collective regional response. Consequently, the negotiators introduced into the Charter the principle of the 'inherent right of individual and collective self-defence' in case of armed attacks. The aim was to assure 'regionalist' regional arrangements or agencies of their freedom to respond to aggression from outside their region without being hobbled by any Security Council stalemate.

The provisions agreed upon in the Charter reflect the 'mild discouragement' of regionalism, allowing regional security arrangements to maintain peace and security complimentary to the primary role exercised by the Security Council in this field. On the one hand, the Charter (Article 24) confers the Security Council with the primary (therefore not exclusive) responsibility for maintaining peace and security and the authority to allow the use of force, controlled through the veto power of its permanent members. But on the other hand, Articles 52 (pacific settlement), 53 (enforcement) and 54 (reporting obligation) allow regional 'agencies and arrangements' to take initiatives in this sphere, as long as they inform the Security Council (pacific settlement) or are granted authorisation (enforcement). Article 51, however, by guaranteeing states' rights to act in self-defence or in 'collective self-defence', opens the door for regional organisations to use force to defend member states without prior UN authorisation (Brian 2004). While the basic authorisation for regional actions is set up in the Charter, no specific mechanism is offered when regions are still in their inception phase. Only two regional organisations were relevant (League of Arab States and Organisation of American States).

The charter drafters did not anticipate how regional organisations would develop, nor pondered how power sharing and the nature of subsequent conflicts and peace management operations would change worldwide. Indeed, the Cold War made it almost impossible for the UN to pursue its role as the primary authority for peace and security (Wulf 2009). Similarly, Chapter VIII was left dormant: the division of the world did not allow for regional response as it would too often lead into freezing of action. As regional organisations played minor roles in conflict management, the absence of a lasting and well-defined relationship with the UN was not of particular consequence. Regional conflicts were managed by the major powers, which promoted their geopolitical advantage.

However, the organisations themselves started developing independently of the UN and its charter. Indeed, during the Cold War, regional organisations started booming and blooming, more for economic integration than for peace and security objectives. By the end of the 1980s, a global network of regional and sub-regional agencies was in place.[1] The creation and development of these regional 'arrangements and agencies' proceeded largely independently of the UN Charter provisions, reflecting rather the political and security exigencies of each region at a particular point in time. The organisations developed completely detached from the largely 'dormant' Chapter VIII framework, with different mandates, geographical areas to cover, structures and resources.

In the 1980s, the nature of conflicts began to change, increasing in numbers and complexity and involving non-state actors, weak states and polarised societies. The UN was unable to respond to these new conflicts nor was it able to devise new modes of response; the regional organisations themselves started developing their own instruments to respond to security threats, even if they were not originally mandated to do so – this being one of the characteristics of the so-called 'new regionalism'.[2] Thus, they adapted and did so, once again, independently of the UN Charter. Indeed, most organisations now responding to conflicts were not originally conceived for security purposes, and their mandates did not necessarily fit Chapter VIII.

The EU, NATO, AU, ECOWAS, SADC, Intergovernmental Authority on Development (IGAD) and PIF all have undertaken military interventions in recent years (e.g. NATO in Bosnia and Kosovo, ECOWAS in Sierra Leone and Liberia, the AU in Sudan). Furthermore, they have been developing early warning mechanisms to deal with possible conflicts – in such a way that some of them can already be described as more or less effective conflict management regimes. At the same time, the UN has seen an immense growth in its security responsibilities, to which it is no longer able to respond effectively. The UN peacekeeping system faces operational, managerial and political crises as the burden increased over ten times in the last 10 years.[3] In 2008, the number of UN military and police personnel in missions had risen to over 100,000. Simultaneously, other international organisations (e.g. NATO, AU, the EU) become heavily involved in peacekeeping. Excluding Iraq, there were approximately 75,000 non-UN 'peacekeepers' worldwide in 2008 (Gowan 2008). As the UN reaffirmed its commitment and 'responsibility to protect populations from genocide, war crimes, ethnic cleansing and crimes against humanity' in 2006,[4] the stretching of resources became even clearer. Further, the UN is also committing more resources in the peacebuilding area, with the creation of the Peacebuilding Commission in 2006. And the need to replace the small UN office in Timor-Leste with a considerably larger multidimensional mission (UNMIT) sparked new debate about the shortcomings of past international peacebuilding efforts.[5]

8.3 Putting Global-Regional Cooperation on the Agenda

In the 2005 World Summit Outcome Document,[6] the General Assembly decided to 'expand consultation and cooperation between the UN and regional and subregional organisations through formalised agreements between the respective secretariats and, as appropriate, involvement of regional organisations in the work of the Security Council'. This decision goes back to the long-standing history of relations between the UN and regional organisations (Eide 1966; Graham and Felício 2006). As the UN realised it was no longer capable of responding to so many and so different peace challenges, and was confronted with the danger of loss of prominence, pertinence and relevance, it started reforming its peacekeeping doctrine including the regional organisations. In order to 'share the load' in a coordinated manner, the UN started developing a process of multilateral dialogue in the attempt to move from an ad hoc relationship to an organised and systematic collaboration under Chapter VIII of the Charter.

Agenda for Peace, its supplement and the Brahimi Report all show this change in doctrine towards the sharing of responsibilities with regional organisations, putting regional organisations inside the UN agenda. A framework of cooperation with the regional organisations was called for in 1992 by Russia, in 1993 by the Security Council and in 1994 by the General Assembly, leading to the commencement of high-level meetings with the regional organisations.[7] In 1993, the Security Council invited regional organisations to study ways of strengthening their functions in peace and security and improve coordination with the UN.[8] In response, the then UN Secretary-General, in 'An Agenda for Peace', called for a greater involvement of regional organisations in a dual attempt to lighten the burden of the Security Council and to contribute to a deeper sense of participation.[9] The 'Supplement to an Agenda for Peace' further highlighted the advantages and potential for the division of labour in using the regional arrangements for the mechanism of peace discussed in that document (preventive diplomacy, peacekeeping, peacemaking and post-conflict building).

Since then, a formal cooperation between regional organisations and the UN has also started developing at the initiative of the Secretary-General, who convened the so-called 'High-Level Meetings' with regional organisations involved in security matters from all continents. Between 1993 and 2006, seven such meetings took place and were chaired personally by the Secretary-General. Discussions focused on challenges to international peace and security, the role of regional organisations in peacebuilding activities and practical measures to promote greater coordination and cooperation in peacekeeping and peacebuilding.

8.4 The High-Level Meetings with the Regional Organisations

There were no preconceived topics at the first two High-Level Meetings (HLMs) between the UN Secretary-General and the regional organisations. At the first meeting, it was agreed to have a flexible and pragmatic approach to the partnership. At the second meeting, the suggestion was endorsed that knowledge and expertise gathered by regional organisations in the areas of peacekeeping and peacemaking should be shared. The meeting also discussed the problem of impartiality of regional organisations when dealing with conflicts in their region.[10] The third meeting in 1998 discussed conflict prevention; the fourth in 2001 peacebuilding; and the fifth in 2003 dealt with new threats to international peace and security including international terrorism. A crucial moment in this history was April 2003 when Kofi Annan called for the UN and regional organisations to 'redouble their efforts' to ensure peace and security. Later that year, at the fifth High-Level Meeting in July 2003, the Secretary-General offered a 'new vision of global security' that rested upon a 'network of effective and mutually reinforcing multilateral mechanisms' – regional and global.

During the fifth High-Level Meeting, a suggestion was also made to hold the High-Level Meeting on an annual basis and that they should be 'soundly prepared'. Six working groups were then established; each led by one UN department or agency. Further, and thanks to a grant provided by the Belgian Ministry of Foreign Affairs, the sixth High-Level Meeting in July 2005 was prepared by UNDPA in association with the Bruges-based unit UNU-CRIS of the UN University. UNU-CRIS provided research and analytical support in the form of a series of background papers for the six working groups that were established in the areas of peacekeeping, civilian protection, respect for human rights in counter-terrorism, dialogue of civilisations, disarmament and the reform of the partnerships between the UN and regional and other intergovernmental organisations.

The sixth meeting in 2005 was therefore the result of much more concerted efforts, having discussed the recommendations of the Secretary-General's High-Level Panel on Threats, Challenges and Change related to regional organisations. The 2004 report of the High-Level Panel on Threats, Challenges and Change paid special attention to the issue of cooperation between the UN and regional organisations and recommended that consultations and cooperation between them should be expanded and could be formalised into an agreement. The Panel also emphasised that authorisation from the Council for regional peace operations was required in all cases. The Secretary-General fully endorsed the recommendations in his *In Larger Freedom* report and indicated his intent to conclude the memoranda of understanding with regional organisations to streamline the operational partnership.

In July 2005, participants agreed on the need to make a difference between joint activities under the umbrella of the high-level meetings under Chapter VIII of the UN Charter and cooperation with other intergovernmental organisations under other provisions of the Charter. They also agreed to meet henceforth on an annual basis, to coordinate meetings with the relevant thematic debates of the Security Council and to establish a standing committee to act as an initiator of ideas, a mobiliser of political will and sustainable direction and a monitor for ensuring the implementation of decisions made. At the end of the meeting, a joint statement was issued that called for a closer and more institutional cooperation. This idea was taken up in the September 2005 meeting of the World Summit.

After the sixth High-Level Meeting, a standing committee was created in order to support this process. In February 2006, the first Standing Committee meeting was held in New York and prepared also in cooperation with UNU-CRIS. The sixth meeting also proposed a study of the capacities of regional organisations in peace and security as it was recognised that there was lack of institutionalised knowledge of such capacities.[11]

The seventh and most recent meeting took place in 2006. The overall theme was to improve coordination and avoid both duplication and competition. For this meeting, a report of the Secretary-General was prepared by the UN Secretariat in collaboration with UNU-CRIS.[12]

Two observations can be made regarding these high-level meetings. First, the attendance at the meetings doubled from 10 in 1994 to 20 in 2006. This certifies that regional organisations attached importance to this process of dialogue. Second, during that period, both the Security Council and member states showed a growing interest in the process and in making it more concrete. Remarkably, this process has come to almost a complete standstill in 2007, and the UNDPA unit responsible for organising the high-level meetings was dissolved. As such, it seems that after a period of convergence in the approach, we have now entered again a period of divergence (Baert and Van Langenhove 2008: 351).

8.5 The UN Security Council and Regional Organisations

Upon completion of the fourth High-Level Meeting in February 2001, the Security Council issued a statement encouraging the UN and partner organisations to establish consultative processes.[13] It was underlined, at this meeting, that successful peacebuilding is predicated on an effective and unambiguous division of labour, based on the comparative advantages of the different implementing bodies. Since then, the Security Council has convened a number of meetings with regional organisations.

In April 2003, under Mexico's Presidency, the Security Council agreed that a dynamic relationship between the regional organisations and the Council needed to be developed.[14] As a result, a 'framework for cooperation' between the UN and regional agencies has been agreed. Graham and Felício (2006) have identified nine normative principles of that cooperation:

(a) A flexible and pragmatic approach to regional crises, with no universal model
(b) UN primacy in all crises
(c) A clear division of labour between the UN and regional agencies
(d) Regular consultations between the UN and regional agencies
(e) Mutual support in diplomatic and operational activities
(f) Joint operational deployment where appropriate
(g) Regional impartibility in handling conflicts
(h) Common conflict prevention modalities
(i) Common peacebuilding principles

In July 2004, during its Presidency of the Security Council, Romania took the important step of moving the process forward by encouraging debates on the role of regions within the functioning of the Security Council. Furthermore, on 20 July 2004, a second 'open meeting' between the Secretary-General and regional organisations identified new methods of cooperation in conflict resolution and stabilisation processes. In the Presidential Statement issued at this occasion, the Secretary-General invited regional organisations

> to take necessary steps to increase collaboration with the UN in order to maximise efficiency in stabilisation processes, and encouraged enhanced cooperation and coordination among regional and sub-regional organisations themselves, in particular through exchange of information and sharing experience and best practices.[15]

Clearly, the interest in UN-regional organisations partnerships has grown considerably to such an extent that in October 2005, under the Romanian Presidency, the Security Council adopted its first resolution on this issue. Resolution 1631 expressed the Council's determination to take appropriate steps to further develop the cooperation between the UN and regional organisations in maintaining international peace and security. It also invited the Secretary-General to submit a report to the Security Council on the opportunities and challenges facing this cooperation. This was an important step forward as it was 'the first document on cooperation to carry such significant legal and political weight' (Felício 2007: 69).

In September 2006, under the presidency of Greece, a Security Council meeting with regional organisations was held for the first time at the ministerial level. The statement by the President of the Security Council proposed to establish a 'Regional-Global Security Mechanism' and invited all regional organisations to enhance their working relations with the Secretariat. Both the sixth high-level meeting and the Security Council Resolution 1631 (2005) suggested that the Secretary-Generals' and the Security Councils' meetings should coincide for better efficiency and substantive complimentary of agendas, and these meetings were indeed coordinated in September 2006.

This was also an opportunity to present the Report of the Secretary-General, 'A Regional-Global Security Partnership: Challenges and Opportunities', pursuant to UNSC Resolution 1631.[16] This report described the Secretary-General's conviction that the time is ripe for the establishment of a more effective partnership operating in close cooperation with the Security Council based on a clear division of labour reflecting the comparative advantage of each organiser. The report also identified two main challenges to be addressed in order to make the partnership more effective: (a) classification of the respective roles of the UN and all its partner organisations in peace and security and (b) capacity building.

The Secretary-General's recommendations on conflict prevention and peacebuilding received unanimous support. It was also felt, in the overall, that there was need for recommendations on capacity building (namely for African organisations) and for the role of regional organisations in the Peacebuilding Commission. But the Secretary-General's recommendation that the international community should make a distinction between Chapter VIII organisations and other intergovernmental organisations proved to be more far-reaching and complex. Many speakers supported bringing more clarity to the definitions (OAS, AU, LAS, OIC and Commonwealth). But others (some of the P-5, the EU and COE) preferred a status quo. Russia in particular seemed suspicious that any change of terminology might cause unforeseen political consequences – e.g. the possibility of giving more legitimacy and status to organisations like NATO. Member states and organisations such as China, the USA, the EU and Council of Europe preferred a flexible and pragmatic approach, result oriented and less formal in nature, avoiding creation of new structures and not confined to a particular modality or mechanism.

In 2007, South Africa tried to use its membership of the Security Council as an opportunity to further develop the relationship between the UN and regional organisations. On 28 March 2007, the Security Council held another open debate on the issue, resulting in a presidential statement focusing upon the cooperation between the UN and the AU (S/PRST/2007/7). This UN-AU cooperation has also been the key issue in the second Report of the Secretary-General that was published in 2008.[17] By doing so, the debate shifted from a comprehensive approach that tried to establish a general partnership between the UN and regional organisations to an ad hoc approach, now more focused on one of the previously supported recommendations, capacity-building, and on one region – Africa.

8.6 The 2008 UN Secretary-General Report on Regional Organisation: A Little to the South

In 2007, Ban Ki-Moon succeeded Kofi Anan as the eighth Secretary-General of the UN. Like his predecessor, Ban Ki-Moon has shown a great interest in the cooperation between the UN and regional organisations. However, there is a conspicuous difference in the modality adopted by the incumbent Secretary-General to the issue of cooperation. Rather than continuing the virtually biennial high-level meetings, the current UN Secretary-General has not held another of such meetings 3 years into his tenure. However, on 7 April 2008, the Secretary-General issued one of the most comprehensive reports on UN and regional organisations to date.[18] On the one hand, the report addresses several contours of the relations between the UN and regional organisations while, on the other hand, it focuses on UN's relations with the African Union.

The exclusive focus of the 2008 UN/RO report on the African Union can potentially be construed as an attempt by the organisation to jettison its prospecting for a greater understanding between it and regional organisations in general. Nonetheless, nowhere in the report is it explicitly stated that the UN will not continue holding its high-level meetings or that the organisation has abandoned its search for a better understanding of its relations with regional organisations in general. In fact, one possible interpretation of the exclusive concentration on the AU is that by so doing, the UN is able to test the veracity and applicability of the several thoughts and principles it has developed, over the last 10 years, about its cooperation with regional organisations. To that effect, the UN can be regarded as having adopted its relation with the AU as a prototype or a pilot edition of a much wider desire to converge with regional organisations.

The UN/RO 2008 Report has all the making of a very important instrument. The report not only acknowledges the deepening perplexity of the UN as the exact nature of its relations with regional organisations, it also, rather mercurially, speaks to some of the challenges of the UN's own collective security which are hardly mentioned in literature let alone in the UN's own documents. Thus, the organisation magnanimously reflects that '[t]he real challenge is to find ways to replace the improvised, at times *selective* resource-skewed approach with more planned, consistent and reliable arrangements…'.

The 2008 report also ponders the specific thematic areas of cooperation between the UN and regional organisations. Thus, the Secretary-General speaks about the need to strengthen relations in such diverse areas as capacity building for peacekeeping and peace support operations, conflict prevention and mediation, disarmament and nonproliferation, peacebuilding and human rights. Furthermore, the Secretary-General invites the Council, once again, to consider demarcating Chapter VIII organisations from the more amorphous ones. Certainly, there is a world of benefits to be reaped from a clear distinction between those organisations which operate within the perimeters of Chapter VIII and those that are outside of it. For a start, such clarification will tackle the hop-in-hop-out regime adopted by such organisations as NATO, which step into Chapter VIII whenever it pleases it and steps out to avoid legal obligations. More so, a conceptual categorisation of regional organisations will go a long way in illuminating the rather opaque nature of the legal relations between the UN and these organisations.

Be that as it may, the Secretary-General's desire for a greater legal clarity flies in the face of daunting politics of the Council. While it is yet uncertain whether the Security Council will buy into this Secretary-General's quest, precedents are not so reassuring. It is clear that the Security Council has neither the appetite to shut out potential collaborators just so that it can satisfy increasingly otiose provisions of Chapter VIII nor does it have a great craving for upsetting the status quo which some of its permanent members, such as Russia, petulantly favours.

On 12 January 2010, the Secretary-General held a retreat with heads of regional organisations on the theme of 'Cooperating in times of crisis: crisis prevention and mediation'[19] at Greentree (hereafter cited as Greentree retreat). The Greentree retreat is particularly important for many reasons. First, it was the first time the Secretary-General would directly raise, with regional organisations, the issue of women representation at the level of leadership of the organisations. Second, the Secretary-General raised some questions which go to the root of the relations between the UN and regional organisations. Among others, the Secretary-General asks:

> how we can balance the interoperability between our organisation with recognition of how different we are; when enforcement action is authorized, how can we ensure that it is undertaken in accordance with article 53 of the Charter? [h]ow can we ensure that the Council is kept fully informed of activities in international peace and security, as provided for in the Charter's Article 54?[…]

The fact that the Secretary-General recognises the need to enhance compliance with Chapter VIII provisions – especially articles 53 and 54 is remarkable and perhaps signifies a greater era of operationalisation of Chapter VIII framework in general. In the past, the Security Council has not particularly evinced concern about the fact that regional organisations hardly kept the Council informed of actions they take or plan to take under Chapter VIII just as it had been, to all intent and purposes, contented with 'welcoming' actions taken by regional organisations without its authorisation.

Another remarkable point in the Greentree retreat is that the regional organisations which were present used the medium to 'inform' the UN about their perceptions either about certain principles contained in their own constituent instruments or the UN Charter itself. As regard the former, the Chairperson of the AU Commission, Jean Ping, said that 'on such issues as crimes against humanity, genocide and impunity, the AU did not need to be called in by the host government of its Member States; it could intervene automatically'. In regard to Chapter VIII of the UN Charter, Mr. Amre Moussa, representing the League of Arab States, observed that while 'it might not be possible to amend Chapter VIII of the United Nations Charter…the Security Council and the General Assembly should establish procedures and arrangements to reflect the current responsibilities of regional organisations'. The LAS representative made this point in connection with his observations that there were shortfalls between what Chapter VIII empowers regional organisations to deal with and what these organisations are now currently confronted with.

Although this is not the place to embark on a legal analysis of the full implications of these statements coming, as it were, from most senior officials of two important regional organisations, it is certain that regional organisations have become more emboldened in the way they perceive their relations with the UN and how they understand the principles of their own constituent instruments and the UN Charter as well.

The considerable interest taken by the current UN Secretary-General in the strengthening of UN/AU relations manifested in the unprecedented steps the UN took in respect of this relation just a few months into the tenure of Ban Ki-Moon. Between March and April 2007, the UN provided professional training to some AU staff Peace and Security secretariat, and on 11 June of the same year, the UN Security Council held its first ever joint meeting with the AU PSC in Addis Ababa, Ethiopia and issued a joint communiqué to that effect.[20]

Thus far, the method adopted by the UN in consulting with regional organisations has taken as unpredictable a route as the unveiling of its relations with these organisations was in the first 50 years of its life. From an unsure and uncertain 'relations' in the early 1990s (Liberia and Sierra Leone, for instance), it moved into holding high-level meetings with regional organisations in a joint effort to prospect for the best way forward. In the last 3 years, the Security Council has shifted its focus a little more to the south. The fact that Africa has a disproportionate amount of conflicts, compared to other regions, and a high number of regional actors (AU, ECOWAS, SADC, IGAD), partly justifies the shift in the Secretary-General's attention.

8.7 Conclusions: The Complexities of a Difficult Partnership

The above short historical overview shows that, in recent years, there has been increased talk about extended cooperation between the UN and regional organisations. Next to a limited amount of concrete cooperation cases,[21] there have been attempts to formalise or streamline such cooperation processes, also at the level of the Security Council. There are some good reasons for this. First, the UN Charter allows for dealing with security issues at a regional level. It therefore makes sense to profit from that possibility. Second, the present geopolitical situation is moving towards a multipolarity which reinforces the importance of regional stability. And on top of this, it is more and more acknowledged that the UN cannot take the burden of being the sole provider of security. Its capacity for preventive diplomacy, peacemaking and peacekeeping is limited. The current widening of the security concept to human security and the embracing of new doctrines such as 'responsibility to protect' makes it even more difficult for the UN to deal with all these tasks. Hence, to call upon regional organisations seems a logical solution. And indeed, there is growing interest in this partnership as shown by the attendance both at the high-level meetings and Security Council meetings.

However, as a greater number of interested organisations attended the meetings, the density of the relationship became clearer. The organisations present had different representation schemes, sometimes sitting three times at the table (the EU), had different mandates and focused on different issues, according to their different mandates and capacities. And very often the same states were represented by different organisations.

The development of the regional-global security mechanism is clearly hampered by an array of complexities, pertaining to uncertainties over the meaning of concepts such as 'region', 'agency' and 'arrangement'; the structural duplication of regional agencies and other organisations (involving overlapping of membership); ambiguity over their objectives (involving, inter alia, improvised and occasionally competing mandates); and contention over the area of application of their functions.[22]

The UN Secretary-General Report 'A Regional-Global Security Partnership: Challenges and Opportunities' was meant to help overcome these complexities, having recommended formalised partnerships and clearer division of labour. The report described the Secretary-General's conviction that 'the time is ripe for the establishment of a more effective partnership operating in close cooperation with the Security Council based on a clear division of labour reflecting the comparative advantage of each organisation'.[23] While the challenge of capacity building was supported by all organisations and member states alike, the challenge of clarity was overlooked – for the preference of a 'pragmatic and flexible approach', more suitable to the most resourceful organisations (often the same with the weaker mandates to act in peace and security, especially out of area).

The complexities of the relationship between the UN and regional organisations bring us back to the issues of definition of the latter (to be looked at in detail in Chap. 17) and to the fact that today's regional organisations dealing with peace and security are very different in nature, very confusing to study, and consequently, a clear division of labour can only be achieved after the definitional issues are overcome. The change in the title of the high-level meetings itself is a show of these confusing definitions – the UN having felt obliged to include '*other intergovernmental organisations*' in order to assure accuracy in the attendance list, as more and more organisations, less regional in nature, asked for a seat at the table.

Moreover, the organisations involved in peace and security, are very different in their capacities. More often, the more regional in nature, with more clear mandates and legitimacy to act in their own region, are the ones with less capacity to do so. Indeed, not all parts of the world have regional organisations that are capable of performing regional peacekeeping operations. A capacity survey of 21 regional organisations, conducted by UNU-CRIS in 2008 concluded that not all regional organisations have a legal mandate to operate on peace and security issues and those which do have, in turn, a wide variety of instruments to their disposal.[24]

These complexities seem to show a further need to build an institutional framework that organises relations between the UN and these different organisations. As shown above, the so-called high-level meetings and the joint meetings with the Security Council have been attempts to set up such a framework. But today, this process has come to a standstill. As the dialogue was deemed 'too heavy and bureaucratic', a moment of reflection took over, with no high-level meetings taking place since September 2006 and the dissolution of the specific unit responsible for the cooperation inside the UN Secretariat.

The lack of a dialogue and an oiled cooperation may lead to the worst outcome, the UN losing a grip on its primary responsibility – peace and security. The UN was created to save humanity from the scourge of war.[25] Unable to do so on its own and unable to rely on an equal, healthy, well-coordinated partnership with the regional organisations, the UN may lose its credibility as a global actor for peace and security. The outcome may be disastrous, as the global legitimacy for action in peace and security may also be lost. One should not forget that the potential benefits of involving regional organisations in peace and security also bring the risks of partiality and strengthening of regionally dominant hegemons. This can only be avoided through a strong cooperation under the umbrella of the global legitimate body, the UN.

Up to now there have been two main drivers for the process of increased cooperation between the UN and regional organisations: the UN Secretary-General and the UN Security Council presidencies. A number of European states such as Romania and Greece have so far been active in pushing the agenda. Belgium has also contributed, be it in a more 'soft' way by supporting the scientific support to the high-level meetings (Van Langenhove 2009). Given the growing importance of the EU within the UN system, there is a huge potential for EU member states that take permanent or non-permanent seats in the Security Council to continue to explore 'multi-level governance' partnerships between the UN and regional organisations.

EU member states would very much benefit from using their membership in the Security Council to organise further meetings with the regional organisations, pushing for new decisions in this field and giving a new mandate to the Secretary-General in this field. If the Secretary-General would take up the project of re-establishing high-level meetings and following the conclusions of the report on cooperation with regional organisations beyond the issue of capacity building, a clearer and more structured relationship would also be possible. A stronger hand of the global body in the way regional security builds up will bring more efficiency to peace operations and more legitimacy to the global body's main job – saving humanity from the scourge of war.

Notes

1. For more on the growth and development of regional organisations, see Graham and Felício (2006: 62–64).
2. For a comprehensive discussion of the concept of new regionalism, see Hettne (2003). See also Farrell et al. (2005) and Abass (2004).
3. See Gowan (2008: 459). See also Johnstone et al. (2006).
4. UN Summit UNGA, 2005 World Summit Outcome, Resolution adopted by the General Assembly (A/RES/60/1), 24 October.
5. For further reading on this topic, see Wiharta (2007).
6. United Nations, 2005 World Summit Outcome, Resolution adopted by the General Assembly (A/RES/60/1), 24 October.
7. See Graham and Felicio (2006: 64–65).
8. United Nations, Security Council, Note by the President of the Security Council (S/25/84), 29 January 1993.
9. United Nations, Secretariat, An agenda for peace: Preventive diplomacy, peacemaking and peacekeeping: Report of the Secretary-General (A/47/277-S/24111), 17 June 1992.
10. United Nations, Secretariat, Secretary-General's statement at the opening of second meeting between UN and regional organisations (SG/SM/5895), 15 February 1996.
11. This 'capacity survey' was undertaken by UNU-CRIS, a unit of the United Nations University located in Belgium. Results of that survey were published in 2008. See http://www.cris.unu.edu/fileadmin/user_upload/capacity_survey.pdf and also Tavares (2009).
12. United Nations, Secretariat, A regional-global security partnership: challenges and opportunities. Report of the Secretary-General (A/61/204/-S/2006/590). 28 July 2006.
13. United Nations, Security Council, Statement by the President of the Council (S/PRST/1995/9), 22 February 1995.
14. United Nations, Security Council, 4579 Meeting (S/PV.4739), 11 April 2003.
15. United Nations, Security Council, Statement by the President of the Security Council (S/PRST/2004/27), 20 July 2004.
16. United Nations, Secretariat, A regional-global security partnership: Challenges and opportunities. Report of the Secretary-General (A/61/204-S/2006/590), 20 September 2006.
17. United Nations, Secretariat, Report of the Secretary-General on the relationship between the UN and regional organisations, in particular the African Union (S/2008/186), 7 April 2008.
18. S/2008/186.
19. Notes on file with the authors. The retreat was held at Greentree.
20. S/2007/421.
21. For an overview, see Graham (2008)
22. For further reading, see Graham and Felício (2006).
23. United Nations, Secretariat, A regional-global security partnership: Challenges and opportunities. Report of the Secretary-General (A/61/204-S/2006/590), 20 September 2006.
24. See http://www.cris.unu.edu/fileadmin/user_upload/capacity_survey.pdf.
25. United Nations Charter, Preamble.

References

Abass, A. (2004). *Regional organizations and the development of collective security: Beyond Chapter VIII of the UN Charter*. Oregon: Hart Publishing.

Akindele, R. A. (1976). *The organization and promotion of world peace: A study of universal-regional relationships*. Toronto: University of Toronto Press.

Baert, F., & Van Langenhove, L. (2008). Nieuw veiligheidspartnership in de maak. Verenigde Naties en regionale organisaties. *Internationale Spectator, 62*(2), 351.

Bebr, G. (1955). Regional organizations: A United Nations problem. *The American Journal of International Law, 49*(2), 166–184.

Brian, L. J. (2004). The UN, regional organizations and regional conflict: Is there a viable role for the UN? In R. Price & M. Zacher (Eds.), *The United Nations and global security* (pp. 227–243). Basingstoke: Palgrave Macmillan.

Buzan, B. (2000). "Change and insecurity" reconsidered. In S. Croft & T. Terriff (Eds.), *Critical reflections on security and change* (pp. 1–17). Soutgate: Frank Cass.

Eide, A. (1966). Peacekeeping and enforcement by regional organizations: Its place in the United Nations System. *Journal of Peace Research, 3*(2), 125–145.

Farrell, M., Hettne, B., & Van Langenhove, L. (Eds.). (2005). *Global politics of regionalism: Theory and practice*. London: Pluto Press.

Felício, T. (2007). A regional-global mechanism for peacebuilding. Setting the framework. In *Security sector reform in post-conflict peacebuilding: A closer partnership between the UN and regional organisations*. Geneva: UN.

Goodrich, L. M. (1949). Regionalism and the United Nations. The Unites States and the Atlantic Community. *Proceedings of the Academy of Political Science, 23*(3), 47–56.

Gowan, R. (2008). The strategic context: Peacekeeping in crisis. *International Peacekeeping, 15*(4), 457.

Graham, K. (2008). Regionalisation and responses to armed conflict, with special focus on conflict prevention and peacekeeping. In A. F. Cooper, C. W. Hughes, & P. De Lombaerde (Eds.), *Regionalisation and global governance. The taming of globalisation?* (pp. 159–186). London: Routledge/Warwick Studies in Globalisation.

Graham, K., & Felício, T. (2006). *Regional security and global governance*. Brussels: VUB University Press.

Grewe, W. G. (1995). The history of the United Nations. In B. Simma (Ed.), *The Charter of the United Nations: A commentary* (pp. 1–12). Oxford: Oxford University Press.

Haas, E. (1969). *Tangle of Hopes: American Commitments and World Order*. Englewood Cliffs: Prentice Hall.

Hettne, B. (2003). The new regionalism revisited. In F. Söderbaum & T. Shaw (Eds.), *Theories of new regionalism: A Palgrave reader* (pp. 22–42). Basingstoke: Palgrave.

Johnstone, I., Jones, B., & Gowan, R. (2006). *Annual review of Global Peace Operations 2006: Briefing Paper*. New York: Center on International Cooperation.

Laakso, L. (2002). Introduction. In L. Laakso (Ed.), *Regional integration for conflict prevention and peace building in Africa*. Helsinki: University of Helsinki.

Padelford, N. J. (1954). Regional organizations and the United Nations. *International Organization, 8*(2), 203–216.

Schlesinger, S. C. (2003). *The founding of the United Nations*. Boulder: Westview Press.

Simma, B. (Ed.). (1995). *The Charter of the United Nations: A commentary*. Oxford: Oxford University Press.

Tavares, R. (2009). *Regional security: The capacity of international organizations*. London: Routledge (Global Institutions Series).

Thakur, R., & Van Langenhove, L. (2008). Enhancing global governance through regional integration. In A. F. Cooper, C. W. Hughes, & P. De Lombaerde (Eds.), *Regionalisation and global governance: The taming of globalisation?* (pp. 17–42). London: Routledge.

Van Langenhove, L. (2009). The UN Security Council and regional organisations: A difficult partnership. In J. Wouters, E. Drieskens, & S. Biscop (Eds.), *Belgium in the UN Security Council: Reflections on the 2007–2008 membership* (pp. 165–174). Intersentia: Antwerp.

Wiharta, S. (2007). *Peacekeeping: Keeping pace with changes in conflict. SIPRI yearbook 2007: Armaments, disarmament and international security*. Oxford: Oxford University Press.

Wulf, H. (Ed.). (2009). *Still under construction: Regional organization's capacities for conflict prevention* (INEF-Report 97). University Duisburg Essen.

Chapter 9
The UN and the League of Arab States: A Point of View on Future Interaction

Amre Moussa

The UN and the League of Arab States are, together, a historical twin. The two organisations were born in the same year, an indication to the fact that the growth of regional organisations and that of the global organisation have been simultaneous processes. Both organisations are fundamental components of the larger family of international organisations actively affecting, though certainly influenced by, international relations.

The scope of activities of the League of Arab States, like that of the UN, is comprehensive. It covers all aspects of international cooperation: security, economic development, financial institutions, trade, education, culture, agriculture, telecommunication, environment and health. In brief, whatever aspect of human activities in the region falls within the competence of the League.

But the League of Arab States is something more than merely a 'regional' organisation. The establishment of the League was meant, and remains, to fulfil the aspirations of millions of Arabs towards independence, economic and social progress and interactive identity. The idea and the drive towards Arab nationalism, mostly in the second half of the twentieth century, have never known xenophobia or zealous fanaticism. The independence of the Arab States, an outcome of consistent struggle, led to both the creation and growth of the League, and the League has consolidated the principle of equal sovereignty among its members who are all members of the UN. The Arab League has always identified itself with the UN and the international system. The respect for the UN Charter and the commitment to UN Resolutions constitute a consensus within the League.

As much as the UN has benefited from the experience of other international organisations, the League of Arab States has been nourished with the practice of the UN. Each of them is a melting pot of member states, but the two are melting together. Member states of the League of Arab States believe, as all others, that economic

A. Moussa (✉)
Secretary-General of the League of Arab States (2001–2011), Cairo, Egypt

P. De Lombaerde et al. (eds.), *The United Nations and the Regions: Third World Report on Regional Integration*, United Nations University Series on Regionalism 3, DOI 10.1007/978-94-007-2751-9_9, © Springer Science+Business Media B.V. 2012

and social development is indispensible for the maintenance of international peace and security. Respect for human rights is being promoted by the League.

It is important to note, in this respect, that the summit and the ministerial conferences of the League of Arab States have been consistently translating the principles of the Millennium Development Goals into regional action. Plans are charted in cooperation with UN regional commissions. Timetables are defined in the activities of numerous working groups. There is hardly any area of innovation in the activities of the UN which has not been reflected in the work of the League. An Arab Charter on Human Rights, an Arab Parliament, a more efficient Arab Economic and Social Council, a process of democratisation and a forum for non-governmental organisations (NGOs) are significant examples.

Needless to say, the League of Arab States has made its contribution to plans for reforming the UN. And this has proven to be a reciprocal process. Contributing to the elaboration of plans for UN reform suggests, at the same time, the idea for Arab League reform. The two organisations which were borne simultaneously are growing up simultaneously.

This is being carried out progressively, and the Arab League has been consistently reforming its organs with a view to securing more efficient functions. This range from modifications in the League's voting procedure to the restructuring of its main organs. The League's activities have been expanded to include new areas so vital for peace and progress such as the dialogue among civilisations, where the League of Arab States has become an active partner, and the adoption of modern mechanisms for overall reform in the Arab World in implementation of the basic document on reform and modernisation adopted in 2004 at the Tunis Arab Summit.

Meetings between the Secretary-Generals of both the UN and the League of Arab States have been effective in elaborating uniform conceptual approaches to issues on the agenda of both organisations, thus helping positive responses to plans and actions necessary to tackle the fluidity and complexity of regional and international situations.

From the standpoint of the League of Arab States, the resolution on cooperation between the UN and the League of Arab States, adopted at the regular session of the General Assembly of the UN, is more than a routine exercise. The link between the two organisations is determined by the Charter, and the cooperation between them is operated in accordance with that resolution. As previously said, the relationship between both organisations does not stop at cooperation; it should be a relationship of interaction. And interaction is a rather complex process which requires sophisticated methodology capable of ensuring that the Charter principles of both organisations are fully respected.

The Arab states, having entrusted the League with the arduous task of the settlement of disputes and having intensified its role in the transition towards sustainable peace and development, are consolidating an overall process of change which, in turn, presents many challenges to be met. In this respect, new avenues for joint action between the League and the UN shall continue to be explored. The ultimate goal remains to be the wider coherence of the constructive relationship between the UN and regional organisations.

Chapter 10
UN Cooperation with Regional Organisations in Peacekeeping Operations

Ademola Abass*

10.1 Introduction

The development of the United Nations (UN), in its first 50 years, shows little or no history of the UN cooperating with regional organisations in peacekeeping operations. In fact, prior to 1990, no single resolution of the Security Council referred to regional organisations. However, from 1991, such references proliferated, and by 1993, the Security Council, in Resolution 866, marked 'the first peacekeeping mission undertaken by the UN in cooperation with a peacekeeping mission already set up by another organisation'. This chapter discusses the UN cooperation with regional organisations in peacekeeping operations. Particular attention is focused on the legal basis, and the nature and principles emerging from this cooperation.

The frequency and the increasing fluency, with which the UN and regional organisations have cooperated in peacekeeping operations since the early 1990s, make two paradoxical facts easily forgettable. First, that peacekeeping, which is nowhere mentioned in the UN Charter – but which has become a principal referent point for UN's functioning – was discovered purely by accident. Second, regional organisations, which have today become leading actors and formidable partners of the UN in peacekeeping operations, were not in the original contemplation of the world order programmed to emerge from the ruins of World War II.[1] Indeed, the eventual inclusion of regional organisations in the UN Charter owed much to their suspicion of the UN (or some of its member states) rather than to any flattering desire for cooperation.

These two historical facts would haunt the UN's relationship with regional organisations from the start of its life until the closing decade of the twentieth century.

---

* The views expressed here are the author's and in no way represent the United Nations.

A. Abass (✉)
United Nations University Institute on Comparative Regional Integration Studies (UNU-CRIS), Bruges, Belgium
e-mail: aabass@cris.unu.edu

P. De Lombaerde et al. (eds.), *The United Nations and the Regions: Third World Report on Regional Integration*, United Nations University Series on Regionalism 3,
DOI 10.1007/978-94-007-2751-9_10,

On the one hand, there was a great reluctance, on the UN's part, to utilise regional organisations for maintaining international peace and security as Chapter VIII of the UN Charter preordains. This lack of appetite for regional organisations was partly due to the practical impossibility of expecting a Cold War–polarised Security Council to authorise regional military operations, even if such operations were of purely peacekeeping nature, and partly because of the inchoate provisions of Chapter VIII, the defining matrix of UN's relationship with regional organisations. On the other hand, regional organisations were, during this period, mostly preoccupied with forging economic integration amongst their members, leaving the rather Herculean task of collective security and peacekeeping to the UN. After all, it is the Security Council that the Charter explicitly invests with the primary responsibility for maintaining international peace and security.[2]

In the early 1990s, the UN broached a *rapport* with regional organisations in peacekeeping operations. This somewhat uncertain step so much quickened in later years that calls began to be made that the world's most inclusive organisation should make use of its regional counterparts to realise the collective security goals of its Charter which, in the UN practice till then, had been liable to frequent veto seizures.[3] While the UN has not gone (and may perhaps never go) as far as ceding its overall peace maintenance responsibility to regional organisations, evidence continues to manifest a phenomenally growing cooperation between it and regional organisations in peacekeeping operations, although, when circumstances permit (for instance, as with the EU's Operation Artemis in Congo), the UN occasionally delegates hard core collective security tasks to regional organisations (Abass 2007a, 2008).

Despite that huge strides have been made in the UN cooperation with regional organisations in peacekeeping operations from Africa to Asia, Europe to the Americas, certain problems, avoidable and unavoidable alike, continue to dog the relationship. Divergence in mandates, misplaced priorities and excruciating capacity limitations have had as much debilitating impacts on the operational cooperation between the UN and regional organisations as have indeed the enthralling politics of the Security Council itself. In addition, there is a lack of clarity about the legal basis and the nature of the relationship between the UN and regional organisations in peacekeeping operations, which frequently leads to confused analysis.

Broadly speaking, one could identify at least five thematic areas in which the UN currently cooperates with regional organisations; these are consultation, diplomatic support, generic operational cooperation, co-deployment and joint operation (Boutros-Ghali 1992). But this chapter is concerned only with the cooperation between the UN and regional organisations in peacekeeping operations. That said, the identified five thematic sub-categories are by no means mutually exclusive, and as will be seen later, two or more models do coexist in any interaction between the UN and regional organisations; and there is a lot to be said for overlapping between them. It is, however, not the intention of this chapter to delve into the UN cooperation with regional organisations in peace building, humanitarian action, conflict prevention and mediation and human rights, all of which deserve separate attention.

First, an attempt is made to establish the legal basis for UN cooperation with regional organisations. This is followed by a historical overview of the relationship.

A third part discusses some specific models of UN/regional organisations cooperation in peacekeeping, but rather than delve into details, emphasis is placed here on principles emerging from such interaction. Thus, given that it was in Liberia that the UN first entertained some kind of relationship with a regional organisation, certain matters arising from that operation (which was a co-deployment model, as replicated in Georgia) are juxtaposed with the UN/AU mission in Darfur, which became the first time that the UN would combine its forces with regional forces to jointly execute a similar peacekeeping mandate. Ensconced between these two extreme operational models were the UN engagement with the Organisation of American States (OAS) in Haiti and the Organisation for Security Cooperation in Europe (OSCE) in Nagorno Karabakh, on the one hand, and with the North Atlantic Treaty Organisation (NATO) in the Former Yugoslavia, on the other.

10.2 The Legal Bases for UN and Regional Cooperation in Peacekeeping

10.2.1 The Debate About Chapter VI or Chapter VI½: A Plea for Common Sense

The best place to commence a discussion of the legal basis for UN/regional organisations cooperation, in *whatever* form, is an analysis of the legal framework that made any kind of relationship between the two systems at all possible. Chapter VIII of the UN Charter, containing Articles 52–54, embodies the basic guidelines for the UN/regional organisations' relationship. The provisions of these articles are diverse, but together they seek to map out a rudimentary outlay of UN/regional organisations interaction.

Previous chapters have analysed these provisions, but it is still worth considering them from a more legal perspective for the purposes of this chapter. As above mentioned, Article 52 empowers regional organisations to settle disputes amongst their member states using purely nonmilitary means. The nature of the 'settlement' is set out in Article 33(1) of the Charter, obligating parties to try to solve disputes by peaceful means.

Notably, the word 'peacekeeping' is not found in the peaceful means enumerated in Article 33(1). The view has nonetheless been expressed that the pacific settlement, envisaged by this provision, provides a legal basis for regional peacekeeping operations, by the omnibus phrase 'or other peaceful means of their own choice'.

But the view has also been expressed that peacekeeping operations cannot be subsumed under Chapter VI as it is. The assertion – which has gained some currency in academic discourse – that peacekeeping is a Chapter VI½ operation – being, as proponents believe, not totally peaceful as Chapter VI anticipates, and not enforcement in the language of Chapter VII – is nebulous and somewhat incongruous. Chapter VI (Article 33(1) especially) talks about *other peaceful means* of disputants' *choices*. Classical peacekeeping, which is *only* possible at the volition of disputing parties, falls squarely within those peaceful means and does not require an expansion or a fanciful stretching of that provision for reconcilability with Chapter VI. It is only when peacekeeping operations cease to be an exercise of disputants' freewill – such as, robust peacekeeping/peace enforcement – that one can perhaps speak of them in a beyond – Chapter VI language – and even then, there is a crossover from Chapter VI (probably) to Chapter VII with no stopover in between. You cannot speak of peace enforcement or robust peacekeeping and speak of Chapter VI or VI½: peace enforcement is the moment when an original peacekeeping operation becomes an enforcement action, the moment a Chapter VI action transforms into a Chapter VII scenario: it is as simple as that.

Much as it may provide the platform for understanding regional organisations' involvement in peacekeeping, an exegesis of Article 33(1) prescriptions, one way or another, does not calibrate the legal basis of UN cooperation with regional organisations in peacekeeping. For whether or not one believes that regional peacekeeping is legally ascertainable within the perimeters of Article 33(1), or that its crucibles inhere elsewhere, this in no way concerns the UN itself. Peacekeeping operations, construed in their archetypal orthodoxy, and in the way that Article 52 contemplates settlement of regional disputes (whether taken on a unilateral or multilateral basis),[4] do not require UN legitimation.[5] Article 52 is nonetheless important since the UN often cooperates in peacekeeping operations initiated entirely by regional organisations, and therefore, the legality of such cooperation could well depend on whether the concerned regional peacekeeping operation is, in itself, legal.

10.2.2 Chapter VIII as the Basis for UN/Regional Organisations Peacekeeping Cooperation: A Plea for Clarity

Chapter VIII is commonly cited as the legal authority for UN cooperation with regional organisations in peacekeeping operations. Even the UN Secretary-General's latest report (April 2008) pandered to this interpretation.

Article 53 provides that the Security Council 'shall, where appropriate, utilize such regional arrangements and agencies for *enforcement action* under its authority'.[6] This article clearly forbids regional organisations to take any such action that is not legally permissible under Article 33(1) when settling regional disputes within Article 52 regulatory framework. Such actions, generically referred to in Article 53 as *enforcement actions*, certainly include the use of military force by regional organisations against their member states, although there is considerable doubt as to whether they also include non-forcible sanctions (White and Abass 2006; Akehurst 1967; Walter 1997). The only (possible) exception to this prohibition is if regional enforcement actions are authorised by the Security Council. To cement the injunction of Article 53 and avoid a *fait accompli*, Article 54 obligates States, not only regional organisations, to keep the Security Council informed of any action they take or contemplate to take.

If one were to be exact – as the present remit requires – Chapter VIII cannot be regarded as the apt legal authority for UN cooperation with regional organisations in *peacekeeping* operations, even if it incontrovertibly remains the most authoritative legal basis for cooperation between the UN and regional organisations in general. The rationale for this assertion is first and foremost self-evident in the Charter. To begin with, Chapter VIII does not talk about cooperation between the UN and regional organisations for *peacekeeping purposes*. It (possibly) authorises regional peacekeeping (for those who insist on finding legal cover for peacekeeping under the Charter)[7] which, in any case, does not concern the UN; hence, no reference is made to the Security Council in Article 52 vis-à-vis regional pacific actions. But Chapter VIII speaks in Article 53, *only* of the UN utilising regional organisations for *enforcement* actions, which, as generally accepted amongst international lawyers, do not include peacekeeping operations.

The clear mention of 'enforcement action' in Article 53 is legally consequential to the point in review. An application of the *exclusion unis* rule (the mere mention of a thing is to the exclusion of all others) makes the argument plausible that the explicit empowering of the Security Council to utilise regional organisations for the enforcement actions excludes peacekeeping operations from the ambit of that provision. In light therefore that Chapter VIII limits the UN cooperation with regional organisations to enforcement actions, the question remains: where does the UN derive its authority to cooperate with regional organisations in peacekeeping operations? To answer this question, it is necessary to look beyond Chapter VIII of the UN Charter.

10.2.3 Peace Enforcement/Robust Peacekeeping: A Possible Chapter VII- or Chapter VIII-Plus Authority?

Classical peacekeeping can be defined as the consensual interposition of neutral, lightly armed, impartial troops in the buffer zone or partitioning line, dividing disputing states for the primary, but not exclusive purpose of supervising the latter's compliance with a ceasefire agreement. This, a *posterio* definition, irreverently elucidates the orthodox conception of peacekeeping as an impartial, neutral and consensual operation. As the UN Secretary-General noted in his 1956 Report:

> peacekeeping would be limited in operations to the extent that consent of the parties concerned is required under generally recognized international law. While the General Assembly is enabled to *establish* the force with the consent of those parties which contribute units to the force, it could not request the force to be *stationed* or *operate* on the territory of a given country without the consent of the Government of that country.[8]

However, with the exception of a few instances, the practice of peacekeeping, in over 50 years since the UN deployed its first peacekeeping mission (UN Emergency Force, UNEF 1) between Israel and Egypt in the Suez Canal crisis, has been all but classical. The light-arming of UN peacekeepers (apparently, to visibly signal their peacekeeping nature) often makes them soft targets, leading quickly to abandoning impartiality principle in favour of fiercely engaging those who fire on then, a situation that, more often than not, compromises the neutrality of peacekeepers.[9]

The failure of classical peacekeeping to achieve prescribed mandates inspired the UN to introduce robust peacekeeping (alternatively referred to as peace enforcement), a concept that anticipates imposing ceasefire agreements on recalcitrant parties. Reasons for robustly enhancing classical peacekeeping mandates include to facilitate the delivery of humanitarian assistance to victims of conflicts (as was the case in Somalia in 1994), to assist regional sanction regimes to achieve maximum effect (as with Resolution 1132 supporting ECOWAS in Sierra Leone) and to preserve lives and property (as seen in the UN Protection Mission in Yugoslavia (UNPROFOR)).[10]

Interestingly, in its original conception of peacekeeping operation, the UN had precociously envisaged the possible emergence of robust actions. In paragraph 9 of the Secretary-General 1956 Report, it was stated that the requirement for host state consent 'does not exclude the possibility that the Security Council could use a force within the wider margins provided under Chapter VII of the United Nations Charter'.[11] But the UN fell short of articulating what this 'wider margin' might imply, perhaps, not willing to fetter the development of Chapter VII in practice.

In legal terms, peace enforcement, on the basis of Chapter VII, provides at least a supplementary legal basis for the cooperation between the UN and regional organisations in peacekeeping operations. Whereas Chapter VIII (Article 52) entitles a regional organisation to resolve disputes amongst their member states through non-military measures enumerated in Article 33(1), the Security Council is entitled, under Chapter VII, to latch onto a regional peacekeeping operation and upgrade the regional organisations' mandate to include the use of force to protect the integrity of the mandate whatever this might be. In most cases, the Security Council has acted in this way *ex post facto*.[12]

It might be argued, and quite rightly too, that such situation, as just described, qualifies as an enforcement action, therefore falling under Article 53 rather than a peacekeeping operation. Surely, an enhancement of a traditional regional peacekeeping operation qualifies as an enforcement action under Chapter VIII. Nonetheless, the operation, which the Security Council so enhanced with a robust mandate, is, *ab initio*, a peacekeeping one; despite the enhanced mandate, consent and impartiality of the peacekeepers are still essential to the legality of the operation at inception, from concerned regional organisation's standpoint. But because the Security Council cannot authorise a regional organisation's peacekeeping operation on the basis of Chapter VIII, the enhancement is irrelevant as a legal basis for the UN cooperation with regional organisations in peacekeeping.

However, once robustness enters, *pacificity* immediately flies out of the window. To then argue, as some have done, for coexistence of 'consent and impartiality on one hand, and the need to use force on the other' (Rose 1998) in *the same peacekeeping mission* is a recipe for conceptual and operational disasters. In fact, 'it would be irresponsible if commanders had given enforcement orders to troops, which were sent, trained, equipped and deployed as peacekeepers' (Biermann and Vadset 1999). The only relevance of 'consent and impartiality' to an original classical peacekeeping operation that metamorphosed into a robust action is to establish its legality at inception. Nothing is more anomalous in international law than the doctrine of consensual robust peacekeeping.

Regional organisations cannot by themselves, except (arguably) in very rare circumstances,[13] transform a peacekeeping operation into, or authorise, an enforcement action as the Security Council can do. Therefore, the Security Council's riding on a classical regional peacekeeping operation (started under Chapter VIII) with a robust mandate (derived through the wider margins of Chapter VII) is what can be appropriately termed as a 'Chapter VIII-Plus' legal basis for cooperation between the UN and regional organisations in peacekeeping operations. It is 'Chapter VIII' to the extent that such operation initially derives from regional organisations' competence (under Article 52) to *solely* authorise classical peacekeeping operations in their regions. The 'Plus' element derives from the Security Council energising the operation (somehow on the basis of its Chapter VII powers) to deliver the requisite mandate.

10.3 Possible Non-Charter Bases for UN/Regional Organisations Cooperation in Peacekeeping

10.3.1 Subsidiary Soft Law: The Secretary-General Guidelines from 1956 to 2008

Just as the UN contemplated, well in advance, the possibility of peace enforcement, so did the organisation ponder an out-of Charter legal basis for peacekeeping. Setting out the principles for UNEF in 1956, the then UN Secretary-General stated that:

> an emergency international United Nations force can be developed on the basis of three different concepts…it can, in the first place, be set up on the basis of principles reflected in the constitution of the United Nations itself…a second possibility is that the United Nations charge a country…a third possibility, an international force may be set up in *agreement* among a group of nations.[14]

The report noted that peacekeeping would function 'on the basis of a decision reached under the terms of the resolution "Uniting for Peace", the force…would be limited in its operations to the extent that consent of the parties concerned is required under generally recognized international law'.[15]

While there has been much controversy about whether the *Uniting for Peace* resolution, which generally empowered the General Assembly (GA) to decide on a course of action whenever the Security Council is immobilised by veto, entitles the GA to authorise enforcement action, it is fairly settled that the GA is able to authorise peacekeeping operation, considering that no use of force is intended for this genre. Such GA powers derive clearly from Articles 10–14 of the Charter, subject to Article 12 prohibiting the Assembly from dealing with such matters as the Security Council may be exercising on.

The importance of the 1956 Secretary-General Report on the law of peacekeeping hinges principally on its standard-setting values, if not an outright normative essence: it was the first of those reports which, complemented by periodic high-panel studies, would constitute a bundle of soft laws that, together with the sparse UN Charter provisions and entrenched norms of general international law, today form the corpus of peacekeeping legislation.

On 31 January 1992, the Secretary-General of the UN issued the first piece of guidelines to govern, amongst others, the UN's relationship with regional organisations. The *Agenda for Peace*[16] speaks to the need for greater cooperation between the UN and regional organisations, much beyond the confines of enforcement actions, the only such cooperation explicitly recognised by Chapter VIII. The *Agenda* views UN cooperation with regional organisations more in terms of decentralisation, delegation and cooperation of the roles rather than in any form of master/servant dichotomy.[17] But the *Agenda* also stresses the primordial essence of Chapter VIII in the evolution of that relationship:

> But in this new era of opportunity, regional arrangements or agencies can render great service if their activities are undertaken in a manner consistent with the purposes and principles of the Charter, and if their relationship with the United Nations, and in particular the Security Council, is governed by Chapter VIII… regional action as a matter of decentralisation, delegation and cooperation with the United Nations efforts could not only lighten the burden of the Council but also contribute to a deeper sense of participation, consensus and democratisation in international affairs…and should the Security Council choose specifically to authorize a regional arrangements or organisation to take a lead in addressing a crisis within its region, it could serve to lend the weight of the United Nations to the validity of regional efforts.

This passage touches on many vital points. First, it relates to the claims made above concerning the limited legal basis Chapter VIII offers to the UN cooperation with regional organisations in peacekeeping operations. The *Agenda* recognises there is a raft of areas in which the UN and regional organisations can cooperate, aside from enforcement action. But in the latter respect, the *Agenda* itself seems to be unduly restrictive in that, in speaking of the Security Council choosing to authorise a regional arrangement or organisation to take the lead in addressing a crisis *within its region*, the *Agenda* gives the arguably wrong impression that the Security Council can only utilise regional organisations in crises occurring in *their* regions. Apart from the absence of any Charter justification for such a narrow interpretation of Article 53, the fact that the Security Council authorised the European Union (with France as the Framework nation) to intervene in the crisis in the DRC in 2003 undermines the position of the *Agenda* in this respect.

Second, the *Agenda* affirms that for any meaningful cooperation to exist between the UN and regional organisations, an identification of some operational models between the UN and regional organisations is indispensable. Although such models were not included in the *Agenda*, the *Supplement to the Agenda*, issued 3 years later, identified the five sub-categories which are already mentioned above.[18] What is instructive to note here is that the *Supplement* proposes areas of cooperation that well go beyond enforcement action. This, indeed, was the first time that a UN guideline (even in the form of a soft law instrument) has envisioned UN cooperating with regional organisations beyond enforcement action, apparently in an *ex post* recognition of practices in Liberia and other places.

Between 1994 and 2008, the UN adopted further reports dealing more generally with the various aspects of UN cooperation with regional organisations. Although most of these reports did not contain normative principles such as present in the 1956 version, the *Agenda* for Peace and its *Supplement*, they do set out, sometimes ambiguously, the content of the relationship. An important piece of guidelines that emerged during this period was the 30 November 1998 statement of the Security Council's President (S/PRST/1998/35) which not only brought in sub-regional arrangements into the purview of regional organisations that the UN may cooperate with on the basis of Chapter VIII but which also affirmed the Security Council's readiness to examine appropriate measures whenever regional or sub-regional organisations are being considered for conflict resolutions. Aside from this, it was the Security Council Report in April 2008 that proposed most far-reaching steps yet towards consolidating the UN cooperation with regional organisations in peace-keeping operations. But since this report, as with a few others, form the basis of a separate discussion, its analysis is differed to later.

10.4 The UN/Regional Organisations Peacekeeping Cooperation: From Liberia to Darfur

10.4.1 Liberia and the Errors of Beginning

As with the discovery of the first UN peacekeeping operation, UN cooperation with regional organisations emerged, to some extent, somewhat unexpectedly. A vicious civil war exploded in Liberia in 1989, led by a former Cabinet Minister, Charles Taylor, who, under the auspices of his National Patriotic Front of Liberia (NPFL), contested and won a democratic election and became the country's president in 1997.

Shortly after the outbreak of the war, the then incumbent President, Samuel Doe, invited the UN to intervene in the conflict. The UN promptly declined the invitation. According to its SG Pérez de Cuellar, the nature of the Liberian crisis (a civil war) was not such that the UN could intervene. Under Article 2(7) of the UN Charter, the organisation is forbidden to intervene in matters which fall within the domestic jurisdiction of its member states, and civil wars, no matter how brutal, are considered to be such matters. Indeed, it was not until about 1993, precisely in Haiti and later in Somalia, that the UN took a more purposive approach to interpreting the rule in Article 2(7) of its Charter and was able to intervene in such matters when certain humanitarian thresholds were crossed.

The UN's refusal to intervene in Liberia provided an opportunity for the then little-known ECOWAS, an economic grouping of some 16 West African states of varied economic and political clouts, to concoct an ad hoc monitoring group, ECOMOG, with the mandate to supervise a ceasefire agreement that had just been brokered between the Liberian government and the several rebel factions involved in the conflict.[19]

The wider legal implications of ECOWAS' intervention in Liberia, under the law of use of force, have been well covered in analyses to merit any details here. What is most crucial for our purpose now is the nature of the interaction between the UN and ECOWAS in Liberia. Despite UN's formal decline to intervene in the Liberia conflict, it deployed, in 1993, the United Nationals Observer Mission in Liberia (UNOMIL) with the mandate, inter alia, to supervise the implementation of the Cotonou Peace Plan by ECOWAS.[20] UNOMIL experienced severe problems mainly due to its weak mandate and the haphazard relationship with ECOWAS, leading to its downsizing in 1994. In 1996, a new Abuja II Peace Agreement was negotiated, and under this, ECOWAS protected UNOMIL forces in return for the latter complementing its efforts in Liberia.

UNOMIL's mandate was to oversee ECOWAS' so-called peace monitoring role in Liberia. ECOWAS' mandate, although practically weak and ill-advised at the time, was partly legally defensible under the general international law of peacekeeping, but viscerally controversial under the Charter. To a large extent, ECOWAS' mission in Liberia fulfilled some of the criteria of peacekeeping operations – at least at the time of deploying ECOMOG. The mission was invited by the Head of State of Liberia at the time (in accordance with the requirement of host state consent), the troops were lightly armed and the mission was apparently impartial.

However, analysing ECOWAS intervention under the Charter rules proved problematic. ECOWAS asserted that its mission in Liberia did not depend on the consent of any party to the conflict although it was invited by Liberia at the time. According to the ECOWAS Chairperson at that time 'we do not need the permission of any party involved in the conflict to implement the decisions reached in Banjul' (Africa Research Bulleting 1990). This disclosure meant that ECOMOG's role was more a disguised enforcement action against the NPFL – being an operation executed in spite of the latter's predilection.

Furthermore, right from arriving in Monrovia, ECOMOG engaged elements of the NPFL rebel group in fierce battle, apparently in response to the latter's attacks. Whereas acting in self-defence is an acceptable exception to peacekeepers' avowed neutrality and nonuse of force, ECOMOG's pursuit of an all-out war against NPFL, far beyond the dictates of self-defence, seriously undermined those principles and called ECOWAS' real motive into question. And, without doubt, by militarily preventing Charles Taylor's forces from marching into the Liberian power house – ECOWAS unabashedly violated the principle that peacekeepers cannot influence the outcome of conflict.

The impact of these developments on the UN cooperation in this operation is quite telling, even if the lessons learnt are far enriching. To start with, it is conceptually difficult to ground the UN/ECOWAS cooperation in Liberia under any of the five distinct thematic models for cooperation identified in the Supplement to the Agenda. To some extent, it does appear that the operation falls under the 'co-deployment model' given that both the UN and ECOWAS deployed separately. The problem, however, is that co-deployment presupposes working towards the realisation of the same goals and objectives. But while ECOWAS had clearly intended an enforcement action in Liberia, the UN was apparently supporting a peacekeeping mission. To argue, therefore, that the UN cooperated with ECOWAS in the latter realising an enforcement mandate, without the Security Council approval, is to argue that the UN was an accomplice in violating its own Charter. The only way one can make sense of such an argument is to posit, as it is often done, that the Security Council, by so doing, retroactively approved ECOWAS' use of force in Liberia, a view generally accepted given that Article 53 does not prescribe any temporal limitation to the Security Council authorising a regional enforcement action. Furthermore, the vicissitudes of UN/ECOWAS deployment in Liberia arguably did not afford the UN the luxury of seriously considering the modality for cooperating with ECOWAS.

10.4.2 Yugoslavia: The Gale of Confusion in UN/NATO 'Peacekeeping' Cooperation

A year before the UN deployed to Liberia, the Security Council had authorised states, under Resolution 770, to take

> nationally or through regional agencies or arrangements all measures necessary to facilitate in coordination with the UN the delivery by relevant UN humanitarian organisations and others of humanitarian assistance to Sarajevo and wherever needed in other parts of Bosnia and Herzegovina.

One organisation that responded to the Security Council's clarion call was NATO. NATO is *not* a regional organisation under the framework of Chapter VIII, being an organisation established exclusively (at least until its reorientation/re-strategisation in 1999)[21] as a collective self-defence mechanism.[22] Of course, one can argue that the Security Council simply did not want to get involved in the legal or doctrinal debate about NATO and Chapter VIII and that, in any case, considering the virtual inability of the Security Council to activate Chapter VII enforcement action then, it had limited options. Yet, such tactful approaches, while politically expedient, do not aid the understanding of UN/regional organisations' relationship; much more, they are fraught with ambiguities.

The nature of the relationship between the UNPROFOR and NATO forces in Yugoslavia, being the point of interest to this endeavour, entailed different dynamics than the Liberian experience.

As mentioned above, Resolution 770 invited states to assist in the realisation of humanitarian assistance in Yugoslavia, acting nationally or through regional arrangements. NATO responded. However, UNPROFOR was already on ground as at the time Resolution 770 was adopted,[23] and was mandated, as it were under Resolution 743, to perform pure peacekeeping operations.[24]

But there are several incongruous features associated to Resolution 743 which established UNPROFOR, such that make an appreciation of its nature and purpose daunting. First, in the preambular paragraph 7, the Resolution had recalled the provision of Article 25 and Chapter VIII. The Security Council, in reciting Article 25, set the tone for the decisions it took under Resolution 743: it was a decision intended to bind UN member states as an obligation. But then Resolution 743 established a peacekeeping operation (not an enforcement action), and it is unlikely that the Security Council can compel UN member states to contribute to a peacekeeping operation as a matter of obligation under Article 25, especially considering that peacekeeping is not explicitly provided for in the Charter. The only link between Article 25 and UNPROFOR was if by its recital the Security Council intended to remind the UN member states of their general obligation (under Article 25) to implement its decisions. In the present context, that decision only related to the sanctions imposed by virtue of Resolution 713 (1991).

In any case, there is no reference in Resolution 743 to Chapter VII of the UN Charter. This implies that as regards its overriding mandate, UNPROFOR was neither a *decision* of the Security Council (in the sense of binding UN members under Article 25) nor was its mission envisaged to be an enforcement action. Whether the Security Council deliberately decided to avoid reference to Chapter VII is unclear, but its attitude is consistent with its decision under operative paragraph 2 of Resolution 743 to establish UNPROFOR in accordance with the UN peacekeeping plan.

Had the UN maintained faith with the underlining peacekeeping guidelines it subscribed to when establishing UNPROFOR, the serious problems it subsequently ran into might have been avoided. However, subsequent resolutions adopted after 743 fell under Chapter VII with many of them clearly encouraging UNPROFOR to use force.

The divergent mandates between UNPROFOR and NATO generated different reactions between the two organisations to the situation in Yugoslavia. From the start, NATO had to cooperate with UNPROFOR in order to enforce the flight ban on the airspace of Bosnia and Herzegovina. Yet, UNPROFOR strategies for discharging its overall mandates were as varied as the number of peace agreements it was meant to help implement.[25] In the Washington Framework Agreement of 1994, which established the Muslim-Croat Federation, the intention was for UNPROFOR to discharge a classical peacekeeping mandate in which the warring factions can be separated.[26] The same applies to the Dayton Accord of 1995, establishing the Inter-Entity Boundary Line (IEBL) on the basis of a ceasefire agreement concluded by parties with UNPROFOR in 1995.

However, despite that UNPROFOR was intended to operate as a peacekeeping mission, alongside NATO's enforcement action, occasions arose whereby UNPROFOR crossed the peacekeeping line. NATO's aerial action, following its Council decision on 19 November 1994, to bomb Bosnian Serb positions, provoked brutal reaction from the Serbs, leading to the call by the UN Secretary-General Boutros-Ghali for a tough action. Following a series of hostage-taking of UNPROFOR personnel – in response to NATO's bombing of Serbian positions – UNPROFOR eventually requested NATO airstrikes around Pale in Sarajevo, following the expiration of a UN ultimatum for Bosnian Serbs to return weapons removed from UN premises.

Whatever the political permutations of UNPROFOR might be, one of the problems faced by the mission was the imbuing of a peacekeeping mission with an enforcement mandate in the same operation. Surely, the use of force by UNPROFOR and its calling on NATO to help it attack some parties to the conflict was beyond the issue of self-defence. While this brings the NATO/UNPROFOR relationship close to ECOWAS/UNOMIL, the major difference is that the UN cooperation with ECOWAS was on a legally deficient ground since the latter undertook enforcement action masquerading as a peacekeeping operation. Whether this illegality was cured by the subsequent approval by the Security Council is a different issue altogether. Furthermore, while the UN relied heavily on ECOWAS forces protecting its own force in Liberia, UNPROFOR reliance on NATO was to the extent of the latter, undertaking actions which were, in reality of enforcement nature, thus acting more as an agent, of the UN. And it was obvious that in the former Yugoslavia, the UN was as confused as it could ever be as to what best action it should take: its intervention machinery was firmly on a roller coaster, partly propelled by the multiple winds of revolt exploding all around it and partly steamrollered by the enthralling politics in New York.

10.4.3 UN and AU in Darfur: New Development in UN/Regional Organisations Cooperation in Peacekeeping

The ambiguities, confusion and uncertainties that characterised UN cooperation with regional organisations in Liberia and Yugoslavia, climaxed in the bewildering conflict ensuing in the Darfur region of Sudan. A full analysis of the UN/AU engagement in Darfur has been pursued elsewhere, and it is impossible, in the limited space of the current endeavour, to do justice to that remit.[27] Be that as it may, there are some fundamental issues that have emerged so far, in the UN/AU cooperation in Darfur that are of significant interest to this chapter.

At inception – that is, shortly after the outbreak of conflict in Darfur in 2003 – the AU decided, without wasting much time, to intervene in the conflict.[28] Memories of the UN's tragic prevarication in Rwanda especially were fresh, and opinions in African capitals favoured deploying the AU immediately. However, this engulfing enthusiasm was not matched by a readiness of AU member states to provision the organisation with the huge resources, both human and materials, it required to undertake the daunting task of intervening in a province the size of France. Consequently, it came down to a few states, particularly Nigeria, to contribute the lion share of the total troops needed in Darfur.

The effectiveness of the AU Mission in Darfur (AMIS) continues to generate wide and wild debates amongst academics and non-state actors. Assessments of AU's performance depends, as is often the case in this kind of situation, on who is looking at what the organisation is doing in Darfur, from what standpoints and perspectives, and to whose benefits the analysis of AU's actions. What is certain though is that even the AU's harshest critics cannot escape from the fact that but for the timely intervention of the Union, it is highly unlikely that the UN would have stepped into the foray when it eventually did, if at all it would, with consequences that are perhaps better imagined.

However, following series of meetings and talks, the UN took over AMIS and established the United Nations-African Union Mission in Darfur (UNAMID) towards the end of 2007. UNAMID is the first joint operation in which the UN actually took control of the mandate and its implementation with a regional organisation.

The cooperation between the UN and the AU started when, during its 66th meeting, the AU Peace and Security Council endorsed '*the conclusions of the Addis Ababa High Level Consultation on the Situation in Darfur*' on 16 December 2006,[29] providing for a three-phased UN support for the AU mission in Sudan.[30] The most significant of the three-level UN support to the AU is the establishment of the UNAMID.

Security Council Resolution 1769, adopted on 31 July 2007, established UNAMID. If fully deployed, UNAMID will be the largest UN mission in history. It comprises nearly 26,000 personnel with as many as 19,000 military, 360 observers and 3,372 police officers.[31]

UNAMID stands out clearly in the advent of UN cooperation with regional organisations for many reasons. First, it would be the first joint operation between the UN and a regional organisation with both organisations committed to implementing the same mandate from the start. A more important feature of UNAMID is with regard to the funding of the mission. Although the AU had substantially funded AMIS through the EU financial assistance to the AU, under the ninth European Development Fund (EDF), UNAMID's funding has come substantially from assessed contributions by UN members amongst other means. The fact that the UN will underwrite the UNAMID expenses is, in itself, a success in the UN cooperation with regional organisations.

Furthermore, the history of UN's supporting continent-wide organisations in Africa, in particular, shows that the question and the role of funding in the dynamics cannot be taken for granted. The Organisation of African Unity (OAU)'s 1981 peacekeeping mission in Chad fell apart partly because the UN could not help the organisation generate the resources it needed to implement its mandate in that country.

Yet, despite the relative clarity in the cooperation between the UN and AU in Darfur, a UNPROFOR-type bedlam could probably have occurred (or, at least been precipitated) were it not for the paradoxical (even if self-serving) efforts of China. The Security Council Resolution 1769, adopted under Chapter VII of the UN Charter, had

> authorised [UNAMID] to take *necessary action*, in the areas of deployment of its forces and as it deems within its capacities to protect its personnel, facilities, installations and equipment, and to ensure the security and freedom of movement of its own personnel and humanitarian workers.

This mandate would probably have served the basis for UNAMID troops (or its commanders) using force beyond the legal parameters of peacekeeping operations.

China, however, objected to any understanding of Resolution 1769 as creepily authorising enforcement action.[32] Surely, this is a self-defeating episode for the UN since, it is crystal clear that once again, the UN is keeping the peace in a situation where there is no peace to keep. Nonetheless, with the critical understanding that the UNAMID mandate is a peacekeeping one, there is at least some certainty of what the UN might not do (enforcement action) under 1769, although what it could actually do (in terms of effective protection of lives and property in Darfur) remains to be seen. At the time of writing, UNAMID is still engaged in Darfur. Therefore, it may not be until the close of the mission that a full picture of its contribution to the developing of UN cooperation with regional organisations in peacekeeping can be fully appreciated.

10.5 The Secretary-General 2008 UN/Regional Organisations Report: A Shuttle in the Crypt

In 1994, the UN Secretary-General convened the first High Level Meeting between the UN and regional organisations to discuss how best to improve cooperation with regional organisations (these meetings are further discussed in Chap. 8).

In April 2008, the UN Secretary-General issued an important report on the relationship between the UN and regional organisations, in particular the AU, in the maintenance of international peace and security (hereafter UN/RO Report).[33] Through the UN/RO Report, the UN seeks 'more planned, consistent and reliable arrangements' with regional organisations.

But more than a self-admonishing instrument, the UN/RO Report is, on another level, an instrument through which the UN seeks to strengthen and realise the much-vaunted need to develop the capacity of regional organisations in peacekeeping operations. In substance, the UN/RO Report emphasises the nature and structure of partnership between the UN and regional organisations (para. 71). Interestingly, the report also speaks of drawing a distinction between 'regional organisations for Chapter VIII activities and all other regional organisations' activities', and also, of identifying 'regional security mechanism either by membership, focal area and/or mandate'[34] (para. 71(d)). It is worth noting that this is the first time the UN has attempted to separate regional organisations falling under Chapter VIII from those that do not.

From an analytical standpoint, one could see the immediate benefits in the clarification of regional organisations' status under Chapter VIII. Such moves would surely delight many international lawyers who detest the fact that in the absence of such clarification, organisations like NATO are able to pick and chose when to and not to work with the UN and, more importantly, when to escape the constraint of Chapter VIII on regional enforcement actions. For in claiming that it is not a regional organisation under Chapter VIII, NATO has been able to avoid the need to seek Security Council's authorisation, for instance, in its action against Serbia and Montenegro in 1999 during the Kosovo crisis.

Be that as it may, the crucial issue is whether the UN really wants to get involved in a debate that is, to all intent and purposes, an academic exercise. The fact that NATO has consistently claimed not to fall under Chapter VIII has not in any way hindered its cooperation with the UN either after the bombing in Kosovo (pursuant to Resolution 1244) or in the international effort to exterminate Al Qaeda in Afghanistan. Furthermore, the fact that NATO claimed to be established under Article 51 is far from foreclosing the debate under Chapter VIII. The *travaux préparatoires* of the UN Charter suggests that the right of self-defence (under which NATO claimed to have been established) was actually included in the Charter for the protection, first and foremost, of regional organisations, such as the Inter-American System. The right of self-defence was not intended to entitle regional organisations postdating the UN Charter to make a dubious distinction between organisations governed by Chapter VIII and those governed by Article 51. Article 51 is a shield, not a sword, and it would be difficult to see a regional organisation which claims that because it acts under Chapter VIII, it could not enjoy the right of self-defence under Article 51. NATO's argument – that it does not fall under Chapter VIII – therefore is both dubious and fraudulent. It is the uncritical nature of legal analysis of regional organisations vis-à-vis Article 51, and more importantly, the tragic failure of legal inquiry to carry the Kelsen and Beckett's pioneering debate on NATO's status under the UN Charter to its logical conclusion that allowed for NATO's perfidious interpretation to triumph for more than 50 years.

It would be a wasteful effort for the Security Council to attempt identifying regional organisations under Chapter VIII according to membership, focal area and/or mandate. It has long been recognised, amongst legal specialists, that the UN avoided laying down trite criteria of regionalism under Chapter VIII in order to allow states to associate as they like. To base an identification of regional organisations on the criterion of membership is to create mammoth problems for organisations like NATO consisting of countries from Europe to the North America, or CENSAD. Similarly, 'focal area and mandate' criteria fly in the face of multitasking organisations as ECOWAS.

As part of the new system, the General Assembly approved the establishment of the African Union Peace Support Team (AUPST) which came into operation in January 2007. AUPST is mandated to provide necessary expertise and transfer of technical knowledge to the AU Peace Support Operation Department (PSOD). Other areas of cooperation envisaged by the UN/RO Report include possible annual meetings between the Security Council and the AU Peace and Security Council (para. 73(b)), training staff and increasing desk-to-desk interactions between the two organisations.

10.6 Concluding Remarks

Cooperation between the UN and regional organisations, active in peace and security, is a relatively new phenomenon. The unremitting stretching of the UN resources by exponential rise in the number of peacekeeping operations it has conducted since the 1990s means that the UN desires a strong partnership with regional organisations in peace.

There are many reasons why this cooperation needs to be more structured, precise and focused. As at present, the cooperation between the UN and regional organisations, as shown above, is on *ad hoc* basis and haphazard. The extremely lose and hop-in-hop-out style of UN's engagement with regional organisations is at variance with the vision expressed by the World Summit in 2005 in which the UN and regional organisations cooperation should develop through formalised agreements.[35] Hopefully, the supplementary mechanisms the 2008 UN/RO refers to in paragraph 71(e)[36] will address this penitent problem and help the UN in devising a more structured cooperation regimen with regional organisations.

The adoption of supplementary regulatory frameworks will go a long way in shoring up the terse and laconic provisions of Chapter VIII. As it stands today, the UN Charter does not speak volumes, or even near enough, about what nature the UN cooperation with regional organisations should take; nor do the provisions of Chapter VIII, the legislative framework governing UN's interaction with regional organisations, offer much help in understanding the legal basis of that relationship. The vacuum has been filled by dangerous practices and outright abominations. Encouraging UN peacekeeping forces commanders to use force beyond the scope of self-defence in a pure peacekeeping operation is as dangerous as the UN relying on partial and biased regional organisations to afford its peacekeepers protection from enemy fire.

Many regional organisations desire and – indeed – need to be more proactive in maintaining peace and security in their regions. But these organisations must continue to coordinate their activities with the UN. Regional organisations should desist jumping into conflicts first before undertaking a painstaking reconnaissance of their ability and capability and of the advantage of taking the UN on board from the start off point. Of course, the sometimes painful, sometimes tragic prevarication of the UN, in the face of calamities, does leave regional organisations with little choices. But the go-it-alone response of regional organisations to the frequent do-nothing posture of the UN could itself be symptomatic of the current nature of their engagement which, it is hoped, will be addressed in not too distant future.

Notes

1. For an excellent account of the emergence of regional organisation after the World War II, see, in particular, Russell (1958a, b).
2. Article 24(1).
3. See, in particular, Tascan (1998).
4. The phrases 'unilateral' and 'multilateral' are used here to denote respectively a peacekeeping operation taken by a single state and one that is taken by two or more states in respect of a dispute.
5. The assertion, therefore, by the Lesson Learnt Unit of the Department of Peacekeeping Operation that 'UN support provides legitimacy to operations by a regional or sub-regional organisation/

arrangement' must be understood to refer to political legitimacy in contradistinction from legality. A peacekeeping operation initiated by a regional or sub-regional organisation on the basis of Article 52 of the UN Charter is certainly made more politically important with UN credence, such is not legally held over the legal barrel by the absence of such legitimacy. See UN Department of Peacekeeping Operations (DPKO) (1999).

6. Emphasis added.
7. See, for instance, Economides and Taylor (2007).
8. See the second and the final report of the Secretary-General on the Plan for An Emergency International United Nations Force requested in the resolution adopted by the General Assembly on 4 November 1956 (A/3276) and on 6 November 1956 (A/3302).
9. For a good review of why the principles of traditional peacekeeping suffer, see Biermann and Vadset (1999:15).
10. On the changing nature of UN mandates in Yugoslavia, see Economides and Taylor (2007).
11. Ibid, at paragraph 9.
12. For instance, in Liberia and Sierra Leone, the Security Council adopted resolutions that welcomed enforcement actions by ECOWAS in circumstances that warranted legal analysts to conclude that the Security Council retroactively endorsed those operations.
13. As I have argued elsewhere, regional organisations are able to use force against their own members where the constitutive treaty of that organisation permits such a use of force. Usually, parties to such a treaty, including the state against which force is being used, would have given their consent in advance to legitimatise the use of force by their regional organisation. Such uses of force, as I have argued elsewhere, do not conceptually fall foul of Article 2(4) of the UN Charter. It is not a use of force that violates the territorial integrity or political independence (or in any other way) of the concerned state. For a full analysis, see Abass (2004), particularly Chap. 6.
14. Secretary-General Report, 1956, supra, at paragraph 4.
15. Ibid., paragraph 8.
16. An Agenda for Peace (1992) International legal Materials 953; An Agenda for peace: Preventive diplomacy, peacemaking and peacekeeping. Report of the Secretary-General pursuant to the settlement adopted by the Summit Meeting of the Security Council on 31 January 1992 (New York: United Nations 1992).
17. The Security Council Report, The UN and Regional Organisations, also acknowledges this fact stating that 'when the UN Charter was negotiated, there was debate over the place of regionalism in the new organisation. The outcome was Chapter VIII which acknowledges the scope for contribution of regional organisations to the settlement of disputes, but in a subordinate capacity, and there is some ambiguity about the exact nature of regional arrangement'. Available at <http://www.secutitycouncilreport.org>, p. 2.
18. Supplement to An Agenda for Peace issued on 3 January 1995.
19. A/DEC.3/8/90, First Session of the Community Standing Mediation Committee, Banjul, Gambia, 1990.
20. See Report of the UN Secretary-General on Liberia, UN Doc S/26422, 9 September 1993, at p. 4.
21. On whether the approval by the North Atlantic Council that NATO could undertake tasks beyond the prescriptions of Article 5 of the Washington Treaty, see, in particular, Nigel White (2000).
22. For an early analysis of the place of NATO in the Chapter VIII framework, see Kelsen (1950) and Becket (1950).
23. UN Doc S/RES/743, 21 February 1992.
24. Operative paragraph 2.
25. See From Stoltenberg – Owen to Dayton. An Interview with Thorvald Stoltenberg, in Biermann and Vadset, supra at 6.
26. For a comprehensive analysis of UNPROFOR's various engagements, see Bierman and Vadset (1999a, b).
27. See Abass (2007b).

28. Technically, the decision of the AU to decide was at the request of the Sudanese Government, thus conditioning AU's intervention as necessarily a peacekeeping operation. The debate, therefore, as to why the AU should not have undertaken a humanitarian intervention in Darfur is *non-sequitur*.
29. PSC/AHG/Comm. (LXVI) Communiqué of the Peace and Security Council, 30 November 2006 (hereafter The 'Conclusions').
30. High Level Consultation on the Situation in Darfur: Conclusions, available at HTTP: <http://www.amis-sudan.org/PSCCommuinque/061116_Conclusions%20of%20the%20High%20Level%20Consultation%20on%20the%20Situation%20in%20Darfur.doc> visited on 20 January 2007.
31. Resolution 1769, Operative paragraph 2.
32. S/PV.5727, p. 10.
33. S/2008/186, 7 April 2008 (hereafter the 'UN/RO Report').
34. Paragraph 71(d), UN/RO Report.
35. See the *World Summit Outcome*, GA Res. 60/1, 24 October 2005, paragraph 170.
36. On the nature and structure of partnership, paragraph 71(e) states that the Security Council shall, amongst other things, engage 'in consultations on options for a structured cooperation between the United Nations and regional organisations involved in regional peace operations, including a possible mechanism aimed at enhancing interactions with the Security Council'.

References

Abass, A. (2004). *Regional organizations and the development of collective security: Beyond Chapter VIII of the UN Charter*. Oxford: Hart Publishing.

Abass, A. (2007a). Extraterritorial collective security: The European Union and Operation Artemis. In M. Trybus & N. White (Eds.), *European Security Law* (pp. 135–156). Oxford: Oxford University Press.

Abass, A. (2007b). The United Nations, the African Union and the Darfur Crisis: Of apology and Utopia. *Netherlands International Law Review, 54*, 415–440.

Abass, A. (2008). European Union crisis management in Africa: Progress, problems and prospects. In S. Blockmans (Ed.), *The European Union and crisis management: Policy and legal aspects* (pp. 327–343). Cambridge: Cambridge University Press.

Africa Research Bulletin: Economic, Financial and Technical Series, 34(8), September 15, 1990.

Akehurst, M. (1967). Enforcement action by regional organisations with special reference to the organization of American States. In *42 British yearbook of international law* (p. 175). Oxford: Oxford University Press.

Becket, E. (1950). *The North Atlantic Treaty, the Brussels Treaty and the Charter of the United Nations*. London: Stevens & Sons.

Biermann, W., & Vadset, M. (1999). *UN peacekeeping in trouble: Lessons learned from the former Yugoslavia*. Aldershot: Ashgate.

Boutros-Ghali, B. (1992b). *An agenda for peace* (A/47/277 - S/24111). New York: The United Nations.

Economides, S., & Taylor, P. (2007). Former Yugoslavia. In M. Berdal & S. Economides (Eds.), *United Nations interventions 1991–2004* (pp. 65–68). Cambridge: Cambridge University Press.

Kelsen, H. (1950). Is the North Atlantic Treaty a regional arrangement? *American Journal of International Law,* 162.

Rose, M. (1998). Military aspects of peacekeeping. Lessons learned from Bosnia, from a commander's perspective. In W. Biermann & M. Vadset (Eds.), *UN peacekeeping in trouble: Lessons from the former Yugoslavia* (pp. 153–157). Aldershot: Ashgate.

Russell, R. B. (1958a). *Foreign relations of the United States: The conferences at Malta and Yalta*. Text of invitation in US State Department.

Russell, R. B. (1958b). *A history of the United Nations Charter: The role of the United States 1940–1945*. Washington, DC: The Brookings Institution.
Tascan, J. (1998). Searching for OAS/UN task sharing opportunities in Central America and Haiti. In T. Weiss (Ed.), *Beyond task-sharing opportunities with regional security arrangements and service-providing NGOs*. London: Macmillan Press Ltd.
UN DPKO. (1999). *Cooperation between the United Nations and regional organizations/arrangements in a peacekeeping environment, suggested principles and mechanisms* (p. 10). March 1999, Lesson learnt Unit.
Walter, C. (1997). Security council control over regional action. In *Max Planck yearbook of United Nations law* (Vol. 1). Heidelberg: Max-Planck-Institute.
White, N. D. (2000). The legality of bombing in the name of humanity. *Journal of Conflict and Security Law, 5*(1), 27.
White, N. D., & Abass, A. (2006). Countermeasures and sanctions. In M. Evans (Ed.), *International law* (2nd ed., pp. 510–532). Oxford: Oxford University Press.

Chapter 11
The False Promise of Regional Organisations?

Rodrigo Tavares

11.1 Introduction

In 1994, in his landmark article 'The False Promise of International Institutions', John Mearsheimer reviewed liberal institutionalism, collective security and critical theory to evaluate whether the claim that institutions cause peace is convincing. He concludes that it is not – 'institutions have minimal influence on state behaviour, and thus hold little promise for promoting stability in the post-Cold War world' (1994/1995: 7). Realism reigned supreme. Although I will not attempt to engage with Mearsheimer's theory, I am nonetheless sympathetic to his attempt to critically review standard canons in international relations.

Over the last years, considerable attention has been given to the role of regional organisations in conflict management. Although the United Nations (UN) remains the main source of international legitimacy on the use of military force, the global body has been devolving power to regional actors to resolve their own local conflicts. In 1992, UN Secretary-General Boutros-Ghali noted that the post-Cold War era was characterised by problems regarding the 'logistics, equipment, personnel and finance' of increasingly demanded peacekeeping missions, 'all of which could be corrected if Member States so wished and were ready to make the necessary resources available'.[1] The answer was regional task sharing, also called regional subcontracting or subsidiarity.

A new wave of regionalist scholarship has arisen in response. Even if the published work is vast and focuses on a wide range of different subjects, such as the capacity, history or experience of these organisations (Tavares 2009; Alagappa and Inoguchi 1999; Diehl and Lepgold 2003; Pugh and Sidhu 2003; Weiss 1998; Boulden 2003; Graham and Felício 2006; International Peace Academy 2006), the

R. Tavares (✉)
United Nations University Institute on Comparative Regional Integration
Studies (UNU-CRIS), Bruges, Belgium
e-mail: rmtavares@gmail.com

P. De Lombaerde et al. (eds.), *The United Nations and the Regions: Third World Report on Regional Integration*, United Nations University Series on Regionalism 3,
DOI 10.1007/978-94-007-2751-9_11,

general tone is sympathetic to regional task sharing. For example, Lake and Morgan have observed that 'efforts to cope with violent conflicts, as well to achieve order and security, will primarily involve arrangements and actions devised and implemented at the regional level' (1997: 5). In August 2009, in his latest report on the work of the organisation, the Secretary-General confirmed the 'deepening of our [UN] cooperation and partnership with regional bodies along a vast spectrum of activities' and looked forward to 'continued collaboration'.[2]

Critical voices on the role of regional organisations do exist, however. Diehl, for instance, has pointed out that 'regional organisations have some notable disadvantages vis-à-vis global efforts, especially the UN, at conflict management [and] are ill-designed to conduct enforcement and peacekeeping operations or facilitate judicial solutions to conflicts' (2003: 74). An undersecretary-general of the UN in charge of peacekeeping, Marrack Goulding, also warned that most regional organisations lacked the experience, bureaucratic structures and resources necessary to conduct peacekeeping effectively (2003: 217). I will not oppose the view – transversal to most contributors to this volume – that regional organisations are prominent actors in conflict management. As the apologists of regional subcontracting often note, due to regional organisations' cultural and geographical proximity to the conflict, they are deemed more likely to understand the factual background of disputes and to share the applicable norms and procedures. In this chapter, however, I am mostly interested in exploring the institutional and operational limitations of regional security agencies so that at the end one has a more comprehensive view of the benefits and disadvantages of regional subsidiarity. The analysis will be concentrated on five main subject areas: capacity, partiality, hegemony, overlapping/absence of institutions and mandate.

11.2 Capacity

The capacity of an organisation to engage with peace and security depends on two aspects: first, the constitutional provisions according to the mandate to become active, and second, the institutional mechanisms through which it can function and exercise that mandate. Presently, most regional organisations operate in peace and security under a clear legal mandate (e.g. the Constitutive Act of the AU, the Treaty of the EU or LAS' Mechanism for Conflict Prevention, Management and Resolution between Arab States). Yet some other organisations – such as the Community of Portuguese Speaking Countries (CPLP) and the Caribbean Community (CARICOM) – have not refrained from carrying out peace and security missions, although they lack a legal mandate altogether. The foundational treaty of CARICOM, the Treaty of Chaguaramas, provides no legal mandate to CARICOM to engage in the security dominion. Nevertheless, the organisation has developed some functions in this field, mostly in less traditional areas of security (transnational crime), and has been involved in security crises that endangered the stability of its member states, such as in Haiti. The CPLP, on the other hand, has sent peacemaking missions to Guinea-Bissau in 1998, São Tomé and Príncipe in 2002 and again Guinea-Bissau in 2004, but its statutes do not endow the organisation with a mandate to operate in the security sphere.

In terms of institutional capacity, most organisations are faulty. This has not prevented some to argue that regional subcontracting could be the answer to the increasing operational, financial and political problems of the UN to conduct peacekeeping missions. Even if sometimes only rhetorically, the UN has often underlined the importance of task sharing. In the latest debate on the topic, the Security Council for instance emphasised that

> [...] the growing contribution made by regional and subregional organisations in cooperation with the United Nations can usefully support the work of the Organisation in maintaining international peace and security, and stresses in this regard that such contribution should be made in accordance with Chapter VIII of the Charter of the United Nations.[3]

Some argue, however, that the Council's inclination towards formal subcontracting is not always well intentioned, but rather motivated by the 'desire to turn a blind eye' to a particular conflict corner in the world (Berman 1998: 3). Indeed, greater participation by regional organisations 'cannot be an excuse for the Security Council to shirk its responsibility' (Boulden 2003: 30), because only the Council has the competence to provide a regional operation with legitimacy. Either way, to become viable partners, regional organisations need to have large resources and capacity. Hansen, Mitchell and Nemeth have demonstrated so quantitatively. Using data on territorial (1816–2001), maritime (1900–2001) and river (1900–2001) claims from the Issue Correlates of War (ICOW) project in the Western Hemisphere, Europe and the Middle East, they have shown that international organisations are more likely to help disputing parties reach an agreement if they have more democratic members, if they are highly institutionalised and when they use binding management techniques (2008). Nonetheless, most regional organisations, especially in Africa, are far from having those characteristics. Let us pause on the AU for a moment. The organisation has set itself an ambitious aim to develop an African Peace and Security Architecture (APSA), and in addition to creating the necessary decision-making bodies in Addis Ababa such as the Peace and Security Council, the Military Staff Committee, an early warning mechanism, and the Panel of the Wise, APSA will comprise of the African Stand-by Force (ASF) based on five regional brigades to be established by each of the subregional organisations (ECOWAS, SADC, IGAD, ECCAS, UMA). The ASF will have both military and civilian components. In practice, however, the AU has only available poor human and financial resources to allow all these organs to operate effectively. The 2007 Audit of the AU has indicated that 'inadequate in-house leadership and weak management systems have resulted in poor supervision in the Commission, within and between departments, and low morale among staff' (2007: p. 47). Although local dynamics call for caution, the UN Secretary-General normally opts for an oratorical tone. In 2008, he observed that the increase in the interface and synergies between the UN and the AU has shown that 'regionalism as a component of multilateralism is necessary and feasible' and that 'there is now the possibility of a shared role for maintaining international peace and security'.[4] More critical views are, hence, necessary. A first step was taken by the 2008 Prodi report, which highlighted that

> [...] there is a growing anomalous and undesirable trend in which organisations lacking the necessary capabilities have been left to bear the brunt in terms of providing the international community's initial response, while others more capable have not engaged.[5]

Therefore, if the UN has a clear intention to devolve power to regional organisations, in particular the AU, that needs to be expressed on the ground. A 'shared role' with the AU implies a stronger UN presence in Addis Ababa, the headquarters of the AU. For the moment, UN presence is scattered: the Department of Political Affairs (DPA) liaison office, DPKO capacity building cell, joint AU/UN UNAMID cell and UN technical assistance to AU SPMU (Strategic Planning/management cell). If it wants to serve as a credible partner in the establishment of a strengthened partnership, the UN has to increase its capacity from a qualitative (more coherence) and quantitative (more resources) perspective.

11.3 Partiality

Most interventions by regional bodies are not impartial, as member states generally participate in military interventions for reasons of personal or national interest rather than humanitarian motivations or out of a primary interest in preserving regional stability. When an organisation intervenes to mitigate a local conflict (pacific settlement), as this does not need to be authorised by the Security Council, who assures that the intervention is legitimate, the conduct is fair, and that its objectives are morally sound? Sometimes an intervention opens a Pandora's box that permits states to use military means to tackle security problems not related to the initial purposes of the intervention, as was the case with a Senegalese campaign against Casamance forces in northern Guinea-Bissau (under ECOWAS) and with Angola's firm determination to cut off supply lines to rebel UNITA members in Congo (under SADC). In East Timor, the interests of Indonesia and its behind-the-doors pressure led ASEAN member countries, with the exception of Singapore which initially abstained, to always vote with Indonesia in UN resolutions on East Timor (Martin 2003: 51). In Sudan, although President Omar al-Bashir claimed that he had invited IGAD to intervene and mediate in the North/South conflict because he believed that the regional organisation would be neutral 'without loopholes through which colonialism could penetrate on the pretext of humanitarianism' (Murithi 2009), in practice, he expected that his best friends would dominate the deliberations in the mediation committee. As regional organisations are formed by states, they are considered to be more supportive of governmental positions when they intervene in civil conflicts. For example, during the political crisis in Bolivia, in September 2008, Bolivian opposition leaders wrote a letter in which they disparaged the OAS for 'demonstrating partiality and lack of objectivity, proven on several occasions'.[6] In several other examples, states' underlying interests have largely compromised the ability of the regional organisation to serve the population's needs. In the case of the Central African Republic, the pursuit of national interests was camouflaged by the mission's official mandate itself: the mandate of CEMAC was initially defined as protecting President Patassé from coups rather than ensuring the population's security (Meyer 2009).

Empirical research has often concluded that weak and developing states regionalise but do not integrate. As they tend to be obsessed about sovereignty, they coalign to serve common statist interests (Ayoob 1995: 4). Hence, regional organisations 'have generally reproduced regional tensions within their structures rather than ameliorated them through neofunctional integration' (Kelly 2007: 220). For instance, Capie argues that ASEAN has done purposefully little to address the illicit trade in small arms and light weapons in the region. Linking small-arms action to 'transnational' issues permitted and even encouraged some action, but also served to close off discussion of sensitive 'internal' issues, such as military and police complicity in unlawful weapons transfers, and ruled out transparency measures that could impact on the legal arms trade (2008). Jones and Smith corroborate the fragility of ASEAN to serve as an effective agent of peace by demonstrating that the norms and practices that ASEAN promotes, rather than creating an integrated community, can only sustain a pattern of limited intergovernmental and bureaucratically rigid interaction (2007).

Moreover, the Charter says that the interventions have to be 'consistent with the Purposes and Principles of the United Nations' (Art. 52), but this motto remains so vague that regional organisations may try to play it out. For example, in 1948, LAS claimed that it was acting to uphold the principles of the UN when it intervened in an attempt to reverse Israel's declaration of independence. In 1999, US Secretary of State Madeleine Albright strongly refuted the idea that NATO intervention in Kosovo had no legitimacy on the grounds that the North Atlantic Council was a more legitimate voice on the use of force than the Security Council, which included many non-democracies (and thus included countries that defended principles inconsistent with the purposes and principles of the UN).

But it is in peacekeeping – mostly due to its anticipated capacity to bring about instant change – that is more vulnerable to be hijacked by member states to advance their national interests. In fact, it is difficult to identify one single regional peacekeeping intervention where a partaking country did not promote in some degree its national interests. The case of Africa is paradigmatic. In all interventions carried out by ECOWAS, SADC, ECCAS, CEMAC or the AU, the contributing countries aimed at projecting their national agendas. Much has been written about the partiality of the hegemons – Nigeria, Australia, South Africa and Ethiopia – in regional conflict management (see below). But if one also dissects the agendas of the smaller contributors, we may also identify plain evidences of *realpolitik*. The contribution of Mozambique to the AU mission in Burundi is a case in point. Why did a poor country with an ill-prepared army decide to adventure into distant foreign lands? First, peacekeeping is a business and the government wanted to keep the national army satisfied. The increase in salaries, the exposure to new technologies and armament and the learning of new military doctrines elevates the living conditions of the military.

And a content military decreases the likelihood of disturbances at home. Second, and despite the embarrassingly poor resources, the Mozambican political leadership was led by a desire to reward African countries over their key contributions to ONUMOZ (United Nations Operation in Mozambique, 1992–1994).[7] Encouraged by the end of the civil war (1975–1992), Mozambique wanted also to demonstrate to its African counterparts (and to the international community) that it was no longer a country that needed to be aided but a country that could come to the rescue of other countries. It was, therefore, a struggle for international visibility.

Additionally, African leaders often adopt a strategy of personalisation of politics, and strong links between heads of state – based either on empathy or animosity – are recurrent. It would be difficult to understand Angola and Zimbabwe's military deployment in Congo if we did not account for the personal bond between Eduardo dos Santos and Robert Mugabe. The same holds for the good relation between President Babangida and Samuel Doe of Liberia; between Charles Taylor and Ghaddafi of Libya, Boigny of Côte d'Ivoire and Campaore of Burkina Faso; or between President Diouf of Senegal and Joao Vieira of Guinea-Bissau. This type of personalisation is 'hardly the ideal basis for peacekeeping' (Obi 2009). Even more neutral organisations, such as the European Union, have been used to camouflage national agendas, as was the case with the intervention in Chad/Central African Republic, arguably led by French energy and political interests. Some research also brings into focus the ambiguity of the EU's normative power. For instance, Merlingen argues that EU's self-styled mission for humanity inscribes the very agency of those it seeks to empower in relations characterised by epistemic violence, the technologisation of politics and administrative arbitrariness (2008).

11.4 Hegemony

The issue of partiality is more striking when a region is dominated by a hegemonic power, as Australia in PIF, the United States in OAS, Nigeria in ECOWAS, Russia in CIS or South Africa in SADC. The issue of hegemony is a double-edged sword. On the one hand, there is indeed the danger that hegemonic powers will seize the decision-making apparatus of the organisations and render them paralysed or play them out to convey national agendas. But on the other hand, peacekeeping is a costly business, and regional organisations are largely dependent on the military resources of the larger states. The likelihood of a regional-body intervening military is exponentially increased if the national interests of the subregional hegemonic power are favourable to the intervention. South Africa, Nigeria, Ethiopia, the United States and Australia have all capitalised on their membership of subregional organisations to cynically pursue their national interests under the cover of international altruism. Some of these interventions are primarily national operations and become 'regional' only after an organisation 'acknowledges', 'supports' or 'approves' the intervention (often even retroactively). The South African intervention in Lesotho (SADC), the Russian interventions in Abkhazia and Tajikistan (CIS) or the Australian mission to the Solomon Islands (PIF) were not strategically planned and monitored in the headquarters of an organisation but rather in the corridors of power in Pretoria, Moscow, or Canberra. National operations only become 'regional' due to administrative and political astuteness. One may illustrate with Nigeria's role in Liberia. When troops under rebel leader Charles Taylor attempted to topple the Liberian president, ECOWAS employed an ex post facto sanctioned inexperienced peacekeeping force to restore social order. The regional hegemon leading the operation was Nigeria, which at that time was run by a dictator who had personal interests in swaying the conflict to his and his allied friends' benefits (Adibe 1997). If one moves from Africa to Asia, the same dynamics might be detected. An important factor that has helped to assure the survival of the CIS is that it has evolved into a mere instrument of Russian hegemony in Eurasia. There is no doubt that Russia was, and remains, the most powerful player within the CIS; to a large extent, Russia provides the key rationale behind the organisation's existence.

11.5 Too Many or Too Few

In some regions, there are too many organisations willing to intervene, such as in Europe, Central Asia, the Caribbean or in all subregions in Africa. The issue of overlapping would not be problematic if there were a clear division of labour between them, but this is seldom the case. At the initial steps of European institutionalisation, a sharing of responsibilities did exist between the COE (conflict prevention and human rights protection), NATO (collective defence and counter-insurgency), OSCE (peacebuilding and election monitoring) and the EU (soft security and civilian crisis management), but this is hardly the case now: NATO is involved with peacebuilding in Afghanistan and with civilian crisis management in Iraq, whereas the EU has embraced post-war reconstruction in the Balkans and robust peacekeeping in Africa. Ironically, there is an ongoing inter-regional dialogue between these organisations illustrated by the existence of joint programmes, high-level meetings and MoUs. But the dialogue is mostly about establishing close cooperation based on their shared priorities rather than on a true division of labour. The EU and the OSCE might have an old and active collaboration based on experience sharing in the field of human rights and the rule of law, but if the EU's interests prompt it to deploy a peacebuilding mission, for example, in the Balkans or the Caucasus, that decision will not take OSCE's interests, capacities or willingness to intervene into major consideration. At best, they would establish some type of field collaboration. In Central Asia, regional security bodies have mushroomed over the last years, not due to a need to fulfil a niche but to create yet another organisation to satisfy the temporary objectives of a lead nation. In Eastern Africa, the overlapping of early warning mechanisms has reached an almost anecdotal level: although IGAD has established a well-functioning early warning mechanism (Conflict Early Warning and Response Mechanism (CEWARN)), the East African Community has also developed a draft Protocol on Early Warning and Response

Mechanism. Perversely, as Kenya and Uganda are members of both organisations, what regional body shall they report to? And how should they proceed if they receive contradictory instructions from the regional organisations on how to respond to the imminent conflict? In South America, the OAS, UNASUR, Rio Group and the Andean Community have a mandate to engage in peace and security, but the division of labour between them is far from settled. The problem of overlapping leads to unaccountability, resource ineffectiveness and political competition.

In some other regions, the problem is the opposite: there is no, or no suitable, regional body to which a requisite intervention might be delegated. Despite the proliferation of integration and cooperation arrangements, there are indeed some parts of the world which are devoid of any kind of regional agency with a mandate to conduct security operations. For instance, if a conflict breaks out in Mongolia or if a regional intervention is requested to tackle the Israeli-Palestinian conflict, no local regional organisation would be able to intervene. In some others regions, the problem is not so much the lack of an organisation but the lack of a legal mandate to carry out peace operations. This is the case of the South Asia Association on Regional Cooperation (SAARC). With the UN playing a negligible role in South Asia or in the Middle East, the provision of security in these regions is contingent on the capacity of the state to do so. But if in theory the state is still the most prominent political actor and the bedrock of social organisation and social protection, there is a long list of states that can no longer perform their basic security and development functions and that have no effective control over their territory and borders. This raises the question of the 'fairness' of the ongoing process of devolution, and of expecting regional bodies to complement the work of the UN. With states, regional organisations and the United Nations hiccupping in their capacity of providing security in some regions, how are development and protection ensured? Decentralisation and delegation are only acceptable if they are paralleled by an equal dedication on the part of the UN to promote the formation and strengthening of institutions where they are currently non-existent or weak. Geography should not define people's security.

11.6 Mandate

Although there are currently 38 organisations with a mandate to carry out peace and security missions (Tavares 2009: 10–11), they vary widely in terms of *where* and *how* they can operate. There is indeed an acute need for the UN to provide guidelines on who should be empowered to do what and under what circumstances. Aware that the global institution cannot remove itself from its responsibility to provide a clear framework of security provision, Kofi Annan in his report *A Regional-Global Security Partnership* pledged to take the partnership 'to a new level of clarity, practicality and seriousness' (2006: 16). But this is far from being accomplished and the Security Council itself often authorises Chapter VIII organisations to operate under Chapter VII (e.g. the African Union Mission in Somalia (AMISOM)), disarranging further what it is already malfunctioning.

There is a need of identifying with some rigour who qualifies as a Chapter VIII organisation and what are the principles that define the exact area of possible intervention of a Chapter VIII agency. The UN Charter declares that regional agencies and arrangements can only intervene in 'local disputes', but what counts as a local dispute? Is it both inter-state and intra-state? Does it only encompass the total area covered by member states? Or is an organisation entitled to intervene in a state even if it might not be a member of that organisation although it is clearly situated in the region and therefore it meets the requirements for 'local'? The League of Arab States intervened in Israel in 1948, and today, it is an active player in the Israeli-Palestinian peace process. But Israel is not one of its 22 members. In another striking example of lack of juridical clarity, the CIS has tagged itself as a Chapter VIII agency and has intervened in Tajikistan and Abkhazia in that capacity. But the CIS's home-grown definition of peace operation (*mirotvorchestvo*) is at odds with current UN doctrine and practice. If according to the Charter, the Security Council ought to authorise peace enforcement but not pacific settlement/traditional peacekeeping, the Russian idea of peace operations bewilders this distinction, which certainly allows for unaccountability to flourish. In another case of a malfunctioning regional intervention, ECOWAS in Liberia, the Security Council disregarded the legal basis for the establishment and deployment of ECOMOG. While atrocities were being committed, the Security Council's statements or resolutions did not shed any light upon the mandate of the operation.[8] Given these discrepancies, Hettne and Söderbaum question the conception that a region is simply an intermediate actor that undertakes tasks determined at the multilateral level. In their view, some kind of horizontal and more balanced combination of regional and global agencies, each having its own basis of authority, 'should provide the predominant future form of global security governance' (2006: 231).

11.7 Conclusion

No general account can afford to make a final judgement on the capacity of regional organisations as each has its own specificities and calls for a particular type of cooperation with the UN. This chapter aimed to demonstrate, nonetheless, that simply mandating peacekeeping operations to regional organisations is critical. When assessing the advantages and disadvantages of both UN-peacekeeping and regional peacekeeping, the complementary nature of both levels of operation becomes obvious. This essay therefore argues that task sharing is not to be dismissed per se, but that certain forms of UN task sharing could make peacekeeping operations more efficient. One possible route is joint operations with regional arrangements, a method that has been considered a 'possible model for the future' (Boutros-Ghali 1995: 86). Although the joint AU/UN mission in Darfur is facing critical challenges, a revised model may still be replicated elsewhere. Ultimately, however, either regional task sharing or UN peacekeeping is dependent on better and more resources. Clearly, the political intensions outweigh the operational means.

Notes

1. Report of the Secretary General: An Agenda for Peace: Preventive Diplomacy, Peace-making and Peacekeeping, 17 June 1992 (A/47/277-S/24111), paragraph 50.
2. Report of the Secretary-General on the work of the Organisation, 4 August 2009 (A/64/1), para 148.
3. Presidential Statement S/PRST/2007/42 (6 November 2007).
4. Report of the Secretary-General on the relationship between the United Nations and regional organisations, in particular the African Union, in the maintenance of international peace and security, 7 April 2008 (S/2008/186), Summary.
5. Report of the African Union-United Nations panel on modalities for support to African Union peacekeeping operations (the 'Prodi Report') (A/63/666-S/2008/813), paragraph 11.
6. 'South American Presidents Unite to Defend Bolivia Against Destabilization' (Venezuelanalysis.com. 17 September 2008).
7. ONUMOZ was established to help implement the General Peace Agreement, signed by the President of the Republic of Mozambique and the President of the Resistência Nacional Moçambicana (RENAMO). Eight African countries took part in the mission.
8. See Letter Dated 90/08/09 from the Permanent Representative of Nigeria to the United Nations Addressed to the Secretary-General, S/21485, 10 August 1990; Letter Dated 90/12/14 from the Permanent Representative of The Gambia to the United Nations Addressed to the Secretary-General, S/22025, 20 December 1990; Note by the President of the Security Council, S/22133, 22 January 1991; Note by the President of the Security Council, S/23886, 7 May 1992; Security Council resolution 788, 19 November 1992; Security Council resolution 813, 27 August 1998; Security Council resolution 856, 10 August 1993; Security Council resolution 866, 22 September 1993.

References

Adibe, C. E. (1997). The Liberian conflict and the ECOWAS-UN partnership. *Third World Quarterly, 18*(3), 471–488.

Alagappa, M., & Inoguchi, T. (Eds.). (1999). *International security management and the United Nations*. Tokyo: United Nations University Press.

Annan, K. (2006). *A regional-global security partnership: Challenges and opportunities* (Report of the Secretary General. A/61/204 – S/2006/590). New York: United Nations.

Ayoob, M. (1995). *The third world security predicament: State making, regional conflict, and the international system*. Boulder: Lynne Rienner.

Berman, E. (1998). The security council's increasing reliance on burden-sharing: Collaboration or abrogation? *International Peacekeeping, 4*(1), 1–21.

Boulden, J. (Ed.). (2003). *Dealing with conflict in Africa: The United Nations and regional organizations*. London: Palgrave Macmillan.

Boutros-Ghali, B. (1995). *Report of the Secretary General: Supplement to an agenda for peace* (Document A/50/60 – S/1995/1). New York: United Nations.

Capie, D. (2008). Localization as resistance: The contested diffusion of small arms norms in Southeast Asia. *Security Dialogue, 39*(6), 637–658.

Diehl, P. F. (2003). Regional conflict management: Strategies, necessary conditions, and comparative effectiveness. In F. P. Diehl & J. Lepgold (Eds.), *Regional conflict management* (pp. 41–77). Lanham: Rowman and Littlefield.

Diehl, P. F., & Lepgold, J. (2003). *Regional conflict management*. Oxford: Rowman & Littlefield.

Goulding, M. (2003). *Peacemonger*. Washington, DC: Johns Hopkins University Press.

Graham, K., & Felício, T. (2006). *Regional security and global governance: A study of interactions between regional agencies and the UN Security Council with a proposal for a regional-global security mechanism*. Brussels: VUB Brussels University Press.

Hansen, H. E., McLaughlin, M. S., & Nemeth, S. C. (2008). IO mediation of interstate conflicts: Moving beyond the global versus regional dichotomy. *Journal of Conflict Resolution, 52*(2), 295–325.

Hettne, B., & Söderbaum, F. (2006). The UN and regional organizations in global security: Competing or complementary logics? *Global Governance, 12*, 227–232.

High Level Panel of the Audit of the African Union. (2007). *Audit of the African Union*. Addis Ababa: African Union.

International Peace Academy. (2006). *Building partnerships for crisis prevention, conflict resolution and peace-building between the United Nations and regional organizations*. New York: International Peace Academy.

Jones, D. M., & Smith, M. L. R. (2007). Making process, not progress: ASEAN and the evolving East Asian regional order. *International Security, 32*(1), 148–184.

Kelly, R. (2007). Security theory in the "new regionalism". *International Studies Review, 9*, 197–229.

Lake, D., & Morgan, P. (1997). *Regional orders: Building security in a new world*. Pennsylvania: Pennsylvania State University Press.

Martin, I. (2003). Is the regionalization of peace operations desirable? In M. Pugh & W. P. Singh Sidhu (Eds.), *The United Nations and regional security: Europe and beyond*. Boulder/London: Lynne Rienner.

Mearsheimer, J. J. (1994/1995). The false promise of international institutions. *International Security, 19*(3), 5–49.

Merlingen, M. (2008). Everything is dangerous: A critique of 'normative power Europe'. *Security Dialogue, 38*(4), 435–453.

Meyer, A. (2009). Regional peace operations in Central Africa: FOMUC's limited security contribution and new expectations on MICOPAX. *African Security, 2*(2–3), 158–174.

Murithi, T. (2009). IGAD on the ground: Comparing interventions in Sudan and Somalia. *African Security, 2*(2), 136–157.

Obi, C. (2009). ECOWAS on the ground: Comparing peacekeeping in Liberia, Sierra Leone, Guinea-Bissau and Cote D'Ivoire. *African Security, 2*(2), 119–135.

Pugh, M., & Singh Sidhu, W. P. (2003). *The United Nations and regional security*. Boulder/London: Lynne Rienner.

Tavares, R. (2009). *Regional security: The capacity of international organizations*. London/New York: Routledge.

Weiss, T. G. (Ed.). (1998). *Beyond UN subcontracting: Task-sharing with regional security arrangements and service-providing NGOs*. Basingstoke: Macmillan.

Chapter 12
From International and Regional Organisations to Global Public Policy

Jean-Marc Coicaud and Jin Zhang

It has been the tendency in recent years to see regional organisations as a way to help overcoming the limitations of international organisations in addressing the global challenges at hand, particularly in the areas of security, development and environment. In this perspective, it is thought that where international organisations are unable to deliver, regional organisations can be part of the solution. Without disregarding altogether this point of view, the authors of this chapter believe that, to a large extent, it is much more problematic than it appears. For the most part, regional organisations, as they exist today, have neither the adequate resources nor the mandates and policies to make this a possibility across the board.

That being said, it does not follow that one should give up on the idea of having the norms of international cooperation and the goods that they are meant to produce and nurture becoming more of a reality in the future. On the contrary, this leads us to suggest that reframing the nature and role of international and regional organisations, and their relations, in terms of global public policy could arguably contribute to improving the situation. To be sure, to the supporters of traditionalist conceptions of international relations, including realists, this line of thinking will seem even more of a utopia than current international and regional arrangements. Still, we believe it is worth exploring it as an option.

The end of the Cold War brought about high hopes for international organisations. This especially applied to the United Nations (UN). With the collapse of the Soviet Union and the logic of competition and confrontation associated with the East–west bipolarity, many felt that, finally, the time had come for it to play a central role. After having been relegated to a sideshow status for more than 40 years, the UN, capitalising on its unique position, was going to be more than a hardly

J.-M. Coicaud (✉)
Rutgers University, New York, USA
e-mail: jeanmarc.coicaud@rutgers.edu

J. Zhang (✉)
Formerly with UNU-ONY, New York, USA

P. De Lombaerde et al. (eds.), *The United Nations and the Regions: Third World Report on Regional Integration*, United Nations University Series on Regionalism 3,
DOI 10.1007/978-94-007-2751-9_12, © Springer Science+Business Media B.V. 2012

relevant 'talking shop'. In its own way, it was going to be one of the movers and shakers of international politics. As such, Boutros Boutros-Ghali's *Agenda for Peace*, published in the spring of 1992,[1] offered in the field of collective security a blue print for the revitalised role of the UN.

It nevertheless did not take long to realise that the situation had not changed drastically at the global level despite the fall of the Berlin Wall. By the end of the 1990s, this was illustrated by the ambiguous track record of the UN.

On the one hand, in the years immediately following the end of the Cold War, the initiatives of the UN increased to reach levels unseen before. Peacekeeping operations constitute a case in point. While between the late 1940s and the late 1980s, the UN launched 18 peace operations, during the 1990s, it established 35 operations.[2] This trend continued in the 2000s, although at a slightly lower level; by March 2009, the UN led 18 peace operations around the world, with 115,311 troops, police, military observers, international and local civilian personnel and UN volunteers on the ground.[3] In addition, in the aftermath of the Cold War, the mandates of UN peacekeeping operations grew significantly. In contrast with previous decades, in the context of which peace operations were by and large limited to the deployment of peacekeepers meant to serve as a buffer between the parties at war, UN peacekeeping operations came to address a whole range of policies. They came to encompass, before conflicts, measures designed to prevent them from happening, during conflicts, humanitarian aid and use of force while trying to establish peace and, after conflicts, the reconstruction of countries.

On the other hand, it is not as if the UN had been demonstrating much effectiveness in its increased collective security activities. For a few years into what was supposed to be its showcase period, it was accumulating more failures or mixed results than successes (Coicaud 2007a, b). The track record was particularly dismal in the Balkans and Africa. In the Balkans, and more specifically in Bosnia, in the middle of 1995, after 3 years of UN involvement to stop the war, the conflict was still underway, with no clear end in sight. As for Africa, the debacle of the UN peacekeeping operation in Somalia, in the fall of 1993, followed a few months later, in the spring of 1994, by the inability of the UN to stop the genocide in Rwanda, showed the extent of its shortcomings. This state of affairs put on full display the operational limitations of the UN and, perhaps more importantly, the unwillingness of the international community, i.e. of its key member states – and first and foremost the permanent members of the UN Security Council – to support the UN all the way.

As a matter of fact, even at the normative level, what had begun as a promising decade for the UN turned into a show of relative weakness. For example, the *Agenda for Peace* was supposed to be completed by two other agendas, one dealing with development and the other with democratisation. However, member states were unable to agree on what to do about development and democracy, and they could also not reach a consensus on what exactly these notions meant. As a result, the UN Secretary-General presented half-baked documents on these questions, half-baked documents which could not really be used as a basis for action (Boutros-Ghali 1994, 1996).

It is in this context that regional organisations came to be seen as a possible complement, if not as an alternative, to the UN and, more generally, international institutions. The role that, in subsequent years, was given to regional organisations in the Balkans and Africa is quite telling from this point of view.

In the Balkans, it is the North Atlantic Treaty Organisation (NATO) and the European Union (EU), more than the UN, which emerged as key players. Concerning Bosnia, at the Dayton peace meeting that took place in November 1995 to establish the post-war conditions and rebuild the country,[4] the UN, apart in particular from responsibilities in rebuilding local police, was given a largely formal monitoring role. The multinational military Implementation Force (IFOR), in charge of helping to ensure compliance of the military aspects of the Dayton Peace Accords, was placed under the command of NATO, with a grant of authority from the UN. As for the EU, it became the cornerstone of economic and political reconstruction (Dobbins et al. 2008: 139–172). A few years later, NATO and the EU would also be given leading roles in the management of the Kosovo crisis. Although the UN would assume a significant role there, namely through the office of the Special Representative of the UN Secretary-General and the UN Interim Administration Mission in Kosovo (UNMIK), the military force of NATO was critical in making it possible to defeat the Serbs in the spring of 1999 and maintain peace afterwards. Equally critical was the assistance of the EU to rebuild Kosovo. In the 2000s, in Afghanistan, the role of NATO and the EU, the latter being one of Afghanistan's largest donors, as part of the multinational efforts to get rid of the Taliban and stabilise the country came as a confirmation of their new global role.

In Africa, regional organisations acquired as well important responsibilities, at times not simply in complement of the work of the UN, but as a substitute to it. In this regard, it is not only the African Union and a number of other African sub-regional organisations which got a role in trying to put nations on track for peace and development.[5] It is also regional organisations out of the area, especially, once again, the EU (Dobbins et al. 2008: 25–48, 73–100, 101–138).

Nevertheless, it would be erroneous to infer, as it seems to be largely the case today, from the growing place of regional organisations that they are the answer to the limitations of the UN and of international institutions as a whole. For, without minimising their contribution, three factors, indeed, call for caution. They are the resources at hand, the mandates and the policies of regional organisations. Chapter 11 focuses on some of these factors, namely resources and mandates. We propose further analysis of these issues as they have proved crucial in the balancing of the regional/global approach to security, development and the environment.

To be sure, it is not surprising that NATO has come to be seen as a possible solution for the difficulties that the UN encounters to deliver concrete results on the ground in terms of collective security. Its resources, financial and operational (from a military, logistic and manpower standpoint) are sizable. For example, in the middle of the 2000s, it had an annual civilian budget of 167 million US dollar and a military budget of 1 billion US dollar (Dempsey 2005). In addition, the costs of NATO missions, not covered by the civilian and military budgets, are financed by the countries that send soldiers or equipment. Considering the strong political support that NATO tends to receive from its members, particularly from the United States, this is an asset. However, this commanding position of NATO is not the norm for regional organisations. It is an exceptional situation, enjoyed, whatever their field of specialisation, by very few regional organisations, the EU being one of them in the area of institutional and economic integration. That is to say that when it comes to resources, most regional organisations are walking on thin ice, so to speak. Take for instance the case of Africa, where the international community is increasingly reluctant to be seriously involved and where, consequently, the African Union (AU) is presented as a way to fill the gap. In comparison to the 2009 annual budget of 177 billion US dollar (€ 133.8 billion)[6] of the EU (European Commission 2009: 5), the approved budget of the African Union for 2009 of a little more than 164 million US dollar appears very little in order to address at the regional level the needs of the continent.[7]

Furthermore, it is not as if, in comparison to the track record of international institutions, the results of regional organisations were stellar themselves. This applies both to fragile and strong regional organisations. In this perspective, considering its overall meagre resources, one cannot be surprised by the difficulty the AU has, in the context of the AU/UN Hybrid operation in Darfur (UNAMID), to make a difference.[8] But one has also to recognise that might and money are not a guarantee of success for powerful regional organisations. The contribution of NATO in Afghanistan has not been seen as a resounding success,[9] as have not been entirely convincing either the recent involvements of the European Union beyond its own area of collective security, especially in Africa (Dobbins et al. 2008: Chap. 9).

Then there is the question of the relations between the mandates of regional and international organisations. Ideally, these mandates should be compatible (so that contradictions and competition do not undermine their respective values and goals), convergent (so that mandates go in the same direction), complement each other (so that the comparative advantages of international and regional organisations allow division of labour) and in synergy (so that the governance architecture they outline and endorse are mutually beneficial and reinforcing) – so that, as a whole, win-win situations are created, private and public goods and healthy relations among them are produced and made sustainable at the global and regional levels (Kaul et al. 2003; Estevadeordal et al. 2004). In this regard, one would think that having states being at the same time members of regional organisations and of international institutions which have a universal membership would help to harmonise the mandates and their relations and achieve these objectives.

Yet, more often than not, reality is different. Although harmonisation and consolidation of mandates is frequently the stated official approach, even though it is one to which significant importance is given, the tensions are unmistakable.

It should not come as a surprise considering that, in the end, weak or lack of coordination is not simply a systemic problem which exists between states, or between states and international organisations. It is also one at work between regional and international organisations, as well as between regional organisations and states external to the region.[10] This originates in the fact that the principal mandates of regional organisations, like member states at their level, have first and foremost the purpose of taking care of their primary customers or constituents – the states and people of the region. In this perspective, when they have to choose between their responsibilities towards their own and the ones vis-à-vis the international realm, they rarely fail to choose the former over the latter.

Nowhere more than at the policy level is this visible. Here the ambiguous attitude of the EU is a case in point. For its normative and institutional commitment to universal values of human rights, at the European level as at the global level, namely in its support of the UN, and its development, aid efforts are only one side of the story. Equally and ultimately more significant are its self-centred policies and politics – putting Europe first, even if it means for 'strangers' the de facto denial of access to the rights it claims to be universal and unconditional. As Stiglitz (2006) once facetiously indicated, thanks to European agricultural subsidies, the average European cow gets two dollars a day, a striking fact considering that two dollars per day is the international poverty line, as set by the World Bank. Hence his remarks that it appears to be better to be a cow in Europe than a poor person in a developing country (Stiglitz 2006: 85).[11]

Of course, the point is not to say that regional organisations, and states at their level, should give up on servicing their immediate customers and embrace the global realm at the expense of their constituents. The current nature of socialisation forbids it. The mechanisms of identification, representation, participation and, in general, political accountability, essentially taking place at the national level and, to some extent, at the regional level (at least for the regions were coordination if not integration are making headways), make it impossible.

Rather, the point is stressing the fact that the present organisation and relations existing between international and regional institutions, and states, are neither designed nor functioning at an optimal level. They are not conceived and implemented according to modalities dovetailing as much as possible the pursuit of private and public goods in the national, regional and international realms. More than anything else, the various layers of the current governance architecture and its institutions are all too often set as part of an either/or logic of a system of economic, social and political management based more on selective than universal inclusion. In the process, by overlooking the interest of all actors, individuals and states, it is the interest of each that tends to be minimised, if not undermined. In the end, indeed, the best way to look after the interest of each, to secure and expand it as much as possible, is to take into account the interest and right of others, to factor in the demands of justice (Coicaud 2007a, b). At any rate, this is one of the lessons taught by inclusive modern democratic policies, which, as such, have come to use public policy as a key approach to take rights seriously at the national level.

In this regard, it might be that what has worked in the national setting could be seen as a resource for the international realm. Henceforth, our suggestion is to explore the idea of global public policy in order to address the international structural challenges we face today[12] and to see if this idea could be called upon to bridge the gap existing at the international level between reality and the norms of justice and the security, development and environmental (and others) rights associated to them.

In putting forward this suggestion, we do not ignore the enormous intellectual '*chantier*'[13] to be initiated, the enormous intellectual work to be done to demonstrate the conceptual and practical possibility and viability of the idea of global public policy. We are not blind either to the political and policy dilemmas, namely generated by trying to balance the national and international interests keeping in mind the goal of making it a win-win situation for each and everyone it carries (see, for instance Coicaud 2001). Nor are we oblivious to the profound transformation that this would require in our modalities of thinking about the nature, role and interactions among institutions, about the extent and limits of moral and political communities and, ultimately, about the 'we' *versus* 'them' divide. Also, how is it that a global public policy approach, that is more ambitious in terms of coordination and integration than the global governance arrangements of today, could be more successful than them in debunking the entrenched vested interests committed to the status quo or even to going backward? How could this approach manage to capture the attention, to be taken on board and implemented by decision-makers considering that most of the time they have their eyes more on the short-term, narrow and badly understood as a result interest of their country or simply on the next election around the corner than on the big picture?[14]

Despite this statement of professed lucidity, chances are that many will see the suggestion of exploring the feasibility of global public policy as a naïve, if not a crazy one. A naïve and a crazy one … may be … but not a foolish one. Indeed, the economic, political, social, security and cultural costs of the contemporary situation are not so minimal that we could afford not being intellectually and politically bold.[15] As a matter of fact, these costs and the systemic pathologies they reveal not only make it worth exploring alternatives, they make it imperative.

More than 20 years ago, speaking before the 42nd Session of the UN General Assembly, on 21 September 1987, Ronald Reagan put forth his vision of the world's future, laying out what he characterised as his 'fantasy': 'In our obsession with antagonisms of the moment, we often forget how much unites all the members of humanity… I occasionally think how quickly our differences worldwide would vanish if we were facing an alien threat from outside this world'.[16] Well, if when it comes to the alien threat, we will have to continue to wait, the threat within is already very much upon us. With our current way of organising societies and their relations producing alarming disintegration, we are running out of time. It is urgent to revisit our modes of thinking and acting.

Notes

1. See also Boutros-Ghali (1992a, b, 1995a, b).
2. http://www.un.org/Depts/dpko/dpko/list/list.pdf
3. http://www.un.org/Depts/dpko/dpko/bnote.htm
4. The Dayton Peace Accords, or the General Framework Agreement for Peace in Bosnia and Herzegovina, was signed in December 1995.
5. On this issue, see Gandois (2009), for example, Chaps. 1, 5 and 6.
6. Based on the exchange rate of 30 April 2009.
7. Assembly of the African Union (Addis Ababa, Assembly/AU/Dec.208 (XII), 1–3 February 2009), p. 1.

8. For instance, as of 31 March 2009, almost 2 years after its establishment in July 2007, only two-thirds of the planned 26,000 AU/UN peacekeeping force had deployed in Darfur. See Lederer (2009).
9. Refer for example to Schneider (2008). Moreover, in early April 2009, on the occasion of a NATO summit meeting marking the 60th anniversary of the alliance, President Obama had difficulty convincing European NATO countries to send more troops to Afghanistan. On this, see Erlanger and Cooper (2009).
10. Needless to say, problematic coordination is also an issue at the regional level itself.
11. Panagariya (2005) notes that the average Japanese cow receives 7.50 US dollar in subsidies.
12. This suggestion builds on an intuition by Habermas (2001), under the notion of 'world domestic policy'.
13. A 'building site' in English.
14. The authors are now preparing an article on these issues.
15. The international economic crisis is the latest illustration of this state of affairs.
16. http://www.reagan.utexas.edu/archives/speeches/1987/092187b.htm

References

Boutros-Ghali, B. (1992a). *An agenda for peace: Preventive diplomacy, peacemaking, and peace-keeping.* Report to the Secretary General pursuant to the statement adopted by the Summit Meeting of the Security Council on 31 January. New York: United Nations Department of Public Information.

Boutros-Ghali, B. (1992b). *An agenda for peace* (A/47/277 - S/24111). New York: The United Nations.

Boutros-Ghali, B. (1994). *An agenda for development* (A/48/935). New York: The United Nations.

Boutros-Ghali, B. (1995a). *An agenda for peace: Supplement* (A/50/60 - S/1995/1). New York: The United Nations.

Boutros-Ghali, B. (1995b). *Supplement to an agenda for peace: Position paper of the Secretary-General on the occasion of the fiftieth anniversary of the United Nations.* New York: United Nations, http://www.un.org/Docs/SG/agpeace.html

Boutros-Ghali, B. (1996). *An agenda for democratization.* New York: United Nations.

Coicaud, J.-M. (2001). Conclusion: International organizations, the evolution of international politics, and legitimacy. In J.-M. Coicaud & V. Heiskanen (Eds.), *The legitimacy of international organizations* (pp. 519–552). Tokyo/New York/Paris: United Nations University Press.

Coicaud, J.-M. (2007a). The extent and limits of peace operations in the 1990s. In J.-M. Coicaud (Ed.), *Beyond the national interest: The future of UN peacekeeping and multilateralism in an era of U.S. Primacy* (pp. 13–34). Washington, DC: United States Institute of Peace Press.

Coicaud, J.-M. (2007b). Quest for international solidarity: Benefits of justice versus the trappings of Paranoia. In H. G. Brauch, J. Grin, C. Mesjasz, P. Dunay, N. C. Behera, B. Chourou, U. O. Spring, P. H. Liotta, & P. Kameri-Mbote (Eds.), *Globalisation and environmental challenges: Reconceptualising security in the 21st century.* Berlin/Heidelberg/New York/Hong Kong/London/Milan/Paris/Tokyo: Springer.

Dempsey, J. (2005, April 18). Budget Cuts Worry NATO General. *International Herald Tribune*, Paris.

Dobbins, J., Jones, S. G., Crane, K., Chivvis, C. S., Raddin, A., Larrabee, F. S., Bensahel, N., Stearns, B. K., & Goldsmith, B. W. (2008). *Europe's role in nation-building: From the Balkans to the Congo.* Santa Monica: Rand Corporation.

Erlanger, S., & Cooper, H. (2009, April 5). Europeans offer few new troops for Afghanistan. *The New York Times,* New York.

Estevadeordal, A., Frantz, B., & Nguyen, T. B. (Eds.). (2004). *Regional public goods: From theory to practice.* Washington, DC: Inter-American Development Bank and Asian Development Bank.

European Commission (2009). *General Budget of the European Union for the Financial Year 2009*. Luxembourg: European Commission.

Gandois, G. (2009). *The Emergence of Regional Security Organizations in Africa. A Comparative Perspective of ECOWAS (Economic Community of West African States) and SADC (Southern African Development Community), PhD thesis*. Oxford: Oxford University.

Habermas, J. (2001). *The Postnational Constellation: Political Essays*, Cambridge, MA: The MIT Press.

Kaul, I., Conceição, P., Le Goulven, K., & Mendoza, R. U. (Eds.). (2003). *Providing global public goods: Managing globalization*. Oxford: Oxford University Press.

Lederer, E.M. (2009). UN Chief Says Over 1 Million at Risk in Darfur, *The Washington Post*, April 21.

Panagariya, A. (2005). Agricultural Liberalization and the Least Developed Countries: Six Fallacies. *The World Economy*, 28(9).

Schneider, M. L. (2008). *Strategic chaos and Taliban resurgence in Afghanistan*. International Crisis Group, April 2, http://www.crisisgroup.org/home/index.cfm?id=5370&l=1

Stiglitz, J. E. (2006). *Making globalization work*. New York: Norton & Norton.

Chapter 13
Hybrid Missions: A Promising Model Resolving the Global-Regional Debate

Vesselin Popovski and Annette Fath-Lihic

13.1 Introduction

There has always been a dilemma whether the United Nations (UN) or regional organisations are better suited to preserve peace and help former parties to reconcile after conflicts. The demand for legitimacy, efficiency and impartiality has driven the preference towards the UN – a global organisation with a strong 60 years record of peacekeeping. Regional organisations have been seen as less equipped but also as probably less unbiased when it comes to peacekeeping. However, the UN peace operations have also incurred shortages, and some recent failures – Darfur and the Democratic Republic of the Congo among the others – re-activated the debates how to engage regional organisations closely.

These debates have been far from being only academic; they concern large populations at risk. An emerging occurrence of hybrid missions – where UN peacekeepers operate in parallel with regional organisations under an agreed framework – may suggest a possible workable model. There were some best (or rather good) practices already, but the opportunity of hybrid missions is still to be explored. This chapter will offer some initial framework of understanding and assessing the current hybrid missions.

Recent figures suggest that there are more than 110,000 military, police and civilian personnel at present deployed as part of 19 existing UN peace operations directed and supported by the Department of Peacekeeping Operations (DPKO) (United Nations Department of Public Information 2008). The indicators are that there will be even a greater demand to deploy and sustain more UN peacekeepers.

V. Popovski (✉)
United Nations University-ISP, Tokyo, Japan
e-mail: popovski@unu.edu

A. Fath-Lihic
International IDEA, Stockholm, Sweden

P. De Lombaerde et al. (eds.), *The United Nations and the Regions: Third World Report on Regional Integration*, United Nations University Series on Regionalism 3,
DOI 10.1007/978-94-007-2751-9_13, © Springer Science+Business Media B.V. 2012

The role of the UN peacekeeping missions in conflict management and in the transition from conflict to peace will remain crucial.

However, the UN peace operations' performance in some recent missions has made the world organisation subject to severe criticisms, based on the fact that UN peacekeeping deployments are marked by a lack of flexibility and limited rapidity. The approval of mandates is also often delayed, and a consensus in the UN Security Council on sensitive questions of peace enforcement and intervention can rarely be reached. Furthermore, troop contributions of developed states to UN peacekeeping missions, especially in Africa, have declined in recent years, while a rapid growth in the contributions of troops by developed states has taken place.[1]

In response to these criticisms, new thinking about peacekeeping has evolved, and concept and practice of UN peacekeeping have undergone substantial changes. While traditionally UN peacekeeping deployments generally operated under the principles of impartial, non-forcible intervention with the consent of the conflict parties and the precondition of an agreed peace, more recent peacekeeping missions have increasingly been undertaken in the context of internal wars.

13.2 External Actors

The challenges posed by different types of conflicts – internal and interstate wars – and uncertain bases of intervention must be considered in the context of a more complex, diverse cast of players on the international stage from that which existed at the birth of the UN's mandate. The UN shares more and more of the burden of peacekeeping missions with non-UN components. The increased involvement of various external actors in hybrid peacekeeping missions constitutes a trend that started in the 1990s with different variants.[2] This cooperation may involve hybrid peacekeeping missions in collaboration with the North Atlantic Treaty Organisation (NATO), the Organisation for Security and Cooperation in Europe (OSCE), the European Union (EU), the African Union (AU), the Economic Community of West African States (ECOWAS), the Organisation of American States (OAS), the Commonwealth of Independent States (CIS) and individual states. No two of the peacekeeping missions have been identical (Brahimi 2006).[3]

There is an obvious necessity for partnership between the UN and external actors in their response to international peace and security threats. The growing number of regional organisations, the engagement of multinational forces and the involvement of individual states on the international stage result in wider participation and increase the use of and need for hybrid peacekeeping missions.

13.3 Definition

Hybrid peacekeeping missions can be defined as missions where the UN and a non-UN component share the responsibility of peacekeeping under an agreed framework. Each type of hybrid peacekeeping mission can be differentiated according to the nature of the non-UN component, which consists of either regional organisations, multinational forces or individual states. In terms of a formal relationship, hybrid peacekeeping operations vary among the sponsoring operations, including integrated, coordinated, parallel and sequential operations, or by the functional features of the mission, which themselves can be divided into short-term military support, civilian-military division of labour, linked peacekeeping-observer operations, handover operations and actual integrated operations (Jones and Feryal 2004: 17).

13.4 Examples

13.4.1 UNAMID

One example of a hybrid peacekeeping mission is the UN-African Union (AU) peacekeeping force in Darfur (UNAMID), which can be considered an integrated mission rather than coordinated. It is a specific example of an organisation that has enjoyed greater legitimacy from the host than a normal UN mission.

On 31 July 2007, the UN Security Council unanimously approved the deployment of a joint AU-UN operation to Darfur. With some 26,000 military and police personnel, it will be the largest UN operation since the interventions in Yugoslavia and Somalia in the 1990s, and the most expensive.[4] The new force, replacing an AU mission of 7,000, is mandated to 'support early and effective implementation of the Darfur Peace Agreement, prevent the disruption of its implementation and armed attacks, and protect civilians'.

The resolution authorising UNAMID calls for a single chain of command, provided by the UN, but with dual selection and reporting procedures between both organisations. This is a novel arrangement, the first ever true hybrid mission between the two organisations, posing potential for disagreements and confusion in the field. There has also been disagreement over the make-up of the force's 26,000 uniformed personnel, with Khartoum insisting on an 'African' force. The UN must remain adamant that troops be selected based on operational requirements, not purely political calculations. However, it should be noted that despite the authorisation of UNAMID, the government in Khartoum has continued its bombing raids on South Darfur villages and militia attacks are ongoing, making the task ahead for this experiment in hybrid missions a daunting one (St. Pierre and Smith 2007).

13.4.2 EULEX

Another example of a UN hybrid peacekeeping mission is the newly established European Union Rule of Law Mission (EULEX) in Kosovo, which was post-facto brought into a UN Charter framework.[5]

Kosovo declared independence in February 2008, following 9 years of administration by the UN Mission in Kosovo (UNMIK), which governed the province after Serbian forces were compelled to leave following a NATO bombing campaign.

Kosovo's population is 90% Albanian, and the remaining 120,000 Kosovo Serbs have refused to cooperate with Kosovo Albanian-run institutions.

Also in February 2008, the EU agreed to send a Rule of Law mission, known as EULEX, to Kosovo to take over from UNMIK and oversee the police, judiciary and customs, but its deployment was delayed due to tense political negotiations and objections from Serbia and later Kosovo.

UN Secretary-General Ban Ki-Moon convinced Serbia to accept the new mission, which they perceived as a violation of their territorial integrity, by presenting the 'six-point plan' whereby police, customs officers and judges in Serb-run areas of Kosovo would remain under the UN umbrella, while their Albanian counterparts would work with EULEX.

Kosovo, even though it had pledged to cooperate with EULEX, said the plan violated its constitution and would result in a de facto partition of the fledgling state.

The eventual Security Council statement evaded this problem by failing to mention the six-point plan, despite earlier pressure from Russia.

Today it is unclear how EULEX will operate, and the takeover of UN functions remains to be negotiated. However, in the fulfilment of its mandate, the EULEX Kosovo mission will fully respect Resolution 1244 (United Nations Security Council 1999) and will operate under the overall authority and in the status neutral framework of the UN. The EU's lack of commonality and cohesiveness in both capability structure and decision-making is the EU's greatest challenge in crises management (Eide 2006: 46).

13.5 Advantages

The increasing use of hybrid peacekeeping missions raises political and legal questions as well as managerial and operational challenges. Hybrid missions have advantages and disadvantages.

The potential advantages of hybrid peacekeeping operations are reasonably clear in deductive terms. As more external actors acquire deployment capacity, more options are made available to respond quickly and efficiently to the complex nature of differing conflicts. This allows for more expertise and know how when choosing the most suitable mechanism for a particular situation. Hybrid peacekeeping operations are believed to be more robust and capable than pure UN missions, especially because the external actors have showed more willingness to undertake deployments under Chapter VII (Durch and Berckman 2007). Hybrid missions can alleviate the UN's peacekeeping responsibility by dividing the human and financial contribution between the UN and the non-UN component or by assigning the latter with the entire mandate (St. Pierre 2007: 23). The availability of personnel, funding and equipment are also important factors. External actors are more likely to provide resources since their political, security and economic interests are often directly engaged.

General hybrid peacekeeping missions allow for more flexible responses to a conflict resulting from their regional and local capacity. However, external actors have distinct roles and identities, and varying organisational capacities. Therefore, it is necessary to clarify the exact role of non-UN components, especially regional organisations, in hybrid peacekeeping missions. This is essential due to the implications that their involvement has for UN peacekeeping both at the administrative and field levels.

13.6 Disadvantages

In turn, it also has to be said that the potential disadvantages of hybrid peacekeeping missions include the fact that a regional actor's interest is directly engaged in a local conflict, thus complicating operations in which the organisation plays a facilitating role. Particular states in the region might have taken sides in the conflict in question, which might be tightly tied to wider regional competition for power. Moreover, the distribution of power in specific regions is often asymmetrical, and regionally dominant states often treat regional organisations as instruments of regional hegemony. Impartiality, frequently deemed necessary in peacekeeping, is more difficult to achieve in a hybrid peacekeeping mission than in a purely UN operation.

Therefore, a number of principles should guide hybrid peacekeeping missions in the future so that the UN is able to gather and sustain the necessary political support for its primary task to maintain international peace and security.

Given the trend towards Hybrid Operations, it is crucial to mention that these operations should adopt the concepts, principles and practices of the UN. The UN will lose credibility if it compromises its core values. The challenge for the UN is to ensure the necessary leadership and make its future peace operation efforts both more effective and legitimate.

The characterisation of the advantages and disadvantages of the use of external actors leads to the expectation that hybrid peacekeeping mission may be less impartial, more forceful, driven more by self-interest and less reflective of the constraints imposed by international norms related to intervention and consent, legitimacy, the use of force and humanitarian action. The UN, and in particular DPKO and the Secretariat, still has limited capacity to manage the hybrid nature of peacekeeping missions with their growing civilian component.

As a result, hybrid peacekeeping missions will remain for now inconsistent and on an ad hoc basis driven by interests of multiplier components. Considering the strengths and added value that non-UN components bring to UN missions, it is most likely that participation of different actors will continue in future. Still, the contributions of external actors are expected to remain modest in size and financial support but will nevertheless serve to enhance UN peacekeeping missions positively.[6]

13.7 Conclusion

The international community has yet to realise the full potential of – or issues with – hybrid peacekeeping missions.

A wider international participation in UN missions is necessary for reasons not only of legitimacy but also of capacity and solidarity.

Therefore, it is important that more efforts are committed to strengthening regional and local peacekeeping capacities. As a first step, the UN has to effectively mobilise and utilise local and international resources for peacekeeping operations under its auspices.

Apart from this process, the relationship between the UN and non-UN components should be more formalised. There is still confusion about the exact nature of hybrid peacekeeping missions. The best approach may be through a combination of established modalities for partnership with the UN and case-by-case analysis. However, the challenge of institutionalising hybrid missions in order to ensure flexible responses to conflicts remains great. It requires creative practical solutions and the continuous support and willingness of external actors to get involved in peacekeeping missions. The UN remains the only body capable of combining political, military and humanitarian functions in order to reduce, and even eliminate, the misery of conflict.

Notes

1. 'It should be noted that if we highlight UN-authorised operations, Western troop contributions to these operations more than outweigh the decline in contributions to UN-commanded operations – suggesting that responsibility for skewed regional patterns of troop deployments lies primarily with the Security Council, especially the permanent members, rather than with a broader set of developed state troop contributors.' Jones and Feryal (2004: 7)
2. The potential role of external actors was underscored by the 2004 Report of the Secretary-General's High Level Panel on Threats, Challenges and Change and the Secretary-General's 2005 report In Larger Freedom. The first report called for a greater reliance on Chapter VIII of the UN Charter, which refers to operations authorised by the Security Council but led by other actors, such as regional organisations. In Larger Freedom suggested the establishment of formal agreements between the UN and regional organisations in order to work together in predictable and reliable partnerships (United Nations 2004; 2005).
3. The report recommends that forces must only be deployed if and when they have been given realistic and achievable mandates and only when it is clear that they will be provided with the resources necessary to achieve those mandate objectives.
4. Costs for the first year alone are expected to exceed 2 billion US dollars, a full third of the UN's 2006–2007 peacekeeping budget.
5. The European Union (EU) has conducted 16 missions under the European Security and Defence Policy (ESDP) deploying military, police and civilians to the Balkans, Africa, Southeast Asia and the Middle East. Some of the missions were conducted in close cooperation with the UN.
6. Western states continue to avoid greater engagement in UN peacekeeping operations, both financially and in terms of military, police and civilian personnel. The 'Hybridisation' of UN peacekeeping operations does not free Western states from their obligations towards the UN.

References

Brahimi, L. (2006). UN peace operations in the 21st century. A few personal thoughts. In H. Ojanen (Ed.), *Peacekeeping – Peacebuilding. Preparing for the future* (pp. 13–20), http://www.fiia.fi/fi/publication/27/peacekeeping_-_peacebuilding/

Durch, W., & Berckman, T. C. (2007). Définition et délimitation des opérations de paix. In J. Coulon (Ed.), *Guide du maintien de la paix* (pp. 17–47). Quebec: CEPES.

Eide, E. B. (2006). From peacekeeping to peacebuilding. In H. Ojanen (Ed.), *Peacekeeping – Peacebuilding. Preparing for the future* (pp. 13–20), http://www.fiia.fi/fi/publication/27/peacekeeping_-_peacebuilding/

Jones, B., & Feryal, C. (2004). *Evolving models of peacekeeping, policy implications and responses. Report prepared for the United Nations Department of Peacekeeping operations.* New York: Peacekeeping Best Practices Unit.

St. Pierre, K. (2007). Hybridizing UN-Peace operations. The role of the European Union and Canada. *Review of European and Russian Affairs, 3*(2/2007), 21–37.

St. Pierre, K., & Smith, J. G. (2007). *Finally... a UN mission in Darfur. The first step in a long, difficult journey.* http://www.stimson.org/spotlight/finallya-un-mission-in-darfur-the-first-step-in-a-long-difficult-journey/

United Nations. (2004). *A more secure world: Our shared responsibility. Report of the Secretary General's high-level panel on threats, challenges and change* (A/59/565). http://www.un.org/secureworld/report2.pdf

United Nations. (2005). *In larger freedom: Towards development, security and human rights for all. Report of the Secretary General* (A/59/2005). http://www.un.org.largerfreedom/

United Nations Department of Public Information. (2008, October). *United Nations peacekeeping operations. Background note of 30 September 2008* (DPI/1634/Rev. 88).

United Nations Security Council. (1999). *Resolution 1244* (S/RES/1244), http://www.unmikonline.org/misc/N9917289.pdf

Chapter 14
ASEAN, the United Nations and the Security of Southeast Asia: Problems, Prospects and Paradox

See Seng Tan

14.1 Introduction

This chapter assesses the relationship between the Association of Southeast Asian Nations (ASEAN) and the United Nations (UN) with respect to the peace and security of Southeast Asia. By and large cooperative in orientation, their partnership in conflict management is nonetheless defined by a paradox.

On the one hand, ASEAN's 'minimalist' brand of regionalism, with its soft or weak institutionalism, has invited criticisms regarding the organisation's perceived inefficacy in conflict management. Particularly, trenchant charges have been issued at ASEAN for its inability and/or unwillingness to intervene in political crises in East Timor in 2006 and Myanmar in 2007. But where the Association is concerned, its longstanding adherence to the principle of non-interference – whether in terms of relations between outside powers and ASEAN countries, or relations between ASEAN members – constitutes a key basis of ASEAN's regional diplomacy. This ostensibly precludes any form of interventionism by the Association, unless it 'invites' extra-regional actors to participate or it is 'invited' by the member country in question to intervene.

On the other hand, where instances of intervention have in fact taken place, ASEAN – or ASEAN countries participating in UN-sanctioned or supported missions and/or 'coalitions of the willing' – have on occasion demonstrated a willingness to temporarily contravene the Association's non-interference doctrine. Indeed, a recent study has gone further to argue interference by ASEAN countries in one another's domestic affairs as more commonplace than previous thought (Jones 2010). Against this backdrop, what are the problems and prospects of ASEAN-UN collaboration in

S.S. Tan (✉)
Rajaratnam School of International Studies, Nanyang Technological University, Singapore, Singapore
e-mail: issstan@ntu.edu.sg

P. De Lombaerde et al. (eds.), *The United Nations and the Regions: Third World Report on Regional Integration*, United Nations University Series on Regionalism 3, DOI 10.1007/978-94-007-2751-9_14,

regional security management, particularly in a contemporary era where new global norms, such as the 'responsibility to protect' and human rights, are on the rise?

The UN has long acknowledged the relevance of regional organisations in the management of international security. Indeed, the idea that regionalism and international security are interrelated predates the UN. For example, the Covenant of the League of Nations, in its Article 21, notes the validity of regional understandings for the establishment and maintenance of international peace and security. Chapter VIII of the UN Charter refers to the importance of regional arrangements or agencies for international peace and security insofar as regional actions adopted are appropriate and consistent with the purposes and principles of the UN.

In the UN Secretary-General's report *An Agenda for Peace* published in 1992, it was recognised that the security efforts of regional organisations, when pursued in creative and flexible ways that complement those of the UN, could foster lasting and positive impacts on their respective regions. These cooperative arrangements 'could not only lighten the burden of the [UN Security] Council but also contribute to a deeper sense of participation, consensus and democratisation in international affairs'.[1] Indeed, regional organisations were regarded by Boutros Boutros-Ghali as crucial to his vision of a global preventive diplomacy regime. In a key respect, that vision has been partially realised through the establishment within many if not most regional institutions of high councils, special envoys, observer and fact-finding missions and other instruments of preventive diplomacy. In this respect, efforts to ensure Southeast Asia's security have long been understood in terms of the maintenance of an intricate balance between global forces and regional conditions (Buzan 2003).

How does ASEAN measure against that vision, and what are the problems, prospects and paradox of ASEAN-UN collaboration with respect to the peace and security of the Southeast Asian region? In that respect, I make the following three arguments. First, as a regional security institution, ASEAN, despite its lofty declarations, is at best designed for a minimalist brand of regionalism. Second, notwithstanding the Association's institutional incapacity and apparent lack of political will to overhaul its longstanding conventions, ASEAN's best, though limited, efforts at conflict management and institutional reform have arguably occurred when it contravened its non-interference policy and actively intervened in the internal affairs of its member states. To that end, prominent individuals and groups in various Southeast Asian quarters have called for a fundamental rethinking of the so-called ASEAN Way, a rudimentary code of conduct based on flexible consensus, consultation, informality and sovereignty principles that has guided regional relations for four decades. In particular, appeals for the Association's members to go 'beyond the ASEAN Way' (as the title of a recent study has it) (Caballero-Anthony 2005) have focused on the norm of non-interference.[2] Moreover, institutional developments, such as the introduction in November 2007 of a legal charter and continued efforts at building a regional community in Southeast Asia with three pillars – economic, political security and sociocultural – by 2015, have raised hopes for the foreseeable emergence of a more robust regionalism therein. However, the jury is still out on whether such a transition from a 'soft' to a 'hard' regionalism, as it were, would effectively occur.

Third, to the extent that ASEAN and its member states have engaged in interventionism – the third Indochina conflict, the peace missions in Cambodia, the UN Transitional Authority in Cambodia (UNTAC) and, in East Timor, the UN Transitional Administration in East Timor (UNTAET) – they have done so, if not directly under the rubric of the UN, then certainly and only with the broad support of the wider international community. This stance is unlikely to change for the foreseeable future. But for a region that has long insisted (at least Indonesia has) on 'regional solutions for regional problems' and the importance of regional autonomy (Sukma 2004), reliance on extra-regional actors offers yet another paradox that could complicate collaborative efforts in regional conflict management.

14.2 The ASEAN Way of Regionalism

By most accounts, regionalism in Southeast Asia today has advanced considerably since ASEAN was formed in August 1967. Despite an institutional mandate of regional economic cooperation, the formative years of the Association were largely marked by a relative weak track record in intra-ASEAN economic cooperation. Nonetheless, this did not mean the original ASEAN-5 (Indonesia, Malaysia, the Philippines, Singapore and Thailand) were therefore languishing in their development; after all, the 1980s came to be known as the 'decade of development' in reference to the economic dynamism of East Asia, not least that of the ASEAN-5 economies and Brunei.[3]

However, much of ASEAN's development and prosperity had considerably less to do with intra-ASEAN economic cooperation than the proliferation of extra-regional trade links especially with the West and Japan, the politics of the Cold War (which, in economic terms, favoured the ASEAN region) and the like. To the extent ASEAN cooperation mattered at all, it came, ironically, in the area of regional security. Confronted with the prospect of communist subversion from within and invasion from without (Vietnam), ASEAN, a creature of the Cold War, chose neither the path of alliance, on one hand, nor the path of autonomy and non-alignment, on the other. Instead, the Association opted for a *via media* of sorts: a regional organisation that engaged in the rhetoric of autonomy and neutrality – leading to treaties such as the Zone of Peace, Freedom and Neutrality (ZOPFAN) and the Southeast Asian Nuclear Weapons Free Zone (SEANWFZ) – while maintaining a security dependence on great and middle powers – America for all the ASEAN states but especially the Philippines and Thailand; Britain and the Five Power Defence Arrangements (FPDA) for Malaysia and Singapore (Acharya 1992).

The seeming lack of overall strategic coherence within ASEAN, as evidenced by the diverse (and even divergent) security outlooks and strategies among its member countries, is rendered possible by the ASEAN Way, which essentially permits ASEAN states to pursue their own development and security policies without interference for the most part from one another.[4] In this respect, a code of conduct that requires minimal obligations of members to their organisation has worked relatively well so long as everyone, especially regional heavyweights like Indonesia, play by the rules. On the other hand, those who argue the prospect of order and community in Southeast Asia highlight the rise in interstate cooperation, economic integration of the region and an emerging sense of regional identity as indicators of Southeast Asia's evolution from a region of revolt to a region in community, if only embryonic (Osborne 1970; Acharya 2001). They do not disregard the role of the USA in Southeast Asia, but they argue that realist colleagues have overstated the American contribution to regional security at the expense of ASEAN's relatively successful brand of regional diplomacy (Acharya and Tan 2006).

It is rather telling that at least till the end of the Cold War, ASEAN's greatest success as a regional organisation had to do with a single issue, namely, its diplomatic resistance to and mobilisation of international pressure against Vietnam's invasion and occupation of Cambodia in the Third Indochina War.[5] And while Vietnam and the other new ASEAN members (Laos, Cambodia and Myanmar) have since the mid-1990s joined the Association – an enlargement that has not been without difficulties, including establishing a two-tiered membership (Than and Gates 2001) – the Association's longstanding concern over extra-regional influences has not abated, not least in the light of the rise of China, India, as well as Japan as Asia's powers. Here too, the ASEAN Way plays a crucial function, to the extent extra-regional powers accept and abide by it. In this regard, ASEAN has sought to extend its code of conduct in principally two ways: first, through institutionalising regional relations with the great powers by way of pan-Asia institutions such as the ASEAN Regional Forum and two, through securing the declaratory commitment of external powers to the ASEAN Treaty of Amity and Cooperation (Leifer 1996a, b). Hence, both intra-regionally and extra-regionally, the ASEAN Way of regionalism has perceptibly contributed to the security and stability of Southeast Asia, even as pressures to move ASEAN beyond its longstanding *modus operandi* have of late risen.

14.3 Beyond the ASEAN Way

Despite its apparent utility, facets of the ASEAN Way have come under challenge in ways both subtle and direct. Much has been made of ASEAN's diplomatic success during the Third Indochina Conflict as vindication of the viability of the ASEAN Way. That said, the Association's conduct at that time could paradoxically be understood as a contravention of its own non-interference policy, particularly with respect to its political-military interventionism against Vietnam and Pol Pot's Cambodia. While it could be argued that those Indochina states were not part of ASEAN till the mid-1990s – indeed, Vietnam was a strategic foe throughout the 1980s – the Association's key treaties and documents make clear that non-interference also includes the extra-regional dimension.

In the post–Cold War period, a fair bit of this had to do with attempts on the Association's part to deal with some of the problems that came with membership enlargement in the 1990s, as well as growing complexity in relations among the original ASEAN members due to the vagaries of globalisation that, at times, fostered the impression, to borrow another's phrase, of 'sovereignty under siege' (Beeson 2003). Take for example the following instances. In the wake of the 1997 political crisis in Cambodia and a decade-long attempt to engage the State Law and Order Restoration Council (SLORC) regime in Myanmar, then Deputy Prime Minister of Malaysia Anwar Ibrahim called for ASEAN to play a more proactive role in crisis management. Using terms like 'constructive intervention' and 'constructive involvement', Anwar envisaged a host of interventionist measures aimed at electoral, administrative and legal reforms that would prevent simmering problems from becoming full-blown crises (Capie and Evans 2002: 92) – in other words, modalities of preventive diplomacy endorsed by the UN and, increasingly, adopted by regional organisations such as the European Union and the African Union. Following the 1997 financial crisis and regional haze problem that plagued the southern parts of archipelagic Southeast Asia, Foreign Minister of the Philippines Domingo Siazon Jr. called for ASEAN to reconsider its non-interference principle, while in 1998, Foreign Minister of Thailand Surin Pitsuwan advanced his 'flexible engagement' concept, which stressed public commentary and discussion of domestic policies of ASEAN states that would adversely affect their fellow members (Narine 2002: 168). A final example is the call by political analyst Rizal Sukma, author of a widely cited paper that partially became the basis of the Association's plan to establish the ASEAN Security Community by 2020. Among the many ambitious proposals Sukma recommended, he argued that it is 'important that ASEAN develops the capacity to undertake a peacekeeping role in internal conflict, provided such a role is based on the consent by state concerned' (Sukma 2003).

Significantly, these calls were either moderated – in the case of constructive intervention – or roundly rebuffed by others on various counts – in the case of flexible engagement – principally out of concern that the non-interference principle would be undermined should such calls be heeded.[6] In Anwar's case, he took pains to insist that constructive intervention did not contravene the non-interference norm, whereas in Surin's case, his initial enthusiasm for his idea was such that he believed it was 'time that ASEAN's cherished principle of non-intervention is modified to allow ASEAN to play a constructive role in preventing or resolving domestic issues with regional implications'.[7] As a compromise, extant and anticipated engagement among ASEAN states was subsequently downgraded to 'enhanced interaction', a less controversial quiet diplomacy that fell short of the open forums Surin had appealed for (Haacke 2003; Kraft 2000). Likewise, Sukma's call for an ASEAN peacekeeping force to deal with serious regional crises and conflicts, although significantly qualified as justifiable only on the basis of local consent, was however viewed with considerable caution on the part of Singapore and Thailand.[8] On the other hand, others note that elements of preventive diplomacy have played and continue to play a part in the management of intramural disputes between ASEAN member states (Emmers and Tan 2011).

Self-regulated efforts to modify the ASEAN Way have taken on a collective orientation in recent times in response to perceived challenges to Southeast Asia brought about by the rise of China and India. As noted, the Association formulated and has begun implementing its plan for an 'ASEAN Community' by 2015. In July 2008, ASEAN reportedly took a step closer to establishing itself as a UN-like legal body, following the collective decision to appoint permanent representatives to be based in Jakarta (Koh 2008a). This move came shortly after ASEAN's historic creation of a charter that was unveiled in November 2007. But whether the 'new' ASEAN, adorned with a legal personality and aspiration to become a regional community, can contribute meaningfully to the peace and security of Southeast Asia is still unclear, as the extant policy debate suggests (e.g. see Desker 2008 and Koh 2008b). ASEAN's apparent failure to persuade the junta in Naypidaw against the latter's brutal crackdown on pro-democracy protests in September 2007 and obdurate refusal to accept international humanitarian assistance following the devastation wrought by Cyclone Nargis upon Myanmar was, for some, patent proof of ASEAN's irrelevance to regional security (Guo 2008: 12–14; Katanyuu 2006; Ramcharan 2000). Subsequent assessments in the wake of the junta's acceptance of ASEAN as a conduit for the transmission of foreign aid to Myanmar were considerably kinder towards the Association (Baldwin 2009). As a non-contractual institutional form – particularly so where ASEAN political-security cooperation is concerned – ASEAN's brand of minimalist regionalism has essentially limited what the Association can accomplish in terms of conflict management. Conceding that the Association simply lacks the capacity to induce political change in Myanmar by itself, Singapore's Foreign Minister George Yeo reportedly noted: 'We in ASEAN don't have the heft' (cited in Weitz 2008). But more debatable is the direction taken by drafters of the charter to institutionalise and legalise the ASEAN Way, thereby potentially rendering it more difficult for interventionism within the region to take place.

Finally, it is worth noting that all the ASEAN states adopted the 'responsibility to protect' (R2P) doctrine at the UN World Summit of 2005. Theirs were declaratory commitments at best; their reactions to UN Security Council (UNSC) Resolution 1674, which reaffirmed the R2P and endorsed the use of appropriate measures where necessary to ensure its implementation, were considerably more lukewarm. Clearly, the Association is not about to abandon its non-interference principle. But what this arguably implies, however, is an embryonic openness among some ASEAN governments to the idea of sovereignty as including the element of responsibility towards their fellow Southeast Asian societies. The establishment of the ASEAN Defence Ministers' Meeting (ADMM) in 2006 and that of the ADMM+8 (comprising the ASEAN-10 and eight ASEAN dialogue partner countries) in 2010 reflects the region's growing concerns over the threat posed by transnational challenges – financial crises, viral epidemics, natural disasters, climate change, maritime-based concerns and so forth – and the need to better prepare and equip ASEAN states to respond effectively to such. Principally characterised as a regional enterprise in 'capacity building' and practical security cooperation, the likelihood that the ADMM and ADMM+8 processes could end up altering the way ASEAN does business cannot be discounted. But for change to come at all, it would likely happen in an incremental way.

14.4 Conclusions

To the extent that ASEAN and its member states have engaged at all in interventionism – for example, the Third Indochina Conflict, the UNTAC mission in Cambodia and UNTAET mission in East Timor, facilitating the efforts by UN envoys Razali Ismail and Ibrahim Gambari to engage Myanmar – they have done so, if not directly under the rubric of the UN, then certainly and only with the broad support of the wider international community. This too is in a sense paradoxical given ASEAN's longstanding concern with extra-regional interference in Southeast Asian affairs. Regarding humanitarian emergencies and disaster relief, the ready response by ASEAN countries, say, on behalf of their stricken neighbours during the Boxing Day 2004 tsunamis imply that ASEAN states can and do act in non-conflict situations without the UN's joint participation. However, where disaster relief for politically sensitive areas are concerned, not least Myanmar during Cyclone Nargis, UN involvement has proved necessary. One of the latest efforts includes the formation of the ASEAN-UN-Myanmar Tripartite Core Group Emergency Rapid Assessment Team (ERAT), which would enable quick systematic assessments of disaster situations in remote delta areas.[9]

Despite regional circumspection over prospects for extra-regional interventionism, the perceived need among regional governments for ASEAN-UN collaboration to manage conflict situations in Southeast Asia is unlikely to change for the foreseeable future. Recent bilateral tensions, such as the Cambodian-Thai border dispute over the area surrounding the eleventh-century Preah Vihear Temple, are a stark reminder of ASEAN's constraints in conflict prevention and management. So long as ASEAN regionalism remains minimalist and the ASEAN Way stays in place, notwithstanding attempts towards institutional change, it is unlikely that more ambitious efforts at ASEAN-UN cooperation would develop, much less succeed.

Notes

1. See Section VII, No. 64 of the *An Agenda for Peace: Preventive Diplomacy, Peacemaking and Peacekeeping*, Report of the Secretary-General pursuant to the statement adopted by the Summit Meeting of the Security Council on January 31, 1992 (A/47/277 - S/24111, 17 June 1992), http://www.un.org/Docs/SG/agpeace.html
2. For a discussion on this, see Katsumata (2003).
3. See, for example, the collection of essays in Morley (1999).
4. See, for example, Leifer (1989) and Emmers (2003).
5. Richard Stubbs (1988) refers to that success as making even more glaring the fact that ASEAN, at twenty years old, constituted little more than a 'single issue organisation'.
6. See, for example, ASEAN founding father denounces 'flexible engagement, Asian Political News, 20 July 1998. http://findarticles.com/p/articles/mi_m0WDQ/is_1998_July_20/ai_50189443
7. Speech at Thammasat University, 12 June 1998, cited in Funston (2000: 18)

8. 'ASEAN looks closer into security cooperation', Asian Political News, 9 March 2004, http://findarticles.com/p/articles/mi_m0WDQ/is_2004_March_9/ai_114410626
9. 'Secretary-General of ASEAN Dr. Surin Pitsuwan: ASEAN-UN to Deploy 200 Assessment Team Members to Irrawaddy Delta', Yangon, 4 June 2008, http://www.aseansec.org/21613.htm

References

Acharya, A. (1992). Regional military-security cooperation in the Third World: A conceptual analysis of the Association of Southeast Asian Nations. *Journal of Peace Research, 29*(1), 7–21.

Acharya, A. (2001). *Constructing a Security Community in Southeast Asia: ASEAN and the Problem of Regional Order*. London and New York: Routledge.

Acharya, A., & Tan, S. S. (2006). Betwixt balance and community: America, ASEAN, and the security of southeast Asia. *International Relations of the Asia-Pacific, 6*(1), 37–59.

Baldwin, K. (2009). ASEAN finds new purpose with Cyclone Nargis Response. *AlertNet*, May 1. http://www.alertnet.org/db/an_art/55076/2009/04/1–125433–1.htm

Beeson, M. (2003). Sovereignty under siege: Globalisation and the state in southeast Asia. *Third World Quarterly, 24*(2), 357–374.

Buzan, B. (2003). Security architecture in Asia: The interplay of regional and global levels. *The Pacific Review, 16*(2), 143–173.

Caballero-Anthony, M. (2005). *Regional security in southeast Asia: Beyond the ASEAN way*. Singapore: Institute of Southeast Asian Studies.

Capie, D., & Evans, P. (2002). *The Asia-Pacific security lexicon*. Singapore: Institute of Southeast Asian Studies.

Desker, B. (2008, July 18). Is the ASEAN charter necessary? *The Straits Times*, Singapore.

Emmers, R. (2003). *Cooperative security and the balance of power in ASEAN and the ARF*. London: Routledge.

Emmers, R., & Tan, S. S. (2011). The ASEAN regional forum and preventive diplomacy: Built to fail? *Asian Security, 7*(1), 44–60.

Funston, J. (2000). ASEAN and the principle of non-intervention: Practice and prospects. In D. Dickens & G. Wilson-Roberts (Eds.), *Non-intervention and state sovereignty in the Asia-Pacific* (pp. 9–22). Wellington: Centre for Strategic Studies.

Guo, X. (2008). *Dealing with Myanmar: A unity of divided interests*. Stockholm: Institute for Security and Development Policy.

Haacke, J. (2003). The concept of flexible engagement and the practice of enhanced interaction: Intramural challenges to the 'ASEAN Way'. In J. Haacke (Ed.), *ASEAN's diplomatic and security culture: Origins, development and prospects* (pp. 165–190). London: Routledge.

Jones, L. (2010). ASEAN's unchanged melody?: The theory and practice of non-intervention in southeast Asia. *The Pacific Review, 23*(3), 479–502.

Katanyuu, R. (2006). Beyond non-interference in ASEAN: The Association's role in Myanmar's national reconciliation and democratization. *Asian Survey, 46*(6), 825–845.

Katsumata, H. (2003). Reconstruction of diplomatic norms in southeast Asia: The case for strict adherence to the 'ASEAN Way'. *Contemporary Southeast Asia, 25*(1), 104–121.

Koh, L. (2008a, July 20). Asean stepping closer to UN-like union. *The Straits Times*, Singapore.

Koh, T. (2008b, July 21). Response to Barry Desker's criticism of ASEAN charter. *The Straits Times*, Singapore.

Kraft, H. (2000). The principle of non-intervention: Evolution and challenges for the Asia Pacific region. In D. Dickens & G. Wilson-Roberts (Eds.), *Non-intervention and state sovereignty in the Asia-Pacific* (pp. 23–41). Wellington: Centre for Strategic Studies.

Leifer, M. (1989). *ASEAN and the Security of South-East Asia* (London: Routledge)

Leifer, M. (1996a). The ASEAN regional forum: Extending ASEAN's model of regional security. *Adelphi Paper*, 302. Oxford: Oxford University Press/IISS.

Leifer, M. (1996b) France joins the Treaty of Amity and Cooperation (TAC) in southeast Asia. http://www.ambafrance-au.org/spip.php?article2101

Morley, J. W. (Ed.) (1999). *Driven by growth: Political change in the Asia-Pacific region* (Rev. ed.). Armonk/New York: M. E. Sharpe.

Narine, S. (2002). *Explaining ASEAN: Regionalism in southeast Asia*. Boulder: Lynne Rienner.

Osborne, M. (1970). *Region in Revolt: Focus on Southeast Asia*. Rushcutters Bay: Pergamon Press.

Ramcharan, R. (2000). ASEAN and non-interference: A principle maintained. *Contemporary Southeast Asia, 22*(1), 160–188.

Stubbs, R. (1988). ASEAN at twenty: The search for a new consensus. *Behind the Headlines, 45*(3).

Sukma, R. (2003). *The future of ASEAN: Towards a security community*. http://www.indonesiamission-ny.org/issuebaru/Mission/asean/paper_rizalsukma.pdf

Sukma, R. (2004). Indonesia and regional security: The quest for cooperative security. In S. S. Tan & A. Acharya (Eds.), *Asia-Pacific security cooperation: National interests and regional order* (pp. 71–87). Armonk: M. E. Sharpe.

Than, M., & Gates, C. (Eds.). (2001). *ASEAN enlargement: Impacts and implications*. Singapore: Institute of Southeast Asian Studies.

Weitz, R. (2008). Cyclone Nargis exacerbated ASEAN's Myanmar dilemma. *World Politics Review*, http://worldpoliticsreview.com/Article.aspx?id=2360

Chapter 15
The UN and Regional Organisations: Finding a Balance Between the UN and the African Union in Dealing with Peace and Security in Africa

Marie Muller and Maxi Schoeman

The world has come a long way since the adoption of the UN Charter and the initial debate in the early 1940s on the place of regionalism in dealing with international peace and security. The wording of Chapter VIII resulted over time in various interpretations of the nature of the relationship between the UN and regional organisations involved in regional conflicts. These ambiguities are based on references to 'recognising and/or authorising' actions of regional organisations in maintaining or restoring peace and security. Since the end of the Cold War, though, and the rise of ideas regarding the global governance of peace and security, increasing attention has been paid to this relationship and ways in which to improve, encourage and develop more effective joint strategies for conflict prevention, peacekeeping and peace building. In this regard, the African continent, as a region experiencing what at times seem to be endemic insecurity, incidences of state failure, human suffering and armed conflict, has become a particular focus of attempts at strengthening UN-regional relations. In March 2007, South Africa took the initiative, as Security Council president at the time, to hold an open debate on the UN's relationship with regional organisations and in particular the African Union in the maintenance of peace and security and prevention of armed conflict.

What have come out of this debate, as well as a range of other initiatives stretching back to the early 1990s, are, amongst others, the report of the *High Level Panel on Threats, Challenges and Change* (United Nations 2004), the Secretary General's follow-up report, *In Larger Freedom* (United Nations 2005), various open debates on the topic in the Security Council, the establishment of a Ten-Year Capacity-Building Programme for the African Union focusing on peace and security and, most recently, Security Council Resolution 1809 (2008). This resolution emphasises and acknowledges the importance of the relationship between the UN and regional organisations and 'expresses its [the Security Council's] determination to take effective steps to further enhance the relationship between the United Nations

M. Muller (✉) • M. Schoeman
University of Pretoria, Pretoria, South Africa
e-mail: Maxi.Schoeman@up.ac.za

P. De Lombaerde et al. (eds.), *The United Nations and the Regions: Third World Report on Regional Integration*, United Nations University Series on Regionalism 3,
DOI 10.1007/978-94-007-2751-9_15,

and... in particular the African Union'. Other aspects emphasised in the resolution are the encouragement of inter-regional cooperation, of building peacekeeping capacity in Africa and its subregions, and the fact that 'common and coordinated efforts undertaken by the United Nations and... in particular the African Union... *should be based on their complimentary capacities...*' (emphasis added). Our viewpoint relates specifically to these latter two initiatives: the Ten-Year Capacity-Building Programme and Resolution 1809/2008.

The 'diminishing capability' of the UN in particular (in Africa, the Rwanda genocide of 1994 is a tragic case in point; more recently, the Darfur crisis comes to mind) necessitates a more active and even innovative role for regional organisations, not so much in an instrumental way as in a relationship of partnership with the UN. This dwindling capacity has to do with a lack of political will on the part of member states to become fully involved in keeping the peace and maintaining security. There is some debate about the optimal relationship between the UN Security Council and regional actors in international security: is the Security Council the senior party to the extent that it mandates (regional) security operations and takes overall and final responsibility for the conduct of such operations (what has been referred to as 'UN primacy in all crises')? Or are regions, in the words of Hettne and Söderbaum (2006: 229), 'becoming the most relevant actors in the global security architecture' – a development which demands, according to them, a move away from the (orthodox) 'undemocratic plurilateralism' of the Security Council towards a 'horizontal combination of regional and global agencies' (2006: 231) with regional organisations having their own bases of authority, resulting in 'genuinely shared responsibility'?

We would argue for the former position; the UN should retain primacy in all crises, especially with reference to the peace and security situation and condition of the African continent. This arrangement finds its clearest expression in Article 52 which provides the legal framework for the involvement of regional organisations in the maintenance of international peace and security. This is not to negate 'genuinely shared responsibility'. But when one considers regional peace and security within a framework of global governance, attempts at 'equalising' the relationship between the UN as a (or *the*) global institution and regional organisations would undermine the ideals and principles of collective security which, in its fullest implications and meaning, comprise *all* members of the international community – be these states or regions or people and be it as protectors or protected.

For the sake of promoting good global citizenship and in light of the increasing and urgent need for dealing with the world as 'a single entity' within the framework of human security and the interconnectedness of threats and attempts to address these issues (international migration, spillover effects of civil wars, global warming – the list is long) for which states are too small, genuine collective security is of the utmost importance.

Regional organisations per se, whether in 'horizontal combination' with global institutions such as the UN or acting on their own, are not necessarily more democratic, representative or just than the Security Council. What is clear, though, is that current international efforts to strengthen relationships between the UN and regional organisations in the field of peace and security are to be commended.

The UN Security Council remains, as stated in the 'Joint Communiqué agreed by the UN Security Council and AU Peace and Security Council' (June 2007), the organisation with 'primary responsibility for the maintenance of international peace and security'. Yet it is mandatory for the Security Council to be reformed in order to be more representative of its membership. It is quite conceivable that a more just and equitable system of representation, also with regard to the contentious issue of the great power veto, might actually make a huge contribution to a more productive and efficient relationship of burden sharing between the UN and regional organisations. So, we argue that fair and just representation 'at the top' would contribute substantially to a more dynamic, productive and successful relationship between the UN and regional organisations. This is particularly true in the case of Africa which, sadly, is home to the majority of armed conflicts internationally.

The importance of a global institution such as the UN in socialising members, and by extension, their populations, into shared value systems should not be underestimated. Regional bifurcation too easily leads to 'exceptionalism'. Global summits and conventions on a range of issues, from global warming to racism to sustainable development to addressing HIV-AIDS to issues of human rights, attest to the way in which, however slowly, values and principles underlying the notion of a common humanity have been taking hold internationally. In this sense, a strong relationship between the UN and African regional/subregional organisations with the UN as 'senior partner' (representative of the international community) could encourage the inculcation of such common values, especially with regard to the protection of civilians (women and children in particular), in armed conflicts and situations of gross violations of human rights.

So, for instance, it is seldom acknowledged that UN Security Council Resolution 1325/2000 was adopted during Namibia's chairpersonship of the Council. This resolution, which affirmed the crucial role of women in conflict prevention and resolution, has become the loadstar of international attempts, programmes and policies to ensure that gender concerns are entrenched in all activities related to peacekeeping, peacemaking and peace building. It remains a sterling example of the positive interaction between the regional and global levels. In building the partnership for the maintenance of security on the African continent (and elsewhere!), renewed emphasis should be placed on ensuring that gender concerns are in fact entrenched in all activities. The UN as a global socialising agent has a crucial role to play in engendering a universally accepted set of norms (a consensus on values) to deal with conflict prevention, management and resolution.

Any erosion of the principles and ethos of collective security as a global system in the name of subsidiarity (the practice of utilising the 'most effective' level of authority for dealing with a problem) might result in 'divided responsibility' – the antithesis of collective security. The implications of shifting responsibility to regional organisations – even if cloaked in terms of 'shared' responsibility – especially in the case of Africa, could very likely result in the long run in a disengagement from the continent by other members of the international community and the continent being marginalised or, worse, isolated and treated as some kind of aberration in the global system – the only region that always has to be treated differently.

In other words, placing too much responsibility on Africa to solve its own crises could lead to an easy way out for the international community: whenever they would not want to get involved, they could refer to the continent's responsibility to maintain peace and security. In a continent so mired in poverty, this is not a viable solution to dealing with issues of peace and security. Africa contributed 7,000 peacekeepers to the Darfur operation – it was estimated that at least 26,000 would be necessary. Given that the continent has 12% of the world population, its troop contribution in this case is proportionally significant, and it contributes troops to a number of other peacekeeping operations, both on the continent and in other regions of the world. Making the argument that in the absence of other resources necessary for effective peacekeeping Africa is actually only 'making up' by concentrating on their 'comparative advantage' is also not a satisfactory argument. One of the reasons for the poor performance, if not failure, of the Darfur peace mission is exactly the fact that the international community has not contributed the necessary 'hardware' and logistical support to assist the peacekeepers in their task. Reports of (African) peacekeepers in Darfur having to wear blue plastic bags on their heads because they were not issued with blue helmets would have been funny had it not implied the underlying lack of international sincerity in 'sharing responsibility'.

Assumptions that regional organisations are better placed to deal with conflicts and threats to peace and security do not necessarily hold water. In the case of Africa, training of African peacekeepers for continental operations by the USA, France and Britain is cynically viewed as a 'win-win' solution: Africa provides the troops, and the West, not keen to get involved in 'hotspots', provides training and other forms of support. Regional 'solutions' are not necessarily 'better' than international solutions on the basis that the region 'understands' better, is more familiar with the problems or is more trusted and legitimate than outsiders. This latter argument includes the 'facts' that regional peacekeepers know the local languages and are familiar with local culture, traditions and history, thereby being, ostensibly, more 'efficient' than peacekeepers from outside the region who may be perceived as external impostors. Often, though, it is the very 'familiarity' and presence of regional troops/peacekeepers that may exacerbate a conflict. Many intra-state conflicts also have a clear cross-border character (such as in the Great Lakes region and in the Horn of Africa). The level of success of peacekeepers seems not to be so much dependent on the origin of the force or its familiarity with the situation (as neighbours). Rather, the issue of impartiality is of crucial importance and often regional members have difficulty in remaining impartial, or are perceived to be partial, as was the case with the Southern African Development Community (SADC) intervention in Lesotho in 1998 – an operation that seriously damaged relations between South Africa and Lesotho and tarnished South Africa's image as a peacekeeper.

Another assumption is that a regional peacekeeping framework is mandated from within, rather than being imposed from 'above', and therefore would be more relevant and successful as security actors and agents. Yet, this is not necessarily true, and one should be weary of romanticising the ability and capacity of regional organisations, especially in the case of Africa, to take on the lion's share of operations and efforts to deal with issues of peace and security. Golaszinski (2004: 4) sounds a clear warning:

> For Africa the path of military intervention by regional organisations without an unequivocal and significant involvement of the international community is a dangerous way to go and may over time undermine the global responsibilities of the UN Security Council for peace and security. At the same time, the AU, like its predecessors, might become hostage to a coalition of weak, failing and undemocratic states, which are incapable of providing security beyond that required to protect the self-serving interests of their presidents.

The above warning note is of particular importance in the case of complex humanitarian crises such as identified with a view to the development of the doctrine of the Responsibility to Protect (R2P). In such instances, the international community is called upon to intervene in the internal affairs of a member country without any clear provisions for such intervention in the UN Charter. For the successful development of R2P, it is essential that the relationship between the UN and regions remains that of the UN as 'senior' partner that will diffuse good practices globally.

Not only the international community should be careful of marginalising Africa, though. Africans should also take into account these possible repercussions of what has already become known as 'African solutions to African problems'. This slogan, adopted (understandably so) during the 1990s after the botched UN/USA intervention in Somalia and the failure to intervene in the Rwanda genocide which cost the lives of 800,000 people, nevertheless goes against the grain. Security is indivisible, and though Africa has been let down (with grave consequences) in the past, it cannot take responsibility for solving its own crises, especially as the continent has always been so much involved in its duties as an international citizen. So, for instance, Africa provides more than 75% of UN peacekeepers and 40% of UN peacekeeping troops, with at least 80% of these troops involved in operations on the continent. Little wonder then that the AU is unable to provide sufficient forces for a Somali peace operation.

The possibility of an 'Africanisation' of peace operations should be guarded against. The Ten-Year Capacity-Building Programme for the African Union will certainly enhance the ability and capabilities of the continent to deal with issues of peace and security, but some concerns remain. Without international logistical and financial support, training for such operations will not bear fruit. Another concern is the underlying purpose of such capacity building – is it to strengthen the African Union in its capacity as a contributor to international peace and security, or is it aimed at shifting responsibility for African peace and security onto the continent? In this capacity-building process, as so often in the past, it would seem that Western powers/regional organisations (the USA, UK, France, Denmark, Norway and others and the EU) are taking the lead. What is the position of other UN members and, more particularly, that of the remaining permanent members, China and Russia?

In our current era, we are witnessing the evolution of highly complex and hybrid peacekeeping missions, involving securing the peace through the deployment of armed forces, the consolidation of peace agreements by incorporating civilian personnel and the need for post-conflict reconstruction and development (PCRD).

But conducting these complex missions will continue to demand the full involvement and leadership of the UN. The failure of 'robust' peacekeeping (Somalia in the early 1990s is a case in point) has much to do with the indecision of the permanent members (and not only the West) in providing financial, material and personnel resources in a timely manner. Yet this is no reason to expect regions to cope with such crises largely on their own.

Full and equal partnership between the UN and regional organisations under Chapter VIII of the Charter is not yet on the cards. What is needed in Africa is increasing cooperation with the UN between the African Union (and subregional organisations) and the Security Council, with the international community assisting in strengthening the continent's capacity to prevent and/or resolve conflicts peacefully and to conduct PCRD. But the UN is not something separate from Africa and its various regional organisations – the UN belongs to all, and all are, in the name of collective security, responsible for the maintenance of peace and security everywhere.

References

Golaszinski, U. (2004). *Africa's evolving security architecture.* Friedrich Ebert Stiftung: Dialogue on globalisation. http://mocambique.fes-international.de/downloads/Africa%20Security%20Architecture.pdf.

Hettne, B., & Söderbaum, F. (2006). The UN and regional organisations in global security: Competing or complementary logics? *Global Insights. Global Governance, 12*(2006), 227–232.

Joint Communiqué Agreed by the UN Security Council and AU Peace and Security Council. (2007, June 16). Addis Abeba.

United Nations. (2004). *A more secure world: Our shared responsibility. Report of the Secretary General's high-level panel on threats, challenges and change* (A/59/565). http://www.un.org/secureworld/report2.pdf.

United Nations. (2005). *In larger freedom: Towards development, security and human rights for all. Report of the Secretary General* (A/59/2005). http://www.un.org.largerfreedom/.

United Nations Security Council. (2000). *Resolution 1325* (S/RES/1325). http://daccess-ods.un.org/TMP/9137172.html.

United Nations Security Council. (2008). *Resolution 1809* (S/RES/1809). http://daccess-dds-ny.un.org/doc/UNDOC/GEN/N08/308/12/PDF/N0830812.pdf?OpenElement.

Part III
Regional Organisations, Human Security, Sustainable Development and Human Rights

Chapter 16
Reconceptualisation of Security and Regional Dimension of UN Activities: Towards a Mediterranean Environmental and Human Security Initiative

Hans Günter Brauch

16.1 Introduction

There have been three major political and scientific debates on the conceptualisation and reconceptualisation of security and on the creation of a global security architecture:

- The debate and negotiations at the Versailles peace conference that resulted in the adoption of the Versailles Treaty and of the Covenant of the League of Nations (Holsti 1991; Kissinger 1994)
- The post-war policy planning in the USA, the US-British consultations and the negotiations on a UN Charter in Dumbarton Oaks (1944), Chapultepec (1945) and in San Francisco (1945) that resulted in a new collective security system (Russell 1958; Brauch 1996)
- The debate on the reconceptualisation since the end of the Cold War that resulted in a widening, deepening and sectorialisation of security

With the adoption of the UN Charter in San Francisco in June 1945, the second debate resulted in a threefold legal framework for a post-WWII security system architecture:

- A global collective security system with a powerful UN Security Council that was based on the assumption that its five permanent member states would act together in containing any aggressor with the use of force (Chapter VI: Pacific settlement of disputes; Chapter VII: Actions with respect to threats to the peace, breaches of the peace, and acts of aggression)
- Regional arrangements and agencies for dealing with the maintenance of international peace and security (Chapter VIII)
- Collective self-defence against an attack against a member of the UN (Art. 51).

H.G. Brauch (✉)
Free University of Berlin, Berlin, Germany
e-mail: hg.brauch@onlinehome.de

P. De Lombaerde et al. (eds.), *The United Nations and the Regions: Third World Report on Regional Integration*, United Nations University Series on Regionalism 3,
DOI 10.1007/978-94-007-2751-9_16, © Springer Science+Business Media B.V. 2012

Due to the Cold War systemic competition between the Soviet Union and the West (USA, UK, France), the global collective security system has been paralysed since the outset. In 1990, the UN Security Council for the first time legitimated the use of force against Iraq after its takeover of Kuwait if Iraq failed to respond to an ultimatum by 15 January 1991.

After the UN and the Organisation for Security and Co-operation in Europe (OSCE) failed in solving the conflict in Bosnia-Herzegovina (1994–1995) after the disintegration of Yugoslavia with the US-led military activities against the Bosnian Serbs and in 1999 in the NATO operation against Yugoslavia after the humanitarian crisis in Kosovo as well as with the US-led NATO operation in Afghanistan and the US-led war in Iraq in 2003, the efforts to develop and vitalise the collective security system of the UN had failed, and within Europe, the operation shifted from OSCE back to NATO and increasingly to the Mediterranean Environmental and Human Security Initiative (MEHSEC), which took over NATO operations in Bosnia and Kosovo.

Already prior to the end of the Cold War, a few scientists (Krell 1981; Buzan 1983) noted a widening of the security concept and agenda. With the end of the Cold War, a wide reconceptualisation of the security concept has taken place both in the policy debates of decision makers and in the conceptual discourses of social scientists (Brauch et al. 2008, 2009, 2010). In these debates and analyses, the interaction between the global and regional levels of action and analysis was also highlighted.

This chapter tries to combine the conceptual security discourse with the inter-level (global-regional) debate, and in so doing, it narrows the focus to the environmental dimension of human security in the Mediterranean and develops some conceptual ideas for a suggested *Mediterranean Environmental and Human* (MEHS) initiative in the realm of environment and development policy that could link global and regional organisations dealing with soft security issues. This raises the following research questions: (a) How did the UN Charter conceptualise security in 1945? (b) How does the reconceptualisation of security since 1990 impact on the relationship between the UN and regional organisations on security issues? and (c) How did the debate on human security impact on the relationship between the UN as a global collective security system and regional organisations?

According to Arnold Wolfers (1962: 150), 'Security, in an *objective* sense, measures the absence of threats to acquired values, in a *subjective* sense, the absence of fear that such values will be attacked'. In an inter-subjective sense, security refers to 'what actors make of it' (Wendt 1992; Hintermeier 2008: 660). Securitisation, according to Wæver refers to:

> the discursive and political process through which an intersubjective understanding is constructed within a political community to treat something as an existential threat to a valued referent object, and to enable a call for urgent and exceptional measures to deal with the threat
>
> (Wæver 1995, 1997, 2008)

And it helps to analyse 'how does the politics of a given issue change when it shifts from being a normal political issue to becoming ascribed the urgency, priority and drama of "a matter of security"' (Buzan et al. 1998; Wæver et al. 2009).

This chapter covers both the world and macro regions and global and regional organisations, by focusing not only on 'regional arrangements or agencies for dealing such matters related to the maintenance of international peace and security' but also on functional organisations dealing with new challenges posed by global environmental change and environmental pollution for human beings and humankind. This argument will be developed from a European perspective.

16.2 Conceptualisation of Security in the UN Charter

The establishment of the UN as a system guaranteeing peace and security was the result of a long-term and careful post-war planning in the US State Department since 1939, where President Franklin D. Roosevelt took a leading architectural role by calling in 1943 for a system of 'four world policemen' that became the permanent members of the UN Security Council. To get Stalin's consent, he agreed to a veto power for these policemen what has paralysed the collective security system during the Cold War but also in several post–Cold War crises in Kosovo (1999) and Georgia (2008). In January 1944, in a message to the US Congress, Franklin D. Roosevelt argued that the new international organisation should provide certain benefits for 'economic security, social security, moral security, in a family of nations', and he stressed that 'an equally basic essential to peace is a decent standard of living for all. Freedom from fear is eternally linked to freedom from want'.

Two competing regional approaches for the post-war security system were considered during World War II. In the informal Anglo-American discussions since 1943, Prime Minister Churchill and Foreign Secretary Eden proposed three nearly autonomous regional councils for Europe, the Western Hemisphere and the Pacific. During the Chapultepec Conference on War and Peace in Mexico City (21 January–8 March 1945), several Latin American countries called for a stronger regional approach 'relating to the maintenance of international peace and security'. At the San Francisco conference, Latin American and Arab countries as well as Australia and New Zealand called for regional autonomy and applications of enforcement measures that are reflected in the final compromise wording of Chapter VIII of the UN Charter.

The concepts of 'international peace and security' are repeatedly used in the Covenant and in the UN Charter. According to the Preamble and Article 1(1) of the Charter, the goal of the UN is 'to maintain international peace and security'. This term is repeated in the Charter articles on the powers of the UN organs (Arts. 11, 24, 33(1), 36(1), 39). The meaning of the notion 'peace and security' is crucial, in at least two respects:

> First, where there is a danger to international peace and security, or a threat to the peace, UN organs are entitled to act. Second, as action is to be taken to maintain or restore international peace and security, the type of measure which may be adopted also depends on the definition of these terms. If and to the extent that the meaning of this notion changes, the activities

> of the UN are bound to change as well. This raises the fundamental question of possible modifications of that interpretation, or in other words, of static or dynamic interpretation
>
> (Bernhardt 1995: 1419; Bothe 2008: 475)

In a legal interpretation of the security concept in the Charter, Wolfrum (1994: 51) points to the subjective and objective elements of 'international security', the pursuit of which 'implies a transformation of international relations so that every state is assured that peace will not be broken, or at least that any breach of the peace will be limited in its impact'. In addition, he referred to the 'defining characteristic of the concept of collective security [as] the protection of the members of the system against a possible attack on the part of any other member of the same system', and he noted that

> the distinction drawn between the concepts of collective security and collective self-defence has been blurred to some extent in practice, and it also has lost relevance with respect to the United Nations' because due to the universal nature of the UN system 'any distinction based upon external or internal acts of aggression [have been rendered] meaningless.

16.3 Global Reconceptualisation of Security Debate

The understanding of the 'security' concept has gradually changed after the end of the Cold War in the policy debate, in the declarations and behaviour of governments and international organisations as well as in the scientific discourse and analyses. This reconceptualisation of security has resulted in: (1) a *widening* (from the narrow political and military focus to economic, societal and environmental dimensions); (2) a *deepening* (from the exclusive focus on the state and international state-centred organisations to sub-state and supra-state perspectives as well as people-centred human security approaches) and (3) a *sectorialisation* of security that started with energy security (after the oil shocks in the 1970s) and then shifted to food and health security during the 1980s and 1990s and since 2000 to water security concepts that were used by international organisations, governments and policy and scientific experts (Albrecht and Brauch 2008, 2009).

Within the environmental dimension of security, a gradual securitisation of issues of global environmental change has evolved since the year 2000: first of water security, followed by desertification and climate change where the year 2007 has become a turning point that was triggered by the release of the four reports of the Fourth Assessment Report of the Intergovernmental Panel on Climate Change (IPCC), the tabling of climate change as an international security issue to the Security Council by the UK (17 April 2007) to the European Council by the German EU presidency in June 2007, by Greece as a human security issue during its presidency of the Human Security Network (May 2007–2008), while the US debate has focused on the impacts of climate change on US national security (Brauch 2009; Brauch et al. 2008, 2009, 2010).

What has been the impact of this fundamental reconceptualisation of security and of the progressing securitisation of issues of global environmental change on the UN, its machinery and on regional organisations?

16.4 Impact of This Policy Debate on the UN and the Regional Organisations

The regional perspective to international peace and security was reintroduced by UN Secretary-General Boutros-Ghali in his *Agenda for Peace* (1992, 1995) that offered a new regional perspective. The approach suggested was partly taken up by the OSCE and the EU in Europe and by the African Union (AU), but it did not result in regional systems of security that combined legitimacy with the needed military and economic capabilities.

The narrow understanding of collective security – as reflected in Chapters VI, VII and VIII of the UN Charter – that prevailed when the chapter was adopted defined 'regional arrangements and agencies' as regional systems of collective security, e.g. the League of Arab States, the Organisation of American States (OAS), the Organisation of African Unity (OAU) or now the AU and OSCE. Secretary-General Boutros-Ghali in 1992 pointed to a wider understanding that includes 'undertakings by a group of States to deal with a matter appropriate for regional action which also could contribute to the maintenance of international peace and security'. He argued that this includes:

> treaty-based organisations, ... regional organisations for mutual security and defence, organisations for general regional development or for cooperation on a particular economic topic or function, and groups created to deal with a specific political, economic or social issue of current concern.

He noted that such organisations often 'possess a potential that should be utilised in serving the functions covered in this report: preventive diplomacy, peace-keeping, peacemaking and post-conflict peace-building'. This flexible understanding includes regional organisations such as the European Union and the Economic Community of West African States (ECOWAS) that have increasingly performed such tasks since the 1990s.

The High Level Panel on *Threats, Challenges and Change* (United Nations 2004) noted that 'the Security Council has not made the most of the potential advantages of working with regional and sub-regional organisations'. This report noted that 'alliance organisations as NATO... have undertaken peacekeeping operations beyond their mandated areas' that should be 'authorised by and accountable to the Security Council'.

The Panel also recommended that the Economic and Social Council (ECOSOC): 'establish a Committee on the *Social and Economic Aspects of Security Threats*, and that it uses its powers to commission research and develop a better understanding about the economic and social threats to peace, and about the economic and social aspects of other threats, such as terrorism and organised crime'. Several of the five regional economic and social Commissions (Economic Commission for Europe (ECE), Economic Commission for Africa (ECA), ESCWA, ESCAP, ECLAC) work on policy areas that now reflect a widened understanding of security, e.g. ECA is working on security aspects of HIV/AIDS and ECE has joined the ENVSEC Initiative that focuses on issues of environmental security.

Several ideas were taken up in the Report of Secretary-General Kofi Annan of March 2005 on *In Larger Freedom* (2005) and incorporated into the Outcome Document on UN reform approved by the General Assembly in September 2005 (A/RES/60/1, 25.10.2005). With regard to strengthening the African Union, the UNGA supported 'the efforts of the European Union and other regional entities to develop capacities such as for rapid deployment, standby and bridging arrangements'.

The widening of the understanding of security within the UN as well as the progressing securitisation of selected policy fields or tasks has resulted in a highly flexible and more complex institutional security architecture that combines multiple horizontal networks and vertical links, as the suggested new ECOSOC committee on the *Social and Economic Aspects of Security Threats*, that require more coordinating efforts.

The institutional road map between global and regional organisations has been further complicated by the deepening of the security concepts and the shift from a 'state-centred' understanding of security that is embodied in the UN Charter to 'people-centred' human security approaches and efforts.

16.5 Human Security: The UN and the Regional Organisations

Since 1994, 'human security' has evolved as a new security concept on the international policy agenda due to two major reports (UNDP 1994; CHS 2003). By shifting the focus from the 'state-centred' perspectives of national, international and global security to a 'people- or human-centred' perspective, the security concept was *deepened* vertically, and the exclusive focus on the state was questioned by adding the individual human being, communities, society or humankind as new referent objects (Table 16.1). Kofi Annan (2005) distinguished three pillars of human security: freedom from fear, freedom from want and freedom to live in dignity, to which Bogardi and Brauch (2005) added a fourth: 'freedom from hazard impacts'.

Since the late 1990s, two different concepts were promoted in the political realm. The governments of Canada, Norway and the European members of the *Human Security Network* (HSN) preferred a narrow concept focusing on 'freedom from fear' that dealt with humanitarian initiatives and human rights (Fuentes and Brauch 2009; Black and Swatuk 2009). The government of Japan and the *Friends of Human Security* (FHS) opted for a wider concept that includes with 'freedom from want' the human development agenda (Shinoda 2009).

Table 16.1 Contextualising human security concepts, pillars and policy agendas

Security dimension ⇒ (widening) level of interaction ⇓ (deepening)	Referent object (security for whom?)	Military	Political	Economic	Societal	Environmental
Global security International/regional National security	World of states	Primary focus of the Copenhagen School (securitisation: a 'move' to put policy issues of utmost importance that require extraordinary measures on the agenda of the state or of international governmental organisations (IGOs)) Securitising actors: states and societal bodies (e.g. IPCC)				
Village/community/society Human security (sectorialisation)	Humankind, peoples, people, community, human being, individual	Sectoral security concepts cut across dimensions and referent objects ◀Energy, water, food, health, livelihood security▶				
Four pillars			Freedom to live in dignity			
		Freedom from fear	Freedom from want			Freedom from hazard impacts
		Protection	Empowerment			
Policy agendas		Humanitarian law, disarmament, landmines, small arms, cluster bombs	Human rights, democratic governance, rule of law	Human and sustainable development	Resilience, reduction of social vulnerability	Early warning Disaster response Disaster preparedness
Scope (wide)		UNDP (1994), CHS (2003), Friends of Human Security (2006–) Japan, Mexico (co-chairs) Some member states of the Human Security Network (1999–)				
Scope (focus during their presidencies of the HSN and the ministerial in their country)		Norway (1999), Switzerland (2000), Canada (2005), the Netherlands (left in 2007)	Austria (2003) human rights education, Slovenia (2007) children in armed conflicts	Jordan (2001), Chile (2002), Mali (2004), Thailand (2006), Costa Rica (South Africa)	Ireland (2009) gender security	Greece (2008) climate change

Several proponents of a narrow human security concept (Mack 2004a, b; Krause 2004, 2008; Mac Farlane and Khong 2006) opposed its horizontal widening to include other policy agendas of development and environment policy. No agreement exists in science and politics on definitions, referent objects, scope and boundaries as well as on policy goals and human security agendas (Brauch 2009). In the social sciences, the concept has been widely discussed in *development* (Picciotto et al. 2007; Ulbert and Werthes 2008) and *peace studies* (Tadjbakhsh and Chenoy 2006; Thakur 2006, 2007) and to a lesser extent in *environmental* (Page and Redclift 2002; Dodds and Pippard 2005) and *security studies* (Dannreuther 2007; Booth 2007) where many realists totally ignored this discourse (Kolodziej 2005).

16.6 Conclusions and Proposals: Towards a MEHSEC Initiative

The conceptual debates on environmental and on human security have taken place in parallel, and there has been very little interchange among both policy debates and scientific discourses. As this author has analysed the linkages between 'environment and human security' and assessed the emerging 'conceptualising of environmental dimension of human security' elsewhere (Brauch 2005a, b, 2008) in detail, relying on these available analyses, this chapter ends with a policy proposal for European international regional bodies to address the environmental dimension of human security pertaining to challenges posed by global environmental change, especially climate change, water scarcity and desertification.

Overcoming the division between the global and regional level, OSCE, UNDP, UNEP in cooperation with NATO (Observer), UNECE and REC have formed the ENVSEC Initiative with the goal: 'Peacefully resolving the overriding political, economic and social concerns of our time requires a multifaceted approach, including mechanisms to address the links between the natural environment and human security'. Since 2003, ENVSEC has focused its project activities on Central Asia, South-eastern Europe, Southern Caucasus and on Eastern Europe (Cheterian 2009).[1]

ENVSEC combines a classic regional agency under Chapter VIII (OSCE), with two global programmes reporting to ECOSOC (UNDP, UNEP), a regional and social commission of ECOSOC (ECE) and a military alliance under Article 51 (NATO).

A similar cooperative approach is suggested for addressing the causes (increase of global warming due to the burning of hydrocarbons) and facing and coping with the impacts of the projected global environmental change, in particular, in the Mediterranean that will be affected most by temperature increase (and precipitation and yield decline in major cereals), sea-level rise (in the delta areas, in particular, of the Nile, Po et al.) and increase in hydrometeorological hazards (heat waves, drought, forest fires, storms, floods) that have caused severe damage to several

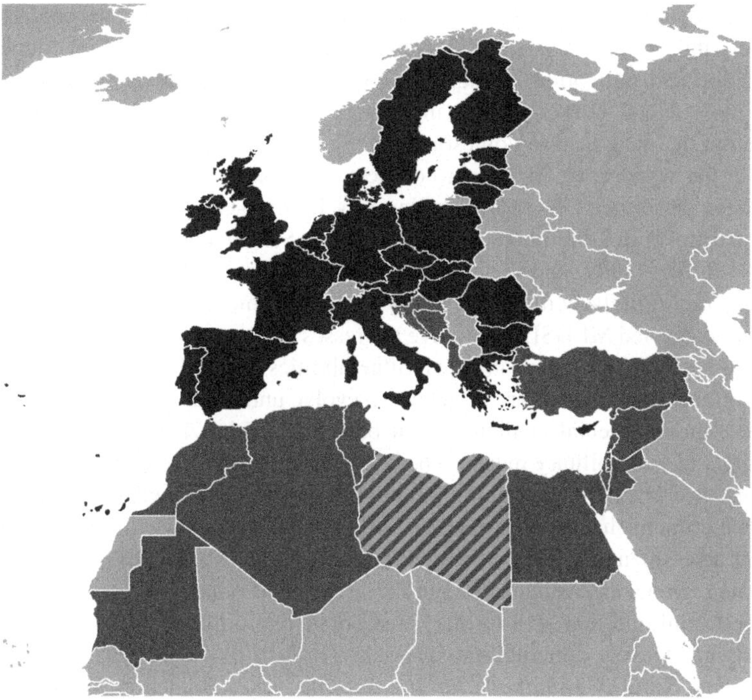

Fig. 16.1 Map of the Union for the Mediterranean member states (Source: Wikimedia Commons; at http://commons.wikimedia.org/wiki/Image:Union_for_the_Med.png)

economic sectors (agriculture, tourism) and for human beings undermining their water, food, health security and forcing them to leave their homes and livelihoods.

In analogy to ENVSEC, a tricontinental and regional *Mediterranean Environmental and Human Security Initiative* (MEHSEC) is suggested as a project of the *European Union* and its new *Union for the Mediterranean* (that was set up on 13 July 2008) (see Fig. 16.1) based on a revitalised and more problem-focused Barcelona Process that could involve, among others, the following regional and global organisations:

- Two regional arrangements and agencies under Chapter VIII: OSCE, Arab League
- UNEP, and its regional Seas Programme for the Mediterranean (Athens), including the Secretariat for the Barcelona Convention (1976) and the Blue Plan
- UNDP and its sub-regional programmes for North Africa and Western Asia
- WMO and the IPCC to bring in the best available scientific expertise on climate change
- UNESCO's natural science programmes focusing on water, desertification, climate change and natural hazards

This proposed MEHSEC Initiative should unite all global and regional organisations with capabilities to analyse, assess available research and develop joint cooperative adaptation and mitigation measures and to develop cooperative measures to deal with the societal consequences, including the environmentally induced forced migration that may lead to domestic hunger and food riots, domestic conflicts and, only in the worst case, in violent conflicts. This proposed initiative takes up the proposals of former UN Secretary-Generals Boutros-Ghali and Kofi Annan with regard to preventive diplomacy. It reflects the first Sustainability Scenario of UNEP's GEO-4 Report (2007) and the proactive global and regional scenarios suggested in the final report of the Millennium Ecosystem Assessment (2005).

This suggested MEHSEC Initiative addresses soft non-military, environmentally induced security threats, challenges vulnerabilities and risks for the whole Euro-Mediterranean region that are projected to evolve until 2025, 2050 and 2100. None of these environmental challenges can be solved with a Hobbesian approach to security and with military means. They can only be overcome by Grotian forward-looking, proactive, functional cooperation that requires knowledge creation (e.g. regional climate change scenarios for the Mediterranean, a Mediterranean climate impact assessment that have so far not been provided by the IPCC due to its three separate regional assessments for Europe, Africa and Asia).

These multiple new non-military and soft environmental and human security 'threats, challenges, vulnerabilities and risks' (Brauch 2005a) that have been mapped in the new *Security Handbook for the Anthropocene* (Brauch et al. 2008, 2009, 2010) require flexible and task-focused institutional arrangements (initiatives, networks and regimes) that should not be limited to state-centred international institutions as new forms of combined global and regional governance with but also without the involvement of governments (Rosenau and Czempiel 1992).

Note

1. http://www.envsec.org/

References

Albrecht, U., & Brauch, H. G. (2008). Security in peace research and security studies. In H. G. Brauch, U. Oswald Spring, C. Mesjasz, J. Grin, P. Dunay, N. C. Behera, B. Chourou, P. Kameri-Mbote, & P. H. Liotta (Eds.), *Globalization and environmental challenges: Reconceptualizing security in the 21st century* (Hexagon series on human and environmental security and peace, Vol. 3, pp. 503–525). Berlin/Heidelberg/New York: Springer.

Albrecht, U., & Brauch, H. G. (2009). Seguridad en la Investigación para la Paz y los Estudios de Seguridad. In U. Oswald Spring & H. G. Brauch (Eds.), *Reconceptualizar la Seguridad en el Siglo XXI* (pp. 503–525). Mexico/Cuernavaca: UNAM/CRIM.

Annan, K. A. (2005, March 21). *In larger freedom: Towards security, development and human rights for all. Report of the Secretary General for Decision by Heads of State and Government in September 2005*, A/59/2005. New York: United Nations, Department of Public Information.

Bernhardt, R. (1995). Interpretation in international law. In R. Bernhardt (Ed.), *Encyclopedia of public international law* (Vol. II, pp. 1416–1426). Amsterdam/New York: Elsevier.

Black, D. R., & Swatuk, L. (2009). Human security in North America: A Canadian perspective. In H. G. Brauch, U. Oswald Spring, J. Grin, C. Mesjasz, P. Kameri-Mbote, N. C. Behera, B. Chourou, & H. Krummenacher (Eds.), *Facing global environmental change: Environmental, human, energy, food, health and water security concepts* (Hexagon series on human and environmental security and peace, Vol. 4, pp. 1095–1104). Berlin/Heidelberg/New York: Springer.

Bogardi, J. & Brauch, H.G. (2005). Global Environmental Change: A Challenge for Human Security – Defining and conceptualising the environmental dimension of human security. In: Rechkemmer, A. (Ed.), *UNEO – Towards an International Environment Organization – Approaches to a sustainable reform of global environmental governance* (pp. 85–109). Baden-Baden: Nomos.

Booth, K. (2007). *Theory of world security*. Cambridge/New York: Columbia University Press.

Bothe, M. (2008). Security in international law since 1990. In H. G. Brauch, U. Oswald Spring, C. Mesjasz, J. Grin, P. Dunay, N. C. Behera, B. Chourou, P. Kameri-Mbote, & P. H. Liotta (Eds.), *Globalization and environmental challenges: Reconceptualizing security in the 21st century* (Hexagon series on human and environmental security and peace, Vol. 3, pp. 475–485). Berlin/Heidelberg/New York: Springer.

Boutros-Ghali, B. (1992). *An agenda for peace: Preventive diplomacy, peacemaking, and peace-keeping. Report to the Secretary General pursuant to the statement adopted by the Summit Meeting of the Security Council on 31 January 1992*, A/47/277 – S/24111. New York: United Nations Department of Public Information.

Boutros-Ghali, B. (1995). *Supplement to an agenda for peace: Position paper of the Secretary-General on the occasion of the fiftieth anniversary of the United Nations*, A/50/60 – S/1995/1. New York: United Nations. http://www.un.org/Docs/SG/agpeace.html

Brauch, H. G. (1996). Democracy and European security order. *Peace Research: The Canadian Journal of Peace Studies, 28*(1), 53–78.

Brauch, H. G. (2005a). *Threats, challenges, vulnerabilities and risks in environmental human security*. Bonn: UNU-EHS. http://www.ehs.unu.edu/index.php?module=overview&cat=17&menu=36

Brauch, H. G. (2005b). *Environment and human security. Freedom from hazard impact*. InterSecTions (2/2005). Bonn: UNU-EHS. http://www.ehs.unu.edu/file.php?id=64

Brauch, H. G. (2008). Conceptualising the environmental dimension of human security in the UN. *International Social Science Journal, 63*(Supplement), 19–28.

Brauch, H. G. (2009). Human security concepts in policy and science. In H. G. Brauch, U. Oswald Spring, J. Grin, C. Mesjasz, P. Kameri-Mbote, N. C. Behera, B. Chourou, & H. Krummenacher (Eds.), *Facing global environmental change: Environmental, human, energy, food, health and water security concepts* (Hexagon series on human and environmental security and peace, Vol. 4, pp. 965–990). Berlin/Heidelberg/New York: Springer.

Brauch, H. G., Oswald Spring, U., Mesjasz, C., Grin, J., Dunay, P., Behera, N. C., Chourou, B., Kameri-Mbote, P., & Liotta, P. H. (Eds.). (2008). *Globalization and environmental challenges: Reconceptualizing security in the 21st century* (Hexagon series on human and environmental security and peace, Vol. 3). Berlin/Heidelberg/New York: Springer.

Brauch, H. G., Oswald Spring, Ú., Grin, J., Mesjasz, C., Kameri-Mbote, P., Behera, N. C., Chourou, B., & Krummenacher, H. (Eds.). (2009). *Facing global environmental change: Environmental, human, energy, food, health and water security concepts* (Hexagon series on human and environmental security and peace, Vol. 4). Berlin/Heidelberg/New York: Springer.

Brauch, H. G., Oswald Spring, U., Mesjasz, C., Grin, J., Kameri-Mbote, P., Chourou, B., Dunay, P., & Birkmann, J. (2010). *Coping with global environmental change, disasters and security – threats, challenges, vulnerabilities and risks* (Hexagon series on human and environmental security and peace, Vol. 5). Berlin/Heidelberg/New York: Springer.

Buzan, B. (1983). *People, states & fear. The national security problem in international relations*. Brighton: Harvester Books/Chapel Hill. University of North Carolina Press (2nd edn. 1991; reprint with new preface 2007).

Buzan, B., Wæver, O., & de Wilde, J. (1998, 2004). *Security. A new framework for analysis*. Boulder-London: Lynne Rienner.

Cheterian, V. (2009). Politics of environment in the Caucasus conflict zone: From nationalizing politics to conflict resolution. In H. G. Brauch, U. Oswald Spring, J. Grin, C. Mesjasz, P. Kameri-Mbote, N. C. Behera, B. Chourou, & H. Krummenacher (Eds.), *Facing global environmental change: Environmental, human, energy, food, health and water security concepts* (Hexagon series on human and environmental security and peace, Vol. 4, pp. 925–938). Berlin/Heidelberg/New York: Springer.

CHS. (2003). *Human security now*. New York: Commission on Human Security. http://www.humansecurity-chs.org/finalreport/

Dannreuther, R. (2007). *International security. The contemporary agenda*. Cambridge: Polity.

Dodds, F., & Pippard, T. (Eds.). (2005). *Human and environmental security. An agenda or change*. London/Steling Va: Earthscan.

Fuentes, C. F., & Brauch, H. G. (2009). The human security network: A global north–south coalition. In H. G. Brauch, U. Oswald Spring, J. Grin, C. Mesjasz, P. Kameri-Mbote, N. C. Behera, B. Chourou, & H. Krummenacher (Eds.), *Facing global environmental change: Environmental, human, energy, food, health and water security concepts* (Hexagon series on human and environmental security and peace, Vol. 4, pp. 991–1002). Berlin/Heidelberg/New York: Springer.

Hintermeier, S. (2008). Reconceptualization of external security in the European Union since 1990. In H. G. Brauch, U. Oswald Spring, C. Mesjasz, J. Grin, P. Dunay, N. C. Behera, B. Chourou, P. Kameri-Mbote, & P. H. Liotta (Eds.), *Globalization and environmental challenges: Reconceptualizing security in the 21st century* (Hexagon series on human and environmental security and peace, Vol. 3, pp. 659–676). Berlin/Heidelberg/New York: Springer.

Holsti, K. J. (1991). *Peace and war: Armed conflicts and international order 1648–1989*. Cambridge: Cambridge University Press.

Kissinger, H. A. (1994). *Diplomacy*. New York: Simon & Schuster.

Kolodziej, E. A. (2005). *Security and international relations*. Cambridge/New York: Columbia University Press.

Krause, K. (2004). Is human security 'more than just a good idea'? *BICC Brief – Promoting Security: But How and for Whom? 30*, 43–46.

Krause, K. (2008). Building the agenda of human security: Policy and practice within the human security network. Rethinking human security. *Int Soc Sci J, 57*(Supplement), 65–80.

Krell, G. (1981). The development of the concept of security. In E. Jahn & Y. Sakamoto (Eds.), *Elements of world instability: Armaments, communication, food, international division of labour* (pp. 238–254). Frankfurt: Campus.

Mac Farlane, S. N., & Khong, Y. F. (2006). *Human security and the UN. A critical history*. Bloomington/Indianapolis: Indiana University Press.

Mack, A. (2004a). The concept of human security. *BICC Brief – Promoting Security: But How and for Whom? 30*, 47–50.

Mack, A. (2004b). A signifier of shared values. *Security Dialogue, 35*(3), 366–367.

Millennium Ecosystem Assessment. (2005). *Millennium ecosystem assessment synthesis report*. Washington, DC: Island Press.

Page, E. A., & Redclift, M. (Eds.). (2002). *Human security and the environment: International comparisons*. Cheltenham: Edward Elgar.

Picciotto, R., Olonisakin, F., & Clarke, M. (2007). *Global development and human security*. New Brunswick/London: Transaction Publishers.

Rosenau, J., & Czempiel, E.-O. (Eds.). (1992). *Governance without government: Order and changes in world politics*. Cambridge: Cambridge University Press.

Russell, R. B., & Muther, J. E. (1950, 1958). *A history of the United Nations charter. The role of the United States 1940–1945*. Washington, DC: Brookings Institution.

Shinoda, H. (2009), Human Security Initiatives of Japan, in: Brauch, H.G., Oswald Spring, Ú., Grin, J., Mesjasz, C., Kameri-Mbote, P., Behera, N.C., Chourou, B., & Krummenacher, H. (Eds.), *Facing Global Environmental Change: Environmental, Human, Energy, Food, Health and Water Security Concepts* (Hexagon Series on Human and Environmental Security and Peace, vol. 4) (pp. 1197–1204). Berlin – Heidelberg – New York: Springer-Verlag).

Tadjbakhsh, S., & Chenoy, A. (2006). *Human security: Concepts and implications*. London: Routledge.

Thakur, R. (2006, 2007). *The United Nations, peace and security*. Cambridge/New York: Cambridge University Press.

Ulbert, C., & Werthes, S. (Eds.). (2008). *Menschliche Sicherheit. Globale Herausforderungen und regionale Perspektiven*. Baden-Baden: Nomos.

UNDP. (1994). *Human development report*. New York: Oxford University Press.

UNEP. (2007). *Global Environmental Outlook, GEO 4*. Nairobi/New York: UNEP. http://www.unep.org/geo/geo4/media/index.asp and http://www.earthprint.com/

United Nations. (2004). *A more secure world: Our shared responsibility. Reports of the Secretary-General's high-level panel on threats, challenges and change*. New York: United Nations.

Wæver, O. (1995). Securitization and desecuritization. In R. D. Lipschutz (Ed.), *On security* (pp. 46–86). New York: Columbia University Press.

Wæver, O. (1997). *Concepts of security*. Copenhagen: Department of Political Science.

Wæver, O. (2008). Peace and security: Two evolving concepts and their changing relationship. In H. G. Brauch, U. Oswald Spring, C. Mesjasz, J. Grin, P. Dunay, N. C. Behera, B. Chourou, P. Kameri-Mbote, & P. H. Liotta (Eds.), *Globalization and environmental challenges: Reconceptualizing security in the 21st century* (Hexagon series on human and environmental security and peace, Vol. 3, pp. 99–111). Berlin/Heidelberg/New York: Springer.

Wæver, O., Buzan, B., & de Wilde, J. (2009). *Politics of security: A comprehensive framework of analysis*. Boulder: Lynne Rienner.

Wendt, A. (1992). Anarchy is what states make of it: The social construction of power politics. *International Organization, 46*(2), 391–425.

Wolfers, A. (1962). National security as an ambiguous symbol. In A. Wolfers (Ed.), *Discord and collaboration. Essays on international politics* (pp. 147–165). Baltimore: John Hopkins University Press.

Wolfrum, R. (1994). Purposes and principles, Art. 1. In B. Simma (Ed.), *The charter of the United Nations. A commentary* (pp. 45–56). Oxford: Oxford University Press.

Chapter 17
The Regional Input for 'Delivering as One'

Kennedy Graham

17.1 Introduction

The aim of this chapter[1] is to explore the implications of the recommendations in the report of the High-Level Panel (HLP) on UN System-Wide Coherence (SWC report) insofar as they relate to regional structures, both UN and non-UN.[2] The analytical and prescriptive content addresses both substantive issues (the nature of the short-comings and recommendations advanced in the SWC report) and structural issues (the breadth of the institutions potentially affected). The chapter argues that, with due regard to the political sensitivities of the challenge, it is possible to engage in reform of the UN whereby greater consistency and coherence can be attained to streamline the operational partnership between the UN and regional organisations. To that end, it proposes that a standardised definition of 'region' be agreed and that a series of regions be identified based on the definition. The chapter also proposes that consideration be given to identifying certain natural 'regional capitals' in Africa, the Arab world, Europe, Asia-Pacific and the Americas. It focuses on the five themes derived from the report's recommendations, assessing their merit and exploring how they might be implemented:

- Regional hubs
- Roles of regional commissions
- Reconfiguration of UN regional setting
- Standardisation of the definition of 'region'
- Co-location of UN regional offices

As previously mentioned throughout other chapters, in an institutional sense, regionalism is of two broad dimensions: on the one hand, those entities that are part

K. Graham (✉)
Member of Parliament, Wellington, New Zealand
e-mail: Kennedy.Graham@parliament.govt.nz

P. De Lombaerde et al. (eds.), *The United Nations and the Regions: Third World Report on Regional Integration*, United Nations University Series on Regionalism 3,
DOI 10.1007/978-94-007-2751-9_17,

of the UN system itself and, on the other hand, those entities that are exogenous to the UN system, which operate autonomously, but which were foreseen in the UN Charter as part of a collaborative institutional network pursuing the common ends of the international community, identified generically in Chapter VIII of the Charter. The basic distinction between the internal UN system and the external UN partnerships underpins the structure of this chapter. The substantive issues explored are thus applied to two institutional levels, namely the UN system (Chapters IX and X entities) and the broader UN partnership network (Chapter VIII entities). The analysis and prescription for Chapter VIII entities is strictly beyond the scope of the SWC report and the ongoing deliberations at the UN. No decisions can be made within that context by the General Assembly or Economic and Social Council (ECOSOC) pertaining to Chapter VIII agencies which are themselves autonomous international organisations or arrangements. Because the goal of consistency and coherence is common to both internal and external aspects of UN functioning, however, and because the international community has an interest in achieving it across all aspects of international activity, it is important that the external aspects be addressed as well. It would be self-defeating to structure a consistent and coherent institutional architecture for the UN system that bore no rational relationship to the nature of the broader UN partnership network. The constituent memberships, moreover, are common to both – the nation-states. So it is open to them to make decisions pertaining to the former within the UN system, as well as recommendations pertaining to the latter, which could then be made binding in the institutional context of Chapter VIII regional organisations.

17.2 The High-Level Report on UN System-Wide Coherence

The UN system is global, vast and complex. It comprises 17 specialised agencies and related organisations, 14 funds and programmes, 17 departments and offices within the Secretariat, 5 regional commissions, 5 research and training institutes and a plethora of regional and country-level structures. Its constituent members are the 192 sovereign member states. Its preamble opens in the name of 'We the peoples' – the whole human family. Its stated purposes – the preservation of peace, the promotion of human rights, and economic and social development – are effectively the core responsibilities of global governance. There is no greater global challenge than to ensure that the UN system can function effectively and efficiently. Partly because of the magnitude of the undertaking, partly because of resource constraints, the UN system is imperfect in structure, method and coordination. As such, it is an easy target for criticism, much of it justified, some of it unfair.

At their 2005 Summit, world leaders agreed on the need for stronger 'system-wide coherence' of the UN system.[3] A series of ten measures were envisaged to this end in policy, operational activities, humanitarian assistance and environmental activities. Three objectives in particular were identified by world leaders:

- To strengthen linkages between the normative work of the UN system and its operational activities
- To ensure that horizontal policy themes (sustainable development, human rights and gender issues) are taken into account in UN decision-making
- To ensure a 'more effective, efficient, coherent, coordinated and better-performing' UN country presence, with appropriate authority and common management

Accordingly, world leaders invited the Secretary-General to 'launch work to further strengthen the management and coordination of UN operational activities … including proposals … for more tightly managed entities in the fields of development, humanitarian activities and environment'. In February 2006, the Secretary-General established a High-Level Panel on UN System-Wide Coherence in these three areas. The SWC report was submitted to the Secretary-General in November 2006.

The case for reform, as set out in the SWC report, rests on the need for efficiency. The multilateral institutions of the 1940s remain with us today but now face a new set of challenges – interdependence with inequality. The UN, having played a crucial role in articulating the Millennium Development Goals (MDGs) in 2000, needed now to take action in helping achieve them. Without ambitious and far-reaching reform, the UN would be unable to deliver on its promises and remain at the heart of the multilateral system. The UN's work in development and environment was often fragmented and weak. Inefficient and ineffective governance and unpredictable funding had contributed to 'policy incoherence, duplication and operational ineffectiveness' across the system. Cooperation between organisations had been hindered by competition for funding, mission creep and outdated business practices. To rectify these shortcomings, the report advanced a series of recommendations, based on four main strategic directions[4]:

- Coherence and consolidation of UN activities, based on the principle of country ownership
- Appropriate governance, managerial and funding mechanisms
- Overhaul of business practices in the UN system to ensure proper focus on outcomes
- Consolidation and delivery of 'One UN' through an in-depth review

The essence of the HLP's vision was for the UN to 'deliver as one' in development, humanitarian assistance and the environment. The UN's normative and analytical expertise, operational and coordination activities, and advocacy role would be more effectively brought together at the national, regional and global levels.[5] The principal recommendation was the establishment of 'One UN' at country level, 'with one leader, one programme, one budget, and where appropriate, one office'. The HLP also recommended an independent task force to further eliminate duplication within the UN system and consolidate UN entities where necessary. A number of 'pilot countries' are now being identified to test the new measures.[6]

17.2.1 Implications for Regionalism: 'A Coherent Regional Institutional Landscape'

The HLP's analysis of regional-level activities of the UN system was frank:

> Signs of fragmentation are also apparent at the regional level. Regional offices of different UN agencies are scattered in different locations, and definitions of regions can differ from one agency to another. In some regions, strong regional and subregional institutions either exist or are rapidly evolving while others have strayed from their original mandates. This calls for a review of the UN's regional roles and settings, including the Regional Commissions, to address regional needs, avoid duplication and overlapping functions and seek a coherent regional institutional landscape.[7]
>
> The regional economic commissions were established to promote economic and social development in their regions. And UN funds, programmes and agencies have developed regional mechanisms to provide technical and management support to their country offices. The result: a broad regional presence for the UN, providing a vast potential of assets and expertise, but increasing duplication, fragmentation and incoherence. Over time, certain regional commissions have continued to meet regional needs while others have lost focus in applying their comparative strength in conducting regional analysis, developing policy frameworks and norms and supporting regional integration efforts and activities – instead of devoting attention to operational activities at the country level. Strong institutional arrangements are now needed to ensure complementarities and build a genuine culture of cooperation among all UN organisations active in each region, as well as between the UN and non-UN regional entities.[8]

To achieve this vision, the HLP advanced the following recommendations:

In the field of governance:

- The important regional work of the UN must be streamlined by establishing regional hubs to support UN country teams and clarifying the roles of regional commissions.[9]
- Review the functioning and continuing relevance of existing regional structures in addressing regional needs, taking into account the different needs of regions and the emergence of strong regional and subregional institutions. The review should also consider options for streamlining and consolidation.[10]

Regarding regional structures and coordination:

- UN entities at the regional level should be reconfigured, and the UN regional setting should be reorganised around two interrelated sets of functions: first, focusing on analytical and normative work and second, focusing on coordinating the servicing of intercountry teams.
- Regional offices of UN entities should be co-located, and the definition of regions among all UN entities should be standardised to ensure consistency and coherence in the work of the UN at the regional level.

These 'regional recommendations' form the substance of this chapter's analysis and prescription. The first requirement is to clarify what standards are expected in attaining 'consistency and coherence' in the UN system.

17.2.2 Postulated Standards: 'Consistency' and 'Coherence' Within the UN System

The goal of 'consistency and coherence' has become a standard cry of the UN system and the broader international community for some years now. The UN General Assembly stresses the need for 'efficiency, consistency and coherence in the unification and harmonisation of international trade law'.[11] The International Conference for Financing for Development stresses the need to enhance the coherence and consistency of the international monetary, financial and trading systems in order to support the MDG goals. The Chair of the UN Commission on Global Migration appeals for 'policy coherence' to ease the suffering that is currently endemic to migration – defining it as 'consistency of laws across nations of origin, transit and destination' (Wright 2004). The call for the UN to be consistent and coherent thus means that it should conform to a regular pattern and hold together institutionally to form a recognisable whole and that its 'voice' (i.e. policy formulation and articulation) and its 'action' (i.e. operational activities) should be clear, logical and consistent. Having regard to these meanings, there would thus appear to be two dimensions to consistency and coherence: institutional and policy. An expert team of the Organisation for Economic Cooperation and Development (OECD) identified four dimensions to policy coherence, namely:

- Internal consistency
- Governmental consistency
- Harmonisation (between policies across all donors)
- Alignment (between donor policy and recipient country strategy) (Picciotto et al. 2005)

Institutional coherence may be seen as a facilitator of policy coherence. It has attracted the most attention in UN reform efforts over the years. It is no accident that the SWC report devotes most of its analysis and prescription to the institutional dimension of the UN system.

17.3 Analysis: Regional Structures of the Contemporary International System

An analysis of the current regional structures of the international system involves two dimensions, namely the current delineations of the various 'regions' and the current locations of the offices of the organisations that serve the 'regions'.

To date, the international community has not developed any definition of a 'region' for either structural or operational purposes. The structure of 'regions' as they currently exist is the result of practical decisions usually taken in the local areas that respond more to national interests and logic than to any overall global 'coherence'. Section 17.1 drew the distinction between the internal UN system and the broader external UN partnership. This basic distinction structures the analysis in this section.

17.3.1 Regions Within the UN System

The UN has used the concept of regionalism in two fundamental ways: electoral and operational. As the evidence below illustrates, the 'regions' employed for these purposes are substantially different. The question warrants exploration whether it is feasible, and whether there is merit, in rationalising the use of the concept of 'region' for all, or some, of the above purposes. The electoral groups are an informal mechanism agreed by General Assembly resolution solely for the purpose of elections to UN bodies. They have experienced an evolutionary development from an informal beginning. Their origin lies in the Gentlemen's Agreement of 1946 for the election to the first General Assembly Session, replicated over the following three years (Daws 1999: 11).

Although the groupings were informally developed for electoral purposes only, their functions, having thus been formalised since the UNGA resolutions, have expanded. The grouping has in fact assumed two functions – electoral and 'caucusing'. The latter function presumes a minimum degree of political concord within a group; in some cases, a group will not undertake caucusing or a state may be a member of a group for electoral purposes only and not participate in a caucus function. Thus, Australia and New Zealand found it inappropriate, in the past, to be a member of their geographical group (Asia-Pacific) and joined the Western Europe group. Canada has no geographical group, the Americas being confined simply to Caribbean-Latin America. Today, Australia and New Zealand are politically closer to the Asia-Pacific region, and there is some prospect of a change in due course.[12] From the UN electoral grouping membership, one can assert the following:

- The electoral groups for Africa, Asia-Pacific and Latin America reflect predominantly geographical consideration, while 'Europe' reflects predominantly political considerations, retaining the Cold War division between Western (WEOG) and Eastern Europe (EEG), further including two Pacific (New Zealand and Australia) and one North American country (Canada), while Cyprus (now an EU Member State) is part of the Asian group.
- The self-exclusion of two countries from any electoral grouping – the USA and Kiribati.[13] The USA declines to be a member of any regional group – yet attends the WEOG for electoral purposes and also remains in it for caucusing.

As noted, the UN maintains in its operational work a variety of institutions: regional commissions, programmes and funds, and specialised agencies. These interact closely, albeit not with a high degree of consistency and coherence. It is instructive, in the context of the HLP's recommendations, to undertake an analytical summary of the current 'regions' employed by each of these three types of entity. The regional economic commissions are perhaps the clearest example of regionalism within the UN system. While they were conceived as instruments of socioeconomic promotion under the Charter itself, the relevant provision did not expressly stipulate that these had to be based on geographical considerations.[14] Yet, the first move to establish such commissions reflected a perhaps instinctual preference for a regional approach. It derived from the recognition of the need to resuscitate economic activity and social stability in the 'areas' devastated by World War II (as with the Covenant of the League of Nations after World War I).[15] In July 1946, the Temporary Sub-Commission on the Economic Reconstruction of Devastated Areas recommended to ECOSOC the establishment of an Economic Commission for Europe. In December, the General Assembly asked ECOSOC to establish an Economic Commission for Europe (ECE) and, separately, one for 'Asia and the Far East' (ECAFE). ECOSOC duly did so in March 1947.[16] Further, in July 1947, ECOSOC requested the Economic and Employment Commission to study the 'general problems' connected with the establishment of 'regional commissions' as a means of promoting the purposes and principles of the UN. ECOSOC concurrently established a committee to study the factors involved in such a commission for Latin America and the Caribbean (ECLA) and established the commission in February 1948. A name change followed over three decades later to include the Caribbean as a separate subregional entity.[17] In September 1951, ECOSOC, noting the valuable work completed by ECE, ECAFE and ECLA over the preceding 5 years, resolved to continue them,[18] and this was endorsed by the General Assembly.[19] The same year, an expert group under the Secretary-General recommended that an economic commission for Africa be established (United Nations 1951: 95). It took another 7 years, however, for ECOSOC to establish ECA.[20]

The commission for West Asia had a more difficult gestation. In October 1947, the General Assembly had invited ECOSOC to study the factors bearing upon the establishment of an economic commission for the 'Middle East',[21] and in December 1948, it had recommended that ECOSOC 'expedite consideration' of the issue.[22] No progress was achieved, however. The creation of ECA resulted in the inclusion of those countries of North Africa that formed a part of the 'Middle East'. The UN Economic and Social Office in Beirut (UNESOB) was subsequently established. UNESOB was regarded as a de facto economic commission and was finally transformed into the Economic and Social Commission for Western Asia (ESCWA) in 1973.[23]

Table 17.1 shows the conceptualisation of 'regions' as observed for functional and operational purposes by the principal entities within the UN system – the Secretariat, the regional economic commissions, the major UN programmes and funds, the major specialised agencies and other related UN organisations. The following may be observed:

Table 17.1 UN system – commissions and programmes: major regional groupings

UN Secretariat	Regional economic commission	UN programmes and funds				UN specialised agencies			
		UNICEF	UNFPA	UNDP	UNEP	IBRD	ILO	WHO	FAO
Africa	Africa	West and Central Africa Southern and Eastern Africa	Sub-Saharan Africa	Africa	Africa	Africa	Africa	Africa	Africa
Middle East	West Asia	North Africa and Middle East	North Africa and Middle East	Arab States	West Asia	North Africa and Middle East	Arab States	East Mediterranean	Near East and Europe
Western Europe Eastern Europe	Europe	Central and Eastern Europe and CIS	Eastern Europe and Central Asia	Europe and CIS	Europe	Europe and Central Asia	Europe	Europe	
Asia-Pacific	Asia-Pacific	East Asia-Pacific	Asia-Pacific	Asia-Pacific	Asia-Pacific	South Asia Southeast Asia	Asia-Pacific	Southeast Asia West Pacific	Asia-Pacific
North America-Caribbean	Caribbean-Latin America	Caribbean-Latin America	Caribbean-Latin America	Caribbean-Latin America	Caribbean-Latin America	Caribbean-Latin America	Caribbean-Latin America	Americas	Caribbean-Latin America

- There is a basic underlying pattern of regionalism observed by the major UN entities, corresponding to the four main continents – Africa, Asia, Europe and the Americas.
- That continental delineation, however, is by no means precise, most particularly the trilateral conjunction of Africa, Europe and Asia. There is significant 'cross lapping' at these regional boundaries – affecting especially the position of the Arab and CIS states.
- While the regional economic commissions hew studiously to geographical terminology, the UN Secretariat itself, surprisingly, retains the Eurocentric term 'Middle East'.

17.3.2 Regions Outside the UN System

As noted earlier, the Chapter VIII entities were envisaged by the framers of the UN Charter as regional bodies that would cooperate with the UN. The Charter refers to 'regional arrangements and agencies'.[24] Such bodies may become involved in international peace and security issues 'as are appropriate for regional action'. But they and their activities must be consistent with the purposes and principles of the UN. By definition, these bodies are regional in nature and scope.

At the time of the Charter's conclusion, and as previously discussed in Chaps. 2 and 8, few such regional arrangements or agencies existed, except for the precursor of OAS and the Arab League, but a plethora of regional and subregional bodies have since then emerged.

In the immediate post–Cold War environment of the early 1990s, with the failure of the international community to support the UN adequately to fulfil all its missions throughout the world, the realisation grew that a greater reliance on regional organisations would be necessary. However, serious problems exist with respect to clarity of the UN regional partnership, made clear after a number of meetings between the Secretary-General and the Security Council with invited regional and other intergovernmental organisations. These are well described in Chap. 8, as is the lack of clear regional terminologies and criteria for partnerships with the UN. This has resulted in a large and uncoordinated group of organisations partnering with the UN, some of which are demonstrably nonregional in nature.

Of the organisations which have attended the Secretary-General's high-level meetings, some 14 might be regional or subregional bodies that could conceivably be seen as 'Chapter VIII organisations'. These bodies, with their memberships, are set out in Table 17.2.

17.4 Current Locations of UN Global and Regional Offices

Closely related to the delineation of 'regions' is the decision of where to site a regional office. As above, the analysis of current locations is shown in the context of both the internal UN system and the external UN partnership network.

Table 17.2 Chapter VIII entities: regionalism outside the UN system

Africa		Arab states		Europe		Asia-Pacific		America	
RO	SRO	RO	SRO	RO	SRO	RO	SRO	RO	SRO
AU	ECOWAS IGAD CEMAC SADC	LAS	GCC	COE	EU	CIS PIF	ASEAN	OAS	CARICOM
1	**4**	**1**	**1**	**1**	**1**	**2**	**1**	**1**	**1**

Other organisations attending:
Cross-regional organisations: OSCE[a], NATO, CSTO, SCO **4**
Transnational organisations: COMSEC, OIC, IOF, CPLP **4**
Functional global agencies: Interpol, OPCW **2**

[a]The OSCE declared itself to be a 'regional organisation' for the purposes of Chapter VIII of the UN Charter, and this was 'welcomed' by the UN General Assembly (A/RES/47/10, 28 October 1992). If, however, strict criteria of membership and territorial jurisdiction are applied, it should be regarded as a cross regional organisation. See Graham and Felício (2006: 133–146)

17.4.1 UN System

The location of UN offices can take the forms of a global UN office headquarter or of a regional UN office.

Table 17.3 illustrates the sites of the principal UN entities (global offices) in the world. Some 16 cities host its 50 different bodies, between offices, programmes and funds, institutes, other UN entities, specialised agencies and related organisations. The global bodies are sited in a particular city for certain political reasons (resistance to global or regional hegemonies) and a strong push from one country to host a UN body, usually for purposes of political prestige and income generation. The outcome of choice, thus, has little to do with regionalism per se. The site of a regional economic commission, however, reflects a conscious decision pertaining to regionalism, denoting a 'regional capital'. Further features of UN institutional locations may be noted from the table:

- The dominance of the North (13 of the 20 hosting cities are located in North America or Europe) over the South (only 4 out of 15 host cities are located in the South – one in Latin America and three in Africa). Further, no headquarters or specialised agency or related organisation is sited in the South.

There are no doubt historical reasons for this – the creation of most UN entities in the 1940s and 1950s before the decolonalisation movement was complete, along with the North's capacity to provide adequate buildings, modern technology and further logistic capacities. Those facts, however, are largely historical relics, and today, the 'Northern skew' of UN locations exacerbates the notion of political and cultural preference, undermining the global legitimacy of the UN system, when some 83% of humanity resides in the South. One of the challenges facing the

Table 17.3 UN system: location of global and regional offices

	Global							Regional
Region	Principal UN organs	UN offices	Specialised agencies	Related organisations	UN programmes and funds	UN institutes	Other UN entities	Regional economic commissions
North America								
New York	UNGA UNSC ECOSOC SECRTR	HQ	–	–	UNICEF UNDP UNIFEM UNFPA	UNITAR	UNOPS	–
Washington	–	–	IMF IBRD	–	–	–	–	–
Montreal	–	–	ICAO	–	–	–	–	–
Europe								
Geneva	–	UNOG	ILO, WHO ITU, WMO WIPO	WTO	UNCTAD UNHCR	UNRISD UNIDIR	UNHRC UNAIDS	ECE
Bern	–	–	UPU	–	–	–	–	–
Vienna	–	UNOV	UNIDO	IAEA	UNODC	–	–	–
The Hague	ICJ	–	–	ICC OPCW CTBTO	–	–	–	–
Paris	–	–	UNESCO	–	–	–	–	–
London	–	–	IMO	–	–	–	–	–
Madrid	–	–	UNWTO	–	–	–	–	–
Rome	–	–	FAO IFAD	–	WFP	–	–	–
Turin	–	–	–	–	–	UNICRI	UNSC	–
Bonn	–	–	–	–	UNV	–	–	–

(continued)

Table 17.3 (continued)

Region	Global							Regional
	Principal UN organs	UN offices	Specialised agencies	Related organisations	UN programmes and funds	UN institutes	Other UN entities	Regional economic commissions
Africa								
Nairobi	–	UNON	–	–	UNEP HABITAT	–	–	–
Addis Ababa	–	–	–	–	–	–	–	ECA
Arabia								
Beirut	–	–	–	–	–	–	–	ESCWA
Asia								
Bangkok	–	–	–	–	–	–	–	ESCAP
Tokyo	–	–	–	–	–	–	UNU	–
Latin America								
Santo Domingo	–	–	–	–	–	INSTRAW	–	–
Santiago	–	–	–	–	–	–	–	ECLAC

'system-wide' rationalisation of the UN will be to reduce this 'Northern skew' for greater legitimacy of the organisation. This deserves to be more explored in depth than that accorded by the HLP.

Table 17.4 below shows the 'site spread' of both headquarters and regional offices of the 25 principal entities of the UN system plus the Secretariat. The following may be inferred:

- New York is the natural headquarter of the UN itself, accounting for the Secretariat and half of its programmes and funds. The other half, however, are located elsewhere (two offices in Europe and two in Africa) and so are the specialised agencies and related organisations, the large majority in Europe. This inevitably works against 'UN consistency and coherence'.
- The 'intra-regional spread' of cities is marked: with 16 in the Americas, 14 in Africa, 14 in Asia and 10 in Europe, plus four in the Arab area. This reinforces the supposition that political rivalry results in a current disbursal of 'UN cities' across a region at the cost of UN consistency and coherence.

Notwithstanding such an 'intra-regional spread', some natural patterns of UN siting may be discerned. The natural 'regional capitals' would seem to be the following (excluding New York as the 'global capital'):

- Africa: Nairobi, Dakar, Addis Ababa
- Arab world: Cairo, Amman
- Europe: Geneva, Bratislava
- Asia-Pacific: Bangkok
- Americas: Washington, Mexico City

The question inevitably arises: to what extent are political considerations (national prestige and rivalry, local income generation) a legitimate factor to take into account within the context of promoting UN consistency and coherence? How many member states that trenchantly critique the coordination and efficiency weaknesses of the UN system would rile at the suggested response that they should surrender their capital city as a UN host in favour of a neighbouring country?

17.4.2 Office Locations Outside the UN System

The host cities of the regional organisations that meet under 'Chapter VIII' auspices reveal some further interesting facts. The comparison between the host cities for Chapter VIII regional organisations and 'Chapter X' UN regional commissions is illustrated in Table 17.5. Except for Africa, there is no consistency.

Table 17.4 UN system: headquarters and regional office locations

	Africa	Arab states	Europe	Asia-Pacific	Americas
UN Secretariat	Nairobi	–	Geneva Vienna	–	***New York***
UN regional economic commissions	***Addis***	***Amman***	***Geneva***	***Bangkok***	***Santiago***
UN programmes					
UNICEF	Nairobi Dakar	Amman	Geneva	Bangkok Kathmandu	***New York***
UNDP	–	–	Bratislava	Bangkok Colombo Suva	***New York***
UNIFEM	Nairobi Kigali Abuja Dakar Johannesburg	–	Bratislava	Bangkok Almaty New Delhi Suva	***New York*** Quito Church (Barbados) Mexico City Brasilia
UNFPA	Addis Dakar Harare	Amman	Bratislava	Bangkok Kathmandu Suva	***New York.*** Mexico City
UNHCR	Dakar Kinshasha Lusaka Pretoria	Cairo	***Geneva*** Stockholm Brussels Vienna Moscow	Beijing Tokyo Jakarta Canberra	Washington Mexico City Caracas Buenos Aires
WFP	Dakar Kampala Johannesburg	Cairo	***Rome***	Bangkok	Panama City
UNEP	***Nairobi*** Nairobi	Manama	Geneva	Bangkok	Washington Mexico City
HABITAT	***Nairobi*** Nairobi	–	–	Fukuoka	Rio de Janeiro
Specialised agencies					
IMF	–	–	–	–	***Washington***
IBRD	Johannesburg	–	–	Almaty Hong Kong	***Washington***
ICAO	Dakar Nairobi	Cairo	Paris	Bangkok	***Montreal*** Lima Mexico City
UPU	Harare	Cairo	***Berne*** Bratislava	Bangkok	San Jose
ITU	Addis	Cairo	***Geneva*** Moscow	Bangkok	Brasilia
ILO	Addis	Beirut	***Geneva*** Geneva	Bangkok	Lima

(continued)

Table 17.4 (continued)

	Africa	Arab states	Europe	Asia-Pacific	Americas
WHO	Brazzaville	Cairo	***Geneva*** Copenhagen	New Delhi Manila	Washington
WMO	Lagos Nairobi	Manama	***Geneva***	Apia	San Jose Asuncion
WIPO	–	–	***Geneva***	–	–
FAO	Accra	Cairo	***Rome***	Bangkok	Santiago
Related organisations					
WTO	–	–	***Geneva***	–	–
IAEA	–	–	***Vienna*** Geneva	–	New York, Toronto

Note: Cities in **bold italics** are the headquarters of each organisation, commission or programme

Table 17.5 Regional host cities: 'Chapter VIII' and 'Chapter X' institutions

Regional organisation (Chapter VIII)		UN regional commission (Chapter X)	
Institution	Host city	Institution	Host city
African Union (AU)	*Addis Ababa*	ECA	*Addis Ababa*
Arab League (LAS)	*Cairo*	ECWA	*Amman*
Council of Europe (COE)	*Strasbourg*	ECE	*Geneva*
European Union (EU)	*Brussels*		
Commonwealth of Independent States (CIS)	*Minsk*		
South Asian Association for Regional Cooperation (SAARC)	*Kathmandu*	ESCAP	*Bangkok*
Association of Southeast Asian Nations (ASEAN)	*Jakarta*		
Pacific Islands Forum (PIF)	*Suva*		

17.5 Prescription: A 'Coherent Regional Institutional Landscape'

The HLP has called for measures that will result in a 'coherent regional institutional landscape' for the UN system. For this to occur, there will be, it is submitted, a requirement for a reconfiguration of the 'regional setting' of the UN's activities, agreement on a standardised definition of a 'region' and identification of specific regions, and agreement on one city within each region to act as a regional hub where UN regional offices can be located. These prescriptive measures are explored in this section.

From the views expressed by world leaders at the 2005 Summit and by others in the course of the HLP's consultations, it is clear that fundamental change is required and expected of the UN system. With respect to the regional dimension of the issue, three questions are to be addressed:

- Whether the concept of 'region' can be clarified and agreement reached sufficiently for a coherent group of regions to act as a common structure for all of the UN's activities

- If so, whether that coherent, reconfigured 'UN regional setting' might apply not only to socioeconomic (developmental, humanitarian and environmental) aspects of the UN's operations but also to security and human rights – the other two 'pillars' of the UN
- If so, whether that regional coherence can embrace both the UN system and the exogenous regional institutional architecture identified above

In addressing these questions, much depends on what stakeholder interests are served in each purpose. As noted earlier, there are two functions performed through regionalism within the international community – electoral and operational. The latter may be further identified as of two purposes – socioeconomic and security operations. Each of these provides the contextual setting for the fundamental values required in determining the most appropriate form of regionalism. In UN terms, the two most fundamental values that the international community is striving to promote in its regional and global institutional architecture are legitimacy and effectiveness.

Legitimacy is most critical for representational purposes, while effectiveness is dependent primarily on efficiency – through consistency and coherence. Thus, while 'optimal representation' is critical for the purposes of electoral groupings in the UN system, 'optimal efficiency' is most critical for the purposes of operational effectiveness – in both socioeconomic and security functions. The judgements to be made in this respect require a degree of subtlety. The electoral groupings, for example, were, as noted, originally devised for the purposes of distributing seats on UN bodies. Over the years, they have acquired two associated functions. First, the electoral dimension has come to imply a 'representational element' – but it is left unclear to what extent a member state duly elected to a UN body is expected to 'represent' all other members of that group. And is that 'representativeness' more easily achieved in less sensitive areas than others – such as most socioeconomic functions compared with security? Much depends on the body to which a member state is being elected.

If, for example, Australia, Canada and New Zealand were to relocate into their geographical rather than their current political groups, what might this mean for their representation abilities and that of their new colleagues? Might Australia be credibly expected to 'represent' Indonesia in the Security Council? Might Venezuela duly act on behalf of Canada in global aid, trade and investment bodies such as UNDP or the World Bank? Having regard to these considerations, what might be the definition of a 'region' that could satisfy all purposes and meet all values postulated for consistency and coherence within the UN system and its broader partnership network?

17.5.1 A Standardised Definition of 'Region'

The lack of a standardised definition of 'region', as discussed in Chaps. 2 and 8, continues to seriously hamper both the development of an effective collaborative 'global-regional' partnership between the UN and regional entities and the achievement of 'consistency and coherence' within the UN system itself. It is instructive, therefore, to once again consider the history of the efforts to date by the international community to develop the concept of 'region' in a political and legal sense before considering what might be done to reach a standardised definition.

17.5.1.1 Approaching the Concept of 'Region': A Brief Review

In 1919, the architects of the League of Nations had perhaps a clearer, if more rudimentary, concept of a 'region' than their mid-century successors. For them, a region was, at least for the purposes of international security, Europe or America. Most of Asia, Africa and the Pacific remained colonised. In the mid-twentieth century, the architects of the UN had to confront a more comprehensive notion of 'region' and adopt a more focused concept of regional security.

At the San Francisco Conference, a majority of delegations in fact favoured a decentralised regional structure. The strong preference of the United States for a centralised global body prevailed, but the concerns of the Latin American and Arab countries resulted in a compromise arrangement. The largely nascent regional organisations of 1945 were acknowledged as having a role in security but 'mildly discouraged' from being too assertive in that role as already noted in previous chapters. During this formative time, however, the concept of a 'region' that could be universally applicable around the world was never agreed upon. At San Francisco, a definition was advanced by Egypt and considered by delegates:

> There shall be considered, as regional arrangements, organisations of a permanent nature grouping in a given geographical area several countries which, by reason of their proximity, community of interests or cultural, linguistic, historical or spiritual affinities make themselves jointly responsible for the peaceful settlement of any disputes which may arise … as well as for the safeguarding of their interests and the development of their economic and cultural relations. (Russett 1967: 4)[25]

Thus, three key criteria are advanced for the definition of a 'region' under the UN Charter, namely geographical proximity, community of interest and common affinities. Neither this nor any other definition of a 'region' has been officially agreed at the UN. While this leaves scope for diplomatic flexibility, it does nothing to enhance clarity in law or policy. Although never adopted, the 1945 draft definition serves today as good a definition of a 'region' as any. Therefore, this chapter proposes the reintroduction of this definition onto the agenda of the General Assembly as part of the forthcoming deliberations of the SWC's report. Having regard to the considerations identified above, and employing the 1945 definition of a 'region', it is, in the author's assessment, possible to determine the importance of each criterion for each UN purpose. This is shown in Table 17.6.

This table illustrates the following:

- For legitimacy to be guaranteed in electoral groupings, there must be a high level of community of interest and common affinities among all member states within a group.

Table 17.6 1945 Definition: relative weighting of criteria

	UN system		Regional organisation
		Operational	
Function	Electoral	Socioeconomic	Security
Principal value	Legitimacy	Efficiency	Legitimacy and efficiency
Geographical proximity	Desirable	Necessary	Necessary
Community of interest	Necessary	Desirable	Necessary
Common affinities	Necessary	Desirable	Necessary

- For efficiency to be genuinely achieved in socioeconomic operations within the UN system, a high degree of geographical proximity is required, over and above common interests and affinities.[26]
- For the UN and exogenous Chapter VIII regional organisations to be both legitimate and efficient, a high degree must exist in all three criteria – proximity, interest and affinity.

17.5.1.2 Contemporary Approaches to 'Region': Prospects of Consensus

Achieving clarity over the concept of 'region' for the purposes of a regional-global security system should not be beyond the reach of the international community. Considerable effort has recently been invested in clarifying the concept of 'region' and applying it in a practical way to the current institutional architecture of global and regional bodies. Three reports, in particular, are notable in this respect: the Secretary-General's HLP, the UNU's 1999 seminar on 'Equitable Geographical Representation' and the United Nations University Institute on Comparative Regional Integration Studies/Vrije Universiteit Brussel (UNU-CRIS/VUB) research project on a 'Global-Regional Security Mechanism'.

In 2004, the High-Level Panel on Threats, Challenges and Change identified, for the purpose of possible future Security Council composition, the obvious four 'regions': Africa, America, Asia and Europe.[27] That broad-brush approach, however, suffers from two shortcomings. First, it disregards the complicating factor of two other 'regions' whose notions of separate linguistic, cultural or spiritual affinities have taken institutionalised form, namely the Arab world (i.e. North Africa–West Asia, which could be termed 'Arabia') and the Pacific.[28] Second, it overlooks the fact that 'Asia' is so vast and, apart from the southeast, has no institutionalised embodiment of security organisation.

In March 1999, the UNU convened a seminar in New York, entitled 'What is Equitable Geographic Representation in the Twenty-first Century?'. In the course of that discussion, a new regional configuration to suit contemporary realities was advanced which identifies nine regions for the purposes of UN electoral groups: Eurasia, Asia-Pacific, Mediterranean-Gulf, North Europe, South Europe, North Africa, Southern Africa, Americas and the Caribbean (O'Brien 1999).

In 2006, UNU-CRIS produced a book reflecting the research work undertaken in its 'Regional Security and Global Governance' project. Taking as its cue the Secretary-General's call for the construction of a 'regional-global security partnership', the project explored a set of 'security regions' that could partner with the UN under Chapter VIII of the Charter. A series of nine 'security regions' was envisaged, composed of Sub-Saharan Africa, Europe, Arabia, Central Asia, South Asia, East Asia, Southeast Asia, the Pacific and the Americas. In six of the nine regions, a 'regional organisation' already exists for collaborating with the UN in the maintenance of international peace and security, namely, the African Union (AU), League of Arab States (LAS), Council of Europe (COE), Association of Southeast Asian Nations (ASEAN), Pacific Islands Forum (PIF) and the Organisation of American States (OAS).

Clearly, the global overview of regionalism is however not perfect or even complete. In Asia, three regions either lack an associated organisation (East Asia) or the organisation is weak (CIS in Central Asia) or not mandated for a security function (SAARC in South Asia). The case of Europe is complex with a great number of organisations (EU, Council of Europe, OSCE, NATO) having competing and duplicative mandates.

Whatever number of 'regions' is decided, the interests of the major stakeholders must be met in seeking a common regional structure: UN electoral groupings, UN socioeconomic operations and UN security operations. It needs to be considered whether the various considerations behind each of these three stakeholder interests warrant a different regional structure or whether a common regional structure can be applied to all. This requires determining what criteria are important to each of the three.

17.5.2 Identification of Regional Hubs and Co-location of Regional Offices

Identifying regional hubs and co-locating regional offices will carry major implications for both the structural and operational dimensions of the international institutional architecture. Achieving consistency and coherence requires that any changes made reflect a set of principles or criteria that are transparent and applicable across the board. The identification of regional hubs and location of regional offices is dependent on the prior identification of regions themselves; agreeing on regional capitals cannot be achieved without agreement on the region they will be serving. This is not an easy task. To reach agreement on the world's 'regions', the development of a set of principles for the purpose seems necessary. Criteria for deciding a 'region' should, in the author's view, be those advanced in the 1945 definition: geographical proximity, community of interest and common affinity. Applying these criteria produces the following challenges:

- Africa is a geographically intact region with natural boundaries whose only requirement is agreement that its northeast extremity is Egypt with the Suez Canal

and the Red Sea. But do the common affinities and community of interests require that North Africa, with the Arab states, form a separate region? If it did, there is no natural geographical boundary between these two 'regions', and the separation factor becomes the political fiction of the nation-state.
- Asia, comprising 60% of humankind, is such a vast and heterogeneous area that it would seem to qualify as several regions – West Asia, Central Asia, South Asia, Northeast Asia and Southeast Asia. Is this distinction based on geographical or political differences? Would West Asia join with fellow Arab States as an 'Arab region' comprising 'North Africa/West Asia' as the World Bank group does? What are the qualifying 'common affinities' – historical, cultural and religious? With what degree of transparency and formality might they be proclaimed?
- How is Europe and Asia to be separately delineated? Where are Turkey, Georgia, Armenia, Azerbaijan and Russia – in Europe or (Central) Asia?
- Should the Pacific be regarded as a separate 'region', given its relatively small size, or should it be simply a sub-region of Southeast Asia?

Agreement would need to be reached on these issues. To some extent, they are already answered in a de facto way, through autonomous decisions made over the years with regard to Chapter VIII regional organisations. Yet these decisions have not, hitherto, been formalised in any way and have borne no relationship to decisions made within the UN system pertaining to regional structures. Principles used to assist decision-making in this regard might be the following:

- Agreement on the identification of 'regions' within the UN system for Chapters IX and X entities and, where appropriate, sub-regions
- Recommendation to the broader UN cooperative network that the same structure of regions should be adopted by Chapter VIII entities
- Identification of one capital city in each region to act as regional hub and location of the UN Regional Office and, where appropriate, capital cities for subregions to act as subregional hubs and UN Subregional Offices

Application of the above criteria would suggest the following regions and UN regional and subregional offices, as depicted in Table 17.7.

The above schema is fraught with political hazard – not dissimilar to the regional rivalry that attends the issue of UN Security Council permanent membership. Where does it leave Algiers, Paris, Islamabad, Jakarta, Tokyo, Canberra and Brasilia?

One of the problems of achieving consistency and coherence in the internal/external UN institutional network concerns the sensitivity of using the term 'capital' in reference to cities hosting UN offices. New York is often described, not least by its inhabitants, as the 'world's capital'. While this may be partially acceptable because of the unique status of that particular city (it is not the capital of the host country); this is not the case elsewhere. The notion of regional 'capitals' carries a sensitivity that is highly political and can act as an obstacle to reaching

Table 17.7 A possible schema of regions and regional offices

Region	Sub-region	Regional office	Subregional office
Sub-Saharan Africa	–	*Addis Ababa*	–
–	West Africa	–	*Abuja*
–	East Africa	–	*Nairobi*
–	Central Africa	–	*Kinshasha*
–	Southern Africa	–	*Pretoria*
'Arabia'	–	*Cairo*	–
–	Maghreb	–	*Tunis*
–	Mashreq	–	*Amman*
–	Gulf	–	*Doha*
Europe	–	*Geneva*	–
–	Northern Europe	–	*Stockholm*
–	Western Europe	–	*Brussels*
–	Central Europe	–	*Vienna*
–	Eastern Europe	–	*Bratislava*
Central Asia	–	*Astana*	–
South Asia	–	*New Delhi*	–
Northeast Asia	–	*Ulaanbaatar*	–
Southeast Asia	–	*Bangkok*	–
Pacific	–	*Suva*	–
–	Micronesia	–	*Palikir*
–	Melanesia	–	*Port Vila*
–	Polynesia	–	*Apia*
America	–	*San José*	–
–	North America	–	*Washington*
–	Caribbean	–	*Kingston*
–	Central America	–	*Managua*
–	Andes	–	*Quito*
–	Southern Cone	–	*Buenos Aires*

agreement on the question of hosting. As Table 17.6 illustrated, of the nine cases of potential comparison between 'Chapter VIII' regional organisations and 'Chapter X' UN regional commissions, there is consistency in choice of host cities in only one case. This gives rise to difficulties and challenges in promoting consistency in the regional institutional architecture of global politics in the twenty-first century.

Further, it needs to be considered whether the aims of the Chapter VIII and Chapter X entities are sufficiently common to warrant consideration of 'broad consistency and coherence' between them. The purposes of the AU, for example, and that of the ECA are closely comparable – even though those of the AU are considerably broader than those of the ECA. It would seem that part of the future work in strengthening consistency and coherence within the UN system could usefully extend to ensuring operational compatibility between the broader aims of Chapter VIII organisations and the more sectorally focused economic and social aims of the UN regional commissions.

17.6 Conclusions: Towards a 'Coherent Regional Institutional Landscape'

If the prescriptive measures outlined above are to be discussed and agreed upon, what process might be followed by the international community? To some extent, that process is already underway. In transmitting the SWC report to the General Assembly, the Secretary-General saw the recommendations as opening the way to a 'decisive realignment of the UN system'.[29] In March 2007, a regional high-level consultation on UN system-wide coherence was convened in Jakarta. In April, the Secretary-General submitted his own report on the SWC report to the General Assembly.[30] In his view, the UN needed more coherence and synergy so that it could 'perform as one and be more than the sum of its parts'. The vision of a more coherent UN was predicated on overcoming fragmentation and uniting the system's assets to enable it to 'deliver as one at all levels' but particularly at the country level in line with the principle of country ownership. The proposals themselves should be pursued as 'an integrated and coherent whole' since many were interconnected.

In April 2007, the General Assembly discussed, during its 61st session, the reports of the HLP and the Secretary-General. In May, the Assembly's president appointed two UN ambassadors (Barbados, Luxembourg) to co-chair the intergovernmental consultations on the reports of the HLP and the Secretary-General. In June, the Assembly convened its first informal meeting to consider the SWC report. In the Jakarta conference co-hosted by Norway and Indonesia in March 2007, agreement was reached on four points:

- Predictable funding for all national programmes
- Simplification of the administrative process of programme delivery
- Alignment of UN programmes with national programmes
- National ownership of the UN programmes at the country level[31]

In this debate, a number of points were made. In the summation of the General Assembly president, there was broad agreement that the UN system had a critical role to play in development, that the UN must remain at the heart of the multilateral development process, that the UN system's development activities must be strengthened and that the UN can develop more and better development activities.[32]

To facilitate progress in strengthening UN system-wide coherence, the author suggests that the recent deliberations should be followed by another resolution submitted to the UN General Assembly proposing the establishment of a task force to develop the 'regional recommendations' of the SWC report. The mandate of such a task force could be to develop a standardised definition of a 'region' for the purposes of UN operations, to identify specific regions derived from the definition and to co-locate regional offices.

This task would be a politically sensitive and diplomatically arduous one. It would, if it were to be implemented, take considerable time – perhaps 5–10 years. But it is not impossible, and it is directly in line with the original conceptualisation of the need for greater consistency and coherence in the UN system and with the greater thrust of the HLP.

Notes

1. This chapter is a shortened version of Graham (2008).
2. Delivering as One: Report of the Secretary-General's High-Level Panel on UN System-wide Coherence in the Area of Development, Humanitarian Assistance, and the Environment, United Nations, New York (advance, unedited version), 9 November 2006.
3. UNGA Resolution 1, adopted 16 September 2005.
4. A fifth recommendation calls for urgency in the implementation of these four directions.
5. SWC Report, p. 2.
6. The first eight 'pilot countries' are Albania, Cape Verde, Mozambique, Pakistan, Rwanda, Tanzania, Uruguay and Vietnam.
7. SWC Report, p. 10.
8. Ibid., paragraphs 66 and 67, p. 34.
9. Ibid., paragraph 54, p. 28.
10. Ibid., paragraph 56, p. 29.
11. UNGA Resolution 161, paragraph 6 (a), adopted 16 December 1996.
12. 'Australia has also long argued that the UN electoral system needs to be updated to reflect changes in the international system. In particular, the old divide between East and West Europe should be adapted to reflect the new converging European reality. The Panel's proposals for a distribution of Council seats between four new major regional electoral groups – with Australia to join the Asia Pacific group – is a good start and one that we strongly support'. Address by Foreign Minister Alexander Downer, 19 January 2005. Available at: http://www.foreignminister.gov.au/speeches/2005/050119_reforming_un.html.
13. Kiribati considers itself to be part of the Asian group, but this has not yet been formalised. Source: Correspondence with Kiribati Foreign Ministry official (June 2007).
14. UN Charter, Article 68.
15. No definition of a 'region' was advanced at Versailles. Indeed, the Eurocentric focus of post-war planning a century ago is shown by the sole reference to 'region' in the Covenant – that the special necessities of the 'regions devastated during the war of 1914–18' shall be borne in mind in rebuilding post-war commerce (League of Nations Covenant (1919), Article 23). It is notable that the Covenant used the term 'regions' while the UN Charter referred to 'areas'.
16. UNGA Resolution 46 (I) of 11 December 1946 and ECOSOC Resolutions 36 (IV) and 37 (IV) of 28 March 1947, establishing ECAFE and ECE, respectively. The additional phrase 'Far East', in contra-distinction to 'Asia', originated in the use by the British Empire of the division between its imperial possessions (the 'Near East' encompassed the lands of the Ottoman Empire, the 'Middle East' encompassed North Africa/Southwest Asia, 'Asia' covered South Asia, and the 'Far East' denoted what is now known as East Asia and Southeast Asia). It was

used as UN terminology until its quintessential Euro-centricism was repudiated and ECAFE changed to ESCAP (Economic Commission for Asia and the Pacific) in 1974.
17. ECOSOC Resolutions 106 (VI) of 25 February 1948 and 1984/67 of 27 July 1984, respectively.
18. ECOSOC Resolution 414 (XIII) of 20 September 1951.
19. UNGA Resolution 526 (VI) of 26 January 1952.
20. ECOSOC Resolution 671 A (XXV) of 1958, on the recommendation of the General Assembly, UNGA Resolution 1155 (XII) of 26 November 1957.
21. UNGA Resolution 120 (II) of 31 October 1947.
22. UNGA Resolution 199 (III) of 4 December 1948.
23. ECOSOC Resolution 1818 (LV) of 1973.
24. 'Nothing in the present Charter precludes the existence of regional arrangements or agencies for dealing with such matters relating to the maintenance of international peace and security as are appropriate for regional action, provided that such arrangements or agencies and their activities are consistent with the Purposes and Principles of the United Nations'. UN Charter, Article 52.1.
25. UNCIO XII, pp. 850 and 857, 8 June 1945, in Simma (1995: 688–689).
26. Experience has shown that common interest and affinities alone do not necessarily make for efficiency. Some countries that possess these characteristics are not among the most efficient in economic terms, and the same might be asserted for regions. Obversely, proximity acts as a positive factor in promoting efficiency – a negative correlation obtains between distance and efficiency.
27. The Panel offered two alternative options for an enlarged Security Council of 24 states, both models reflecting that regional division.
28. The shortcoming of this approach is the overlap of 'Arabia' with Africa (i.e. North Africa) and Asia (West Asia). Here, geographical precision cedes to the political imperative of the cultural-spiritual affinities of a 'region'.
29. SG/SM/10724 & GA/10530, 9 November 2006.
30. A/61/836, 3 April 2007.
31. CEB Briefing Note, p. 6.
32. Ibid., p. 1.

References

Daws, S. (1999). The origins and development of UN electoral groups. In R. Thakur (Ed.), *What is equitable geographical representation in the twenty-first century? Report of a seminar held by the International Peace Academy and the United Nations University, 26 March 1999, New York, USA* (pp. 11–29). Tokyo: United Nations University Press.

Graham, K., & Felício, T. (2006). *Regional security and global governance: A study of interaction between regional agencies and the UN security council with a proposal for a regional-global security mechanism*. Brussels: VUB Press.

Graham, K. (2008). Towards a Coherent Regional Institutional Landscape in the United Nations?, *BRIGG Papers*, (1).

O'Brien, T. (1999). Electoral group reconfiguration and present day realities. In R. Thakur (Ed.), *What is equitable geographic representation in the twenty-first century? Report of a seminar held by the International Peace Academy and the United Nations University, 26 March 1999, New York, USA* (pp. 30–39). Tokyo: United Nations University Press.

Picciotto, R., et al. (2005). *Striking a new balance: donor policy coherence and development cooperation in difficult environments*. Background paper commissioned by the Learning and Advisory Process on Difficult Partnerships of the Development Assistance Committee of the OECD, London: Department for International Development. http://www.oecd.org/dataoecd/31/62/34252747.pdf

Russett, B. (1967). *International regions and international system: Study in political ecology.* Chicago: Rand McNally.
Simma, B. (1995). *The United Nations charter: A commentary.* Oxford: Oxford University Press.
United Nations. (1951). *Measures for the Economic Development of Under-Developed Countries.* Report by a Group of Experts Appointed by the Secretary-General of the United Nations. New York: UN Publications.
Wright, S. (2004). Migration policy coherence needed, U.N. official says. *MIT Tech Talk, 49*(6), 6.

Chapter 18
UN System-Wide Coherence and the Regions: The Quest for Reforms

Eric Maertens

18.1 Introduction

Roughly since 1997,[1] the United Nations (UN) has struck a remarkable accommodation between far-reaching initiatives to reform its operational activities, supported by those inclined for more radical changes, and an incremental-steps approach which seems to be now growing in popularity among its membership. But, though most states agreed on the need to improve the overall coherence of the UN system, the debate has revealed steep default lines crossing the agenda. Positions vary significantly on the link between core normative and operational roles of the UN in the development, humanitarian and environment fields, on the mainstreaming of cross-cutting issues (human rights, gender and sustainable development) and, more prominently, on the governance of these activities.

This chapter is not intended to embark on a detailed, chronological analysis of the UN System-Wide Coherence (SWC) reform and of the positions adopted by its membership.[2] It will, instead, relying on the ongoing debate, pinpoint some of the key questions that affect the search for coherence in addressing needs from different regions, and, notably, the relationship with the regional governance levels and integration.

E. Maertens (✉)
UNU-CRIS, Bruges, Belgium
e-mail: emaertens@wanadoo.fr

P. De Lombaerde et al. (eds.), *The United Nations and the Regions: Third World Report on Regional Integration*, United Nations University Series on Regionalism 3,
DOI 10.1007/978-94-007-2751-9_18,

18.2 The 2005 World Summit and the High-Level Panel on System-Wide Coherence

As noted by von Freiesleben (2008), in spite of different perspectives between and within the developing and developed world, the World Summit Outcome Document (WSOD) was adopted in September 2005. It led, a few months later, to a request by the General Assembly to the Secretary-General for concrete proposals to achieve its stated goals. In dealing with the SWC and the regional organisations, the Outcome Document looks fairly brief, suggesting apparently that some of the deep structural difficulties needed more substantial examinations after the Summit.

Three paragraphs (168, 169 and 170) provide guidelines to the overall coherence, on the core role of the UN activities and on the links with regional organisations, lining up efforts in four main directions: policy, operational activities, humanitarian assistance and environmental activities.

Within the *policy area*, agreed measures include the strengthening of the linkages between normative and operational activities, coordination between the governing bodies of UN development and humanitarian agencies and the mainstreaming of cross-cutting issues (human rights, gender and sustainable development) in the decision-making process throughout the UN. The second area, on *operational activities*, deals with the field level presence, coordination and improved performance of the UN, which will further on be more concisely reflected into the recommendation by the High-Level Panel (HLP) on the 'delivering as one at country level' or 'One-UN' project.

Within the third area, *humanitarian assistance*, two key objectives were adopted: capacity building for member states, especially developing countries, in responding and managing natural disasters, as well as strengthening the current UN response to humanitarian crisis.

Finally, the fourth area, *environmental activities*, leads the member states to explore the possibility of creating a coherent institutional framework.

Considering the interest at stake, the reference to regional organisations (RO) in paragraph 170[3] looks unsurprisingly brief, revealing a relative lack of focus, leaving also to further consultations the analysis of more practical proposals. With a strong accent on peacekeeping and prevention of conflict, offering the option of placing RO's capacities under the framework of the UN Standby Arrangement System, the UN is mainly invited to build a stronger relationship with ROs and to deepen its cooperation in the economic, social and cultural fields.

Looking ahead, the HLP report on SWC[4] had benefited from extensive consultations on the functioning of the UN system at country, regional and global levels. The HLP reiterative quest for radical reforms is rooted in deep structural difficulties observed in operational activities: '[…] fragmentation and weakness of the UN work in the development and environmental areas, inefficient and ineffective governance, unpredictable funding, competitive search for funding […]' are pointed out as key factors having '[…]contributed to policy incoherence, duplication and operational ineffectiveness across the system'.

Some of these difficulties spring from the UN Charter itself, whose framers explicitly promoted a decentralised structure for the UN.[5] Some are the outcome of member states' behaviours in policymaking at country, regional and global levels. Among the former, without denying the benefits from decentralisation, it must be recognised that it meant a broad reach with varied constituency, different bureaucratic culture and practices, different intergovernmental machinery and specific institutional agendas. Among the latter, the main difficulty stems from the uncoordinated approach by official development assistance (ODA) bilateral and multilateral actors, as well as from the relative disconnection between the UN and the main domestic and regional actors from the finance, trade and economic sectors, who are more inclined to work with the Bretton Woods institutions and the World Trade Organisation (WTO).

Building on five strategic directions (United Nations 2006: 2), the HLP pursued its quest for reform by formulating proposals on eight specific clusters. Two are of primary importance in discussing the regional level of governance: the 'delivering as one at country level' or 'One-UN project', highlighting what the HLP considers as the 'key drivers and incentives for coherence from a bottom-up approach', and the second cluster, on the governance and institutional reform, arguing that, in order for the changes in the first cluster to become effective, they need to be supported by similar coherence at the centre.

By far, the sharpest proposals are set in the first cluster, the 'One-UN' at country level, which, indeed, is seen as the prominent and most effective level of search for coherence, while advocating at the same time that the 'new' system should preserve varied constituency with the presence of 'some' individual UN agencies that can '[…] best achieve their vital role in the provision of global public goods, advocacy, research, promoting best practice and global norms and standards, by operating individually in their specific sectors' (UN 2006: paragraphs 55 and 56).

However, many of the reflections on governance presented in the second cluster[6] are equally relevant, considering that, to deliver lasting changes, more effective mechanisms at the intergovernmental, organisational and regional levels should be inclusive and decisive. But here, against the HLP's suggested measures, especially the establishment of two new bodies, the Sustainable Development Board (SDB) and the Global Leaders Forum (GLF), the majority of member states became critical, underlining the possible erosion of national ownership of the UN intergovernmental processes, duplication of functions and the risks at stake in further weakening the Economic and Social Council (ECOSOC).

18.3 SWC and the Regions

Similar seeds of dissatisfaction can also be traced back to generalities and ambiguities on the way the HLP and the debate on its follow-up address the varied needs of the regions, the link with regional and sub-regional institutions, and regional integration.

First, within the time frame and the context of its own work, centred on a bottom-up approach, detailed proposals on governance and further streamlining at regional and central levels were obviously leading to more analysis. While concurring with the HLP's conclusion for an in-depth technical analysis, the nature and substance of the ongoing debate and default lines[7] on governance and institutional reform will most certainly delay changes in setting more effective regional (and central) mechanisms. It could, in a similar way, create gradual imbalance in reforming the different levels and jeopardise the overall coherence.

The need for such an analysis brought indeed the HLP to recommend that the Secretary-General establish an independent task force, efforts of which would focus on the following three objectives:

- Delineating with clarity the role of the UN, of its funds and programmes and of the specialised agencies, leading possibly to significant savings redirected to the 'One-UN' project
- The reviewing of the current imbalance between assessed and voluntary funding[8]
- The analysis of the functioning and relevance of the existing regional structure of the UN, with options for streamlining and consolidation

It is worthwhile noting that this HLP recommendation was only acknowledged by Secretary-General Ban Ki-moon for further due consideration, in a context where the member states, through the General Assembly, are actually guiding the process on SWC. This was even clearly spelled out by the President of the General Assembly Sheikha Haya Rashed Al Khalifa. In her opening remarks, stressing the importance of the 'One-UN' project, 'she had identified several commonalities among the positions of Member States, including views that the UN should remain at the heart of the multilateral development system and that there is a need for national ownership in the coherence process' (von Freiesleben 2008: 45).

In the second place, the latter objective on reconfiguring the UN regional setting[9] is tightly bound up with progress on the former two objectives. There again, the task ahead in delineating with clarity the role of the UN, within each region, as well as addressing, with some success, the current imbalance in the funding, could not only delay the new regional setting but also lead the UN system to narrow the scope of its regional setting to a mere organisational issue, improving the coordination of services to be provided to the UN country teams. To a certain extent, this possibility has been spelled out by the HLP, in equally brief and general terms, around two interrelated set of functions (UN 2006: paragraphs 67 and 68):

- The analytical and normative work, as well as activities of a trans-boundary nature, for which the regional commissions would act as a catalyst for these functions
- The coordination of services provided to UN country teams, the UNDP acting as the catalyst for these functions

Third and final comment, the UN regional dimension warrants a clear, holistic and systemic strategy on its own, especially on the way the UN normative and operational system can effectively interact with regional organisations and integration processes. Regional integration is on the agenda worldwide. But, it seems rather absent from the whole SWC search, focusing mainly on the coherence between two levels of operations: the UN central and country levels of operations, together with a general statement about reconfiguring the UN regional setting.

Again, at present, excepting the surge of dialogue and activities in UN peace-keeping and security, as well as analytical work performed by the UN regional commissions, UNCTAD, UNU-CRIS and some departments of specialised agencies, the relationship with regional organisations is usually formal, perfunctory and, to a large extent, disconnected from economic cabinets. There are several dimensions to this aspect. One is stemming from the natural constituency of the UN and capacity to influence key domestic and regional economic actors. Another is that, in the last three decades, open regional and sub-regional integration has been gradually acknowledged as a stepping stone in addressing imbalances from both the national and global contexts, with still a predominant, initial accent on economic and open trading regime. Even if there are also some efforts at deeper regional integration, often as a political, social and cultural project, by and large, the UN convening power on economic and trade actors has been traditionally weak.[10] In the social and economic spheres, the decision-making economic actors (Ministry of Finance, Budget, Trade, Monetary authorities) often relate to the Bretton Woods institutions and the WTO. Finally, the level and volume of operational activities addressing regional needs and assistance to regional institutions or regional integration remain quite limited, as a proportion of the UN development assistance flow.

A cohesive regional strategy will also be a key and decisive factor of the development agenda for the years to come. Its relative absence from the HLP report forms part of some of the common threads of the reform proposals, including those launched in other fora[11] and could certainly hamper the SWC debate. It requires, in avoiding fragmentation, to bring together the analytical, normative and operational capacities dispersed in the UN, extending the dialogue with the Bretton Woods institutions and the WTO to reach a better understanding of the added value of the different UN actors.

Such a strategy should also consider that regional arrangements take many different forms, can promote regional goods and, as noted by the World Commission on the Social Dimension of Globalisation (WCSDG), a more equitable pattern of domestic and global markets, in at least three ways:

> first, it can empower people and countries to better manage global economic forces. By effectively increasing the size of domestic markets, integration increases the capacity to withstand economic fluctuations [...] Common frameworks for financial regulation, rights at work, tax coordination and investment incentives are practical regional goals which can help prevent any risk of a race to the bottom [...] Integration can also enhance the negotiating power of smaller countries, acting together [...] Second; it can help build the capabilities needed to take advantages of global opportunities. Investments [...] will often require a critical mass of effort readily achieved at regional levels. [...] Third it can improve the conditions under which people connect to the global economy.
>
> (ILO 2004)

The above three angles deserve a solid space in devising the UN regional strategy and should probably lead to a non-standardised reconfiguration of the UN regional settings in each region, well adapted to the broad reach, the heterogeneity and specificity of the existing integration arrangements.

The same had been stressed by Rosenthal (2005: 36–37) of the work of the regional commissions and their link to the ECOSOC, suggesting that the regional dimension warrants a segment of its own in the General Assembly and that 'the segment or sub-segment on regional cooperation should revolve around the regional dimension of global issues and the global dimensions of regional issues'.

In conclusion, the debate on SWC is clearly revealing that progress is first expected from the focus on the bottom-up approach, encroached in the 'One-UN project', and from the lessons learned through the pilot experiences conducted in eight countries, with the hope that they could even guide the process of reform on governance and institutions. It is however arguable that this bottom-up approach could rapidly reach its own limits, without conducting a deeper analysis of the coherence of regional mechanisms that would support the efficiency and effectiveness of the changes set forth at central and country levels. This requires a clear and systemic regional strategy.

Notes

1. 1997 Report by Secretary-General Kofi Annan on 'Renewing the United Nations: A Programme for Reform' (A/51/950). This report can be perceived as a new starting point of reforms in UN operational activities, rooted in the various outcome documents of major conferences and panels such as the Millennium Declaration (2000), the Monterrey Consensus (2002), the Rome Declaration on Harmonisation (2003), the Paris Declaration on Aid Effectiveness (2005), the 2005 World Summit and the November 2006 High-Level Panel on System-Wide Coherence (SWC) in the Areas of Development, Humanitarian Assistance and the Environment (UN 2006).
2. For a recent and updated review, see von Freiesleben (2008).
3. 'We support a stronger relationship between the UN and regional and sub-regional organisations, pursuant to chapter VIII of the Charter, and therefore resolve:
   To expand consultation and cooperation between the UN and regional and sub-regional organisations through formalised agreements between the respective secretariats and, as appropriate, involvement of regional organisations in the work of the Security Council;
   To ensure that regional organisations that have a capacity for the prevention of armed conflict or peacekeeping consider the option of placing such capacity in the framework of the UN Standby Arrangement System;
   To strengthen cooperation in the areas of economic, social and cultural fields'
   Interesting to note that in the draft outcome document of 5 August 2005 from the GA president, the wording under 'c' included the 'areas of economic, social and human rights'.
4. Report submitted to the SG in November 2006. For a summary of the preparation, composition and content of the HLP report, see von Freiesleben (2008: 40–45).
5. The same reasoning is applied by G. Rosenthal in considering the strengths and weaknesses of ECOSOC in Rosenthal (2005).
6. Which includes also proposals on funding and management.
7. See in particular the report of the two co-chairs to the president of the UN General Assembly on the consultations regarding the SWC (United Nations, September 2007).

8. An ongoing debate addressed, with mixed results, by several UN programmes and agencies, within their own governance machinery.
9. Covering both the role of regional economic commissions and the regional mechanisms that different UN funds, programmes and agencies have established to provide technical and administrative backstopping.
10. Which in recent years brought the UN, its funds, programmes and specialised agencies to devise ways to enhance the dialogue with the Bretton Woods institutions and the WTO, as well as to enter in joint activities.
11. For instance, in the Triennial Comprehensive Policy Review (TCRP), created in the late 1990s to provide guidance on UN operational activities.

References

ILO. (2004). *A fair globalization. Creating opportunities for all.* Geneva: World Commission on the Social Dimension of Globalization, ILO.

Rosenthal, G. (2005, February). The Economic and Social Council of the United Nations. An Issues Paper. *Occasional Paper*. Friedrich Ebert Stiftung.

UN. (2006). *Secretary-General's high-level panel on UN system-wide coherence in the areas of development, humanitarian assistance, and the environment: "Delivering as One Report".* New York: United Nations.

von Freiesleben, J. (2008). *'System-wide coherence' in managing change at the United Nations.* New York: Centre for UN Reform Education.

Chapter 19
The UN and Regional Social Policy

Bob Deacon

19.1 Introduction

In this short chapter, I want to argue that although a set of *global* social reform policies might be the best way to fashion a socially just globalisation, a more politically viable strategy might be to concentrate on building effective *regional* social policies. I will further show that such regional health, education and social protection policies are being developed by many regional associations of government. I will then demonstrate that the UN regional commissions and the regional offices of the UN social agencies (ILO, UNESCO, UNDP, WHO) have with a few exceptions not been at the forefront of these new progressive regional social policies. I add my voice to the call for these UN actors to redirect their efforts around actually existing regional associations of government rather than continuing to focus their social policy interventions on single countries within merely geographically defined regions.

19.2 The Obstacles in the Way of a Progressive Global Social Policy

Critics who warned of the negative social consequences of neoliberal globalisation sought in various ways to propose reforms to globalisation that would ensure that these negative social consequences were addressed. Alternative global social policies were argued for that would ensure more *transnational redistribution* (via global taxes and increased Official Development Assistance (ODA)) to create greater

B. Deacon (✉)
University of Sheffield, UK; United Nations University Institute on Comparative Regional Integration Studies (UNU-CRIS), Bruges, Belgium

P. De Lombaerde et al. (eds.), *The United Nations and the Regions: Third World Report on Regional Integration*, United Nations University Series on Regionalism 3,
DOI 10.1007/978-94-007-2751-9_19, © Springer Science+Business Media B.V. 2012

global equity, more *global social regulation* (via agreed international labour standards) to prevent what was perceived as a race to the bottom and a strengthened *global social rights regime* (with international courts of justice with a mandate to address social rights) to ensure global citizens could take their country to court (Deacon 2007; Held 2004; Yeates 2001, 2008). Some progress has been made in some of these global social policy fields. There is the airline ticket tax and global funds to address many health problems. There is the global social compact, and there are moves to improve the UN social rights system. Progress is slow, however, and moreover, many of these proposed global social policies have become a matter of contestation between some in the Global North and some in the Global South.

A source of this North–south contestation is the wish on many in the Global South to be out from under a northern-driven globalisation. The negative experience of structural adjustment has led to many countries wishing to articulate their own social policies and therefore are resistant to new northern-driven social policies even if these are now progressive ones concerned to implant universal social protection measures and improve social governance. At the same time, even as some countries in the Global South might still need increased ODA to top up weakened government health and education budgets, the overriding wish is to be independent of aid. Similarly in the area of labour and social standards and social rights, there remains a suspicion of the self-interest of the Global North in pushing these onto the global agenda in trade and other deals.

19.3 The Alternative of Progressive Regional Social Policy

This North–south policymaking impasse which is slowing progress on UN governance reform lead me and others to the conclusion that an alternative route to a socially just globalisation might lie through a decentred globalisation based on a federation of world regions each addressing transnational social policies at the regional level (Deacon 2001, 2007; Deacon et al. 2006, 2007; Yeates 2005; Yeates and Deacon 2006; UNU-CRIS 2008). These regional social policies address issues that benefit from intergovernmental cross-border cooperation in areas such as (Deacon et al. 2007: 3):

- Regional social redistribution mechanisms: These can take several forms ranging from intra-regional transfers to overseas development aid (ODA) and can be used to target depressed areas or to redress inequalities.
- Regional regulations: These may include health and labour standards to combat an intra-regional 'race to the bottom', as well as the regulation of private social services and utilities (water, electricity). Regional formations in principle are in a stronger position than isolated governments to negotiate with private providers to ensure access, affordability and quality standards in commercial services and utilities.
- Regional mechanisms that give citizens a voice to challenge rights abuse: The European Union's European Court of Justice or the Council of Europe's Court of

Human Rights could serve as useful models of mechanisms by which citizens can be empowered to challenge the perceived failures of national governments to fulfil their rights.

- Regional cross-border investments: These could address various common social policy priorities, for instance, the production of cheaper generic pharmaceuticals at regional level to benefit from economies of scale or common programmes to avoid cross-border spread of diseases (e.g. malaria).
- Regional technical cooperation in social policy: This provides an opportunity to learn from good practices that have worked at local level and develop innovative local solutions.

These ideas about the importance of the social dimension of regions have also featured in many UN publications. The report '*A Fair Globalisation: Creating Opportunities for All*' of the World Commission on the Social Dimension of Globalisation (WCSDG) claimed that regional integration can contribute to a more equitable pattern of globalisation, but only if regional integration has a strong social dimension (WCSDG 2004). In the July 2006 session of ECOSOC, the UN Secretary-General declared that multi-stakeholder policy dialogues at the national and regional level have to be developed 'with the objective of building national and regional capacity to develop a multi-disciplinary approach to economic and social issues' (UNSG 2006). Earlier that year, UNESCO organised a High-Level Symposium on the Social Policy Dimension of Regionalism in the context of the UNESCO International Social Sciences Policy Nexus Forum (Deacon et al. 2006). The resulting Buenos Aires Declaration called upon

> the regional organisations such as the Common Market of the Southern Cone (MERCOSUR) and the African Union (AU), in association with social scientists and civil society, to further develop the social dimension of regional integration and [called] upon the UN to facilitate inter-regional dialogues.

19.4 Regional Social Policies in Practice

In practice, there is progress in the development of such regional social policies. Many regional associations of government have begun to tackle these cross-border health, education and social protection issues at a regional level. The European Union (EU) represents the most advanced form of regional integration. In terms of regional social policy, the EU has made major advances in the three fields of social redistribution, social regulation and social rights. The Structural Fund/Social Cohesion Fund is the mechanism whereby the EU's funds (which are contributed approximately according to countries' gross national product (GNP) and population size) are allocated to the development of impoverished or economically underdeveloped areas within the EU member states. There are a range of regulations in the fields of occupational health and safety, health services, equal opportunities, labour law and social security and pension schemes, together with social dialogue mechanisms that apply to all countries. In terms of regional social rights, the Community

Charter of Fundamental Social Rights of Workers was established at an earlier stage and was added to in 2000 with the adoption of the Charter of Fundamental Rights. Harmonisation of national social regulations and standards is a precondition to be accepted at the EU and benefit from its internal market and regional transfers. Additionally, the Open Method of Coordination (OMC) is a mechanism whereby national civil servants are encouraged to ratchet up their policies against agreed EU-wide benchmarks and through policy learning processes (de la Porte and Nanz 2004; Chalmers and Lodge 2003). The OMC in the fight against social exclusion was introduced in March 2000; in the area of pensions, it was introduced in March 2001, and in the area of health care, it was introduced in June 2001.

There are some signs of such a regional approach to social policy emerging in the Global South. Despite its recent creation in 2006, the Bolivarian Alternative for Latin America (ALBA) has already developed some social policies to address pressing health problems, illiteracy and emergency relief among member countries, involving regional redistribution and technical cooperation. The Association of Southeast Asian Nations (ASEAN) has a Social Charter consistent with the various commitments undertaken by member countries. ASEAN has however been noted for its limited involvement in social policy beyond encouragement of safety nets in the aftermath of the Asian financial crisis. The Central America Free Trade Agreement (CAFTA) is a new regional formation which is a hybrid of an open or mega-regionalism formation extending to and including the USA but exhibits features of a smaller regional formation with some social protectionist features. The constitution provides for the legal requirement to recognise the ILO's core labour standards. The Andean Community agreed in 2004 on a regional Integral Plan for Social Development that involves technical cooperation on social policy among Andean countries including the exchange of good practice, regional monitoring of the Millennium Development Goals (MDGs) and a number of regional social projects, including the 2005 Andean Social Humanitarian Fund. MERCOSUR has an important labour and social declaration, common regulations on pharmaceuticals, some reciprocal social security entitlements and joint health and safety inspections. Agreements have been signed to recognise education credentials, degrees and diplomas across member countries. There are proposals for a regional social fund, and a few regionally funded projects in border areas exist. In January 2007, in an effort to enhance the social dimensions of MERCOSUR, its Council approved the establishment of the MERCOSUR Social Institute, to be based in Asunción, Paraguay, with the mandate to elaborate regional social policies, to systematise and update regional social indicators and to promote the exchange of good practices in the social field and cooperation mechanisms. The Southern African Development Community (SADC) has developed an infrastructure and capacity for the implementation of sub-regional social policy. In particular, the Social and Human Development Directorate has responsibility for a SADC Social Charter which included among its objectives the 'harmonisation of social policies which.....contribute to productive employment ....facilitate labour mobility' and asserts that 'member states shall ratify and implement the ILO core labour standards...and that member states shall establish regional mechanisms to assist member states'. Additionally, it has elaborated codes of conduct on HIV and AIDS and employment on child labour, on safe use of chemicals and on social security. Finally, in this selective review, the South Asian Association for Regional Cooperation (SAARC) has included social issues on the agendas of its summits. In 2002, SAARC signed a regional convention for the promotion of child welfare and a regional convention on the prevention of trafficking of women and children. The 13th summit of SAARC was held in November 2005. Highlights of the Summit Declaration included the SAARC Decade of Poverty Alleviation, a regional food bank, a Poverty Alleviation Fund, new resolves to address problems of natural disasters and pandemics and the trafficking of women and children.

19.5 Is the UN Supporting Progressive Regional Social Policies?

A review of the extent to which the regional economic commissions of the UN and the regional arms of the UN social agencies (ILO, UNESCO, WHO, UNICEF, etc.) have been in the forefront of helping to fashion these regional social policy initiatives of regional associations of government has revealed that with a few notable exceptions, the driver of these initiatives has not been the UN (Deacon and Macovei 2009). Here, we review the regional economic and social commissions first and the social agencies of the UN second. In general, what is observed with the Economic and Social Commissions is that with notable exceptions, first, the UN continues to focus *on advice to countries within regions rather than advice to regional associations of countries,* and, second, where there is advice to regional associations, *the advice often neglects the social policy dimension of regional social integrations.* What is observed with the UN social agencies are some examples of good practice in one or other region but no systematic coherent planned approach to this work even within the ILO which has done most and which itself argued for the social dimension of regional integration to be taken seriously in its World Report on a Fair Globalisation.

The Economic Commission for Latin America and the Caribbean (ECLAC) among the regional economic commissions has a deserved reputation for excellent policy analysis and policy advocacy work including in the fields of social policy and social protection. *In Globalization and Development: A Latin American Perspective* (Ocampo and Martin 2003: xv), it argued for an agenda for the global era that 'needed to achieve three foremost objectives of a new international order; a supply of global public goods, the gradual correction of international asymmetries, and the progressive construction of a rights-based international social agenda'. That having been said, ECLAC has been rather silent on supranational regional social policies such as cross-border agreements on social security as exists in MERCOSUR or cross-border social funds, as exist in the Andean Community, let alone the new cross-border largesse of Venezuela funding anti-poverty programmes in its neighbouring country. This is surprising when it is recalled that regional integration in Latin America has its origins in the developmental theory that ECLAC promulgated in the 1950s. This loss of focus on regional formations in ECLAC during the 1980s and 1990s was due to the replacement of this regional development strategy with an open- and neoliberal-driven regionalism. However, there are a number of recent examples of ECLAC seeking to reinject a concern with the social dimension of regional economic integration into the agenda. In June 2006, the ECLAC sub-office in the Caribbean convened a high-level ministerial dialogue on social security and sustainable social development which included agenda item 7 on the 'Social Dimension of Regional Integration in CARICOM'. The discussion dealt with cross-border social security agreements, harmonisation of industrial relations, etc. (ECLAC 2006).

Regional integration represents an important topic on the UN Economic Commission for Africa (ECA) agenda. At the 2006 AU Summit, the role of ECA was reaffirmed as a 'key African institution to assist and facilitate the work of the African Union and the Regional Economic Communities (RECs) in advancing the development agenda of the continent' (ECA 2007: 1). In its structural design, the five sub-regional offices of ECA play an important role in implementing regional integration programmes. In 2004, ECA delivered a Policy Research Report 'Assessing Regional Integration in Africa' (ARIA). However, even though the report is considered to be 'a tool for monitoring and tracking progress in achieving integration in key sectors at the sub-regional and regional levels' (ECA 2007: 5), the social dimension of regional integration is not addressed in a distinctive chapter. Under the chapter 'Human Resources and Labour Mobility', the progress in performance in labour mobility within the RECs is underlined. Subsequent ARIA editions have looked at the burning issue of rationalisation of the RECs (2005) and macroeconomic policy convergence (2008) but not social integration.

Starting with 2002, the UN Economic and Social Commission for Western Asia (ESCWA) 'has focused on the issue of integrated social policies with a view to promoting a coordinated and effective social vision that encompasses both the social and the economic priorities of *countries* (my emphasis) in the region' (ESCWA 2005: c). In January 2008, the Policy Frameworks and Instruments team of the Social Development Division convened an Expert Group Meeting in Amman. The meeting gathered regional and international experts in the area of social policy. For the purpose of this meeting, the new ESCWA report on 'Integrated Social Policy Report II: From Concept to Practice' was realised. The review was designed to serve as 'an advocacy tool providing practical direction for social policy makers and practitioners in the region' (ESCWA 2008a: 1). It is important to note that the report tackles the issue of financing social policy in the ESCWA region, which 'remains a challenge for the (…) *countries* (my emphasis) in the region' (ESCWA 2008b: 39). My point is the social dimension of the regional integration process and actually existing regional associations of governments are not directly addressed in the report.

The self-declared role of the Economic and Social Commission for Asia and the Pacific (ESCAP) is to overcome some of the region's greatest challenges and focuses on issues that are most effectively addressed through regional cooperation. The area of work of ESCAP is three-folded: poverty reduction, managing globalisation and tackling emerging social issues. Here, we do find within the work of ESCWA a recent example of the kind of focus on regional associations of countries that I am arguing for. At the end of 2007, ESCAP released the study 'Ten as One: Challenges and Opportunities for ASEAN Integration', which coincided with the ASEAN Summit. Even though the study reaffirms that ASEAN represents a successful example of regional organisations, it also stresses 'the need for ASEAN to narrow the development gaps among its members, through mutual assistance and cooperation, for the benefit of the citizen of all 10 countries' (ESCAP 2007: 5). The report calls on ASEAN to advance a regional strategy for managing the migration phenomenon in a coordinated and integrated manner. Furthermore, it states that 'inadequate social protection systems and standards will make it difficult for poorer countries to cope with the effects of investment integration and to achieve their potential in attracting investment' (ESCAP 2007: 32). From the recommendations stipulated by ESCAP, ASEAN should improve the cohesion policy on the new freedom of movement of people. This will only be sustainable if supported by a cohesion policy aimed at 'narrowing the gaps between winners and losers of the integration process. The policy requires financial transfers for social, economic, and environmental development and strengthening social safety nets'.[1]

Turning to the UN Social Agencies, we do find rather more focus on their part on regional associations of governments. The ILO and UNESCO in particular have taken initiatives in this regard but often not in a coherent and planned way but as part of ad hoc initiatives. The proposition that regional integration might be a stepping stone to a fair globalisation has informed much of the ILO's work on the topic, although there is no unit that has specific responsibility for regional integration, nor has a systematic approach or policy been developed on the issue. The ILO has, however, signed agreements with 14 different regional communities over the years for sharing information and cooperating on matters of mutual concern. In practice, the day-to-day interaction between the ILO and the regional economic communities (RECs) varies dramatically from one region to the next. The social dimension of regional integration is largely dealt with on an ad hoc basis (through a mixture of projects and research) whenever sub-regional developments correspond to ILO policy priorities (e.g. regional labour migration protocols, the European EPA process, regional PRSPs or related development plans, skills and social security portability, regional labour law harmonisation or regional social dialogue). Because of the scattered nature of this work, a survey was initiated in early 2007 to find out what was being done both at the field level and in Geneva on regional integration over the past few years (mainly 2006/2007). This revealed that despite the lack of coordination, there is in fact a great deal being done. Among the projects were those on (1) labour law harmonisation project in CARICOM, (2) promotion of social dialogue in Francophone Africa (PRODIAF), (3) ILO-ASEAN Occupational Health and Safety Network, (4) joint ILO-ASEAN study on the labour impact of the ASEAN Free Trade Agreement, (5) labour migration for integration and development in the EuroMed context and West and East Africa, (6) strengthen the capacity of SADC to promote social dialogue and corporate social responsibility, (7) Ouagadougou

Summit (AU) on employment and poverty alleviation, (8) ILO-ASEAN study on HIV/AIDS in the world of work and (9) comparative analysis of child labour legislation in MERCOSUR.

UNESCO has been surprisingly active in the field of regional social policy and development through the agency of its Social and Human Sciences Sector. This sector of UNESCO convened in February 2004 a High-Level Symposium on the Social Dimension of Regionalism in Uruguay. UNESCO, through its MOST programme, has subsequently organised regional meetings of Ministers of Social Development in three continents. Zola S. Skweyiya, Minister for Social Development in South Africa and chair of MOST, has ensured that the focus of such meetings in Africa has been on regional integration. Within this programme, MOST organised a series of seminars on regional integration policies in the ECOWAS region, called 'Nation-states and the challenges of regional integration in West Africa', which ended with a call to establish a regional integration studies centre in Cape Verde.

At the regional level, UNDP is involved in different projects that are linked with regional social policies. For instance, the UNDP Regional Centres in Bangkok and Colombo (Asia and the Pacific region) is involved in several projects that are worth mentioning. The 2007 Work Plan refers to capacity development programmes directly linked to poverty reduction and achieving the MDGs, and HIV/AIDS, such as 'Support for SAARC: Regional Poverty Profile; data bank for best practices and technical support', 'Capacity support provided to ASEAN, SAARC, SPC and PIFS for regional and inter-country collaboration on HIV', 'Implementation of ASEAN Work Programme-III', 'SAARC HIV Strategy and SPC and PIFS ADIS Strategy', 'Assessment of the legal situation in relation to trafficking, sex work and HIV conducted in SAARC countries' and 'Regional consultation organised on enabling ethical and legal environment in ASEAN and SAARC'. Among other initiatives by UN social agencies focussed on regional associations of countries are those of UNICEF and the WHO. UNICEF issued in 2005 a report on the 'State of the SAARC Child'. This report is a result of the collaboration between SAARC and UNICEF, which started in 1993 with a Memorandum of Understanding. The report focuses on the rate of progress in the region regarding the girls' education in SAARC. In close cooperation with WHO, ASEAN implemented the ASEAN Plus Three Emerging Infectious Diseases Programme. The Ouagadougou Declaration on Primary Health Care and Health Systems in Africa in April 2008 called for WHO in consultation with the member states and other UN agencies to establish a regional health observatory.

19.6 The Need for Regional Bodies of the UN Social Agencies and UN Economic and Social Commissions to Refocus on Regional Associations of Countries

If the argument of this short chapter is valid that a strengthened system of world regional governance with each region adopting a social dimension to its regional integration project is the best way of securing a socially responsible globalisation, then certain things follow for the reform of the governance and practice of UN social agencies and for the UN Economic and Social Commissions. These reforms are needed to elevate regional associations of governments and, within them, the Social and Labour Commissions of regional associations to a more prominent place in the world social governance.

For the ECOSOC, it means convening, on a regular basis, high-level meetings of the Commissioners and Secretariats of regional associations of governments responsible for social development and social and labour policy. These meetings would review best practice in the development of regional social policies of redistribution regulation and rights and cross-border cooperation in the fields of health, education, social protection and allied policy fields.

For the Economic and Social Commissions, it means devoting considerable more resources to working not with governments in the region but with the regional associations of governments of the region. It also means giving equal priority in that work focused on regional associations to social policy issue alongside economic issues.

For the UN social agencies (ILO, WHO, UNICEF, UNESCO, etc.), it means that the World Health Assembly, World Labour Conference and other annual assemblies create a more prominent space within their deliberations and decision-making processes for representatives of the relevant Social 'Policy' Commissioners of regional associations of countries. It also means fashioning a coherent strategy for working on either health, labour education or other social policy topic at the regional association of country level. It also means that the regional offices of the UN agency devote a far greater part of their analytical and technical capacity to working with the secretariats of the regional associations of governments within their territory. This might mean also relocating regional UN social agency offices to the city hosting these secretariats.

Given that in each world region the exact configuration of regional associations of governments is different and the relationship between regional and sub-regional associations of countries varies too and given also that the Ministries and Secretariats with responsibility for social policy have varied name, it is not possible to give precise institutional and location reform proposals. Taking Africa as an illustrative example of a region and the case of SADC as one of several sub-regions, what is proposed is that:

(a) The AU Commission for Social and Labour Affairs together with the Secretariat dealing with Social Policy in SADC and the other African sub-regions attend the proposed UN ECOSOC high-level regional association meetings periodically.
(b) The ECA focuses its support efforts on the AU and SADC and the other sub-regional offices and gives a higher attention to the social dimension of regional and sub-regional integration.
(c) If not already so located, the WHO, ILO, UNICEF, UNESCO and UNDP establish their head regional office in Addis Ababa and establish their sub-regional offices in Gabarone (for SADC), Abuja (for ECOWAS) and similarly for other sub-regions.

These governance, policy and operational reforms will permit appropriate attention to be systematically paid to the development of effective regional and sub-regional social policies which are important building blocks of a global integration project that puts human need and inclusive social development first.

Note

1. See www.unescap.org.

References

Chalmers, D., & Lodge, M. (2003). The open method of coordination and the European Welfare State. *ESRC Centre for Analysis of Risk and Regulation Discussion Papers* (11). London: London School of Economics.

De la Porte, C., & Nanz, P. (2004). The OMC: A deliberative-democratic mode of governance? The case of employment and pensions. *Journal of European Public Policy, 11*(2), 267–288.

Deacon, B. (2001). The social dimension of regionalism. *Globalism and Social Policy Programme (GASPP) Occasional Paper* (8). Helsinki: National Research and Development Centre for Welfare and Health (STAKES).

Deacon, B. (2007). *Global social policy and governance*. London: Sage.

Deacon, B., & Macovei, M. C. (2009). Regional social policy from above: International organizations and regional social policy. In B. Deacon, M. C. Macovei, L. Van Langenhove, & N. Yeates (Eds.), *World-regional social policy and global governance* (pp. 40–62). London: Routledge.

Deacon, B., Yeates, N., & Van Langenhove, L. (2006). Social dimensions of regional integration. A high level symposium organised by UNESCO, MERCOSUR, GASPP and UNU-CRIS. Conclusions, *UNU-CRIS Occasional Papers* (O-2006/13).

Deacon, B., Ortiz, I., & Zelenev, S. (2007). Regional social policy, *UNDESA Working Paper* (37).

ECA. (2007). *Assessment of progress on regional integration in Africa*. Fifth Session of the Committee on Trade, Regional Cooperation and Integration (E/ECA/CRTCI/5/5). Addis Ababa: ECA.

ECLAC. (2006, June 14–15). *Report of the High-Level Ministerial Dialogue – Social Security and Sustainable Social Development in the Caribbean*. St. John's: ECLAC.

ESCAP. (2007). Ten as one: Challenges and opportunities for ASEAN integration. *ESCAP Series on Inclusive Sustainable Development* (1). Bangkok.

ESCWA. (2005). *Towards integrated social policies in Arab countries: Framework and comparative analysis* (E/ESCWA/SDD/2005/4). New York/Geneva: United Nations Economic and Social Commission for Western Asia (ESCWA).

ESCWA. (2008a). *The social policy report II: From concept to practice, Aide Memoire for the Expert Group Meeting*. Amman: ESCWA.

ESCWA. (2008b). *Integrated social policy report II: From concept to practice*. New York: UN-ESCWA.

Held, D. (2004). *Global covenant*. Cambridge: Polity Press.

Ocampo, J. A., & Martin, J. (2003). *Globalization and development: A Latin American and Caribbean perspective*. Santiago de Chile: ECLAC.

UNSG. (2006). *Creating an environment at the national and international levels conducive to generating full and productive employment and decent work for all, and its impact on sustainable*

development, Report of the Secretary-General (E/2006/55). Geneva: UN Economic and Social Council.
UNU-CRIS. (2008). Deepening the social dimensions of regional integration. *IILS Discussion Paper* (188). Geneva: ILO – International Institute for Labour Studies.
WCSDG. (2004). *A fair globalisation: Creating opportunities for all.* Geneva: International Labour Office/World Commission on the Social Dimension of Globalisation.
Yeates, N. (2001). *Globalisation and social policy.* London: Sage.
Yeates, N. (2005). Globalisation and Social Policy in a Development Context: Regional Responses. *Social Policy and Development Programme Paper* (18). Geneva: UNRISD.
Yeates, N. (Ed.). (2008). *Understanding global social policy.* Bristol: Policy Press.
Yeates, N., & Deacon, B. (2006). Globalism, Regionalism and Social Policy: Framing the Debate (O/2006–6). *UNU-CRIS Occasional Papers.*

Chapter 20
The UN and the Regions: The Case of Health Sector Coordination for Disaster Management in the Caribbean

Geert Haghebaert

20.1 Introduction

The Caribbean is one of the most disaster-prone subregions in the world.[1] It experiences multiple natural hazards: tropical storms and hurricanes, floods and flash floods, landslides and mudslides as well as earthquakes and volcanic eruptions. In recent years, repeated hurricanes and tropical storms devastated Grenada and parts of Cuba, Jamaica, Haiti, Dominican Republic and the Bahamas and claimed many hundreds of lives while hundreds of thousands were badly affected. The economical and structural impact on the countries often turns back development efforts by many years.

The Caribbean nations face an uneven battle with nature and have increasingly been developing coordinated action to tackle vulnerabilities and reduce impact of hazards. Assistance in this process, be it operational, technical or financial, is provided by subregional, regional and bilateral and multilateral sources.

Next to its vulnerability to natural hazards, the region faces specific constraints due to inequity, uncontrolled urbanisation and pockets of extreme poverty, while the effective coordination and increasing competition for funding of agencies working in health emergencies is a recognised challenge.[2]

Due to the small size of many countries in the Caribbean subregion, a lack of human and other resources persists also in disaster management, despite many efforts. This issue of economy of scale is especially apparent in the smaller island states where the per capita impact[3] ranks high, where a whole country can be affected by one event and where is little or no margin, e.g. only one hospital.

The geographical and demographical mosaic of countries, bigger and small island states, territories and dependencies in the Caribbean as well as the many regional or subregional bodies and initiatives make official representation and

G. Haghebaert (✉)
Delegation of European Commission, Maputo, Mozambique
e-mail: Geert.HAGHEBAERT@eeas.europa.eu

P. De Lombaerde et al. (eds.), *The United Nations and the Regions: Third World Report on Regional Integration*, United Nations University Series on Regionalism 3,
DOI 10.1007/978-94-007-2751-9_20, © Springer Science+Business Media B.V. 2012

operational coordination complicated for all actors. We are having a closer look at what facilitates operational coordination for emergency preparedness and disaster response in the health sector on a (sub)regional level, more in particular using the example of the UN cluster lead for the region, the Pan American Health Organisation (PAHO).[4]

20.2 Regional and Subregional Bodies Involved in Disaster Risk Reduction or Response

The following regional and subregional bodies are involved in disaster risk reduction or response:

- Organisation of Eastern Caribbean States (OECS)[5]: in the 'St George Declaration', this mini subregion commits itself to environmental sustainable development including integrated disaster management.
- Caribbean Community (CARICOM)[6] is the single most important subregional body of political integration in the Caribbean. It helps to set the agenda for the subregional disaster management agency (CDERA, cf. below). CARICOM's health and social development council has driven several successful collaboration efforts, e.g. eradication of indigenous measles. The 'Agreement between the Caribbean Community and PAHO' (2002) is the basis for collaboration and coordination of common actions and for the recognition of each other's roles.
- The broader Association of Caribbean States (ACS)[7] collaboration has 'natural disasters' as one of the four priority areas where joint actions are developed. The subregional advisor for disasters of PAHO attends the disaster-related meetings of the ACS.
- The Organisation of American States (OAS)[8] developed several initiatives related to disasters. Noteworthy is that it was a regional initiative in 1976 by the ministers of health of its member states that created PAHO's Programme on Emergency Preparedness and Disaster Relief (PED) after a major earthquake in Guatemala. Since 1999, the OAS Inter-American Committee for Natural Disaster Reduction (IACNDR) not only acts as 'a venue for information exchange on natural disaster reduction actions' but also seeks 'mechanisms to enable more efficient and effective preparedness and response measures'.

20.3 The UN System and Health Emergencies in the Caribbean

In addition to their bilateral country contacts, UN agencies meet at least once a year with the CARICOM secretariat separately. Until recently, the only UN agency office specifically for the subregion was PAHO's Caribbean Programme Coordination ('CPC'). Located in Barbados, it originated as an add-on function to PAHO's representation to the OECS countries. The CPC acts as a broker in the multiple subregional platforms for strategic health policy and action. It aims at using the opportunity offered by e.g. the CARICOM political integration process to push topics on the agenda of a number of countries, especially when many lack the economy of scale to develop or follow up certain themes on their own.

PAHO installed its main PED disaster management office for the Caribbean in the CPC. From here it covers practically the entire subregion[9] and liaises with other agencies that cover parts of the subregion. At the end of 2008, no other UN agency had such a specific subregional structure and representation. For example, most UN agencies use country or OECS representations or headquarter representatives to liaise with CARICOM.

UNDP however chairs the Eastern Caribbean Donor Group for Disaster Management[10] (see below) and set up a subregional centre in Trinidad in 2009 which also focuses on disaster risk reduction (DRR). Other UN agencies as UNICEF and OCHA are partially involved in disaster management in the subregion, mostly in workshops, training and occasional appeals.

In Panama, the secretariat of the UN International Strategy for Disaster Reduction (ISDR) is supported amongst others by PAHO and aims at coordinating, promoting and strengthening DRR on a regional, subregional and national level. This ISDR Regional Unit for the Americas strives to provide support to actors throughout the region. One of the main elements of the proposed strengthened ISDR system next to the national coordination bodies are networks or coordination platforms at regional and subregional level including inter-agency task forces and networks of national platforms.

Standard UN protocol channels all official communications through the representations before it reaches the counterparts. Hence, PAHO's disaster management office for the Caribbean counts for formal contacts with the existing PAHO representations based in the Bahamas, Barbados-ECC (for the Eastern Caribbean Countries: OECS members and French territories), the Dominican Republic, Guyana, Jamaica, Suriname and Trinidad and Tobago. The subregional bodies however are formally contacted through the CPC office. These formal channels add complexity in communications, but enable PAHO's national and subregional staff to receive and exchange mutually relevant information and contribute to the overarching institutional priorities as, e.g. DRR.

20.4 Initiatives for Subregional Operational Coordination in Disaster Management

CARICOM's Disaster Emergency Management Agency (CDERA, soon to be CDEMA to reflecting a broader role) is based in Barbados and is the subregion's intergovernmental disaster agency since 1991.

On request of a member state, CDERA is responsible for 'soliciting and coordinating assistance from [...] both within and outside the region'. It acts as the

Regional Coordination Centre for the CARICOM Disaster Relief Unit (CDRU). The main tasks of CDRU include management of relief supplies, emergency telecommunications support and the provision of appropriate personnel for repairing critical lifeline facilities.

CDERA has over the years become the main subregional partner and a vehicle of donor funding and gradually included preparedness, recovery and mitigation. It has also an executing role in different DRR projects as e.g. the Caribbean Hazard Mitigation Capacity Building Programme (funded by CIDA) and together with the Caribbean Development Bank has been mapping the vulnerabilities of critical facilities to inform the redevelopment and reduction of the risk to vital services in Grenada.

CDERA tries to harmonise the work programmes of 16 member states (12 countries and 4 British Overseas Territories) through a comprehensive disaster management (CDM) strategy. Its broad annual CDM consultation now brings together up to 60 national and international agencies to encourage open exchange, alignment and strategic alliances. This resulted e.g. in standard operating procedures between partners in disaster management.

In its strategic plan, CDERA recognises the importance of some subregional initiatives preceding to the CDM strategy as the CARICOM regional framework, the Caribbean Single Market and Economy and the OECS's St George's Declaration of principles for environmental sustainability.[11] This illustrates the broader development issues and links in to the work of e.g. UNDP.

PAHO supported the subregional CDERA initiative from the start and hosted the early offices of CDERA in its premises. It was also the first international organisation to sign a memorandum of understanding with CDERA defining and recognising each others' roles.

As the lead agency in the health sector, PAHO sits on CDERA's 'harmonisation council' of the CDM strategy with the representatives of national disaster offices, donors, FAO and UNDP. This council is a potential key subregional coordinating body. Up until now, many UN agencies take up important supportive roles, but all stakeholders involved wish for increased Caribbean leadership in the different sectors. In this sense, PAHO's subregional disaster office supports common planning for CARICOM's health and disaster coordinators by facilitating and organising a yearly planning and coordination meeting.

Separate but linked subregional initiatives try to enhance coordination. For example, the Eastern Caribbean Donor Group for Disaster Management (ECDG/DM), revamped after the devastating impact of hurricane Ivan in 2004, serves as such a coordinating interface. It is chaired by the UN Resident Coordinator for the OECS and Barbados (UNDP) and includes PAHO/WHO, UNICEF, WB, CDERA, the Regional Security System, donor representatives (OFDA, CIDA, DFID and EU), NGOs and the International Federation of the Red Cross.

On a regional level, PAHO's PED programme is the liaison office for OCHA and all other humanitarian actors and the focal point for the humanitarian reform activities and contacts with the UN Inter-Agency Standing Committee (IASC). PAHO focuses specifically on its health cluster responsibility. More global initiatives as

UN led international appeals and the sending of UNDAC teams and the mobilisation of CERF are not routinely used as they are reserved for major disasters and would need formal international appeals by the Caribbean states.

20.5 Other Development Aspects

Global initiatives for specific themes as disaster management bring together states, donors, technical and voluntary agencies on a supra-regional level and offer a common framework for a regional and subregional coordination and advocacy with national decision makers. Noteworthy is the use of the outcomes of the 2005 UN World Conference on Disaster Reduction, the Hyogo Framework for Action and the UN Millennium Development Goals (MDG). These are not only used as mere references but as elements of advocacy as well as technical and planning elements for key national documents and underpin (sub)regional policymaking and operational coordination.

While PAHO is the coordinator of the disaster preparedness and response working group of the OAS and the health sector cluster lead in emergencies (UN IASC), PAHO's basic strategy is to assist countries in reaching some of the MDGs. 'Disasters are a limiting factor in achieving health sector goals and an impediment to the normal functioning of health services'.

PAHO further contributes regionally by the promotion of inter-country collaboration and mutual assistance agreements, the establishment of memoranda of understanding with other international and regional agencies and the provision of technical information products and services aimed at the region as e.g. the 'CRID' (Regional Disaster Information Centre), training initiatives and workshops for regional and technical staff, regional networks of technical experts in disaster mitigation. Its Supply Management System (SUMA) can collect information on donations arriving in country and provides feedback nationally and regionally; it advocates with regional financial institutions and ensures that the health sector impact is reflected in post-disaster socioeconomic assessments conducted by ECLAC and others.

According to the Inter-American Development Bank (IADB),[12] the poor are particularly vulnerable to 'natural' disasters caused by mismanagement of natural resources, such as informal settlements in areas prone to landslides or floods. It has 'priorities for enhancing regional public goods which include the harmonisation of health and environmental codes, and coordinated regional action on issues of e.g. disease control and disaster prevention' amongst others.

IADB is coordinating closely with PAHO and OAS led working groups on disaster preparedness and response, vulnerability assessment and indexing for natural disasters. The IADB Department on Sustainable Development has focused on assisting Caribbean States in anticipating and/or mitigating real or potential threats to their social, economic and environmental security. Several Inter-American forums link disaster reduction and sustainable development, e.g. the IACNDR, the Inter-American Network for Disaster Mitigation (focuses on best practices) or the Emergency Lending Program of IADB.

20.6 Conclusion

The task of creating an effective strategy for disaster reduction in the Caribbean is 'dauntingly complex'.[13] But major disasters and 'multiple-event, multiple-country disaster years' functioned as wake-up calls in the past and triggered the necessary momentum for regional and subregional initiatives.

The coordination for future activities between regional bodies, UN agencies and other stakeholders in the Caribbean builds on an existing 'analysis of earlier specialised programmes, on the global and regional disaster management agenda and what constitutes now a regional programming framework'.[14] The subregional political integration process offers undeniable opportunities to push for and implement coordinated and standardised action to tackle cross border challenges where economies of scale are of particular and sometimes vital interest to resource poor small nations.

The health and disasters sub-sector not only finds its niche in this framework. Its operational coordination is equally strengthened as it is part of a broader – regional and global – rationale that helps to prioritise the disaster risk reduction agenda and as part of an 'overarching goal of sustainable development'. Disaster risk reduction as a development concern is now broadly accepted. This helps many organisations and (sub)regional bodies to pay particular attention to and prioritise the disaster topic beyond emergency response.

As PAHO states, to reach the goals for disaster risk reduction in a rapidly changing international context, it is necessary to go beyond national and public sector partners and to relate to international, regional and subregional organisations such as disaster management coordination bodies and financing institutions, NGOs, universities and civil society and regional technical networks. An open and franc dialogue and willingness of all stakeholders to connect the existing, different but often overlapping, roles and spaces in multiple platforms will be more than ever necessary.

Notes

1. We will use the term regional for the American continent and subregional for the Caribbean.
2. A secure and disaster resilient health sector in the Americas. Strategic Plan 2008–2012, PAHO.
3. CRED, Annual Disaster Statistical Review, http://www.emdat.be/Publications/publications.html.
4. Regional office for the Americas of the World Health Organisation, see http://www.paho.org.
5. The OECS secretariat is located in Saint Lucia. The organisation has nine members (Antigua and Barbuda, Dominica, Grenada, Guyana, St Kitts and Nevis, St Lucia, St Vincent and the Grenadines, Suriname and Trinidad and Tobago) and two associate members (Anguilla and British Virgin Islands), http://www.oecs.org.
6. The organisation was established in 1973, has its secretariat and is located in Guyana. It has 15 member states (the OECS states plus the Bahamas, Barbados, Belize, Haiti, Jamaica and Montserrat) and 5 associated members (the OECS ones plus Bermuda, Cayman Islands and Turks and Caicos Islands), http://www.caricom.org.

7. The ACS is based in Trinidad and includes all of the OECS and Spanish-speaking states of the Caribbean basin and Central America and the Bahamas, Belize, Haiti, Jamaica. Associate members are Aruba, France, the Netherlands Antilles and Turcs and Caicos, http://www.acs-aec.org.
8. The OAS is based in Washington, DC, http://www.oas.org.
9. This goes beyond CARICOM's membership and includes the Eastern Caribbean, the Bahamas, Belize, Bermuda, Dominican Republic and Jamaica as well the British, Dutch and French Overseas Territories in the Caribbean (exceptions are Cuba, Haiti and the US Caribbean territories).
10. UNDP office for Barbados and the Eastern Caribbean, http://www.bb.undp.org.
11. CDERA, CDM Strategy and Programme Framework 2007–2012, http://www.cdera.org/.
12. Seymour F, Maurer C, Quiroga R. Environmental Mainstreaming: Applications in the Context of Modernisation of the State, Social Development, Competitiveness, and Regional Integration, Inter-American Development Bank Sustainable Development Department Environment Division, 2005.
13. Caribbean Disaster Mitigation Project, CDMP, http://www.oas.org/CDMP/document/papers/cdmptech.htm.
14. CDERA, CDM Strategy and Programme Framework 2007–2012.

Chapter 21
Regionalism and Human Rights at the UN

Richard Gowan and Franziska Brantner

21.1 Introduction

Can the United Nations (UN) promote truly *universal* human rights while maintaining an equitable balance of power between regions?[1] This question has recurred in debates over the composition and credibility of the much-criticised Human Rights Council (HRC), where seats are divided among five regional groups (Africa, Asia, Eastern Europe, Latin America and the Caribbean and the Western Europe and Others Group (WEOG)).

Human rights activists would like to see liberal principles take precedence over regional loyalties in the Council's politics. They believe that seats on the HRC should be distributed to states with good rights records. But this clashes with the principle of regional representation, deeply engrained in the UN's procedures and political culture.

The tension between these principles will come to the fore in 2011, when an inter-governmental review of the HRC will take place. It is possible that not only the human rights community but also some Western governments (including the US) may call for new membership rules for the Council based on human rights criteria rather than regionalism. This initiative would engender extremely stiff opposition from the South.

In this commentary, we argue that attempting to overturn the principle of regional representation at the HRC might be counterproductive as well as unpopular. Rather than try to rewrite the UN's rules, Western governments should aim to work through (and improve) current structures – a quest for a 'better HRC' may do more harm than good.

R. Gowan (✉)
Centre on International Cooperation, New York University, New York, USA
e-mail: richard.gowan@nyu.edu

F. Brantner
European Parliament, Brussels, Belgium

P. De Lombaerde et al. (eds.), *The United Nations and the Regions: Third World Report on Regional Integration*, United Nations University Series on Regionalism 3,
DOI 10.1007/978-94-007-2751-9_21, © Springer Science+Business Media B.V. 2012

21.2 Regionalism's Enduring Strength

In 2005, world leaders agreed to replace the UN's Commission on Human Rights with a new Human Rights Council. The US and European governments and many NGOs argued that, while seats in the Commission had been divided up on a regional basis, membership of the new Council should be based on human rights criteria. Proposals included barring governments that had not ratified important human rights treaties and conventions – until it was realised that this rule would exclude the USA and Australia.

Although alternative criteria were put on the table, these initiatives were all in vain. In 2006, the General Assembly approved a membership formula for the Human Rights Council (HRC) based on the principle of regional representation (see Table 21.1). While the division of seats in the old Commission had marginally favoured liberal states – by giving a near-majority of seats to European and Latin American countries – the Council was weighted towards the African and Asian groups. The Bush administration refused to run for a seat on the HRC, and liberal governments have often struggled to shape its agenda.

Although all applicants for seats are put to a vote by the full General Assembly, it is possible for regional groupings to put forward 'clean slates' of candidates (with only as many candidates as there are seats, making it impossible for any candidate to be blocked). EU governments belatedly tried to create a 'no clean slate' rule for the HRC in 2006, but this failed – in part because they had lost time devising more complicated formulae.

The HRC has developed a highly regionalist flavour. In the 2009 round of HRC elections, for example, there were just five candidates for the five Asian seats available and three candidates for the three Latin American seats. There was a similarly clean slate from the WEOG, in spite of the Europeans' earlier theoretical objections to such tactics. Only the African and Eastern European groups were at all competitive. The Eastern European group (the smallest, but including EU members along with illiberal countries including Russia and Belarus) is the only one that always produces an exciting contest for seats.

The HRC's regulations bear a faint imprint of the efforts to prioritise rights over regionalism. Candidates are expected to present reports on their own human rights

Table 21.1 Distribution of seats on the CHR and HRC

Region	CHR	HRC
Africa	15 (28%)	13 (28%)
Asia	12 (23%)	13 (28%)
Eastern Europe	5 (9%)	6 (13%)
Latin America	11 (21%)	8 (17%)
Western Europe and other groups	10 (19%)	7 (15%)
Total	53	47

Source: Brantner and Gowan (2008b: 39)

situations – but this is not required, and Saudi Arabia was elected without supplying any such report in 2009. In August, a coalition of 74 NGOs (many from the South) warned governments that 'the lack of competition made it practically futile to assess candidates on the basis of the human rights records and pledges'.[2] Regionalism reigns.

21.3 2011: A Chance for Change?

There was good news for the HRC in the 2009 elections, however. In an early gesture of faith in the UN system, the Obama administration dropped the Bush-era boycott and campaigned for an HRC – and won it with 90% support from other states. But American diplomats have warned that they are dissatisfied with the Council and would like to see fundamental reforms. The 2011 review of the HRC (agreed at its foundation) will give them a chance to address their concerns. There have been rumours in Washington that the USA will reopen the question of the Council's membership. Options include raising the use of human rights criteria again – or universalising the HRC's membership to include all UN members, which (in theory) should let countries vote with their consciences.

Veterans of the 2005–2006 debates over the HRC shudder at this. They warn that it might provoke illiberal powers like Russia and China to propose new constraints on the functioning of the HRC – both have worked to limit the Council's interventions in countries like Belarus and Cuba. European diplomats are reportedly wary of reintroducing ideas on the HRC's composition that were defeated in 2006. In the next part of this article, we argue that there are deeper reasons for sticking with regionalism.

21.4 In Defence of Regionalism

Would creating alternative membership rules for the HRC fundamentally alter the way it works for the better? There are a number of reasons to be sceptical. The simplest is that, while countries tend to vote on regional lines in the HRC, this is far from inevitable. Regional groups frequently split on particularly sensitive votes. A 2009 resolution highlighting human rights in North Korea split every regional grouping except the WEOG.

Nor is it clear that universalising the HRC – or even introducing strong criteria for membership – would necessarily dissolve regional loyalties among governments. In the General Assembly, for example, African democracies remain more likely to vote with less free African states than with the West (see Table 21.2). In 2008–2009, only three African countries voted with the EU on human rights votes more than 50% of the time. These included Chad and the Democratic Republic of the Congo, not bastions of liberal democracy.

Table 21.2 Voting coincidence with the EU on human rights: votes in the General Assembly, 2006–2008

	Africa	Asia	Eastern Europe	Latin America and Caribbean	Western Europe and others
Free	46%	65%	100%	51%	91%
Partly free	46%	48%	92%	51%	87%
Not free	46%	39%	37%	34%	n/a

Source: Brantner and Gowan (2008b: 39)

In spite of its universal membership, the General Assembly has become an increasingly difficult environment for liberal states to pursue human rights issues in recent years. This is less because of regional issues than the tactics of well-established political blocs (notably the Non-Aligned Movement) and the increasingly cohesive and assertive Organisation of the Islamic Conference (OIC). The OIC is already a significant force in Geneva, cutting deals with Russia, China and Cuba to vote in favour of resolutions limiting rights in the name of religion. If the HRC were to be universalised, it would almost certainly fall prey to precisely the same divisions as the Assembly immediately.

If Western countries attempted to introduce human rights criteria for membership that reduced the leverage of the OIC, they would inevitably be accused of cultural imperialism – and have no chance of success. It is arguable that dividing the HRC along regional lines protects it from a worse fate: becoming a purely ideological battleground.

During the last round of debate over the HRC's composition in 2005–2006, Southern governments argued that excluding non-democracies would be counterproductive. Those excluded would simply ignore the HRC altogether and use their isolation to win sympathy. Engaging them at the HRC may be distasteful, but opens them to scrutiny.

There is evidence that the present regionalism at the HRC can help limit ideological disputes. Different groups handle this in different ways, either adopting *moderation* (finding consensus on candidate countries that avoid radical positions in the UN) or *ideological pluralism* (choosing a more or less equal mix of liberal and illiberal states).

In recent years, successful candidates for African seats (normally presented as a 'clean slate') have tended to include relatively moderate governments rather than radicals like Zimbabwe.[3] The importance of this moderate tendency was seen in 2009, when the USA persuaded all the African members of the HRC to abstain on a resolution on monitoring human rights in Sudan. This allowed the resolution to pass by a single vote. Had the African countries not voted cohesively, it is probable that it would have been defeated.

If the African group converges on moderate candidates, the Latin American group's clean slates demonstrate a degree of ideological pluralism. In 2009, it put forward Mexico, Uruguay and Cuba. This affirmed the group's long-standing solidarity with Havana, but ensures that it will split on many specific HRC issues, with Cuba rejecting the liberal positions of its groupmates. Something similar takes place in the WEOG. Canada, Australia and the USA tend to be more hawkish in defence of Israel than European states. But the EU members of the WEOG treat it as natural that they should be given turns on the HRC.

The Asian group also demonstrates a degree of pluralism. In 2009, it endorsed a slate of candidates with poor or bad performances on human rights (Jordan, Kyrgyzstan, Bangladesh, China and Saudi Arabia). But in 2008, when it had four seats to fill, it put forward two liberal states (Japan and South Korea), a moderate member of the OIC (Bahrain) and a country with a history of hostility to the West on human rights (Pakistan).

Thus, the four larger regional groupings all make some compromises to ensure that the HRC maintains a certain degree of balance. This gives us an important insight into the nature of regionalism at the UN. The regional groups are to some extent self-regulating entities, following strategies to ensure that ideological competition does not run wild.

Of course, this involves a great deal of horse-trading and compromises that NGOs are right to criticise. And powerful players like the USA are still able to manipulate decisions within regional groups other than their own. Nonetheless, the HRC does not fully live up to its reputation as a venue for regionalised bloc politics: instead, it is normally characterised by a multi-level game of states and regions balancing each other.

The exception is the Eastern European group, which we have noted holds competitive elections. Here, Western efforts have ensured that liberal countries typically defeat candidates like Belarus and Azerbaijan. Human rights advocates argue that this shows the superiority of competitive races to clean slates. But if all the regional groups held open and competitive races, the results would not necessarily favour the liberals – Russia, China and their allies would have a good chance of creating a stronger illiberal bloc.

21.5 Painstaking Diplomacy

It may, therefore, be preferable to stick with the current system of balancing at the HRC than risk outright competition and confrontation there. This certainly leads to unsatisfactory outcomes on many human rights issues, with European and African countries agreeing lowest-common-denominator language on crises like Darfur.

But the most likely alternatives might be worse. In 2007, EU members threatened to walk out of the HRC altogether if a Chinese-led initiative to limit its monitoring of individual countries. This dramatic tactic worked. But what if the Europeans had walked? In their absence, illiberal members of the Council would have been able to make a raft of further alterations to its procedures. An HRC based on uneasy balances may be imperfect and sometimes embarrassing – but upsetting the balance could result in something far worse.

US Ambassador to the UN Susan Rice has argued that 'real change (at the UN) can only come through painstaking, principled diplomacy' (Rice 2009). She meant to contrast this approach to Bush administration's stratagem of 'sitting on the sidelines'. But her words could equally be read as a warning to those who believe that the HRC's difficulties can be resolved by a dramatic revision of its membership rules. Dreams of radical change rarely become realities in the UN system. It may be better to work through current structures.

This means working within the current framework of regionalism. There are many initiatives that liberal governments can pursue to improve that framework. They should encourage activists based in each region to monitor developments within their regional group (so African NGOs should investigate dealing in the African group and so forth). They can launch cross-regional initiatives to ensure that liberal and moderate governments in all groups develop stronger ties and strategies for shaping HRC debates.

Regionalism will persist to be a central principle in how the HRC and other UN forums are constituted. But rather than see regionalism an obstacle to defending human rights at the UN, we should see it as a framework that allows human rights to continue despite increasing ideological divisions among member states. The real battle over the future of human rights at the UN concerns ideas and ideologies, not the question of regionalism.

Notes

1. This commentary draws on arguments previously laid out in Brantner and Gowan (2008a, b) and Gowan and Brantner (2009). Readers should refer to these publications for more detailed references to the instances and data analysed in this piece.
2. The letter (entitled 'Embrace Competitive Elections to the Human Rights Council'), http://www.hrw.org/en/news/2009/08/13/letter-un-member-states-embrace-competitive-elections-human-rights-council
3. In 2008, Zambia, Ghana, Burkina Faso and Gabon were elected as a clean slate. In 2009, Senegal, Mauritius, Nigeria, Cameroon and Djibouti were elected, and Kenya was rejected.

References

Brantner, F., & Gowan, R. (2008a). A missed opportunity? The EU and the reform of the UN human rights architecture. In Z. Laïdi (Ed.), *EU foreign policy in a globalized world: Normative power and social preferences* (pp. 83–102). Abingdon: Routledge.

Brantner, F., & Gowan, R. (2008b). *A global force for human rights? An audit of European power at the UN*. London: European Council on Foreign Relations.

Gowan, R., & Brantner, F. (2009). *The EU and human rights at the UN – 2009 review*. London: European Council on Foreign Relations.

Rice, S. E. (2009, August 12). *A new course in the world, a new approach at the UN. Speech delivered at New York University*, http://www.cic.nyu.edu/Lead%20Page%20PDF/USUN%20PR%20163.pdf

Chapter 22
Conclusions

Francis Baert, Tânia Felício, and Philippe De Lombaerde

The various contributions to this volume have looked at the linkages between the United Nations (UN) and the supranational regions from different angles. In the following paragraphs, we will present some of the conclusions that – according to us – can be extracted from the different chapters, being well conscious at the same time that by doing so, we will undoubtedly do injustice to the richness, nuance, and variety of opinions that can be found in this book.

22.1 General Conclusions

Supranational regional arrangements and organizations are likely to further increase their importance as a governance level in most policy areas. This poses challenges for multilateral institutions in general and the UN in particular.

F. Baert (✉)
United Nations University Institute on Comparative Regional Integration Studies (UNU-CRIS), Bruges, Belgium

Centre for European Studies at the University of Ghent, Ghent, Belgium
e-mail: fbaert@cris.unu.edu

T. Felício
United Nations Integrated Mission in Timor Leste (UNMIT), Dili, Timor Leste

P. De Lombaerde
United Nations University Institute on Comparative Regional Integration Studies (UNU-CRIS), Bruges, Belgium

P. De Lombaerde et al. (eds.), *The United Nations and the Regions: Third World Report on Regional Integration*, United Nations University Series on Regionalism 3,
DOI 10.1007/978-94-007-2751-9_22,

The world of regions is a heterogeneous and dynamic world which complicates the interaction with them, the latter therefore not being less needed (Chaps. 1, 8 and 18).

It should be understood, however, that the definitional/legal *problématique* is not to be solved exclusively by the regions themselves. It is precisely the engagement of multilateral institutions like the UN (and national states) with them, thereby putting forward eligibility criteria, that will institutionalize these relations and by consequence typify the regions.

The Westphalian understanding of sovereignty is seriously challenges by the realities of a globalized world. A new consensus view is needed, and globally representative regional structures and organizations which have played a role as incubators and test grounds for new ideas on sovereignty (in Africa, Europe, and elsewhere) should play a crucial role in this process (Chap. 2).

22.2 The UN and the Regions

Our book shows very clearly, on the one hand, that the linkages between supranational regions and the UN are multiple, varied, and of increasing intensity and, on the other hand, that there are many political, institutional, and operational challenges and unresolved issues.

When assessing regional actorness in the UN General Assembly (UNGA) and UN Security Council (UNSC), an underlying hypothesis is usually that a clear tendency toward regional voting coordination and/or bloc mentality could constitute a basis to build on in the political discussions on institutional reforms and the representation of regions (Chaps. 4 and 5). It was shown, however, that it is difficult to assess and demonstrate regional actorness based on voting behavior in the UNSC for various reasons: the limited number of members of the Council, its consensus-seeking decision-making model, and the representation behavior of the EU (Chap. 5). The lack of comparative analyses of regional patterns in voting behavior was also pointed at.

When focusing on the much more widely studied voting behavior at the UNGA, and the regional patterns therein, it was shown that also in that case voting patterns as such do not clearly demonstrate regional actorness (Chap. 4). Looking at the underlying political coordination process sheds a bit more light on the issue, but regional actorness should not be overestimated. There is historically some evidence of bloc behavior centered around the USA and the former USSR, based on asymmetric power relations. A different model is shown by the EU, based on a more symmetrical coordination process, but for fundamental issues, sovereign interests seem to dominate the regional interest. In recent years, there is no evidence of stronger bloc behavior. Several important decisions in the realm of human rights were indeed reached, thanks to strategies that deliberately sought to break the logic of regions.

In discussions on UNSC reform, the proposals that are circulating often reflect specific national interests of individual countries or ad hoc alliances of countries. These discussions are served by more independent reflections (such as Chaps. 6 and 7) on the deficiencies of the functioning of the existing UNSC, and on guidelines and principles to design a reformed UNSC, as they can help in shaping wider political support, needed to implement any reform. A crucial issue thereby is whether regional representation can be woven into a reform, even if membership is still organized around a (larger) core of permanent members. Weighted representation and voting are interesting paths to explore in our new multipolar world (Chaps. 6 and 7). Regional organizations should, in addition, not be considered as passive objects in these debates; they are likely to become more active actors themselves in global governance reform (Chaps. 7 and 9).

The need for including supranational regions in the UN context should further not necessarily be understood as adding an additional layer of governance; it is well possible to visualize hybrid interactions (involving countries and regions) in a number of policy areas for economic, demographic, or political reasons.

The use of different regional concepts within the UN (as is already done today with the electoral groupings, regional economic commissions, Chapter VIII regional arrangements, and agencies, see Chaps. 1, 8, 16, and 17) is probably inevitable for the time being.

Engaging with regional organizations should however not necessarily weaken the role of the UN; on the contrary, designing and implementing global-regional approaches in different policy areas could ever strengthen its role.

At the operational level, there is certainly scope for more collaboration with regional organizations, given the multiplicity of border-crossing issues, spillover effects, economies of scale, etc.

The promotion of regionalism has historically been on the UN agenda (see Chap. 3 on the Economic Commission for Latin America and the Caribbean (ECLAC), but also in Europe) and it should continue to be high on its agenda. Current regionalisms in Latin America but also in Africa and Asia-Pacific are characterized by complexity, overlap, and incoherence and seem to be in search of (and in need of) a model(s) and consensus views, although these can/should be region-specific and socially constructed. There seem to be opportunities therefore for a more active role of the UN regional economic commissions in steering and supporting regional integration processes in their respective regions (as strongly argued in Chap. 3).

The report on system-wide coherence (SWC) is very brief concerning cooperation with regional organizations. On the one hand, it only calls for a stronger relationship in the context of Chapter VIII of the Charter, and on the other, it recommends a streamlining of the regional structure of the UN (Chaps. 17 and 18).

The latter mainly refers to the coordinating roles of the economic commissions (with respect to analytic and normative work) and the United Nations Development Programme (UNDP) (with respect to services to UN country teams). The SWC report apparently does not further reflect on the regional dimensions of a number of policy challenges or on the growing relevance of regional stakeholders and jurisdictions (Chap. 18).

It has been suggested that the UNGA could establish a task force to explore the possibility to standardize the definition of a region in the UN context and to address related issues (Chap. 17).

22.3 The UN and the Regions in Peace and Security

In the area of security, the UN has long acknowledged the potential and relevance of regional approaches (see Chaps. 1, 8, 14, 16, and 20), although actual cooperation between the UN and regional organizations in peace and security is a more recent phenomenon (Chap. 10).

And in spite of the critical challenges that faced, for example, the UN-AU mission in Darfur, several observers are of the opinion that joint (or hybrid) operations should be further developed as a mechanism (Chaps. 11 and 13).

The involvement of regional organizations can increase the levels of legitimacy, adaptedness, political/cultural sensitivity, and speed of intervention and therefore increase effectiveness of UN intervention (Chaps. 1, 8, 9, 11, and 13). Some observers take a more critical stance and argue that regional policies are not necessarily compatible with the ultimate goal to produce global public goods (Chap. 12). If regional organizations are to play a role globally, their policies and operations should be framed within a logic of global public policies. Other observers also stress that it is essential for the UN to continue to play a central role, even if cooperation with regional organizations is sought (Chap. 15).

Those who see a more important role for regional organizations are of the opinion that this purpose would be served by a revitalization of the HLMs with the UN Secretary-General (SG) and the joint meetings with the UNSC, which could prepare the ground for a more effective regional-global security mechanism under Chapter VIII.

It has been observed also that the cooperation between the UN and regional organizations develops in a regulatory vacuum (Chap. 10). Therefore, supplementary regulatory frameworks could bring more structure, precision, and focus to it. The challenge will consist in combining the institutionalization of joint (hybrid) missions with conserving their flexibility and political pragmatism (Chap. 13).

But independently of the perceived need for more involvement of regional organizations in global governance in the area of peace, we should not overestimate their current capacity (i.e., political and/or economic weight, financial resources, internal coherence, impartiality, etc.) to effectively intervene nor underestimate the significant (institutional, economic) heterogeneity (Chaps. 11–15). In addition, the issue of overlapping memberships is a complicating factor.

It will constitute a challenge to involve regional organizations like the Association of Southeast Asian Nations (ASEAN), with strong positions on noninterference, in regional-global security mechanisms (Chap. 14), but limited pragmatic cooperation can be expected, and a further development in the direction of a rules-based regionalism is a possible scenario for the future (Chap. 14). ASEAN-UN cooperation is in the short term more promising in the less political/politicized areas of human security.

22.4 The UN and the Regions in Human Security, Sustainable Development, and Human Rights

The reconceptualization of the security concept toward "human security" implied a shift from a state-centered perspective to a human-centered perspective (Chap. 16). This opens perspectives for engagement with different governance levels, including the regional one.

The case of health sector coordination for disaster management in the Caribbean is a good example of how the UN interacts in a pragmatic way with different authorities and organizations, including regional organizations, and how it plays a coordinating role at the regional level (Chap. 20).

Further, a need is felt for a regional strategy for the UN in the economic and social spheres, and opportunities are seen for more regional presence for the UN and closer collaboration with regional organizations (Chaps. 18 and 19).

Finally, the case is made for a continuation of the regional framework within which the Human Rights Council (HRC) operates (Chap. 21).

Annexes

P. De Lombaerde et al. (eds.), *The United Nations and the Regions: Third World Report on Regional Integration*, United Nations University Series on Regionalism 3,
DOI 10.1007/978-94-007-2751-9, © Springer Science+Business Media B.V. 2012

Annex Ia: Selected Indicators on Regional Arrangements, Economic Development, and Trade[a]

Regional arrangement	Year of establishment	Official website(s)	Regional share in world GDP[b]	Regional GDP per capita (US dollars)[c]	Intra-regional trade share[d]	Intra-regional trade intensity index[e]	Regional FDI inflow as percentage of regional GDP[f]	Regional FDI outflow as percentage of regional GDP[f]
African Union	2002	http://www.africa-union.org/	2.11	1,263	12.74	6.4	5.91	0.89
African. Caribbean. and Pacific Group of States	1975	http://www.acp.int/	1.85	1,215	16.18	10.5	5.44	0.55
Andean Community	1969	http://www.comunidadandina.org/	0.63	3,448	8.73	16.6	4.52	0.3
Arab Maghreb Union	1989	http://www.maghrebarabe.org/	0.46	2,860	2.7	4.3	4.48	2
Arab Organization for Agricultural Development	1970	http://www.aoad.org/index_en.htm	2.65	4,316	9.35	2.2	5.74	3.67
Asia-Pacific Economic Co-operation	1989	http://www.apec.org/	52.62	10,445	64.42	1.4	2.71	2.62
Association of Caribbean States	1994	http://www.acs-aec.org/	2.94	6,058	8.37	2.9	3.22	0.95
Association of Southeastern Asian Nations	1967	http://www.aseansec.org/	2.42	2,249	24.77	4.2	5.41	3.56
Baltic Sea States Subregional Co-operation	1993	http://www.bsssc.com/	6.01	15,058	21.28	3.1	4.16	4.13

Bay of Bengal Initiative for Multi-Sectoral Technical and Economic Cooperation	1997	http://www.bimstec.org/	2.82	1,042	3.07	1.2	2.51	1.28
Benelux Union	1944	http://www.benelux.be/	2.39	46,496	13.44	2.0	15.53	14.19
Black Sea Economic Cooperation	1992	http://www.bsec-organization.org/	4.69	7,634	17.43	3.9	4.36	2.2
Caribbean Community	1973	http://www.caricom.org/	0.11	3,453	11.74	73.5	7.99	0.55
Central African Economic and Monetary Community	1994	http://www.cemac.int/	0.1	1,393	N.A.[g]	3.2	9.54	0.11
Central American Integration System	1991	http://www.sgsica.org/	0.2	3,138	13.99	57.8	6.18	2.92
Central Asia Regional Economic Cooperation Program	1997	http://www.adb.org/CAREC/default.asp	6.72	2,556	5.46	0.6	2.57	0.72
Central European Free Trade Agreement	1992	http://www.cefta2006.com/	0.25	4,684	9.73	39.1	6.45	0.22
Common Market for Eastern and Southern Africa	1994	http://www.comesa.int/	0.69	808	6.91	15.1	8.29	0.49
Common Market of the South	1991	http://www.mercosur.int/	3.03	6,693	16.42	11.1	2.64	0.54
Commonwealth of Independent States	1991	http://www.cis.minsk.by/	3.11	6,049	22.56	7.4	4.58	3.03

(continued)

(continued)

Regional arrangement	Year of establishment	Official website(s)	Regional share in world GDP[b]	Regional GDP per capita (US dollars)[c]	Intra-regional trade share[d]	Intra-regional trade intensity index[e]	Regional FDI inflow as percentage of regional GDP[f]	Regional FDI outflow as percentage of regional GDP[f]
Community of Sahel-Saharan States	1998	http://www.cen-sad.org/	1.02	1,164	6.3	6.6	7.29	1.13
Council of Arab Economic Unity	1957	http://www.caeu.org.eg/	0.85	2,103	4.89	5.5	5.22	3.33
Council of Europe	1949	http://www.coe.int/	36.13	24,167	70	1.6	5.05	6.67
Council of the Baltic States	1992	http://www.cbss.st/	12.28	22,135	22.87	1.5	2.95	4.97
Cross Border Initiative	1992		0.18	567	8.9	33.7	6.33	0.22
East African Community	1999	http://www.eac.int/	0.09	535	10.23	103.3	4.69	0.12
Economic Community of Central African States	1983	http://www.africa-union.org/root/au/recs/eccas.htm	0.22	873	4.39	648.3	13.18	0.83
Economic Community of the Great Lakes Countries	1976		0.08	2,150	0.09	0.6	11.18	0.57
Economic Community of West African States	1975	http://www.ecowas.int/	0.44	833	8.69	18.8	6.7	0.37
Economic Cooperation Organization	1977	http://www.ecosecretariat.org/	2.11	2,761	6.75	4.4	3.39	0.53
European Economic Area	1994		29.28	40,306	51.8	1.6	4.26	7.13

European Free Trade Association	1960	http://www.efta.int/	1.57	66,598	0.72	0.3	6.86	9.4
European Union	1957	http://www.europa.eu.int/	31.55	33,921	64.3	1.6	5.02	7.11
Eurozone	1999	http://www.ecb.int/	22.71	38,181	47.34	1.6	4.57	6.99
Gulf Cooperation Council	1981	http://www.gcc-sg.org/	1.51	22,200	5.7	1.9	6.01	5.61
Indian Ocean Commission	1984	http://www.coi-info.org/	4.82	30,006	0.92	0.2	6.22	8.77
Indian Ocean Rim Association for Regional Cooperation	1997	http://www.iornet.com/	7.7	2,128	25.07	2.7	3.85	2.31
Intergovernmental Authority on Development	1996	http://www.igad.org/	0.22	582	6	46.7	3.74	0.04
Latin American and Caribbean Economic System	1980	http://www.aladi.org/	6.59	6,188	19.61	3.9	3.16	0.76
Latin America Integration Association	1975	http://www.sela.org/	6.19	6,587	17.01	3.7	2.98	0.7
League of Arab States	1945	http://www.arableagueonline.org/	2.65	4,306	9.35	2.2	5.74	3.67
Mano River Union	1973	http://www.manoriverunion.org/	0.01	363	0.18	22.9	8.87	5.26
Mekong River Commission	1995	http://www.mrcmekong.org/	0.62	1,920	3.61	2.4	5.82	0.61
Melanesian Spearhead Group	1993		0.02	1,309	1.99	196.9	4.7	0.23

(continued)

(continued)

Regional arrangement	Year of establishment	Official website(s)	Regional share in world GDP[b]	Regional GDP per capita (US dollars)[c]	Intra-regional trade share[d]	Intra-regional trade intensity index[e]	Regional FDI inflow as percentage of regional GDP[f]	Regional FDI outflow as percentage of regional GDP[f]
Nordic Council and The Nordic Council of Ministers	1952	http://www.norden.org/	2.67	57,014	20.22	5.9	3.64	6.47
North American Free Trade Agreement	1994	http://www.nafta-sec-alena.org/	30.27	36,151	40.98	2.5	2.53	2.77
Organization of Arab Petroleum Exporting Countries	1968	http://www.oapecorg.org/	0.67	851	5.72	13.9	8.38	0.5
Organisation of Eastern Caribbean States	1981	http://www.oecs.org/	0.01	8,551	4.08	373.9	108.36	416.09
Organisation of Islamic Conference	1969	http://www.oic-oci.org/	6.62	2,358	13.58	1.6	4.35	2.1
Organisation pour l'harmonisation du droit des affaires	1993	http://www.ohada.org/	0.18	685	13.91	130.2	7.35	0.09
Organization of American States	1948	http://www.oas.org/	35.19	20,665	47.85	2.4	2.62	2.48
Pacific Islands Forum	1971	http://www.forumsec.org.fj	2.05	32,571	8.87	7.0	4.35	1.84
Permanent Interstate Committee for Drought Control in the Sahel	1973	http://www.insah.org/	0.08	591	7.99	154.0	4.65	0.11

Permanent Mechanism of Political Consultation and Coordination	1986		6.38	6,256	18.78	3.9	3.14	0.77
South Asian Association for Regional Co-operation	1985	http://www.saarc-sec.org/	2.67	921	3.47	2.2	2.26	1.23
Southern African Customs Union	1910	http://www.sacu.int/	0.57	5,490	6.44	10.7	2.31	0.99
Southern African Development Community	1980	http://www.sadc.int/	0.76	1,993	13.18	18.0	5.27	1.01
West African Economic and Monetary Union	1994	http://www.uemoa.int/	0.39	923	6.81	16.5	6.73	0.24

Source: RIKS© 2010, http://www.cris.unu.edu/riks/web/arrangement

[a]Indicators of year 2007. See Annex II for the membership

[b]Calculated by RIKS© based on UN Statistics Division: GDP at current prices – US dollars series

[c]Calculated by RIKS© based on UN Statistics Division: GDP at current prices – US dollars series and UN National Accounts Main Aggregate Database, Population series. Regional GDP per capita is defined as the ratio of regional GDP to regional population

[d]Calculated by RIKS© based on UN COMTRADE Database, SITC Rev.1. Intra-regional trade share is defined as percentage share of the region's total trade

[e]Calculated by RIKS© based on UN COMTRADE Database, SITC Rev.1. Intra-regional trade intensity index is defined as the ratio of the intra-regional trade share to the region's share in the world's total trade

[f]Calculated by RIKS© based on UNCTAD Foreign Direct Investment online database

[g]Data not available

Annex Ib: Selected Indicators on Regional Arrangements, Human Development

Regional arrangement	Year of establishment	Official website(s)	Regional share in world population[a]	Regional immigration share[b]	Regional emigration share[c]	Share of total migrants in regional population[d]	Share of intra-regional migrants in regional population[e]	Regional human HDI[f]
African Union	2002	http://www.africa-union.org/	13.3	59.8	53.1	1.8	1.1	0.51
African, Caribbean and Pacific Group of States	1975	http://www.acp.int/	12.1	62.0	44.9	2.0	1.2	0.49
Andean Community	1969	http://www.comunidadandina.org/	1.5	22.9	2.1	0.4	0.1	0.80
Arab Maghreb Union	1989	http://www.maghrebarabe.org/	1.3	9.3	1.9	1.3	0.1	0.72
Arab Organization for Agricultural Development	1970	http://www.aoad.org/index_en.htm	4.9	4.5	8.8	5.7	0.3	0.62
Asia-Pacific Economic Co-operation	1989	http://www.apec.org/	40.2	33.1	51.5	2.7	0.9	0.80
Association of Caribbean States	1994	http://www.acs-aec.org/	3.9	43.5	3.6	0.7	0.3	0.81
Association of Southeastern Asian Nations	1967	http://www.aseansec.org/	8.6	50.1	32.7	1.0	0.5	0.73
Baltic Sea States Subregional Co-operation	1993	http://www.bsssc.com/	3.2	9.7	9.7	7.3	0.7	0.85
Bay of Bengal Initiative for Multi-Sectoral Technical and Economic Cooperation	1997	http://www.bimstec.org/	21.6	71.6	37.0	0.6	0.5	0.61
Benelux Union	1944	http://www.benelux.be/	0.4	5.5	10.7	9.3	0.5	0.95
Black Sea Economic Cooperation	1992	http://www.bsec-organization.org/	4.9	59.6	44.7	6.9	4.1	0.76

Caribbean Community	1973	http://www.caricom.org/	0.3	19.6	1.2	1.2	0.2	0.64
Central African Economic and Monetary Community	1994	http://www.cemac.int/	0.6	34.6	45.9	2.5	0.9	0.48
Central American Integration System	1991	http://www.sgsica.org/	0.5	64.0	15.2	2.1	1.3	0.75
Central Asia Regional Economic Cooperation Program	1997	http://www.adb.org/CAREC/default.asp	21.0	17.4	4.9	0.4	0.1	0.76
Central European Free Trade Agreement	1992	http://www.cefta2006.com/	0.4	42.3	13.8	4.4	1.8	0.74
Common Market for Eastern and Southern Africa	1994	http://www.comesa.int/	6.8	42.6	31.0	1.0	0.4	0.49
Common Market of the South	1991	http://www.mercosur.int/	3.6	30.3	27.4	1.0	0.3	0.82
Commonwealth of Independent States	1991	http://www.cis.minsk.by/	4.1	85.5	74.0	9.2	7.9	0.79
Community of Sahel-Saharan States	1998	http://www.cen-sad.org/	7.0	51.8	39.9	2.0	1.1	0.53
Council of Arab Economic Unity	1957	http://www.caeu.org.eg/	3.2	0.1	0.1	2.7	N.A.[g]	0.55
Council of Europe	1949	http://www.coe.int/	11.9	55.5	60.7	7.9	4.4	0.87
Council of the Baltic States	1992	http://www.cbss.st/	4.4	9.6	12.6	8.7	0.8	0.88
Cross Border Initiative	1992		2.6	36.8	38.6	2.3	0.8	0.46
East African Community	1999	http://www.eac.int/	1.3	36.1	52.8	2.3	0.8	0.51
Economic Community of Central African States	1983	http://www.africa-union.org/root/au/recs/eccas.htm	2.0	27.6	18.9	0.9	0.3	0.44

(continued)

(continued)

Regional arrangement	Year of establishment	Official website(s)	Regional share in world population[a]	Regional immigration share[b]	Regional emigration share[c]	Share of total migrants in regional population[d]	Share of intra-regional migrants in regional population[e]	Regional human HDI[f]
Economic Community of the Great Lakes Countries	1976		0.3	1.4	2.3	4.3	0.1	0.48
Economic Community of West African States	1975	http://www.ecowas.int/	4.2	57.3	60.7	2.7	1.6	0.48
Economic Co-operation Organization	1977	http://www.ecosecretariat.org/	6.1	11.5	5.8	2.3	0.3	0.67
European Economic Area	1994		5.8	25.5	43.5	9.6	2.4	0.95
European Free Trade Association	1960	http://www.efta.int/	0.2	0.8	2.3	16.4	0.1	0.96
European Union	1957	http://www.europa.eu.int/	7.4	32.0	45.2	8.1	2.6	0.90
Eurozone	1999	http://www.ecb.int/	4.7	22.6	39.9	9.6	2.2	0.95
Gulf Cooperation Council	1981	http://www.gcc-sg.org/	0.5	1.1	39.7	37.2	0.4	0.86
Indian Ocean Commission	1984	http://www.coi-info.org/	1.3	3.3	10.0	7.9	0.3	0.86
Indian Ocean Rim Association for Regional Cooperation	1997	http://www.iornet.com/	28.8	49.7	48.9	1.2	0.6	0.64
Intergovernmental Authority on Development	1996	http://www.igad.org/	3.1	49.6	40.3	1.2	0.6	0.46
Latin American and Caribbean Economic System	1980	http://www.aladi.org/	7.5	45.8	8.4	0.8	0.4	0.83
Latin American Integration Association	1975	http://www.sela.org/	8.5	53.2	9.1	0.9	0.5	0.82

League of Arab States	1945	http://www.arableagueonline.org/	4.9	4.5	8.8	5.7	0.3	0.62
Mano River Union	1973	http://www.manoriverunion.org/	0.3	21.7	18.2	3.2	0.7	0.41
Mekong River Commission	1995	http://www.mrcmekong.org/	2.6	12.9	15.8	0.8	0.1	0.73
Melanesian Spearhead Group	1993		0.1	4.6	1.0	0.6	0.0	0.57
Nordic Council and the Nordic Council of Ministers	1952	http://www.norden.org/	0.4	22.0	41.3	8.3	1.8	0.96
North American Free Trade Agreement	1994	http://www.nafta-sec-alena.org/	6.7	27.0	80.7	10.3	2.8	0.93
Organization of Arab Petroleum Exporting Countries	1968	http://www.oapecorg.org/	6.3	45.4	35.4	0.8	0.4	0.51
Organisation of Eastern Caribbean States	1981	http://www.oecs.org/	0.0	11.1	2.4	5.4	0.6	0.76
Organisation of Islamic Conference	1969	http://www.oic-oci.org/	22.4	24.4	20.7	2.6	0.6	0.61
Organisation pour l'harmonisation du droit des affaires	1993	http://www.ohada.org/	2.1	59.4	58.5	4.1	2.4	0.44
Organization of American States	1948	http://www.oas.org/	13.6	46.8	73.2	5.6	2.6	0.87
Pacific Islands Forum	1971	http://www.forumsec.org.fj	0.5	12.9	47.7	14.7	1.9	0.86
Permanent Interstate Committee for Drought Control in the Sahel	1973	http://www.insah.org/	1.1	37.5	17.7	2.7	1.0	0.40

(continued)

(continued)

Regional arrangement	Year of establishment	Official website(s)	Regional share in world population[a]	Regional immigration share[b]	Regional emigration share[c]	Share of total migrants in regional population[d]	Share of intra-regional migrants in regional population[e]	Regional human HDI[f]
Permanent Mechanism of Political Consultation and Coordination	1986		8.1	52.5	9.8	0.9	0.5	0.82
South Asian Association for Regional Co-operation	1985	http://www.saarc-sec.org/	23.1	67.8	37.9	0.7	0.5	0.60
Southern African Customs Union	1910	http://www.sacu.int/	0.8	26.6	32.8	2.5	0.7	0.68
Southern African Development Community	1980	http://www.sadc.int/	3.1	47.8	49.6	1.7	0.8	0.51
West African Economic and Monetary Union	1994	http://www.uemoa.int/	3.4	54.5	57.2	2.3	1.2	0.49

Source: RIKS© 2010, http://www.cris.unu.edu/riks/web/arrangement

[a]Data of year 2007. Calculated by RIKS© based on UN National Accounts Main Aggregate Database, Population series

[b]Data of year 2005. This indicator measures intra-regional migration as a share of total immigration within a particular regional arrangement

[c]Data of year 2005. This indicator measures intra-regional migration as a share of total emigration within a particular regional arrangement

[d]Data of year 2005. This indicator measures the stock of intra-regional migrants as percentage of the regional population within a particular regional arrangement

[e]Data of year 2005. This indicator measures the total stock of migrants as percentage of the regional population within a particular regional arrangement

[f]Data of year 2007. This indicator is calculated as the weighted (by population) average of the value of Human Development Indicators (HDI) of members states within a particular regional arrangement

[g]Data not available

Annex II: Membership of Regional Arrangements, as of January 1, 2010

Regional arrangement	Number of members	Member states
African Union (AU)	53	Algeria, Angola, Benin, Botswana, Burkina Faso, Burundi, Cameroon, Cape Verde, Central African Republic, Chad, Comoros, Congo, Cote d'Ivoire, Democratic Republic of the Congo, Djibouti, Egypt, Equatorial Guinea, Eritrea, Ethiopia, Gabon, Gambia, Ghana, Guinea, Guinea-Bissau, Kenya, Lesotho, Liberia, Libya, Madagascar, Malawi, Mali, Mauritania, Mauritius, Mozambique, Namibia, Niger, Nigeria, Rwanda, Sahrawi Arab Democratic Republic, Sao Tome and Principe, Senegal, Seychelles, Sierra Leone, Somalia, South Africa, Sudan, Swaziland, Tanzania, Togo, Tunisia, Uganda, Zambia, Zimbabwe
African, Caribbean and Pacific Group of States (ACP)	79	Angola, Antigua and Barbuda, Barbados, Belize, Benin, Botswana, Burkina Faso, Burundi, Cameroon, Cape Verde, Central African Republic, Chad, Comoros, Congo, Cook Islands, Cote d'Ivoire, Cuba, Democratic Republic of Congo, Djibouti, Dominica, Dominican Republic, East Timor, Equatorial Guinea, Eritrea, Ethiopia, Federated States of Micronesia, Fiji, Gabon, Gambia, Ghana, Grenada, Guinea, Guinea-Bissau, Guyana, Haiti, Jamaica, Kenya, Kiribati, Lesotho, Liberia, Madagascar, Malawi, Mali, Marshall Islands, Mauritania, Mauritius, Mozambique, Namibia, Nauru, Niger, Nigeria, Niue, Palau, Papua New Guinea, Rwanda, Samoa, Sao Tome and Principe, Senegal, Seychelles, Sierra Leone, Solomon Islands, Somalia, South Africa, St. Kitts and Nevis, St. Lucia, St. Vincent and the Grenadines, Sudan, Suriname, Swaziland, Tanzania, the Bahamas, Togo, Tonga, Trinidad and Tobago, Tuvalu, Uganda, Vanuatu, Zambia, Zimbabwe
Andean Community (CAN)	4	Bolivia, Colombia, Ecuador, Peru
Arab Maghreb Union	5	Algeria, Libya, Mauritania, Morocco, Tunisia
Arab Organisation for Agricultural Development (AOAD)	21	Algeria, Bahrain, Djibouti, Egypt, Iraq, Jordan, Kuwait, Lebanon, Libya, Mauritania, Morocco, Oman, Palestine, Qatar, Saudi Arabia, Somalia, Sudan, Syrian Arab Republic, Tunisia, United Arab Emirates, Yemen
Asia-Pacific Economic Co-operation (APEC)	21	Australia, Brunei Darussalam, Canada, Chile, China, Chinese HongKong, Indonesia, Japan, Republic of Korea, Malaysia, Mexico, New Zealand, Papua New Guinea, Peru, Philippines, Russia, Singapore, Chinese Taipei, Thailand, United States, Vietnam

(continued)

(continued)

Regional arrangement	Number of members	Member states
Association of Caribbean States (ACS)	29	Antigua and Barbuda, Aruba, Barbados, Belize, Colombia, Costa Rica, Cuba, Dominica, Dominican Republic, El Salvador, France, Grenada, Guatemala, Guyana, Haiti, Honduras, Jamaica, Mexico, Netherland Antilles, Nicaragua, Panama, St. Kitts and Nevis, St. Vincent and the Grenadines, St. Lucia, Suriname, the Bahamas, Trinidad and Tobago, Turks and Caicos, Venezuela
Association of Southeast Asian Nations (ASEAN)	10	Brunei, Cambodia, Indonesia, Laos, Malaysia, Myanmar, Philippines, Singapore, Thailand, Vietnam
Baltic Sea States Subregional Co-operation (BSSSC)	10	Denmark, Estonia, Finland, Germany, Latvia, Lithuania, Norway, Poland, Russian Federation, Sweden
Bay of Bengal Initiative for Multi-sectoral Technical and Economic Co-operation (BIMSTEC)	7	Bangladesh, Bhutan, India, Myanmar, Nepal, Sri Lanka, Thailand
Benelux Union (BENELUX)	3	Belgium, the Netherlands, Luxembourg
Black Sea Economic Co-operation (BSEC)	12	Albania, Armenia, Azerbaijan, Bulgaria, Georgia, Hellenic Republic, Moldova, Romania, Russian Federation, Serbia, Turkey, Ukraine
Caribbean Community (CARICOM)	15	Antigua and Barbuda, the Bahamas, Barbados, Belize, Dominica, Grenada, Guyana, Jamaica, Montserrat, St. Kitts and Nevis, St. Lucia, St. Vincent and the Grenadines, Suriname, Trinidad and Tobago
Central African Economic and Monetary Community (CEMAC)	7	Cameroon, Central African Republic, Chad, Democratic Republic of the Congo, Gabon, Gambia, Equatorial Guinea
Central American Integration System	7	Belize, Costa Rica, El Salvador, Guatemala, Honduras, Nicaragua, Panama
Central Asia Regional Economic Cooperation (CAREC) Program	8	Afghanistan, Azerbaijan, China, Kazakhstan, Kyrgyz Republic, Mongolia, Tajikistan, Uzbekistan
Central European Free Trade Agreement (CEFTA)	8	Croatia, Macedonia, Bosnia and Herzegovina, Moldova, Serbia, Montenegro, Albania, Kosovo

Common Market for Eastern and Southern Africa (COMESA)	19	Burundi, Comoros, Democratic Republic of the Congo, Djibouti, Egypt, Eritrea, Ethiopia, Kenya, Libya, Madagascar, Malawi, Mauritius, Rwanda, Seychelles, Sudan, Swaziland, Uganda, Zambia, Zimbabwe
Common Market of the South (Mercosur)	5	Argentina, Brazil, Paraguay, Uruguay, Venezuela
Commonwealth of Independent States	11	Armenia, Azerbaijan, Belarus, Kazakhstan, Kyrgyzstan, Moldova, Russia, Tajikistan, Turkmenistan, Ukraine, Uzbekistan
Community of Sahel-Saharan States (CEN-SAD)	28	Benin, Burkina Faso, Central African Republic, Chad, Comoros, Côte d'Ivoire, Djibouti, Egypt, Eritrea, Gambia, Ghana, Guinea, Guinea-Bissau, Kenya, Liberia, Libya, Mali, Mauritania, Morocco, Niger, Nigeria, Sao Tome and Principe, Senegal, Sierra Leone, Somalia, Sudan, Togo, Tunisia
Council of Arab Economic Unity (CAEU)	11	Egypt, Iraq, Jordan, Kuwait, Libya, Mauritania, Palestine, Somalia, Sudan, Syria, Yemen
Council of Europe (COE)	47	Albania, Andorra, Armenia, Austria, Azerbaijan, Belgium, Bosnia and Herzegovina, Bulgaria, Croatia, Cyprus, Czech Republic, Denmark, Estonia, Finland, France, Georgia, Germany, Greece, Hungary, Iceland, Ireland, Italy, Latvia, Liechtenstein, Lithuania, Luxembourg, Macedonia, Malta, Moldova, Monaco, Montenegro, the Netherlands, Norway, Poland, Portugal, Romania, Russian Federation, San Marino, Serbia, Slovakia, Slovenia, Spain, Sweden, Switzerland, Turkey, Ukraine, United Kingdom
Council of the Baltic States (CBSS)	12	Denmark, Estonia, Finland, Germany, Iceland, Latvia, Lithuania, Norway, Poland, Russian Federation, Sweden, European Commission
Cross Border Initiative	15	Burundi, Comoros, Kenya, Madagascar, Malawi, Mauritius, Mozambique, Namibia, Rwanda, Seychelles, Swaziland, Tanzania, Uganda, Zambia, Zimbabwe
East African Community (EAC)	5	Burundi, Kenya, Tanzania, Uganda, Rwanda
Economic Community of Central African States (ECCAS)	10	Angola, Burundi, Cameroon, Central African Republic, Congo, Democratic Republic of Congo, Equatorial Guinea, Gabon, Sao Tome and Principe
Economic Community of the Great Lakes Countries (ECGLC-CEPGL)	3	Burundi, Democratic Republic of Congo, Rwanda

(continued)

(continued)

Regional arrangement	Number of members	Member states
Economic Community of West African States (ECWAS)	15	Benin, Burkina Faso, Cape Verde, Cote d'Ivoire, Gambia, Ghana, Guinea Conakry, Guinea-Bissau, Liberia, Mali, Niger, Nigeria, Senegal, Sierra Leone, Togo
Economic Co-operation Organization (ECO)	10	Afghanistan, Azerbaijan, Iran, Kazakhstan, Kyrgyzstan, Pakistan, Tajikistan, Turkey, Turkmenistan, Uzbekistan
European Free Trade Association (EFTA)	4	Iceland, Liechtenstein, Norway, Switzerland
European Union	27	Austria, Belgium, Bulgaria, Cyprus, Czech Republic, Denmark, Estonia, Finland, France, Germany, Greece, Hungary, Ireland, Italy, Latvia, Lithuania, Luxembourg, Malta, Netherlands, Poland, Portugal, Romania, Slovakia, Slovenia, Spain, Sweden, United Kingdom
Eurozone	15	Belgium, Germany, Ireland, Greece, Spain, France, Italy, Cyprus, Luxembourg, Malta, the Netherlands, Austria, Portugal, Slovenia, Finland
Gulf Cooperation Council (GCC)	6	Bahrain, Kuwait, Oman, Qatar, Saudi Arabia, United Arab Emirates
Indian Ocean Commission (IOC)	5	Comoros, Réunion France, Madagascar, Mauritius, Seychelles
Indian Ocean Rim Association for Regional Cooperation (IOR-ARC)	18	Australia, India, Kenya, Mauritius, Oman, Singapore, South Africa, Indonesia, Malaysia, Madagascar, Mozambique, Sri Lanka, Tanzania, Yemen, Bangladesh, Iran, Thailand, United Arab Emirates
Intergovernmental Authority on Development (IGAD)	7	Djibouti, Eritrea, Ethiopia, Kenya, Somalia, Sudan, Uganda
Latin American and Caribbean Economic System (SELA)	28	Argentina, Bahamas, Barbados, Belize, Bolivia, Brazil, Chile, Colombia, Costa Rica, Cuba, Dominican Republic, Ecuador, El Salvador, Grenada, Guatemala, Guyana, Haiti, Honduras, Jamaica, Mexico, Nicaragua, Panama, Paraguay, Peru, Suriname, Trinidad and Tobago, Uruguay, Venezuela
Latin American Integration Association (LAIA)	12	Argentina, Bolivia, Brazil, Chile, Colombia, Cuba, Ecuador, Mexico, Paraguay, Peru, Uruguay, Venezuela
League of Arab States	22	Algeria, Bahrain, Comoros, Djibouti, Egypt, Iraq, Jordan, Kuwait, Lebanon, Libya, Mauritania, Morocco, Oman, Palestine, Qatar, Saudi Arabia, Somalia, Sudan, Syria, Tunisia, United Arab Emirates, Yemen

Mano River Union (MRU)	3	Guinea, Liberia, Sierra Leone
Mekong River Commission (MRC)	4	Cambodia, Laos, Thailand, Vietnam
Melanesian Spearhead Group (MSG)	4	Papua New Guinea, Fiji, Solomon Islands, Vanuatu
Nordic Council and the Nordic Council of Ministers	8	Denmark, Finland, Faroe Islands (Denmark), Greenland (Denmark), Aland Islands (Finland), Iceland, Norway, Sweden
North American Free Trade Agreement (NAFTA)	3	Canada, Mexico, United States
Organization of Arab Petroleum Exporting Countries (OAPEC)	11	Algeriz, Bahrain, Egypt, Iraq, Kuwait, Libya, Qatar, Saudi Arabia, Syria, Tunisia, United Arab Emirates
Organisation of Eastern Caribbean States (OECS)	9	Anguilla, Antigua and Barbuda, British Virgin Islands, Dominica, Grenada, Montserrat, St. Kitts and Nevis, St. Lucia, St. Vincent and the Grenadines
Organisation of Islamic Conference (OIC)	57	Albania, Algeria, Azerbaijan, Bahrain, Benin, Cameroon, Chad, Cote D'ivoire, Djibouti, Gabon, Gambia, Guinea, Guinea-Bissau, Guyana, Indonesia, Iraq, Kazakhstan, Kuwait, Kyrgyz Republic, Lebanon, Malaysia, Maldives, Mali, Morocco, Mozambique, Niger, Oman, Palestine, People's Bangladesh, Qatar, Saudi Arabia, Senegal, Sierra Leone, Somalia, Sudan, Suriname, Syrian Arab Republic, Tajikistan, Togo, Tunisia, Turkey, Turkmenistan, Uganda, Union Of Comoros, United Arab Emirates, Uzbekistan, Yemen
Organisation pour l'harmonisation du droit des affaires (OHADA)	16	Bénin, Burkina Faso, Cameroun, Centrafrique, Comores, Congo, Côte d'Ivoire, Gabon, Guinée, Guinée Bissau, Guinée Equatoriale, Mali, Niger, Sénégal, Tchad, Togo
Organization of American States (OAS)	35	Antigua and Barbuda, Argentina, Bahamas, Barbados, Belize, Bolivia, Brazil, Canada, Chile, Colombia, Costa Rica, Cuba, Dominica, Dominican Republic, Ecuador, El Salvador, Grenada, Guatemala, Guyana, Haiti, Honduras, Jamaica, Mexico, Nicaragua, Panama, Paraguay, Peru, St. Kitts and Nevis, St. Lucia, St. Vincent and the Grenadines, Suriname, Trinidad and Tobago, United States, Uruguay, Venezuela
Pacific Islands Forum	16	Australia, Cook Islands, Federated States of Micronesia, Fiji, Kiribati, the Marshall Islands, Nauru, New Zealand, Niue, Palau, Papua New Guinea, Samoa, Solomon Islands, Tonga, Tuvalu, Vanuatu

(continued)

(continued)

Regional arrangement	Number of members	Member states
Permanent Interstate Committee for Drought Control in the Sahel	9	Burkina Faso, Cape Verde, Gambia, Guinea-Bissau, Mali, Mauritania, Niger, Senegal, Chad
Permanent Mechanism of Political Consultation and Coordination (Rio Group)	23	Argentina, Belize, Bolivia, Brazil, Chile, Colombia, Costa Rica, Cuba, Dominican Republic, Ecuador, El Salvador, Guatemala, Guyana, Haiti, Honduras, Jamaica, Mexico, Nicaragua, Panama, Paraguay, Peru, Uruguay, Venezuela
South Asian Association for Regional Co-operation (SAARC)	8	Afghanistan, Bangladesh, Bhutan, India, Maldives, Nepal, Pakistan, Sri Lanka
Southern African Customs Union (SACU)	5	Botswana, Lesotho, Namibia, South Africa, Swaziland
Southern African Development Community (SADC)	15	Angola, Botswana, Democratic Republic of the Congo, Lesotho, Madagascar, Malawi, Mauritius, Mozambique, Namibia, Seychelles, South Africa, Swaziland, Tanzania, Zambia, Zimbabwe
West African Economic and Monetary Union (UEMOA)	8	Benin, Burkina Faso, Cote d'Ivoire, Guinea-Bissau, Mali, Niger, Senegal, Togo

Source: RIKS© 2010, http://www.cris.unu.edu/riks/web/arrangement

The manufacturer's authorised representative in the EU is Springer Nature Customer Service Centre GmbH, Europaplatz 3, 69115 Heidelberg, Germany. If you have any concerns regarding our products, please contact ProductSafety@springernature.com

Printed and bound by CPI Group (UK) Ltd, Croydon, CR0 4YY

30/09/2026

02225453-0016